Soldier of
Tennessee

Soldier of Tennessee

GENERAL ALEXANDER P. STEWART
AND THE CIVIL WAR IN THE WEST

SAM DAVIS ELLIOTT

Louisiana State University Press   *Baton Rouge*

Designer: Michele Myatt Quinn
Typeface: Galliard
Typesetter: Coghill Composition
Printer and binder: Edwards Brothers, Inc.

Frontispiece: Wartime drawing of Stewart, courtesy Library of Congress

Library of Congress Cataloging-in-Publication Data

Elliott, Sam Davis, 1956–
    Soldier of Tennessee : General Alexander P. Stewart and the Civil
    War in the West / Sam Davis Elliott.
        p.   cm.
    Includes bibliographical references (p.   ) and index.
    ISBN 0-8071-2340-4 (cloth : alk. paper)
    1. Stewart, Alexander P. (Alexander Peter), 1821–1908.
    2. Generals—Confederate States of America—Biography.
    3. Confederate States of America. Army of Tennessee—Biography.
    4. Tennessee—History—Civil War, 1861–1865—Campaigns.   5. Georgia—
    History—Civil War, 1861–1865—Campaigns.   6. United States—
    History—Civil War, 1861–1865—Campaigns.   I. Title.
    E467.1.S863E45   1999
    973.7′468′092—dc21   98-44178
                                                                     CIP

For Karen, Mary Claire, and Sarah Anne

CONTENTS

ILLUSTRATIONS

PREFACE

A bronze figure of a soldier stands in front of the Hamilton County Courthouse in Chattanooga, green and tarnished, the inscription reading: "A. P. Stewart, Lt. General, C.S.A., 1861–1865." Like so many other courthouse statues, it is noticed by few—an ornament ignored by most people who walk by it: nervous litigants, weary lawyers, couples just married nearby under the large trees on the well-kept lawn. Only children and tourists from out of state seem to really look. Yet the statue, and especially the man it represents, deserve much more attention than they have gotten up to now. A. P. Stewart was a leader in that noble host, the Army of Tennessee.

Stewart's service in the Civil War spanned the time from the earliest beginnings of the Army of Tennessee, in May, 1861, to its final surrender, in April, 1865. Between those dates, he participated in nearly every major battle the army fought, rising in rank from major to lieutenant general. He commanded the Army of Tennessee on its last battlefield, leading its battered remnants at Bentonville, a force numbering not much more than the division he commanded at Chickamauga. At the end of the war, he was the ranking Confederate officer from the state of Tennessee, and, at the time of his death in 1908, the ranking Confederate survivor.

As has often been the case with the Army of Tennessee and the men who served with it, Alexander Peter Stewart has in many ways been ignored by historians and biographers. He is the subject of only one biography, Marshall Wingfield's *General A. P. Stewart: His Life and Letters* (Memphis: West Tennessee Historical Society, 1954). Though invaluable to this study, Wingfield's work contains little analysis of Stewart's role in the war or his performance in the many battles in which he fought. Regardless of whether this dearth of information is attributable to Stewart's own well-known modesty during life or to the sparse treatment accorded the Army of Tennessee relative to its famous counterpart in Virginia, Stewart has received less than his due.

Yet determining Stewart's place in southern history requires more than just an investigation into his life as a soldier. Stewart was a noted educator

long before the war and resumed that role for many years after. A devout
Christian, the general both practiced and preached his religion on the battlefield, in the classroom, and at home. Stewart played a significant role in
the establishment and marking of the Chickamauga-Chattanooga National
Military Park—the nation's oldest and largest. He spent a number of years
in Chattanooga on that task, the quality of his work being exhibited in the
park itself, one of the best, if not the best, Civil War parks in our country.
Almost to his dying day he made significant and lasting contributions to
our knowledge and understanding of the Civil War.

　　As would be the case with any man or woman who lived in the last century, reconstructing the life of General Stewart presents many difficulties.
No source has indicated Stewart's size, so any physical description can only
be derived from photographs or from depictions such as his statue, which
was referred to by those who knew the general as true to life. Unlike many
other high-ranking officers of the Civil War, Stewart left few papers, and
they have not been gathered into a single repository for a researcher to
draw upon easily. Duke University Library is the only research facility to
have a collection described as the "A. P. Stewart Papers," and it consists of
four brief documents, two of which are so fragmentary as to be practically
useless. The Tennessee State Library and Archives, well known for its impressive collection of documents relating to Tennesseans in the Civil War,
has but one of Stewart's letters.

　　Fortunately, materials on Stewart do exist. These include his letters in
the papers of others, his reports in the *Official Records* and in scattered
manuscript collections, the minutes of meetings at the institutions where
he served, and articles relating to him and his troops in the *Confederate Veteran* and similar periodicals. There is also a remarkable (and somewhat disorganized) book compiled by one of his staff officers and a "sketch" of the
Army of Tennessee Stewart wrote in 1886. Discernible effects of his influence survive on the quiet campus of Cumberland University and in the dignified older buildings of the University of Mississippi. And echoes of his
martial spirit resound at the many points where he and his men fought: the
hills around Hoover's Gap and at Perryville, the thick cedars at Murfreesboro, the country cemetery at New Hope Church, the placid fields at Shiloh, the bitter plain at Franklin, the winter-barren side of Missionary
Ridge, and the Tanyard at Chickamauga.

　　As is true of most human beings, General Stewart was a man of great complexity and contradiction. Humble, he was proudly conscious of his own worth. Exalted by his position in the army and as a celebrated educator, he was mindful of the physical and spiritual well-being of the lowliest soldiers and students under his charge. Opposed to slavery, he was unwilling to allow the slaves to fight to preserve the concept of constitutional liberty for which he drew his sword. A soldier known for his quiet competence and lack of political maneuvering, he showed a remarkable aptitude for advancement within an army where politics was high science, and was not above using a degree of political influence to secure advancement. Nonetheless, when he advanced, few begrudged his promotion, as he was perceived by those situated high and low as deserving of his laurels. He spent the most momentous time of his life fighting to overthrow the United States government in the South, yet ended his life working to preserve one of the war's greatest battlefields on behalf of that very government.

Born a Tennessean, Stewart spent the greater portion of his long life living and working in the Volunteer State. Raised to the highest levels of the Confederate army, he recognized, both during and after the war, that he represented Tennessee's participation in the South's failed revolution. At the dedication of the Tennessee monuments at Chickamauga in 1898, he spoke with pride of his Tennessee heritage. Stewart recognized the war in the West as a struggle for Tennessee, the heart of the Confederate heartland, and he emphasized the role of Tennessee troops in the sketch of the Army of Tennessee he wrote twenty-one years after the end of the war. Accordingly, I have titled this book *Soldier of Tennessee*, in order to acknowledge the general's pride of origin and the army in which he fought. Both the Volunteer State and the Army of Tennessee may have had more flamboyant soldiers fight under their banners, but no one more constant.

Regardless of a novice writer's enthusiasm for his subject, it would be impossible for him to complete a project such as this book without the kindness and assistance of others. While one can glimpse, in other published Civil War materials, the complexity of the work required to treat adequately a subject such as General Stewart, it is impossible to appreciate fully that complexity until the work is undertaken. I would have been unequal to the task if it weren't for the help of those listed below.

For their assistance by e-mail, mail, and phone, I would like to thank the staffs of the Alabama Department of Archives and History, Montgomery; the Huntington Library, San Marino, California; the Mississippi Department of Archives and History, Jackson; the Missouri State Archives, Jefferson City; the St. Charles, Missouri, City-County Library, St. Louis; the Howard-Tilton Memorial Library, Tulane University; the United States Military Academy, West Point, New York; the United States Army Military History Institute, Carlisle, Pennsylvania; the University of Arkansas, Fayetteville; and the Western Reserve Historical Society, Cleveland, Ohio. I also appreciate the efforts of the staffs of a number of other institutions who were, after inquiry, unable to locate materials on General Stewart in their collections.

For assistance at the libraries and other repositories I visited, I extend my thanks to the staffs of the Chattanooga–Hamilton County Bicentennial Library; the William R. Perkins Library Special Collections, Duke University; the Woodruff Library, Emory University, Atlanta; the Georgia Department of Archives and History, Atlanta; the Georgia Historical Society, Savannah; Kennesaw Mountain National Battlefield Park; the Library of Congress; the National Archives and Records Administration; the Tennessee State Archives, Nashville; the Hoole Special Collections Library, University of Alabama, Tuscaloosa; the University of Mississippi Archives and Special Collections, Oxford; the Southern Historical Collection, Wilson Library, University of North Carolina, Chapel Hill; and the Hargett Library, University of Georgia, Athens. Also, personal thanks for assistance of this nature to Anne Armor, archivist at my alma mater, the University of the South.

Certain individuals went above the call of professionalism in providing assistance. G. Frank Burns, archivist and historian of Cumberland University, took time out of his summer vacation to discuss General Stewart's time at Cumberland and in Lebanon and to share with me materials in the Cumberland archives. Later, he alerted me to an early photograph of Stewart and helped me secure permission to publish it.

Lynda Crist and the staff of the Papers of Jefferson Davis Project at Rice University provided, as a service of their remarkable website, an extensive list of Stewart-related documents in the project's database, some of which I would have never found without Lynda's kind assistance.

I owe a debt of gratitude to James Ogden III, historian of the Chickamauga-Chattanooga National Military Park. I learned a great deal about

Missionary Ridge through a tour given by Mr. Ogden on one of the anniversaries of the battle, and his assistance regarding materials in the park library and the location of materials outside the library was invaluable.

Many helpful pointers as to the location of newspapers and archival material were provided by Keith Bohannen, of Chattanooga, Tennessee, who went out of his way on my behalf on many occasions. Keith also read portions of my manuscript, and his suggestions substantially improved the finished product.

Other individuals were most kind in sharing materials or insights of great importance. Steven Woodworth of Texas Christian University generously gave me a copy of his essay on the Tullahoma campaign prior to its anticipated publication. R. Hugh Simmons, of Paoli, Pennsylvania, mailed me a copy of his interesting study of Stewart's Corps in its final months. Mrs. Jo Hill, president of the A. P. Stewart Chapter of the United Daughters of the Confederacy, directed me to her chapter's earliest records, and gave me permission to publish a photograph of General Stewart in old age found there. Stacy Allen, of Shiloh National Military Park, pointed to useful information in the park files. John Pat Cox and Stuart Salling, fellow Civil War enthusiasts I met on the Internet, provided copies of valuable materials. Bruce Allardice, of Des Plaines, Illinois, shed light on Stewart's rank and gave me direction as to other materials available. Lynn Bock of New Madrid, Missouri, and Frank Nickell of Southeast Missouri State University provided information about a potential primary source. Eivind Boe copyedited the final manuscript with sensitivity and skill. Blake Magner expertly translated my rough concepts into easily read maps.

Assistance of a more intangible sort came from my law partners, Charles Gearhiser, Wayne Peters, Bob Lockaby, Chuck Tallant, Terry Cavett, Lane Avery, and Wade Cannon, all of whom suffered by my time away from the practice to investigate leads and obtain information. Thanks are also due my parents-in-law, Arvid and Claire Honkanen, for their encouragement. Special thanks go to my parents, Gene and Ruth Elliott, for being patient with my enthusiasm for the Civil War while I was growing up and for their constant support during the time it took to complete this project. My mother went above and beyond the call of duty by proofreading my manuscript not once, but twice.

I have already acknowledged the assistance of Jim Ogden, but perhaps my greatest debt to him is his suggestion that I contact my fellow Chattanoogan, Nathaniel Cheairs Hughes, Jr., for his insights. Well known for his fine writings on the Civil War, Nat Hughes took time from his own work to patiently answer hundreds of questions, make innumerable valuable suggestions, direct me to source materials, introduce me to other historians, read my manuscript, and essentially become a mentor to a novice historian. Simply put, without Nat's guidance, this book would not have been possible.

Finally, my deepest gratitude goes to my wife, Karen, and my daughters, Mary Claire and Sarah Anne. For the past four years they have had to live not only with me, but with General Stewart as well. Their encouragement was endless, their patience boundless, and their love inspiring.

ABBREVIATIONS USED IN NOTES

APS   Alexander Peter Stewart

B&L   Robert Underwood Johnson and Clarence Clough Buel, *Battles and Leaders of the Civil War*. 4 vols. 1884–1887. Reprint, New York: Thomas Yoseloff, 1956.

C-HCBL   Chattanooga–Hamilton County Bicentennial Library, Chattanooga, Tenn.

CCNMP   Chickamauga and Chattanooga National Military Park, Fort Oglethorpe, Ga.

CSR   Compiled Service Record

CV   *Confederate Veteran*

DU   Duke University, William R. Perkins Library, Durham, N.C.

GA   Georgia Department of Archives and History, Atlanta, Ga.

GHS   Georgia Historical Society, Savannah, Ga.

KNBP   Kennesaw Mountain National Battlefield Park, Ga.

LC   Library of Congress, Washington, D.C.

MDAH   Mississippi Department of Archives and History, Jackson, Miss.

NA   National Archives, Washington, D.C.

OR   *War of the Rebellion: A Compilation of the Official Records of the Union and Confederate Armies*. 128 vols. (Washington, D.C.: U.S. Government Printing Office, 1880–1901). *OR* citations take the following form: volume number (part number, where applicable): page number(s).

RG   Record Group

SHC   Southern Historical Collection, Wilson Library, University of North Carolina, Chapel Hill, N.C.

SNMP   Shiloh National Military Park, Tenn.

TCWCC   Tennessee Civil War Centennial Commission

TSLA   Tennessee State Library and Archives, Nashville, Tenn.

UAL   University of Alabama, W. S. Hoole Special Collections Library, Tuscaloosa, Ala.

UAR   University of Arkansas Library, Fayetteville, Ark.

UM   University of Mississippi Archives, Oxford, Miss.

USMA   United States Military Academy

Soldier of Tennessee

— 1 —

Son of the Volunteer State

Rogersville, Winchester, West Point, and Cumberland

My judgment is that if my distinguished friend, Lieutenant General Stewart, who is with us today, honored by all who served under or with him, had been in command of the Army of Tennessee on that fateful day, Chickamauga would not have been a barren victory." Alexander Peter Stewart made a polite nod to the speaker, former Tennessee governor James D. Porter, who was kind to mention him in so favorable a manner, though he took it as no more than a compliment from an old friend. Porter's comment could only moderately increase his self-content, which was already such as he had rarely felt in his seventy-seven years. The work that was celebrated here on the Chickamauga battlefield was as much his as anyone's, and although his stern religion admonished him to avoid pride, it was with no small sense of satisfaction that he saw it come to fruition.

Stewart had first come to these woods and fields thirty-five years before, a major general commanding a division in a retreating army. That army, named for his native Tennessee, had turned on its enemy and fiercely assaulted it for two days, finally forcing the men in blue off this very hill in the early autumn twilight of that glorious September evening. His own division had played its part in what turned out to be the army's greatest victory, spectacularly bludgeoning its way through the blue lines on the first day, and furiously assaulting enemy breastworks on the second. It seemed at the time that the Army of Tennessee had reversed the trend of Shiloh,

Perryville, and Murfreesboro, hard-fought yet fruitless battles, and that Chattanooga, and indeed Tennessee, might be recovered for the new southern republic.

Unfortunately for the Army of Tennessee and the cause it represented, its officers had marred the aftermath of its greatest victory. Their power struggle had left the army ill-prepared for the resurgence of the blue host, the stronger of the contending parties in the contest. When that resurgence had come, the Army of Tennessee had once more been forced from the Volunteer State.

Stewart reflected on the terrible days of fighting in the mud and the rain and the heat in the Atlanta campaign, his division being slowly eroded by sickness, exhaustion, and death. Yet there had been that one great day at New Hope Church, where he and his veterans had stood squarely in the path of a massive attack bent on splitting the gray lines and sweeping into position to move unopposed into Atlanta. In the midst of a terrific thunderstorm, he had ridden back and forth on his old horse, encouraging his men as they repelled the Yankees. Later, he had heard it said that his calm presence inspired his division's stout resistance. This had filled him with pride.

It was also gratifying that his fellow officers had recognized his ability and his zeal for the cause. When that grand old patriot and Episcopalian bishop Leonidas Polk had been killed a few weeks after New Hope Church, the Confederate government had promoted Stewart to lieutenant general to command Polk's Corps. In that capacity, he had served Joe Johnston and John Bell Hood in the futile effort to save Atlanta for the Confederacy. Afterward, there had seemed to be nothing left but to return to Tennessee, where the army had been virtually annihilated on the bloody plains of Franklin and in the cold hills south of Nashville.

The old general sadly recalled the pain of leaving Tennessee for a third time in December, 1864. Those had been hard days, filled with personal sadness and growing despair for the future. Along with what few of his men remained with the colors, he had traveled across the war-torn South to North Carolina, to face the blue host in one last effort to avoid the inevitable. Even in defeat and surrender, however, there had still been the comforting thought that honor had been satisfied.

A college professor before the war, Stewart had returned to the classroom at the war's end, even as he was exploring ways to better his place in life by business ventures. Fate had led him away from Tennessee, first to Missouri, then to Mississippi. He had been useful, as he had been taught long ago, and had at last entered into retirement. During these years of peacetime pursuits, however, the war remained in his memory as the defining event of his life. When the call had come in 1890 to serve as a commissioner for the Chickamauga battlefield park, he had gladly accepted.

Today, May 12, 1898, he spoke as the representative of the United States government, accepting for the reunited nation the monuments to the men who sought to rend it asunder over a third of a century before. Paying tribute to the great deeds of the past commemorated at the park, he gloried in the victories recently won by the now restored United States in its current struggle with Spain. Having said what he supposed the representative of the United States government should say, the old general continued, "I have thought it might be expected and desired that I should say a word for Tennessee and the South. It is a source of both pride and pleasure to me to-day that I am myself a Tennesseean, a son of the great 'Volunteer State' of the Union, every chapter of whose history is a glorious one. . . . I was born and partly brought up in the State in the days when Andrew Jackson was the greatest and foremost figure of the country."[1]

On October 2, 1821, Andrew Jackson, governor of the territory of the Floridas, was making ready to return home, ostensibly to remove his wife, Rachel, to Nashville before the winter set in, but doubtlessly to evaluate the political situation in his Tennessee power base. In Tennessee's recent gubernatorial election, William Carroll had been elected by an overwhelming majority of voters, who were frustrated by the economic depression brought about by the Panic of 1819. Although his friend Carroll had won, Jackson's candidate, Edward Ward, had lost, having been outpolled by Carroll in all but two counties of the Volunteer State.[2]

Hawkins County in upper East Tennessee was typical of the counties

1. The speeches given by Porter and Stewart are described in Bromfield Ridley, *Battles and Sketches of the Army of Tennessee* (1906; reprint, Dayton: Morningside Bookshop, 1995), 602–25.

2. Harold D. Moser, David R. Hoth, and George H. Hoemann, eds., *The Papers of Andrew Jackson*, vol. 5, *1821–1824* (Knoxville: University of Tennessee Press, 1996), 110–11; Charles W. Crawford, ed., *Governors of Tennessee, Vol. 1, 1790–1835* (Memphis: Memphis State University Press, 1979), 130–32.

supporting Carroll, giving him over 84 percent of its vote. The county was populated in large part by people of Scotch-Irish descent: people of Scottish ancestry whose forebears lived in Ireland before coming to America. They were plain people, democratic and personally independent, not likely to sympathize with the large landowning interests represented by Ward. In 1821, Hawkins County had been settled for almost fifty years, but a large portion of Tennessee was still frontier, and still being settled by such simple folk. West Tennessee had been purchased from the Chickasaws only three years previously, and Memphis, on the Mississippi, was only in its second year of existence.[3]

Hawkins County's seat was Rogersville, a town of fifty or sixty houses first laid out in 1789. The town also contained a one-story hewn-log courthouse, a brick jail, a few stores, a Presbyterian and a Methodist church, a brick school named McMinn Academy, and a Masonic lodge. A branch of the state bank under the name of the Rogersville Tennessee Bank had been incorporated four years previously with a capital stock of four thousand dollars. Rogersville had its own newspaper, the *Rogersville Gazette*, a five-column paper with the motto "The Star Spangled Banner, etc."[4]

While the talk in Rogersville on October 2, 1821, no doubt concerned Jackson's politics and the prospects of Governor Carroll, it is likely there was some discussion of the birth that day of the town's newest citizen, another Tennessean of Scotch-Irish descent named Alexander Peter Stewart. Young Alexander was the fourth child of Elizabeth Decherd Stewart and William Stewart, the third to survive infancy. Elizabeth was the daughter of Pennsylvanians Michael and Elizabeth Spyker Decherd, who had moved to Abingdon, Virginia, shortly after the Revolution. There she married William, the grandson and son of Revolutionary War veterans James Stewart, Jr., and James Stewart III, both of Delaware. In 1816, William and Elizabeth had moved a few miles across the Virginia-Tennessee state line to

    3. Anne H. Hopkins and William Lyons, *Tennessee Votes, 1799–1976* (Knoxville: University of Tennessee Bureau of Public Administration, 1978), 15; Will T. Hale and Dixon L. Merritt, *A History of Tennessee and Tennesseans* (Chicago: Lewis Publishing Company, 1913), 2:266, 400–401.
    4. Weston A. Goodspeed, "Sketches of Thirty East Tennessee Counties," *Goodspeed's History of Tennessee* (1887; reprint; Nashville: Elder Booksellers, 1972), 873, 877–79.

Blountsville, where they lived for two years before moving one county west to Rogersville.

Little is known of the Stewart family's stay in Rogersville, where seven of their children were born. Later in life, Alexander Peter Stewart said the schoolhouse he attended from 1827 to 1831 was approximately sixteen by twenty feet with a rock chimney. There was a writing board made of rough lumber and benches made of split logs. Young Alexander was too small to sit on the bench to write, so he stood. The benches provided no support for the children's backs, forcing them to put their arms across one another's shoulders for mutual support. The schoolmaster, probably a Revolutionary War veteran by the name of Crawford, would require the children to recite their lessons loudly so passersby could hear and be impressed with their scholarship. The course of study and the facilities at the Rogersville school were typical of schools all over Tennessee. In fact, the audible recitals of the students would get so loud that the schools were called "loud schools."[5]

While William and Elizabeth Stewart were raising their growing family in Rogersville, Elizabeth's parents and her brothers were establishing a home in Franklin County, Tennessee, almost two hundred miles to the southwest, on the Alabama border. The Decherds migrated from Franklin County down the Tennessee River to Huntsville, Alabama, then northeast back to Tennessee and Franklin County, where they received a large grant of land. In the autumn of 1831, they were joined there by William and Elizabeth Stewart, ten-year-old Alexander, and his seven brothers and sisters.[6]

Franklin County was formed on December 3, 1807, and named for Benjamin Franklin. The eastern part of the county held a mountain to rival any in Hawkins County, a part of the Cumberland Plateau known as Sewanee Mountain. To the west, Franklin County was generally level or had

5. Marshall Wingfield, *General A. P. Stewart: His Life and Letters* (Memphis: West Tennessee Historical Society, 1954), 9–13; Marshall Wingfield, "Old Straight: A Sketch of the Life and Campaigns of Lieutenant General Alexander Peter Stewart, C.S.A.," *Tennessee Historical Quarterly* 3 (June 1944): 99–102; Hale and Merritt, *Tennessee and Tennesseans*, 266–68, 271–72, 300.

6. Wingfield, *Stewart*, 12–13.

gently rolling hills, and was well watered by the Elk River and its tributaries. The rich valley soil made Franklin County one of the leading cotton-producing areas in the state as early as 1810, within a decade or so of its first settlement.[7]

An 1809 act of the Tennessee General Assembly put in motion the eventual establishment of the county seat, Winchester. By the time the Stewart family arrived in 1831, the town's population numbered about six hundred. Its inhabitants lived near and worked in and around a cramped courthouse and brick jail. Commercial establishments included three hotels, a soon-to-fail branch of the state bank, various merchants, a tanyard, a blacksmith shop, a silversmith, a cabinet shop, and two saddle and harness shops. Winchester was prosperous because it was the only substantial settlement on a long stage route. Like the residents of Hawkins County, the early settlers of Winchester and Franklin County tended to be God-fearing people. Camp meetings were held at various locations in the county. A large number of the first settlers were said to be ministers of the gospel. The religious denominations represented early on included Methodists, Presbyterians, Baptists, and Lutherans. A brother of Elizabeth Stewart, Benjamin Decherd, helped organize the Cumberland Presbyterian Church in Winchester, which met in private homes or in the courthouse from its foundation in 1820 until a building was erected in 1827. Benjamin Decherd also organized a Sunday school in 1828, where both white and black children were taught.[8]

In 1809, the General Assembly provided for an academy in Winchester for boys only. When young Alexander enrolled in school there, the institution, named Carrick Academy, occupied a two-year-old building. Alexander's education was financed by either or both of his uncles, Benjamin Decherd and Peter Spyker Decherd. Alexander actually lived with his Uncle Peter, from whom he derived his middle name, during a portion of his years in Winchester.[9]

7. B. C. Rauchle, "A Brief Account of the Early History of Franklin County," *Franklin County Historical Review* 2 (December 1970): 37–39.

8. Weston A. Goodspeed, *The Goodspeed Histories of Giles, Lincoln, Franklin and Moore Counties of Tennessee* (1886; reprint, Columbia, Tenn.: Woodward & Stinson Printing Co., 1972), 789, 790, 800, 803.

9. Wingfield, *Stewart*, 14–15; Edward A. Pollard, *Lee and His Lieutenants* (New York: E. B. Treat, 1867), 711. Wingfield indicates it was Peter who financed the education. Pollard,

Although he may have spent a great deal of time on the Decherd Plantation, Alexander Stewart received solid moral and religious instruction and example from his parents. William and Elizabeth were described as "remarkable for their zeal and piety in the Methodist Church." Elizabeth was noted to be "indulgent, tender and faithful" toward her many children, and like most mothers, she prayed for her children "from infancy." In fact, she "prayed about everything." Like many of the residents of their former home in East Tennessee, the Stewarts disapproved of slavery and never owned a slave; nor did any of their children. After the family's arrival in Winchester, Elizabeth Stewart bore seven more children. Those of Alexander's brothers and sisters who survived to adulthood became teachers, clergymen, merchants, a physician, and soldiers.[10]

In time, William Stewart established himself in Winchester. He owned a general store on the square, was for many years Winchester's postmaster, and for thirty years was the treasurer of Franklin County. By 1838, either William or the Decherds had enough influence to take advantage of the secretary of war's practice of selecting at least one West Point nominee from each congressional district. They secured from Congressman Hopkins L. Turney an appointment to West Point for Alexander Peter Stewart, age sixteen.[11]

On March 6, 1838, Congressman Turney wrote Joel Poinsett, the secretary of war:

> We understand there is at present no cadet at West Point from the fifth Congressional district in Tennessee, we therefore take the Liberty of recommending Alexander P. Stewart of Winchester, Tennessee[.] [H]e is sixteen years of age a good Scholar as any of that age both in the Languages and Sciences and is in every way qualified to

---

somewhat more contemporaneously, states that Stewart was "liberally" educated by Benjamin.

10. Pollard, *Lee and His Lieutenants*, 711; Wingfield, *Stewart*, 11, 15–16, 18, 200–208. Peter Decherd offered the railroad a right-of-way through his land in 1845, and thus was given the right to name two local stations, "Decherd" and "Tulkahoma," the latter for an Indian chief captured by his grandfather. "Tulkahoma" was gradually corrupted to "Tullahoma." Wingfield, *Stewart*, 11; Mrs. Bob C. Hill, "A Brief History of Decherd, Tennessee," *Franklin County Historical Review* 3 (June 1972): 3–4.

11. Wingfield, *Stewart*, 18; Pollard, *Lee and His Lieutenants*, 711.

enter the institution above named. He is of a rispectable [*sic*] family you will be pleased to communicate with Mr. Turney on this subject.

As if to underscore the family's ability to command some political influence, Tennessee senator Felix Grundy endorsed Turney's letter.[12]

After confirming that Winchester was in Turney's district and that the district was in fact due an appointment, Poinsett wrote young Stewart on March 8, 1838, offering a conditional appointment to West Point. On March 26, Stewart replied in neat handwriting that he accepted the appointment, and promised to "endeavor in all things to comply with the Requisitions of your department and of the Academy." This reply bore the endorsement of William Stewart, authorizing his son, A. P. Stewart, to sign the articles a cadet is required to sign. It seems that young Stewart and his father encountered some resistance from Alexander's mother, who worried that her son's religious scruples would be affected by life away at school and in the army. Nonetheless, sometime in the early summer of 1838, A. P. Stewart, age sixteen years, eight months, left Winchester for West Point.[13]

Early in his first year as a cadet, Stewart wrote his oldest sister, Catherine, to console her on the death of her first husband. He described West Point as a place of "fresh mountain air and wild and romantic views and scenery up the Hudson" that would restore her spirits. Stewart wrote that he felt as if he had been away from home for a year or two already, "but my time is all filled up and passes swiftly." A review of the regulations indicates how a cadet's time was "all filled up." The day's studies lasted "not less than nine, nor not more than ten hours." In addition to military subjects, cadets studied French (as befitted a school patterned upon the French model), mathematics, drawing, rhetoric, geography, history, natural philosophy, grammar, chemistry, mineralogy and geology, and engineering.[14]

12. Thomas J. Fleming, *West Point: The Men and Times of the United States Military Academy* (New York: Morrow, 1969), 112; *U.S. Military Academy Cadet Application Papers, 1805–1866*, National Archives Microfilm Publication 688.

13. *USMA Application Papers*; APS to Catherine Jones, January 7, 1877, in Wingfield, *Stewart*, 117.

14. APS to Catherine Hawkins, September 16, 1838, in Wingfield, *Stewart*, 26–27; USMA, *Regulations Established for the Organization and Government of the Military Academy* (New York: Wiley & Putnam, 1839), 16–17.

Stewart and his classmates entered a school as noted for its ability to produce engineers and teachers as for training soldiers. In fact, the academy was criticized because a number of its graduates soon resigned from the army to pursue civilian careers. Jacksonian Democrats denounced the institution as elitist, claiming the academy sought to establish "a military nobility." Subsequent events would prove this criticism to be well-founded, as the members of Stewart's class included such future generals as James Longstreet, William S. Rosecrans, Daniel Harvey Hill, John Pope, Earl Van Dorn, Abner Doubleday, Lafayette McLaws, George Sykes, Richard H. Anderson, John Newton, Mansfield Lovell, Martin Luther Smith, Seth Williams, and Gustavus Woodson Smith.[15]

There is no record of Stewart's social life at the academy, but a letter written a few months after his graduation suggests he enjoyed parties and visiting young ladies. Like many a cadet, he may have even slipped out to patronize the famous Benny Haven's tavern—if for no other reason than to get relief from the constant diet of beef served at the academy. Stewart's roommates were Rosecrans, with whom he was on "somewhat intimate terms," Pope, Longstreet, and his particular good friend, G. W. Smith. Later, Stewart would face Pope and Rosecrans on the battlefield, fight beside Longstreet at Chickamauga, and join Smith in defending Atlanta. Stewart took advantage of his sojourn in the North to visit with various relatives in Baltimore and Pennsylvania, and took a trip with his brother James to see their grandfather James Stewart at his home in Brandywine Hundred, Delaware.[16]

At the end of his first year, in June, 1839, Stewart stood nineteenth in his class. At the end of his second year, he stood tenth, ranking in the top ten in all his subjects except drawing, where he was a middling thirty-fourth. In 1841, at the end of his third year, Stewart had fallen back to nineteenth overall, again doing well in all subjects except drawing, falling to an even poorer forty-third in that troublesome subject. By the time of his graduation, in June, 1842, Stewart ranked twelfth, grading at ninth in

15. Fleming, *West Point*, 98, 112; USMA, *Official Register of the Officers and Cadets of the U.S. Military Academy, 1839.*

16. Wingfield, *Stewart*, 22, 28–29; Fleming, *West Point*, 92–93; Ridley, *Battles and Sketches*, 473; APS to Charles D. McGuffey, November 17, 1905, Chattanooga Historical Society Papers, C-HCBL.

engineering, sixth in ethics, twentieth in infantry tactics, tenth in artillery, and eighth in mineralogy and geology. Stewart also acquired seventy-eight demerits in his final year. Rosecrans ranked fifth, with only nineteen demerits, Smith eighth, Pope seventeenth, and Longstreet, arguably the most competent of his class on future battlefields, fifty-fourth out of fifty-six, with one hundred and two demerits.[17]

On July 1, 1842, Stewart was commissioned a second lieutenant in the 3rd Artillery, which included among its officers at the time a rather quarrelsome first lieutenant from North Carolina, Braxton Bragg, and Bragg's friend from Ohio, first lieutenant William T. Sherman. Given leave before reporting to duty, Stewart returned to Winchester. At the conclusion of his leave, Stewart traveled southeast through north Georgia to Augusta, a district just recently taken from the Cherokees. Stewart later described his trip as a journey across almost "impassable" roads, with poor accommodations and bad food, through territory populated "by as despicable a race of white men as it has yet been my fortune to meet with." Upon reaching Augusta, he had just enough money to purchase a ticket on the railroad to Charleston, but the clerk would not accept a four-dollar bill from North Carolina. Convincing the clerk that he was an army officer carrying important dispatches, Stewart was able to get to Charleston, where he was allowed to stay a few days at Fort Moultrie, enjoying the company of old acquaintances and being introduced to "all the belles of the place." After attending a grand party given by the regiment's officers, he traveled to his post at Fort Macon, North Carolina, going from Charleston to Wilmington by boat, and in the process getting terribly seasick.

Fort Macon was located to protect the Beaufort Inlet, and was relatively new, having only been completed in 1834. A large five-sided work covering eight acres, the fort held thirty-three cannon and could accommodate a garrison of one thousand men. In 1842, it was garrisoned by Company F, 3rd Artillery, whose quartermaster, commissary of subsistence, and post treasurer were Lieutenant Stewart. These weighty duties, performed by a

17. USMA, *Official Register, 1839*; USMA, *Official Register of the Officers and Cadets of the U.S. Military Academy, 1840*; USMA, *Official Register of the Officers and Cadets of the U.S. Military Academy, 1841*; USMA, *Official Register of the Officers and Cadets of the U.S. Military Academy, 1842*; H. R. Shepherd, "Gen. D. H. Hill: A Character Study," *CV* 25 (August 1917): 366–67.

clerk, entitled Stewart to an extra allowance of fourteen dollars a month. During most of his stay at Fort Macon, Stewart was actually the senior officer. He complained about the lack of society, as the nearest town, Beaufort, was a little wooden fishing village. There was very little military work to do except drill the men, who, as old soldiers, required very little drill. Doubtless Stewart, like the other officers of the garrison, enjoyed sailing, fishing, and dining on the abundant game and seafood.[18]

After almost a year at Fort Macon, Stewart was assigned back to West Point as an assistant professor of mathematics, his appointment dating from August 29, 1843. Stewart was one of seven professors and assistant professors of mathematics who taught algebra, geometry, trigonometry, descriptive geometry, analytical geometry, and such subjects as mensuration and fluxions. Stewart's classmates John Newton and William Rosecrans were also on the faculty as acting assistant professors of civil and military engineering.[19]

At the close of the 1844 school year, Stewart went to visit his friend Lieutenant G. W. Smith in New London, Connecticut. During this visit, he was introduced to a young woman from Warren, Ohio, named Harriet Byron Chase. Harriet was twenty-two years of age and the daughter of a Connecticut sailor lost at sea along with his son, Alphonso, near the time of Harriet's birth. Her mother was the daughter of Dr. Rufus Spaulding of Martha's Vineyard, Massachusetts. Stewart and Harriet soon fell in love and planned to marry.[20]

At some point in the 1844–45 academic year, Stewart must have realized, if he had not before, that education was his calling. If he remained in the army, he eventually would be transferred back to the 3rd Artillery from West Point, and move from post to post dragging his wife and family with him. As one of his future staff officers wrote, Stewart's health may have been a concern as well. Thus when an opportunity arose for employment in education outside the army and close to home, he took it. On January

18. Grady McWhiney, *Braxton Bragg and Confederate Defeat*, vol. 1 (1969; reprint, Tuscaloosa: University of Alabama Press, 1991) 33–35; Wingfield, *Stewart*, 31–37, S. G. French, *Two Wars: An Autobiography of Gen. Samuel G. French* (Nashville: Confederate Veteran, 1901), 21.

19. USMA, *Regulations*, 11–12; USMA, *Official Register of the Officers and Cadets of the U.S. Military Academy, 1844.*

20. Wingfield, *Stewart*, 29–30.

22, 1845, the trustees of Cumberland University in Lebanon, Tennessee, elected Stewart professor of mathematics. Stewart's duties at West Point ended February 25, 1845, and his resignation from the army was effective May 31, 1845. Apparently by that date, Stewart was at Cumberland working in his new job.[21]

Before the start of the new school year in September, 1845, Stewart traveled to Warren, Ohio, and married Harriet on August 27, 1845. They returned to Lebanon, a small town established around 1800 about thirty miles to the east of Nashville and about ninety miles north of Winchester. Only three years before, Cumberland University had been established there by the General Assembly of the Cumberland Presbyterian Church. Shortly after Professor and Mrs. Stewart's arrival, the Educational Committee of the Cumberland Presbyterian General Assembly described the school: "It has a fine, large college edifice, a president, four professors, two tutors, and seventy-six students; twenty-one of whom are ordained ministers, licentiates and candidates for the ministry."[22]

The Stewarts came to consider Lebanon home. Except for two interludes in Nashville, Stewart lived in Lebanon until May, 1861. His first son, Robert Caruthers, was born in Lebanon at the home of Stewart's fellow faculty member, Robert Looney Caruthers, on June 14, 1846. Alphonso, doubtless named for Harriet's lost brother, was born August 27, 1848, followed by Alexander Peter, Jr., on February 20, 1859, and Gustavus Woodson Smith Stewart on February 25, 1861.

As made evident by the name of their first-born son, Professor and Mrs. Stewart esteemed their relationship with Caruthers and his wife. A founder of Cumberland University, Caruthers was the first president of its board of trustees. By 1846, he had been a member of the Tennessee legislature and a state's attorney, and had served a term in Congress as a Whig. The next year, he would found Cumberland's law school, and would, by 1852, sit

21. George W. Cullum, *Biographical Register of the Officers and Graduates of the U.S. Military Academy at West Point, N.Y.* (Boston: Houghton, Mifflin, 1891), 2:124; Ridley, *Battles and Sketches*, 473; Winstead P. Bone, *A History of Cumberland University, 1842–1935* (Lebanon, Tenn.: Winstead P. Bone, 1935), 68–69.

22. G. Frank Burns, *Wilson County* (Memphis: Memphis State University Press, 1983), 22, 33–34; Wingfield, *Stewart*, 38; Bone, *History of Cumberland University*, 71.

on the Tennessee Supreme Court. Caruthers would prove to be among the strongest of Stewart's connections to Cumberland University.[23]

Stewart's close relationship to Judge Caruthers would in time be put to the test, as the young family's finances were inextricably linked with those of the fledgling university. Stewart saw himself as having given up an honorable position in the army with a "competent salary" for the university job. But Cumberland's representatives, among them Caruthers, made "flattering expectations" which were "disappointed," so that a substantial portion of Stewart's small salary—about twelve hundred or thirteen hundred dollars—was in arrears by 1849. An opportunity to improve his prospects appearing, Stewart resigned his professorship on October 1, 1849, and took a similar post at the University of Nashville.

Caruthers and Cumberland's president, T. C. Anderson, soon launched a protracted campaign to bring Stewart back to Cumberland. Stewart was understandably disappointed with the financial rewards of teaching to that point, and his main concerns were the long-term financial well-being of his family, getting out of debt, and the wherewithal to build a home. Caruthers, Anderson, and possibly others offered Stewart additional financial guarantees and other commitments to induce him to return to Cumberland, but not before Stewart had investigated the possibility of going to work for a railroad. Writing to Caruthers, Stewart indicated that his sole ambition was a "*permanent* situation, where I can provide myself & my family with a comfortable home, live a useful and respected citizen, and qualify my children to become useful and respected citizens after me." Returning to Lebanon in late October, 1850, Stewart planned to erect a house of a style seen near Harriet's family home in Ohio, "handsome . . . and sufficiently roomy . . . which they build there very cheaply." The home eventually erected by the Stewart family fit that description, and is still in use today.[24]

Stewart's correspondence with a Chicago merchant during that school year suggest renewed efforts by the school's administration and supporters

---

23. Wingfield, *Stewart*, 39, 208, 211, 213; Joshua W. Caldwell, *Sketches of the Bench and Bar of Tennessee* (Knoxville: Ogden Brothers, 1898), 144–46.

24. APS to R. L. Caruthers, February 9, May 13, June 16, July 10, July 16, 1850, R. L. Caruthers Papers, SHC.

to improve Stewart's situation. Stewart placed an order for a "polarscope and reflector" and made a detailed inquiry as to other equipment, "such as would be suitable for illustrating lectures on astronomy, before an *intelligent* audience." Stewart was obviously happy enough with Cumberland's efforts in 1851 to turn down an offer of a position by the Virginia Military Institute, which was subsequently filled by Thomas J. Jackson. Recognizing that there were few qualified engineers in the Southwest, Stewart established Cumberland's School of Engineering in 1852. Notwithstanding these indications that the Cumberland administration was making good-faith efforts to improve matters, apparently prospects there did not proceed at the pace Stewart desired, as he resigned on August 2, 1854, once more to go to Nashville.

Stewart taught at the University of Nashville for the 1854–1855 school year, apparently in the affiliated Western Military Institute. Later in 1855, he took a job as city surveyor for Nashville. In 1856, he returned to Cumberland. About 1858, he was offered the chancellorship of Washington University in St. Louis, but eventually chose to remain at Cumberland in order to stay close to his students. The University of Mississippi also sought Stewart's services during these years. The roots that he and his family put down in Lebanon must have exerted an equally powerful influence, for in addition to these varied opportunities and positions, Stewart apparently had charge of a female school at Lebanon in the late 1850s. As a later sketch of Stewart noted, "The number and variety of these calls attest the high scholarly worth of the man, and the extent of his fame in the South."[25]

Stewart had his share of sorrow as well as happiness in these years. On October 18, 1847, his mother passed away, albeit in an atmosphere of "Christian triumph." Stewart would also lose his brother Samuel to yellow

25. Wingfield, *Stewart*, 39–40; APS to R. L. Caruthers, June 16, 1850, R. L. Caruthers Papers, SHC; APS to J. M. Wrightman, February 12, 1851, Joseph Milner Wrightman Papers, DU; Bruce Allardice, "West Points of the Confederacy: Southern Military Schools and the Confederate Army," *Civil War History* 43 (December, 1997): 310, 324–35; James I. Robertson, Jr., *Stonewall Jackson: The Man, the Soldier, the Legend* (New York: Macmillan, 1997), 103; Bone, *History of Cumberland University*, 79, 95; Burns, *Wilson County*, 100; Pollard, *Lee and His Lieutenants*, 712; Carole Prietto, Washington University archivist, to author, December 2, 1996. Wingfield and Pollard conflict somewhat on the exact dates of Stewart's various prewar jobs.

fever in New Orleans in 1853, and his brother James to the same disease the next year.[26]

Though William and Elizabeth had brought their children up in a home imbued with Christianity (indeed, William Stewart had written to his sons of the great consolation he derived from Elizabeth's faith as she faced her death), Alexander Stewart appears to have had some doubts as a younger man. As a plebe at West Point, Stewart wrote his sister Catherine:

> But we must submit to the decrees of Heaven and learn to bless the hand that afflicts us, for it is for our own benefit; at least I suppose so: and I hope the consideration of that religion you profess will in a great measure alleviate your grief. . . . You speak of my meeting you and Mr. Hawkins in Heaven; I hope I shall do so, but I don't know. This is a strange world and strange ideas sometimes fill my brain.[27]

While at Cumberland, however, Stewart experienced a conversion during an old-fashioned revival. He thereafter became "a man of the deepest piety," and later organized at Cumberland the first college chapter of the Young Men's Christian Association.[28]

Stewart's political leanings were with the Whigs, no doubt due in large part to the influence of Judge Caruthers. In the South, the Whigs were the party of urban and commercial banking interests, and the majority of the planters. The Democrats were mostly supported by the small farmers. The Whig party in the South had such strength as to almost split the vote fifty-fifty in the five presidential elections between 1836 and 1852. As the watershed election of 1860 approached, the Whigs had largely disappeared from the national scene, replaced in the North by the new Republican party. In the South, especially in border states such as Tennessee, old-line Whigs and conservative Democrats turned to the Constitutional Union party, which fielded John Bell of Tennessee as a candidate for president on the sole platform of the Constitution, the Union, and the laws. In the elec-

---

26. Wingfield, *Stewart*, 16–17.

27. APS to Catherine Jones, September 26, 1838, in Wingfield, *Stewart*, 26.

28. Wingfield, *Stewart*, 177; Bone, *History of Cumberland University*, 95–96. At a later point in life, Stewart "became so full of religion that he would conduct prayer meetings." Wingfield, *Stewart*, 177.

tion that followed, Bell carried only the border states of Tennessee, Kentucky, and Virginia, the states most likely to be the scenes of strife between the North and South. Abraham Lincoln's election unleashed forces in the South and in the United States as a whole that would upset the prosperous peace of Professor Stewart's life, and overturn the lives of millions of his countrymen.[29]

29. Wingfield, *Stewart*, 40; J. G. Randall and David Donald, *The Civil War and Reconstruction* (Lexington, Mass.: D. C. Heath, 1969), 47, 102, 104, 132–33.

— 2 —

The Defense of Our Rights

Secession to New Madrid

Secessionists did not have an easy task withdrawing Tennessee from the Union. Stewart observed after the Civil War that in 1861 the people loved the Union and were loyal to the Constitution. A popular vote in February of that year rejected a secessionist convention 91,803 to 24,709.[1] Years later, Stewart explained, "The people were afraid that such a body, convened in the midst of the prevailing excitement, would act hastily, and, by the adoption of an ordinance of secession, withdraw the State from the Union without giving them an opportunity to pass upon such course."[2]

President Lincoln's call to the governors of the various states for 75,000 volunteers after the fall of Fort Sumter changed the attitude of most Tennesseans. Governor Isham G. Harris, an ardent secessionist, defiantly replied to Lincoln, "Tennessee will not furnish a single man for coercion, but fifty thousand, if necessary, for the defense of our rights or those of our Southern brethren." On May 6, the Tennessee General Assembly passed a secessionist "Declaration of Independence and Ordinance," to be ratified

---

1. Stanley F. Horn, *The Army of Tennessee* (1941; reprint, Wilmington, N.C.: Broadfoot Publishing, 1987), 47; Ridley, *Battles and Sketches*, 619; John Berrian Lindsley, ed., *The Military Annals of Tennessee: Confederate* (Nashville: J. M. Lindsley, 1886), 60. Stewart wrote an extensive sketch of the Army of Tennessee for this book, which is a useful overview of the army and provides valuable insight into his view after the war of certain events in it.

2. Lindsley, ed., *Military Annals*, 60.

or rejected by an election on June 8. Also on May 6, the General Assembly passed an act creating the Provisional Army of Tennessee, with an authorized strength of 55,000 men. On May 7, the General Assembly ratified a military alliance with the Confederacy. By June, Tennessee was so far into the Confederate orbit that it was almost impossible for the voters to reject secession. This spawned a popular saying in the state at the time that "Tennessee never seceded; Isham G. Harris seceded and carried Tennessee along with him."[3]

In a broader sense, Harris was merely a vehicle to play out Tennessee's "inescapable dilemma," a phenomenon common to the other states of the Upper South. The voters were forced to choose either the Union without the South or the South without the Union. The vote on June 8 was 104,913 to 47,238 in favor of secession.[4] Whether Harris was the cause or just a vehicle, Tennessee had cast its lot with the Confederacy.

Stewart stated thirty years later that he was "deeply grieved" when South Carolina seceded from the Union. Assuming that his later writings reflect his thinking in 1861, we can conclude that Stewart felt the crisis of 1860–61 was purely a constitutional issue. He deemed the South to be on the side of right, since the 1857 *Dred Scott* decision of the United States Supreme Court recognized slaves as property protected by the Constitution throughout the Union. Notwithstanding his personal opposition to slavery, Stewart was of the opinion that northern states had acted unconstitutionally in refusing to enforce the fugitive slave laws. To Stewart and other southerners, Abraham Lincoln's election foreshadowed the overthrow of the South's "constitutional rights and guarantees, and the ultimate destruction of her entire social and industrial organization."[5]

Stewart thought secession unwise but well within the constitutional rights of the southern people. Twenty-five years later, he posed the ques-

---

3. Ibid.; Randall and Donald, *Civil War and Reconstruction*, 186; Thomas L. Connelly, *Army of the Heartland* (Baton Rouge: Louisiana State University Press, 1967), 26; Nathaniel C. Hughes, Jr., and Roy P. Stonsifer, Jr., *The Life and Wars of Gideon J. Pillow* (Chapel Hill: University of North Carolina Press, 1993), 162; Horn, *Army of Tennessee*, 47. A more moderate view of Harris' role in the secession crisis may be found in Stanley F. Horn, "Isham G. Harris in the Pre-War Years," *Tennessee Historical Quarterly* 19 (September 1960): 195–207.

4. Randall and Donald, *Civil War and Reconstruction*, 186.

5. Lindsley, ed., *Military Annals*, 59; Ridley, *Battles and Sketches*, 620; Wingfield, *Stewart*, 40.

tion, "If [the South's] people thought it in every way better for them to separate from the Union and form a Confederacy of their own, on what *just* ground could they be prevented from doing so? and whence did the Government of the Union derive authority to coerce them?"[6]

Stewart's actions in 1861 were consistent with his description of mainstream thought in the state. He voted against the secession convention in February. He seems to have had hope for the "Peace Convention" held in Washington that month at the behest of moderates of both sides. After Fort Sumter, however, Stewart tendered his services to Governor Harris and was employed by the state military board, making army contracts and organizing training camps. Among his first tasks, Stewart secured property in his native Franklin County as a camp for newly recruited troops. On May 17, 1861, he was appointed major of the Tennessee Provisional Army's artillery corps, ranked by Colonel John P. McCown and Lieutenant Colonel Milton A. Haynes, who were senior in part because of their having graduated from West Point before Stewart. Offered the command of the Provisional Army's 7th Regiment, Stewart declined because he felt himself most useful at the time in the artillery.[7]

Organizing the state's artillery started slowly. On May 9, the Provisional Army's commanding officer, Major General Gideon J. Pillow, complained that although five thousand men were then under arms, he was without any artillery. Major Stewart went to Randolph, in Shelby County north of Memphis, to instruct the new recruits in artillery drill and the management of guns. Batteries were also placed on the Mississippi River there. Stewart was given responsibility for the state's heavy artillery battalion, which, unlike the field artillery units, had a number of large-caliber guns for river defense. Later in the summer, the battalion moved fifteen miles north of Randolph to Fort Pillow.[8]

6. Lindsley, ed., *Military Annals*, 60.

7. Wingfield, *Stewart*, 42; Ridley, *Battles and Sketches*, 473, 619–20; Dillard Jacobs, "Outfitting the Provisional Army of Tennessee: A Report on New Source Materials," *Tennessee Historical Quarterly* 40 (fall 1981): 257, 269; APS to Andrew Johnson, July 10, 1865, APS Pardon Application File, RG 74, NA; Pollard, *Lee and His Lieutenants*, 712; Larry J. Daniel, *Cannoneers in Gray: The Field Artillery of the Army of Tennessee, 1861–1865* (Tuscaloosa: University of Alabama, 1984), 5.

8. Daniel, *Cannoneers*, 3–4; Ridley, *Battles and Sketches*, 474; TCWCC, *Tennesseans in the Civil War* (Nashville, 1964), 1:123.

Confederate forces under Pillow occupied New Madrid, Missouri, on July 28, 1861. Pillow envisioned the town as a base for possible offensive operations in southeast Missouri, whereas newly appointed Major General Leonidas Polk and Brigadier General William J. Hardee, the latter the Confederate commander of northern Arkansas, saw the defensive possibilities of the town. Pillow's troops found New Madrid a "neat little town," with wide and level streets, white houses, and hospitable residents sympathetic to the South.[9] Both New Madrid and nearby Island No. 10 were important links in the Confederate defense of the Mississippi.

On August 15, Stewart and his Provisional Army battalion were mustered into Confederate service and two days later received orders from Polk to relieve McCown at Island No. 10. Pillow disagreed with the assignment, but Polk replied to the effect that it had not been a request, but an order. A report from Island No. 10 on August 20 noted Stewart's presence there.[10]

Stewart's resumed military career to this point reflected an emphasis on Mississippi River defense as conceived by Harris and Pillow at the Provisional Army's inception. Throughout the summer of 1861, the bulk of Confederate forces in the state occupied various forts along the Mississippi. The resulting neglect of the Tennessee and Cumberland Rivers has been considered Harris' worst move as the commander of the state's Provisional Army. Part of this neglect, however, stemmed from Harris' confidence that Kentucky would stay neutral in the coming fight. As long as no Federal troops could enter Kentucky, Tennessee's northern border would need no defense. This theory collapsed when Stewart and other Confederates under Major General Leonidas Polk occupied Columbus, Kentucky, on September 4.[11]

Columbus was considered a prime location for the heavy batteries

9. Hughes and Stonsifer, *Pillow*, 174–81; J. G. Law, "Diary of the Rev. J. G. Law," *Southern Historical Society Papers* 10 (December 1882): 568–69.

10. TCWCC, *Tennesseans*, 1:123.

11. Connelly, *Army of the Heartland*, 39–40; Ridley, *Battles and Sketches*, 623; Larry Daniel, "The Quinby and Robinson Cannon Foundry at Memphis," *West Tennessee Historical Society Papers* 27 (1973): 18, 28; William M. Polk, *Leonidas Polk, Bishop and General* (New York: Longmans, Green, 1893, 1915), 1:70–71. For Polk's background, see Ezra Warner, *Generals in Gray* (Baton Rouge: Louisiana State University Press, 1959), 242–43; Joseph H. Parks, *General Leonidas Polk, C.S.A.: Fighting Bishop* (Baton Rouge: Louisiana State University Press, 1962), 21, 36–37, 71, 135–52.

needed to stop the Federal gunboats then being constructed at St. Louis. While the possession of Columbus was consistent with the Confederate preoccupation with the defense of the Mississippi, its occupation ironically negated Kentucky neutrality, the one factor that made the almost complete emphasis on the Mississippi valid. When he occupied Columbus, Polk failed to occupy Paducah, located at the confluence of the Tennessee and the Ohio. Union brigadier general Ulysses S. Grant moved in, and almost immediately the Confederate position at Columbus was subject to a flanking movement up the Tennessee. The situation was made worse by the Confederate navy's inability to construct ironclad gunboats to counter those the Federals were building.[12]

On September 10, 1861, General Albert Sidney Johnston assumed command of the Confederate West from Tennessee to Kansas. Like Polk, Johnston was an old friend of Confederate president Jefferson Davis' and had known him even before both had entered West Point. Johnston was acclaimed by all as one of the South's great soldiers, Davis being of the opinion that Johnston was his one sure hope of having a good general. When Johnston came to Columbus early in October, 1861, Stewart and McCown called on him at Polk's headquarters. Johnston told the two Tennesseans that he had recommended both for promotion to brigadier general. In fact, Johnston requested Stewart's appointment as a brigadier general to command the defenses at Columbus. While McCown's promotion came through on October 12, Johnston's request regarding Stewart was initially denied by the War Department. Instead, it appointed Colonel Lloyd Tilghman of Kentucky, "whose record shows longer and better service, and who is, besides, as a Kentuckian, especially appropriate to the command at Columbus."[13] Tilghman's "longer and better service" could only have been a reference to his experience in the Mexican War, which Stewart missed.

Accepting this response as a rebuke, Johnston wrote to Simon Bolivar

12. Steven E. Woodworth, *Jefferson Davis and His Generals* (Lawrence: University Press of Kansas, 1990), 36–39; Robert V. Boyle, "Defeat Through Default: Confederate Naval Strategy for the Upper Mississippi River and Its Tributaries, 1861–1862," *Tennessee Historical Quarterly* 27 (spring 1968): 62–71; F. Gilmer to W. W. Mackall, December 9, 1861, Letters Sent, Chief of Engineers, Western Department, 1861–1862, RG 109, NA.

13. Woodworth, *Jefferson Davis and His Generals*, 51; Connelly, *Army of the Heartland*, 59–62; APS to Marcus J. Wright, October 30, 1880, Marcus J. Wright Papers, SHC; Warner, *Generals in Gray*, 199; OR 4:1, 453. All OR citations, unless otherwise noted, are to Series 1.

Buckner about Kentucky and other matters on October 19. Johnston stated that his nomination of Stewart and McCown as brigadier generals was not meant as a slight to Tilghman, but was made because he thought Tilghman would be appointed as a result of an earlier recommendation. He noted that the appointment of at least three competent brigadier generals was needed. Interestingly, on that same day, Polk reported sending "Major Stewart and four artillery officers" for a few days to drill the artillery troops at Dover on the Cumberland.[14]

On November 7, 1861, the aggressive Ulysses S. Grant landed a force above Belmont, Missouri, across the Mississippi from Columbus. Eschewing their fortifications, the Confederates met Grant in the open and were slowly pushed back in obstinate fighting. The Federals overran the camp of the regiment originally stationed at Belmont. Grant then formed a line at right angles to the river, intending to move up the riverbank and capture the disorganized and panicked Confederates. At this juncture, the Federals exposed themselves to fire from the Lady Polk, a huge cannon positioned on the bluff above Columbus, which shot large, conical shells similar in shape to a minié ball. At Stewart's command, the Lady Polk opened fire on the Federals, the first shot striking in front of their line, "throwing up a great cloud of dirt, and ricocheting over the heads of the men." Continued shelling from the heavy guns under Stewart's command slowed the Federal advance. A field battery on the lower end of Columbus added its fire. Timely Confederate reinforcements dispatched by Polk then restored the situation, and the Federals were driven back to their boats.[15]

With understandable hyperbole, Stewart wrote after the war that the battle "was really won by the 'big gun.'" In his report of the Battle of Belmont, Polk stated that the joint fire of Stewart's cannon and the field battery "was so terrific as to dislodge the enemy, silence his battery, and cause him to take up his line of march for his boats." Both Stewart and Captain Melancthon Smith of the field battery were praised "for the skill and judg-

14. William Preston Johnston, *The Life of Albert Sidney Johnston* (New York: D. Appleton, 1878), 415; *OR* 4:463, 468–70. Dover, of course, was the location of Fort Donelson.

15. Shelby Foote, *The Civil War* (New York: Random House, 1958), 1:149–52; Lindsley, ed., *Military Annals*, 66; Ridley, *Battles and Sketches*, 25–26; William D. Pickett, "The Bursting of the Lady Polk," *CV* 12 (June 1904): 277; Nathaniel C. Hughes, Jr., *The Battle of Belmont* (Chapel Hill: University of North Carolina Press, 1991), 140.

ment manifested in the service of the guns under their command, to the joint fire from which I feel not a little indebted for turning the fortunes of the day."[16]

A day or two after the battle, the Lady Polk's crew requested permission to fire a load left in the gun at the close of the battle. Stewart denied the request, feeling it would be better to draw the load out, and Stewart left for his tent outside the fort. Polk then came by on a tour of inspection. The crew made the same request of Polk, who agreed, asking that it be fired up the river so he could see its range. As Stewart was entering his tent, he heard a loud explosion. Looking toward the bluff, he could see a dense column of black smoke rising from the gun position, and correctly surmised that the gun had exploded. The explosion killed eleven, and injured three others, including Polk, who was incapacitated for some time afterward.[17]

Having not heard anything further about his expected promotion to brigadier general, Stewart, at Polk's suggestion, wrote Secretary of War Judah P. Benjamin on November 3 to inquire as to its status. Apparently, Johnston succeeded in explaining the need for another brigadier in addition to Tilghman and McCown, because on November 16, Stewart received a letter from Benjamin dated November 7 informing him that the commission had come through. The only problem had been that Johnston's recommendation had spelled the Tennessean's name as "Stuart," and President Davis simply was not aware of any officer of that name who he felt deserved such a promotion, until Stewart's own letter cleared up his identity. Stewart's commission dated from November 8, 1861. In gratitude, Stewart wrote Polk acknowledging Polk's assistance, and to inquire as to his new duties.[18]

On November 16, General Stewart received orders to report to Albert Sidney Johnston at Bowling Green, Kentucky. Stewart returned to Columbus and assumed command of a "brigade" consisting of the 5th Tennessee Infantry, two infantry battalions, two field artillery units, and the heavy artillery. Stewart's brigade was independent of any divisional organization,

16. Ridley, *Battles and Sketches*, 26; *OR* 3:308–309; Polk Belmont Report, November 10, 1861, Leonidas Polk Papers, LC.

17. Ridley, *Battles and Sketches*, 26–27.

18. APS to Marcus J. Wright, October 30, 1880, Wright Papers; APS to Leonidas Polk, November 16, 1861, APS/CSR, M-331, RG 109, NA; see also *OR* 4:533.

probably because it was the actual garrison of the works at Columbus. Later, Polk gave Stewart the formal title of chief of heavy artillery, a recognition of Stewart's *de facto* role since before Belmont.[19]

Soon after Albert Sidney Johnston had assumed command, he realized the great length of the line he was called on to defend and the dearth of resources available for the job. Because Davis could give him no troops, Johnston spent the winter building the impression that his army was much stronger than it actually was. He advanced his troops as far forward into Kentucky as possible, made numerous raids, and did what he could to create an illusion of great numbers. Johnston's deception worked to the end of January, 1862, when, ironically, the little help Richmond was able to send him brought it all crashing down.[20]

P. G. T. Beauregard had served in Virginia since his successful reduction of Fort Sumter in April, 1861. Beauregard went west as Johnston's second-in-command, where his name and presence would be a morale booster. Beauregard also had an enhanced reputation among the Federals, who heard false reports that he was bringing fifteen regiments from Virginia to reinforce Johnston. Already in the stages of planning an advance down the Tennessee, Ulysses S. Grant was authorized to do so before the phantom Rebel reinforcements arrived. Within two days of Beauregard's arrival at Bowling Green on February 4, Grant was at Fort Henry with 15,000 men and four ironclad gunboats. The loss of Fort Henry, and the subsequent fall of Fort Donelson, split Johnston's line in two.[21]

Empowered by Johnston to direct affairs in West Tennessee, Beauregard met with Polk in mid-February and informed him that a new defensive line would stretch from Corinth, Mississippi, south of the Tennessee River, northwest to Jackson and Humboldt, Tennessee, on to New Madrid and Island No. 10. Beauregard felt Columbus required too many men to garri-

---

19. OR 4:559, 7:727, 854, 906; APS to Leonidas Polk, December 21, 1861, APS/CSR; APS to Leonidas Polk, January 16, 1862, A. P. Stewart Papers, DU.

20. Woodworth, *Jefferson Davis and His Generals*, 54–56, 72, 75–79; Peter Franklin Walker, "Building a Tennessee Army: Autumn, 1861," *Tennessee Historical Quarterly* 16 (June 1957): 99–116.

21. Warner, *Generals in Gray*, 22–23; Woodworth, *Jefferson Davis and His Generals*, 75–79.

son, since New Madrid and Island No. 10 could be held by fewer troops. Over Polk's objections, Beauregard ordered the evacuation of Columbus.[22]

Island No. 10 was the key to the New Madrid area's utility as a defensive point on the river. The position commanded an unobstructed view up the river from a point just south of the Tennessee state line for several miles, along a stretch of the river known as the Seven Mile Reach. Island No. 10 lay at the bottom of the first curve of an inverted S. Down the river, but to the northeast of Island No. 10, on the curve of the inverted S projecting north, lay the town of New Madrid. Prior to the evacuation of Columbus, New Madrid was protected by Fort Thompson, a small fort with several cannon, and two regiments of Arkansas troops commanded by Colonel Edward W. Gantt.[23]

The Federals recognized that New Madrid was the weak point of this defensive system. Its possession would enable them to cut off Island No. 10 from supplies and reinforcements sent from downstream, the only practical way to resupply the island. On February 18, 1862, Stewart's former roommate, Brigadier General John Pope, received orders to organize an expedition against New Madrid and Island No. 10. The new Federal commander characterized most of his 18,000 troops as "entirely raw." By February 28, they were able to set out on a swampy approach to New Madrid.[24]

Probably recognizing the same weaknesses at New Madrid as Pope and his superior Major General Henry Halleck had, Beauregard intended to hold the New Madrid area "only long enough to permit the completion of the stronger and more important works" farther south at Fort Pillow. On February 27, Stewart's fellow Tennessean John P. McCown was ordered to New Madrid from Columbus with his division of five regiments and attached artillery. Beauregard instructed McCown to hold the defenses to the "very last extremity," in order to give Fort Pillow a chance for completion. Beauregard ordered McCown to sink transports to block the nar-

22. Connelly, *Army of the Heartland*, 131–32; Horn, *Army of Tennessee*, 109–10.

23. Horn, *Army of Tennessee*, 110–11; Larry J. Daniel and Lynn M. Bock, *Island No. 10: Struggle for the Mississippi Valley* (Tuscaloosa: University of Alabama Press, 1996), 4–7, 10; Henry Walke, "The Western Flotilla at Fort Donelson, Island Number 10, Fort Pillow and Memphis," *B&L* 1:437 (map); *OR* 8:162–63.

24. *OR* 8:79, 80, 84; Daniel and Bock, *Island No. 10*, 18–19, 38–41, 61.

rower Missouri shore channel, and to place a fire-raft in the middle of the
Tennessee channel to prevent the passage of Federal gunboats by night. Finally, with the exception noted below, McCown would have to conduct
his defense without any further reinforcement.[25]

By the time General Pope and his army appeared in force before New
Madrid, McCown had received a final reinforcement: two regiments from
Fort Pillow—the 40th Tennessee, commanded by Colonel L. M. Walker,
and the uniquely named 1st Alabama, Tennessee, and Mississippi Regiment, commanded by Colonel Alpheus Baker—six gunboats of the Confederate States Navy, and, arriving by steamer from Columbus on March
1, Stewart and his brigade. McCown placed Stewart in immediate command of the forces at New Madrid. Colonel Gantt remained in command
of the existing work, Fort Thompson, with two regiments and two companies of artillery. A work north of the town on Bayou St. John, Fort Bankhead, was just under way when Stewart arrived. It was garrisoned by three
infantry regiments (including Stewart's 5th Tennessee), had one field battery of six pieces, and was commanded by Walker. Stewart later estimated
that there were fewer than 3,000 troops available for duty at New Madrid.[26]

North to south, the Confederate defenses consisted first of Fort Bankhead, which Stewart described as a strong parapet ditch in an irregular line,
beyond which was "a sort of abatis of brush and felled trees." It extended
from the bayou above the town three or four hundred yards to the river.
From there, lines of entrenchments extended below the town to Fort
Thompson, described by both Stewart and Pope as a "bastioned" work
mounting several cannon. While it appears there were substantial works
around New Madrid, C. W. Read, an officer on the supporting gunboats,
described the place as "poorly fortified." Pope felt that the works could
have been carried from the start, but that his troops would have incurred

25. *OR* 8:438; Alfred Roman, *The Military Operations of General Beauregard* (New York:
Harper, 1884), 1:256–57. The inconsistencies of Beauregard's after-the-fact explanation are
explored in Daniel and Bock, *Island No. 10*, 22–24. McCown was a native of Sevierville, Tennessee, who had reached the rank of captain in the 4th U.S. Artillery after being commended
for service in the Mexican War. He had been Stewart's superior in the artillery corps of the
Tennessee Provisional Army and ranked Stewart as a brigadier general in the Confederate service, his commission dating from October 12, 1861. Warner, *Generals in Gray*, 199.
26. *OR* 8:127, 162–63, 169–70, 184–85, 438; Daniel and Bock, *Island No. 10*, 25–26.

heavy losses and could not have held the works once captured because of exposure to gunboat fire.[27]

Stewart's first encounter with the Federals occurred on March 2. Colonel Thomas Jordan, Beauregard's aide, was present on behalf of his chief. Accompanied by other officers, Stewart and Jordan rode out of town, but encountered advance cavalry units from Pope's army. The Rebel officers wheeled about and rode hurriedly back to Confederate lines. Later that afternoon, Stewart met Colonel Baker, who "liked [Stewart] very well." Baker found that Stewart was "quite unexcited and self-possessed." Stewart gamely remarked to Baker: "I wonder what the bloody rascals intend. I don't believe they will come up tonight." Baker was of the impression that Stewart was about thirty-five years old, and observed he had "fine, light colored hair." Noting Stewart was "fair and freckled," Baker correctly guessed Stewart's Scottish ancestry.[28]

On March 3, the Federal infantry appeared in force and established their camp within sight of the town, skirmishing with the Confederate pickets all day. McCown wrote Polk that his position at New Madrid was "critical in the extreme," but that his command was in fine spirits. The Yankee troops were engaged by the Confederate gunboats. Baker, watching from the pilothouse of the *Vicksburg*, was heartened by the sound of their guns. Baker observed Stewart "walking quickly about looking at this and that with great sang froid & I thought exhibiting the coolness and self-possession which is one of the characteristics at least of a good commander."[29]

Pope observed that the Confederates defending New Madrid would not send a significant force of infantry outside their works. There was good reason for Stewart's lack of aggressiveness—lack of numbers. As early as March 3, McCown determined that the Confederate force was too small to risk in the open field. Reports from local citizens considered to be reliable inflated Pope's numbers to 50,000 men, which Stewart discounted to a

27. *OR* 8:81, 163; C. W. Read, "Reminiscences of the Confederate States Navy," *Southern Historical Society Papers* 1 (May 1876): 337.

28. Daniel and Bock, *Island No. 10*, 46; Alpheus Baker Diary, March 2, 1862, Alabama Department of Archives and History. Baker's entry provides the only contemporary physical description of Stewart. Photographs and his lifelike statue in Chattanooga suggest he was approximately five feet seven inches in height and weighed about 150 pounds.

29. *OR* 8:81–82, 127, 162; J. P. McCown to Leonidas Polk, March 3, 1862, Leonidas Polk Papers, Dupont Library, University of the South; Baker Diary, March 3, 1862.

much less exaggerated 25,000. Still, as Stewart's much smaller force of 3,000 was further reduced by sickness, manning over three miles of works against an aggressively skirmishing enemy with superior numbers was all that was possible.[30]

Just over a week after his initial approach to New Madrid, Pope received four heavy guns from the Federal base at Cairo, Illinois. About midnight on March 12, a strong Federal force was thrown forward to screen the construction of an emplacement about three-quarters of a mile from Fort Thompson, the work below the town. Colonel Gantt increased the strength of his pickets and sent an officer to report the movement to Stewart. Anticipating an approach to the fort from the south, Gantt ordered the commander of the fort's artillery, Captain R. A. Stewart, to redirect some of the fort's guns in that direction. By 3 A.M. on March 13, the Federals completed two small redoubts to emplace their heavy guns and rifle pits sufficient for two regiments of infantry.[31]

At dawn, the new Federal battery commenced firing on both Fort Thompson and the gunboats, which promptly returned the fire. For some time, the contest was chiefly between the Federal guns and the gunboats. Pope suffered from an ammunition shortage and wanted to concentrate on disabling the gunboats. On the Confederate side, Gantt's men at the fort were hampered by a combination of early-morning fog and smoke. Pope's guns registered some hits on those boats that approached too close to the fort. When the Rebels were able to return fire, they dispersed a force of Federal infantry massed a half mile away. Overall, very little damage was done, although both sides later recorded minor casualties through the course of a day's cannonading.[32]

More importantly, Pope spent the day extending and advancing his trenches, intending to place his batteries on the river below Fort Thompson during the next night. About midday on March 13, McCown first broached the subject of evacuation with Stewart. In response to an inquiry by McCown as to the practicability of removing the guns at Fort Thompson, Stewart indicated he thought it possible, but would need to take an-

    30. *OR* 8:81, 162–63; Lindsley, ed., *Military Annals*, 196; J. McCown to Leonidas Polk, March 3, 1862, Polk Papers, University of the South.
    31. *OR* 8:82, 163, 166.
    32. Ibid., 82, 166–67.

other look. When he returned to the upper fort at nightfall, Stewart was advised McCown was aboard Commodore George N. Hollins' flagship, the *McRae*. Being delayed, Stewart boarded the *McRae* in the midst of a conference between McCown, Hollins, and several of Hollins' officers. Without hearing the opinions of the others, Stewart was asked about evacuation. He replied that if the Confederates were reinforced within a short time in sufficient strength to enable them to take to the field (in other words, outside the works), they would be able to hold out longer. McCown then indicated that further aid would not arrive for a minimum of ten days. Stewart stated that he did not think the forts could hold out that long, as there were insufficient artillerymen to provide reliefs for the guns. Further, the infantry was also fatigued, from frequent alarms and constant labor on the entrenchments.

Commodore Hollins expressed the view that if an evacuation was to take place, it should be done at once. If Pope was able to complete his work downriver from Fort Thompson, getting transports to the fort, which had been a difficult enough process during the exchange of fire on March 13, would be impossible. After this exchange, McCown, Hollins, and Stewart all agreed upon the need to evacuate New Madrid that night.[33]

McCown assigned to Stewart the task of evacuating Fort Thompson. The gunboats *General Polk* and *Livingston* were to remove the garrison and property downriver to Tiptonville, Tennessee. The gunboats' commander, Lieutenant Jonathan H. Carter, told Stewart they would be sufficient for that purpose. When Stewart reached the fort, he advised Colonel Gantt and his officers of the evacuation. Finding that Gantt deployed no pickets, Stewart ordered Colonel Jabez M. Smith of the 11th Arkansas to take seven companies and advance them as pickets as close to the Federal lines as possible without bringing on a fight. Stewart then ordered the removal of the fort's ammunition and guns. While most of the garrison and the sailors loaded the ammunition, work began on removing the big guns at the fort. After the Rebels moved two of the twenty-four-pounders down to the river, an enormous thunderstorm broke, pummeling the fort with rain for the rest of the night. The resulting mud made it impossible to remove the other heavy guns.[34]

33. Ibid., 82, 127, 163–64, 184–85.
34. Ibid., 128, 164, 167–68.

Stewart found that a combination of the rain, his mere two weeks' familiarity with Gantt and his command, and Lieutenant Carter's nervousness about the safety of his boats made his task extremely difficult. The men became sullen and indisposed to work. Guns were spiked without Stewart's order. At Carter's instance, Gantt embarked his regiment on the boats without Stewart's permission. Once it became apparent the heavier guns could not be removed, Gantt was ordered out with some men to cut up the gun carriages. Colonel Smith and his men were called in and an artillery officer sent to ensure the demolition of the gun carriages. Gantt went into the camp to make sure no stragglers were left, but apparently missed thirteen men from Smith's pickets, who Gantt surmised had taken shelter from the storm and fallen asleep. Once Gantt assured Stewart that all troops were on the boats, Stewart embarked, and between three and four o'clock the morning of March 14, the boats transported his wet but relatively steady men to Tiptonville. At seven o'clock that evening, Stewart was ordered to report to McCown at Island No. 10. McCown placed Gantt and his two Fort Thompson regiments to prevent a Federal crossing to the Tennessee side of the river.[35]

Stewart's report is his only writing on the subject of the defense and evacuation of New Madrid. This may not be surprising, since the defense of New Madrid was generally considered to be a very sorry effort. As the overall commander on the scene, McCown bore particular blame. Beauregard described it as "the poorest defense made by any fortified post during the whole course of the war." Major General Braxton Bragg wrote that the post was "disgracefully abandoned" and wrongly ascribed the evacuation, at least in part, to whiskey. Drunkenness was not McCown's problem, but misinterpretation of Beauregard's instructions appears to have been, at least in part. While Beauregard wanted New Madrid held long enough to allow the completion of the defenses at Fort Pillow, McCown wrote that his "principal object" in holding the town "was to possess a landing for reinforcements to fight the enemy, should I receive them."[36]

Gantt, too, seems to have suffered from New Madrid fallout. Naval officer Read termed him an "Arkansas demagogue" who "took the 'shell

35. Ibid., 128, 129, 164–65, 168.
36. Horn, *Army of Tennessee*, 144; Daniel and Bock, *Island No. 10*, 66; *OR* 8:128; Braxton Bragg to wife, March 29, 1862, Braxton Bragg Papers, LC.

fever' quicker than any man I ever saw."[37] The *Official Records* contain a curious letter from Gantt to General Polk in August, 1862, protesting what was obviously a charge of drunkenness during the evacuation on March 13–14. The letter reads as if Stewart made the charge, although Stewart did not mention that Gantt was intoxicated in his report of the evacuation. Stewart was apparently perturbed, however, by Gantt's loading his regiment at the behest of the frantic Lieutenant Carter without leave. Gantt was later nominated for promotion as a brigadier general, but was never confirmed in that rank. Doubtless this rebuff played a large part in Gantt's switching sides in late 1863.[38]

There is no indication that Stewart's reputation suffered from his involvement at New Madrid. He was pressed, nevertheless, by Beauregard for a report on the evacuation, which he had to defer until after the Battle of Shiloh. While he was not in command, the record is clear that Stewart supported the decision to evacuate the post. It should be considered that, as a subordinate officer, he may not have been made privy to Beauregard's instructions to McCown.

It is difficult to criticize the defense of New Madrid. Outnumbered six to one, the Confederates did not have the mobile force necessary to stop Pope's approach trenches. Once Pope erected a battery on the river below Fort Thompson, his guns would have been able to smash the largely unarmored Confederate gunboats, the one significant Rebel advantage. Without waterborne communications, the New Madrid garrison would inevitably have been exhausted to the point of surrender, just as the garrison of Island No. 10 was three weeks later. Significantly, McCown, Hollins, Gantt, and Stewart all expressed in their official reports the necessity of evacuation on the night of March 13–14. No doubt in sympathy for McCown, and perhaps in hopes of dissipating any lingering doubts over his own participation in the affair, Stewart later passed along to Beauregard McCown's request for a court of inquiry, a request that was denied as "impractical."[39]

37. Read, "Reminiscences," 337.
38. *OR* 8:168–69, 164; Marcus J. Wright, *Arkansas in the War, 1861–1865* (Batesville, Ark.: Independence County Historical Society, 1963), 67; Bruce S. Allardice, *More Generals in Gray* (Baton Rouge: Louisiana State University Press, 1995), 97–98.
39. *OR* 8:127, 162, 163, 167, 184–85; APS to Thomas Jordan, April 3, 1862, APS to P. G. T. Beauregard, April 22, 1862, with endorsement, APS/CSR.

As to Stewart's performance at New Madrid, McCown apparently made most of the significant decisions on defense. Additionally, there seems to be no question that there were insufficient troops for an effective defense against Pope's numbers. But the evacuation of Fort Thompson, which was Stewart's primary responsibility, does not appear to have been a model of efficiency. While Stewart reported that only a small amount of ammunition had been left and the heavy guns had been disabled, Pope reported the capture of a great quantity of ammunition. The Federals were able to get the heavy guns back in operation relatively quickly, and found signs of a "disgraceful panic."[40]

Although Stewart was unable to reinforce his men, keep them dry, or equip them more fully, it *was* in his power to inspire them by example. According to Alpheus Baker's observations, Stewart demonstrated coolness and self-possession to his command. These qualities, which never left him during the war, were stretched to the limit during the evacuation. In light of the hasty decision to withdraw and the need for stealth in the face of the enemy, Stewart performed adequately in the evacuation. The Tennessean's lack of experience at this stage of the war, his unfamiliarity with Gantt and his men, and the adverse weather conditions that plagued the evacuation support this conclusion. Stewart was able to recognize the need to abandon New Madrid, and later forthrightly acknowledged the fact, although he doubtless was aware of the contrary opinions of the Confederate high command.

After the evacuation of New Madrid, Stewart and the 5th Tennessee of his brigade moved downriver to Fort Pillow, Tennessee. The unsuccessful defense of the Mississippi irritated Major General Braxton Bragg, who had moved with troops of his Gulf Coast command to Corinth, Mississippi, to join with Johnston. Authorized to put his own generals at Fort Pillow and Island No. 10, Bragg replaced Stewart with Brigadier General John Villipigue. Released from Fort Pillow, Stewart and some of his regiments moved south to join the Confederate troops concentrating at Corinth, a few miles across the Tennessee-Mississippi line from a Methodist meeting-house known as Shiloh Church.[41]

40. *OR* 8:83, 165.

41. *OR* 10(1):129, 352, also in Daniel Ruggles Papers, MDAH; APS to Thomas Jordan, March 25, 1862, APS/CSR; B. Bragg to wife, March 29, 1862, Bragg Papers; Special Orders No. 468, March 28, 1862, No. 475, March 29, 1862, Polk's Corps, Army of the Mississippi, Special Orders, 1862, RG 109, NA.

— 3 —

No Army Did Better Work

Shiloh

However history may view Albert Sidney Johnston, Alexander P. Stewart believed him a "great commander" whose life and character the school-children of the South would study as a "new classic," in place of the ancient classics.[1] Stewart's admiration for Johnston may indeed have been heightened by Johnston's having been the moving force behind his promotion to brigadier general. Yet there is also every indication that the admiration grew out of a considered and objective opinion. Stewart's postwar writings make it clear that he, having endured the Army of Tennessee's bitter years of defeat, saw the near victory of Shiloh as the army's one chance to truly destroy a Federal army and change the course of the war in the West. Stewart believed that the destruction of the Yankees on April 6, 1862, would have been accomplished had Johnston survived:

> The field had been completely swept, and the foe driven back to the river under shelter of the fire from his gunboats. It needed only the inspiring presence and skillful hand of the master-spirit that had raised and guided the storm of battle to press the enemy to a surrender, and thus put the finishing stroke to one of the most brilliant victories of which the annals of war contain a record. But alas! that mas-

---

1. Lindsley, ed., *Military Annals*, 64; Ridley, *Battles and Sketches*, 622.

ter-spirit was no more of earth. In the very moment of victory, the battle, and with it seemingly the Confederate cause, was lost.[2]

In the six weeks after the fall of Fort Donelson, Johnston, once acknowledged first among Confederate soldiers, was considered by some to be among the most incompetent. The Tennessee delegation in the Confederate Congress called on Davis for Johnston's removal, citing a lack of confidence in his military skill. In his history of the Army of Tennessee, Stewart acknowledged the public indignation heaped upon Johnston and even the army's loss of confidence in its commander. No doubt like other knowledgeable officers, Stewart must have recognized the almost insurmountable problems Johnston faced in the late winter of 1862.[3]

Popularity aside, something had to be done to remedy the situation. The obvious move was to unite the various weak detachments under Johnston's command and defeat the Unionists in detail. Corinth, Mississippi, was chosen as a concentration point, as it lay on the east-west line of the Memphis and Charleston Railroad, termed by one Confederate officer "the vertebrae of the Confederacy." It also lay on the line of the north-south Mobile and Ohio Railroad, the route south from Columbus for Leonidas Polk's forces. Finally, Corinth was within twenty or so miles of the Tennessee River, after Fort Henry an easy steamboat trip for Grant and his own Army of the Tennessee.[4]

William T. Sherman had attempted a raid on the Memphis and Charleston Railroad from the river in mid-March, 1862, but was impeded by the weather. He had set up camp at Pittsburg Landing, Tennessee, on the river

2. Lindsley, ed., *Military Annals*, 74. See APS to M. S. O'Donnell, March 24, 1892, Alexander P. Stewart Letter, Western Reserve Historical Society, Cleveland, Ohio. Stewart's opinion was shared by many other southerners. See Horn, *Army of Tennessee*, 122. Modern analysis suggests otherwise. See Larry J. Daniel, *Shiloh: The Battle That Changed the Civil War* (New York: Simon & Schuster, 1997), 316–17.

3. Connelly, *Army of the Heartland*, 138; Lindsley, ed., *Military Annals*, 71–72; Daniel, *Shiloh*, 49–50; William J. Hardee to Felicia L. Shover, April 3, 1862, William J. Hardee Papers, LC (deploring "abominable slander" against Johnston).

4. Horn, *Army of Tennessee*, 107, 108; Daniel, *Shiloh*, 68. There was some debate between the adherents of Johnston and the adherents of Beauregard as to who chose Corinth as a place to concentrate. See Woodworth, *Jefferson Davis and His Generals*, 95; Connelly, *Army of the Heartland*, 138–39. Stewart chose to side with Johnston. Lindsley, ed., *Military Annals*, 70, 73.

twenty-two miles from Corinth, and recommended to General Halleck that the Federals concentrate their forces there. Grant had moved the remainder of his six divisions to the area. The Federal Army of the Tennessee around Pittsburg Landing totaled about 42,000 men, pending the arrival of Major General Don Carlos Buell's 35,000-man Army of the Ohio from Nashville.[5]

Pittsburg Landing was on the western side of the Tennessee River, where the banks were essentially steep bluffs. Federal troops located there found the site dirty and primitive. By the first of April, five of Grant's six divisions were spread out in unfortified camps between Owl Creek on the north and Lick Creek on the south. The headquarters of Sherman's division was near Shiloh Church, a small hewn-log building about two and one-half miles south of the landing on the main Corinth road. The name *Shiloh* was ironically from an ancient Hebrew word meaning "place of peace."[6]

As part of the reorganization of the troops massing at Corinth, Stewart commanded a brigade built in part around the troops he had evacuated from Island No. 10. Lieutenant Colonel C. D. Venable's 5th Tennessee Regiment went with Stewart to Fort Pillow. This regiment was part of Stewart's Columbus brigade and had garrisoned the upper fort at New Madrid. Colonel Rufus P. Neely's 4th Tennessee was evacuated from Island No. 10, going to Corinth by way of Memphis.[7]

Joining Stewart at Corinth were Colonel James C. Tappan's 13th Arkansas, veterans of Belmont, and Colonel Alexander W. Campbell's 33rd Tennessee. Attached to the brigade was Captain Thomas J. Stanford's battery from Yalobusha County, Mississippi. Like the four infantry regiments of the brigade, the battery had been part of the Columbus garrison. The battery was equipped with two 12-pounder howitzers, three 6-pounders, and one 3-inch rifle. Stewart's new brigade was placed in a division under

5. Horn, *Army of Tennessee*, 117–18; James Lee McDonough, *Shiloh: In Hell Before Night* (Knoxville: University of Tennessee Press, 1977), 96; Woodworth, *Jefferson Davis and His Generals*, 96.

6. David R. Logsdon, ed., *Eyewitnesses at the Battle of Shiloh* (Nashville: Kettle Mills Press, 1994), 2; McDonough, *Shiloh*, 4.

7. TCWCC, *Tennesseans*, 1:183, 184; Lindsley, ed., *Military Annals*, 183–84; Special Orders No. 468, March 28, 1862, No. 475, March 29, 1862, Polk's Corps, Army of the Mississippi, Special Orders, 1862, RG 109, NA.

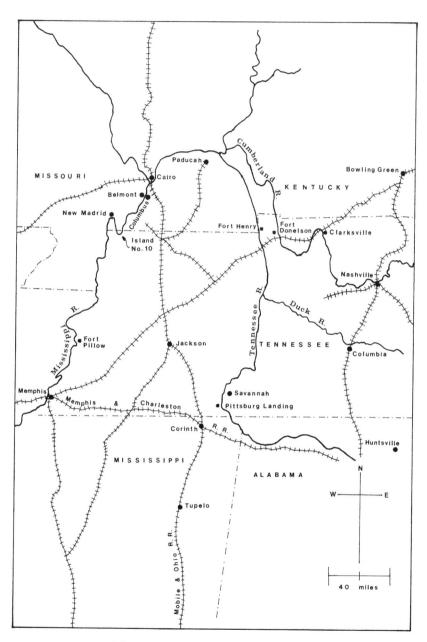

The Mississippi Valley theater, 1861–62
Map by Blake Magner

the command of Brigadier General Charles Clark, a Mississippi planter with experience in the Mexican War. From the start, Clark impressed Stewart as a "vigilant, prudent, capable commander."[8]

Johnston, with the encouragement of Beauregard, divided his army into four corps of unequal size. The First Corps was led by Polk, most of its 9,024 troops from the old Columbus command. The Second Corps was commanded by Major General Braxton Bragg, who commanded the force he had brought from the Gulf coast to Corinth. At 14,868 strong, Bragg's corps was the largest in the army. The Third Corps, the army's smallest at 4,545, was commanded by Major General William J. Hardee. The Fourth Corps, with 6,290 men, was commanded by Brigadier General John C. Breckinridge, former vice president of the United States and Abraham Lincoln's southern Democratic opponent in the election of 1860.[9]

General Bragg was appalled at the army's lack of experience and discipline, terming the troops from the other commands gathering at Corinth a "mob." Stewart was fortunate in that at least two of his regiments had seen some action in the war. On the down side, the men of Stanford's Battery, because of a scarcity of ammunition for practice, had never heard their own guns. General Polk noted that many of his troops had never been under fire before, which was really true of most of the army. After the war, Stewart wrote: "I first joined that army a few days before the battle of Shiloh. It was then mostly without discipline." He further noted that "few of [the army's] rank and file had been in battle before. By far the greater portion of them were raw levies, wholly undisciplined, and very poorly armed."[10]

The purpose of the Confederate concentration at Corinth was simple. As soon as the army's reorganization was accomplished and arrangements made, Grant would be attacked at Pittsburg Landing before Buell could effect a junction with him. Then the Confederate host would cross the river

8. Stewart Sifakis, *Compendium of the Confederate Armies: Florida and Arkansas* (New York: Facts on File, 1992), 93; TCWCC, *Tennesseans*, 1:244; *OR* 4:854; Dunbar Rowland, *Official and Statistical Register of the State of Mississippi* (Nashville: Brandon Printing, 1908), 876; Warner, *Generals in Gray*, 51; APS to William H. McCardle, April 30, 1878, William H. McCardle Papers, MDAH.

9. *OR* 4:854; McDonough, *Shiloh*, 70–72.

10. McWhiney, *Bragg*, 216; B. Bragg to wife, March 29, 1862, Bragg Papers, LC; *OR* 10(1):411; McDonough, *Shiloh*, 17; Lindsley, ed., *Military Annals*, 96, 73.

and defeat Buell, and thereby recover from the effects of the winter's disasters. In his history of the army, Stewart portrayed the planned attack as the "opportunity [Johnston] had been waiting for." With the attack, Johnston "hoped by a decisive blow to silence clamor and censure, and regain all that had been lost."[11]

Stewart's Brigade marched out of its camp near Corinth at around dusk on the evening of April 3, moving nine miles and halting at 12:30 A.M. on April 4. At daylight, the march resumed, but soon halted to allow Hardee's Corps to pass. Stewart camped that night a half mile from Mickey's Crossroads, in an "incessant" rain. On April 5, the whole of Polk's Corps was formed on the road at 3 A.M. in a column of brigades, Stewart's Brigade in front. The darkness and rain delayed the march until dawn. The column then resumed its march on to Mickey's, where again there was a delay until Bragg's Corps cleared the road.[12]

Beauregard's impossibly complex marching orders hindered progress, along with the rawness of the troops and the difficult terrain between Corinth and Pittsburg Landing. Ravines, swamps, and creeks were swollen by the rain. Lieutenant Edwin H. Rennolds of the 5th Tennessee observed that the roads were muddy from the rain and the wagon traffic, that the country was rough and wooded, and that the men were unused to marching. The inexperience of the officers made things even worse. Stewart attributed the delay to the rain and bad roads, and the "misunderstandings unavoidable in a newly organized and undisciplined army."[13]

While Stewart was halted in an open woods on the afternoon of April 5, he saw Johnston riding through the trees with General Breckinridge, and noted Johnston's calm bearing, even in light of the delay of the attack planned for that morning. Later that afternoon, Johnston's demeanor changed when he was informed that Bragg was missing an entire division of his corps. In exasperation, he exclaimed, "This is perfectly puerile!" Disregarding the snarls in the march and the fears of Beauregard and Bragg that surprise had been lost, Johnston ordered at 5:00 P.M. that the attack

11. Horn, *Army of Tennessee*, 119; Logsdon, *Shiloh*, 2–3; Lindsley, ed., *Military Annals*, 73.

12. *OR* 10(1):406, 414, 427.

13. Connelly, *Army of the Heartland*, 135; Logsdon, *Shiloh*, 3; Lindsley, ed., *Military Annals*, 72.

commence the next morning, stating to one of his staff officers, "I would fight them if they were a million."[14]

Sunday, April 6, 1862, dawned cloudless. About 5 A.M., Hardee's skirmishers ran into a reconnaissance party from Benjamin M. Prentiss' Federal division. Only a few of the Federal unit commanders suspected that 40,000 Rebels were on their doorstep, and almost none of the Federal army was disposed to receive the attack. From Hardee's initial contact, a terrific battle developed, which soon involved Bragg's second line. At about 7 A.M., Stewart moved his brigade forward in line of battle, stopping briefly to deposit baggage. Stewart's Brigade was the lead element of Polk's Corps, and was arrayed, left to right, as follows: 5th Tennessee, 33rd Tennessee, 13th Arkansas, and 4th Tennessee, with Stanford and his guns following the two center regiments. As the brigade moved into the Fraley field on the southwest corner of the battleground, a Federal battery fired a shot that severed the flagstaff of the 5th Tennessee and killed one man.[15]

From the "two cabins" area just west of the Fraley field, Albert Sidney Johnston approached unattended. He requested of Polk a brigade to go to the support of Bragg. As Stewart was in the lead, his brigade was detached to go with Johnston. Both Polk and Stewart were impressed with Johnston's demeanor. Directing the brigade to the right, Johnston accompanied Stewart from the north side of the Seay field approximately three-quarters of a mile northeast toward some open woods in front of the abandoned camps of Colonel Everett Peabody's Federal brigade. When Johnston departed, Stewart waited a few minutes for orders and then moved the brigade through the camp and beyond, where a staff officer appeared and directed Stewart to the left and then forward.[16]

It was at this juncture that the cohesion of the brigade began to dissolve. As the 13th Arkansas moved through the camp, the 4th Louisiana of Colonel Randall L. Gibson's brigade fired on a Federal officer who had somehow gotten between the advancing Confederate units. The 4th's fire hit the

14. Ridley, *Battles and Sketches*, 622; Woodworth, *Jefferson Davis and His Generals*, 97; McWhiney, *Bragg*, 226; McDonough, *Shiloh*, 81.

15. Lindsley, ed., *Military Annals*, 73; David W. Reed, *The Battle of Shiloh and the Organizations Engaged*, rev. ed. (Washington, D.C.: Government Printing Office, 1913), 81; *OR* 10(1):427, 433.

16. Ridley, *Battles and Sketches*, 623; Reed, *Battle of Shiloh*, 81; *OR* 10(1):407, 427.

officer, but also hit several members of the 13th. Not realizing it was friendly fire, the 13th fired back, then withdrew and re-formed before advancing again. The 33rd Tennessee likewise fired on other friendly troops. Stewart got his troops under control and moved the 5th Tennessee, 33rd Tennessee, and the 13th Arkansas through the camp, which was that of the 4th Illinois Cavalry, north across a small stream. Leaving the three regiments in order to bring forward the 4th Tennessee, Stewart passed through the left of Stanford's Battery, which was engaged with a Federal battery to the right and front. Due to the lack of roads and the thick undergrowth, Stanford found it difficult to keep up with the brigade and soon became detached altogether.[17]

About 10:00 A.M., Stewart returned to the area where he had left his three left regiments and found they had moved forward up the hill. During the course of the day, these regiments received orders from Hardee, Bragg, Polk, and Brigadier General Daniel Ruggles, illustrating the command confusion brought about by the lack of training and experience and the unwieldy successive alignment of the Rebel corps. Stewart therefore began the fight with only the 4th Tennessee. The 4th was thrown into some disorder by contact with troops of the first line of battle, but re-formed under a heavy fire from Battery D of the 1st Illinois Light Artillery. Then, a staff officer from Bragg told Stewart that Bragg wanted the Federal battery taken. Stewart rode up to Lieutenant Colonel Otho French Strahl and asked if the 4th would take the battery, and received the answer, "We will try."

As the battery was located in the northwest corner of the Review field, Strahl moved forward by the left in order to avoid the open, the regiment following a flag bearing the defiant words "Home Rule." Although this move provided the cover of a small thicket of timber, and the 4th moved at the double-quick, the battery defended itself with canister until the Rebels got within thirty paces of its position and fired a volley. Strahl ordered his men to lie down and reload. Once reloaded, the 4th rushed forward and captured a gun. The victory was costly. The 4th Tennessee lost 31 killed and 160 wounded.[18]

17. Reed, *Battle of Shiloh*, 81; *OR* 10(1):427, 430, 436; Wiley Sword, *Shiloh: Bloody April* (1974; reprint, Dayton: Morningside, 1988), 201.

18. Reed, *Battle of Shiloh*, 81–82; *OR* 10(1):427, 432; A. J. Meadows, "The Fourth Ten-

At a point past 11 A.M., Stewart formed an impromptu command of the 4th Tennessee of his brigade and the 12th Tennessee of Russell's Brigade. His assumption of command of the 12th Tennessee may have been a manifestation of the Confederate tendency that day to create *de facto* commands as the situation required, or may have come about with Stewart's having succeeded to the command of the division, General Clark having been wounded. The two regiments were still under enemy fire, and eventually the 12th Tennessee was compelled to retire to replenish its ammunition. Then, Brigadier General Thomas C. Hindman, commanding two brigades of Hardee's Corps, suggested to Stewart that they join forces to attack the Federals on the east side of the Duncan field, the area that came to be known as the Hornets' Nest. Before the advance started, Hindman was wounded when a cannonball hit his horse, which fell with Hindman underneath. Stewart was directed, likely by Bragg, to assume command. Forming the 4th Tennessee on the left of Hindman's troops, the entire command advanced through the woods into the Duncan field, where they were joined by portions of Brigadier General Patrick R. Cleburne's and Brigadier General Sterling Alexander Martin Wood's brigades. The Confederate line extended somewhat to the left, enabling it to flank the 7th and 58th Illinois out of some cabins in the Duncan field. Stewart's attack failed, his thin lines raked by Federal artillery and small arms fire. However, Stewart's troops stayed engaged until Hindman's troops exhausted their ammunition. By noon, Stewart and the 4th Tennessee were back near the point where the Illinois battery had been captured. Rejoined by the 12th Tennessee, the 4th took position to support Captain Smith P. Bankhead's battery, and repulsed a Federal attack "under an unusually hot fire."[19]

After the Federals were repulsed, the two regiments withdrew across the road. Stewart sent the 4th Tennessee to the rear because its weapons were fouled and its ammunition nearly exhausted. With Polk's help, Stewart then organized a command consisting of Walker's 2nd Tennessee from

nessee Infantry," *CV* 14 (July, 1906): 312; Lindsley, ed., *Military Annals*, 193; Sword, *Shiloh: Bloody April*, 312–13.

19. Reed, *Battle of Shiloh*, 82; *OR* 10(1):415, 428; McDonough, *Shiloh*, 145; Stacy D. Allen, "Shiloh: The Campaign and First Day's Battle," *Blue & Gray Magazine* 14 (winter 1997): 49. Historian Larry J. Daniel places Hindman's wounding before the charge on the Illinois battery. Daniel, *Shiloh*, 179–80. The account used here is chiefly Stewart's, which Reed appears to have accepted.

Bushrod Johnson's brigade (not to be confused with the 2nd Tennessee of Cleburne's Brigade), part of the 11th Louisiana of Russell's Brigade, and another unidentified regiment of Cleburne's. A second assault was then made in the Duncan field area, which gained some success after Bankhead's Battery came forward and opened fire on the Federals near some houses on the side of the Purdy Road.

Afterward, again at Polk's direction, Stewart formed a command of Walker's 2nd Tennessee and his own 5th and 33rd Tennessee regiments, and moved to the left to assist some Louisiana regiments in completing the encirclement of Prentiss in the Hornets' Nest. Once Stewart's men and other Confederates got into Prentiss' rear, they began to pour a terrible fire into the Federal lines. Prentiss soon surrendered, and Stewart moved his troops along the Purdy Road to the area of the Hornets' Nest. A veteran of the 33rd Tennessee recalled the jubilation that accompanied Prentiss' surrender. Prentiss remarked: "Yell, Boys, you have a right to shout for you have captured the bravest brigade in the U.S. Army."[20]

Prentiss' stand, which detained Stewart's various commands and the bulk of the Confederate army for about six hours, probably saved Grant. Nonetheless, there was still an hour of daylight left to try to complete a victory. Troops on the Confederate right could observe from the river bluff the Federal gunboats and thousands of demoralized and skulking Yankees at Pittsburg Landing. Stewart, now on the Confederate right under Breckinridge's command, took position to "aid in the pursuit of the enemy." At this juncture, the gunboats began a "tremendous cannonade of shot and shell over the bank in the direction from where [the Confederate] forces were approaching." But since the river was over a hundred feet below the area of approach, the shells did not affect Stewart's advance.[21]

Events elsewhere on the field intervened to call off the pursuit. At about the time of Stewart's collection of a command for a second assault in the Duncan Field, Johnston was on the right directing attacks on the right flank in the area of the Peach Orchard. Wounded in the leg, Johnston bled to death before he could receive medical attention. Many Confederates, in-

---

20. Reed, *Battle of Shiloh*, 82; *OR* 10(1):428; Logsdon, *Shiloh*, 46; Joseph E. Riley, "The Military Service of Joseph E. Riley in C.S.A." (hereinafter referred to as "Riley Diary"), typescript in 33rd Tennessee File, CCNMP.

21. *OR* 10(1):410, 428; Logsdon, *Shiloh*, 54–55; Sword, *Shiloh: Bloody April*, 344–45.

cluding Stewart, later held the view that Johnston's death led to a relaxation of efforts to complete the destruction of Grant's army. It appears that such was not the case, since Johnston did not appear any more inclined to flank the Hornets' Nest and press for Pittsburg Landing than Bragg.

Upon Johnston's death, Beauregard assumed command. He continued to press the attack, but grew concerned over the condition of his army. Its men had been on the road several days before the battle, had fought long and hard all day, and were disorganized by battle, desertions, and forays for food and plundering. Moreover, Stewart was not the only brigade commander on the Confederate side whose command had disintegrated. Those of Bushrod Johnson, James Patton Anderson, Cleburne, and others were in the same shape. The gunboat fire, which caused a terrific racket, was the last straw. Stewart wrote that his pursuit was "checked by the fire of the gunboat." Beauregard called off the attack, and ordered his troops to fall back to the line of the captured Federal camps. In response to a protest by Tennessee governor Isham G. Harris, who was a volunteer aide at army headquarters and who had been with Johnston at the time of his death, Beauregard insisted that his exhausted men needed rest and food, and could finish Grant the next day. Few modern historians fault this decision, and one even suggested that the mistake was not in calling off the attack, but in not retreating to Corinth.[22]

Beauregard expected to finish off the Federals the next morning, anticipating, based upon false reports, that Buell was too far away to reinforce Grant. Unfortunately for the Rebels, Beauregard's intelligence was faulty, as Grant was joined in the course of the night by Buell and the division of Brigadier General Lewis Wallace. When the confident Confederates awoke the next morning, the Federals were on the move. Stewart started the day in command of several regiments rallied by Beauregard and placed on a hill in front of one of the captured Federal camps, near Beauregard's own

22. Lindsley, ed., *Military Annals*, 74; APS to M. S. O'Donnell, March 24, 1892, Stewart Letter, Western Reserve; Connelly, *Army of the Heartland*, 167–71; Horn, *Army of Tennessee*, 136–37; *OR* 10(1):428; Logsdon, *Shiloh*, 56; Sword, *Shiloh: Bloody April*, 365–66. It is interesting to note that Johnston came as close to beating Grant as anyone in the war, including Robert E. Lee. At Shiloh and in the Wilderness, Lee's great offensive stroke against Grant, an argument can be made that Grant was saved on both occasions by the fall of a Confederate general—in the case of the Wilderness, James Longstreet's accidental wounding by his own men.

headquarters at Shiloh Church. As the Federal attack developed, Beauregard sent Stewart along with the 2nd Tennessee of Cleburne's Brigade and the 13th Arkansas to the right center to support Breckinridge, who was in command of that sector. Stewart attacked and drove the Federals out of an open field they were crossing and into some woods. Stewart then sent to the rear for artillery, and Captain Bankhead once more appeared with two pieces to hold off the Federals while Stewart sent his infantry to the rear to replenish their ammunition. This effort was unsuccessful for some time, until Stewart intercepted a passing ammunition wagon in one of the captured Federal camps and obtained a partial resupply. Then, the Federals opened up a heavy artillery fire upon the two regiments, causing Stewart to withdraw them into a nearby ravine for cover. Once under cover, it was difficult to get the exhausted and not fully resupplied troops back into action. Stewart eventually got the two regiments back into line at the same point they had previously occupied, where they withstood the Federals until their ammunition was once more exhausted.

Again Stewart took his troops out of the line, and when two of his staff officers failed to return with ammunition, he went looking for some himself. After an unsuccessful search, Stewart returned, and learned that the order had been given to withdraw. The Confederate Army of the Mississippi had resisted the attacks of the rejuvenated Federals for the greater part of the day, but by two o'clock it had become evident to Beauregard and his staff that the army was on the verge of dissolution. Orders went out to retreat, and the Army of the Mississippi, exhausted, disorganized, and in the face of the enemy, was nonetheless "slowly and skillfully" withdrawn. Stewart noted proudly in his report that his two regiments were the last to leave his quarter of the field.[23]

The tattered army started for Corinth in a cold rain along the soggy, nearly impassable roads used to advance to the field. In the words of a soldier of the 33rd Tennessee, the men were "all tired down and hungry." Fording the rain-swollen streams brought groans and curses from

23. Connelly, *Army of the Heartland*, 172–75; Horn, *Army of Tennessee*, 137–41; Lindsley, ed., *Military Annals*, 75; *OR* 10(1):428–29; Stacy D. Allen, "Shiloh: Grant Strikes Back," *Blue & Gray Magazine* 14 (spring 1997): 19, 27, 45–46; APS to Leonidas Polk, April 30, 1862, Leonidas Polk Papers, RG 109, NA; APS to M. S. O'Donnell, March 24, 1892, Stewart Letter, Western Reserve.

wounded men being transported in wagons, as the mule teams went belly-deep and water seeped into the wagon beds. Straggling regiments interspersed with walking wounded completed the cavalcade of misery. Fortunately for the Rebels, Grant was so badly battered that there was no meaningful pursuit.[24]

The losses of Shiloh exceeded anything ever seen in North America. A few days later, one of Stewart's men estimated the casualties on both sides to total 100,000 killed and wounded. The actual casualties were bad enough: Confederate casualties totaling 10,699, Federal casualties 13,047. Regardless of the Unionists' greater losses, the battle was a Federal victory. Grant avoided the near destruction of his army by Johnston's troops, which were concentrated for one supreme effort to achieve that purpose and to recover all that had been lost that winter. Nevertheless, the Army of the Mississippi overcame disorganization, lack of training and experience, distance, the elements, and its own unpracticed and, in some cases, inept commanders just to get to the field; that it could then drive Grant to the bluffs of the Tennessee River speaks of heroic determination and valor. While he may have been somewhat prejudiced, Stewart had a solid argument when he wrote, after the war, that "no army on either side during the entire war did better work than was performed by the Army of the Mississippi at Shiloh."[25]

Stewart wrote no evaluation of his own performance. Polk complimented him along with the other brigade commanders of the corps, and elsewhere noted that Stewart on the field was "cool and determined."[26] On April 6, Stewart's Brigade came apart almost too easily, but it must be remembered that it was newly organized, with little cohesion. Likewise, the brigades of other competent brigadiers soon dissolved. Stewart could also be subject to criticism for his participation in the frontal attacks on the left of the Hornets' Nest, but he was there under the command of superiors such as Bragg and Polk. Like many other Confederate commanders on the field,

24. Logsdon, *Shiloh*, 86; W. A. Howard to L. E. Howard, April 11, 1862, W. A. Howard Letters, SNMP.

25. Horn, *Army of Tennessee*, 143; Lindsley, ed., *Military Annals*, 75; W. A. Howard to L. E. Howard, April 10, 1862, SNMP.

26. *OR* 10(1):409, 412.

Stewart extemporized fairly well in organizing commands and carrying on the battle. On April 7, he competently led his *de facto* brigade in a day of bitter fighting against superior numbers. After his slow start at New Madrid, he vindicated Albert Sidney Johnston's confidence in promoting him to brigadier general.

The Federal commander in the West, Major General Henry W. Halleck, personally came to Pittsburg Landing to direct the advance on Corinth. Grant was promoted to the meaningless post of "second-in-command," and his Army of the Tennessee was assigned to Major General George H. Thomas. This force was combined with Buell's Army of the Ohio, Pope's Army of the Mississippi, and new reinforcements from the Midwest, to form a virtual army group of 125,000, which started a glacial advance toward Corinth. For his part, Beauregard was reinforced by Major General Earl Van Dorn's forces from west of the Mississippi, roughly 14,000 poorly armed troops.[27]

Stewart remained in command of the division until April 14, when army headquarters put Brigadier General James H. Trapier, a West Point classmate of Beauregard's, in Clark's place. Stewart obviously perceived the appointment of an officer of equal rank from outside the division over him as a slight. Although Stewart had no objection to Trapier personally, he thought that since seven of the division's nine regiments were from Tennessee, either he or another ranking Tennessean should command the division until Clark returned. Accordingly, he wrote a respectfully mild letter of protest to Polk. Since Clark recovered sufficiently to resume command on April 29, the protest went for naught.[28]

In May, Stewart spent a great deal of time on the defensive lines occupied by his brigade and, as officer of the day on May 17, the corps. Desertions were a problem, and accordingly Stewart tried to trace the routes used by deserters, and gave instructions along the line to shoot any person attempting to move out of the lines without a pass. During the next week, a Federal probe discomfited the new company officers of the 13th Arkansas, causing that regiment to be driven from its picket line. While terming

27. Horn, *Army of Tennessee*, 146–47; Connelly, *Army of the Heartland*, 175–76.

28. Warner, *Generals in Gray*, 309–10, APS to Leonidas Polk, April 23, 1862, Polk Papers, RG 109, NA; Special Order No. 24, April 28, 1862, Polk's Corps, Army of the Mississippi, Special Orders, 1862, RG 109, NA.

the conduct of the officers "reprehensible," Stewart recognized that "The company officers are generally new and inexperienced, and the same is true in all my regiments."[29]

On another occasion, three companies of the 5th Tennessee were on an advanced outpost as the Federals approached. They were almost overrun by a larger Federal force until rescued by Stewart with four companies of the 33rd Tennessee. The reinforced Tennesseans then charged and drove the Federals back.[30]

Halleck's advance soon reached the point where Corinth, a position without any natural advantages, would be invested by an overwhelming force. On the night of May 29, Beauregard quietly withdrew the army without loss to Tupelo, fifty miles to the south of Corinth. This retreat, along with the significant losses of territory in Tennessee, Mississippi, and northern Alabama, brought Beauregard intense scrutiny from Richmond. Beauregard's health, which had been affected by a throat ailment for some months, caused him to take off to a spa north of Mobile, Alabama, without leave on June 19. On June 20, President Davis removed Beauregard as commander and appointed Bragg in his place. To Bragg would fall the daunting task of regaining the initiative in the Confederate West.[31]

29. *OR* 10(2):419, 524, 542; APS to George Williamson, May 1, 1862, APS to Leonidas Polk, May 6, 1862, APS to Charles Clark, May 23, 1862, Polk Papers, RG 109, NA.

30. Lindsley, ed., *Military Annals*, 196–97.

31. St. John R. Liddell, *Liddell's Record*, ed. Nathaniel Cheairs Hughes, Jr. (1985; reprint, Baton Rouge: Louisiana State University Press, 1997), 67; Connelly, *Army of the Heartland*, 179–82.

— 4 —

Veterans from the Volunteer State

Perryville

Braxton Bragg's ultimate failure as the commander of the Army of Tennessee obscures the virtues that even his enemies recognized. One of his officers wrote that Bragg was "firm and impartial," "full of energy," hardworking, and "excited by the purest patriotism, and one of the most honest and unselfish officers of our army." He was the best organizer and disciplinarian the army ever had. Yet the same officer did not think Bragg "was up to the charge of a large army" as a commander. Instead, "as a chief of staff, his services would have been invaluable." Stewart perceived Bragg's chief fault as essentially one of personality. After the war, he wrote that while Bragg was an "able officer . . . [h]is greatest defect was that he did not win the love and confidence of either the officers or men" of his army.[1]

In June, 1862, Bragg inherited an army at Tupelo that had known nothing but retreat and was plagued by desertion, supply problems, and bad officers. Fortunately, the Confederate Army of the Mississippi was not under a direct Federal threat at Tupelo. Federal general Halleck determined to hold the line he had conquered in north Mississippi and garrison the terri-

---

1. A. M. Manigault, *A Carolinian Goes to War*, ed. R. Lockwood Tower (Columbia: University of South Carolina Press, 1983), 158–59; Lindsley, ed., *Military Annals*, 85. For scholarly viewpoints on these issues, see McWhiney, *Bragg*, 390–92; Horn, *Army of Tennessee*, 157; Connelly, *Army of the Heartland*, 205. For Bragg's background, see McWhiney, *Bragg*, 1–25, 33, 90–93, 98; Warner, *Generals in Gray*, 30.

tory captured since February. The lone Federal offensive threat was to the east, as Don Carlos Buell and his Army of the Ohio were slowly advancing along the line of the Memphis and Charleston Railroad through north Alabama to Chattanooga.[2]

Chattanooga, in the center of the corridor from Nashville to Atlanta, was a key railroad center. Not only was it a focal point of Confederate transportation and communications, it was, as events would confirm, an ideal jumping-off point for a Federal advance into Georgia. The only Confederate troops in East Tennessee were Major General Edmund Kirby Smith's Army of East Tennessee. Kirby Smith's 16,000 men faced not only Buell but an aggressive Federal force at Cumberland Gap, the point where the Tennessee, Kentucky, and Virginia state lines come together. By July 22, after only approximately a month in command, Bragg determined to transfer a substantial portion of his army to Chattanooga.[3]

In the month the Army of the Mississippi remained at Tupelo after Bragg assumed command, it was drilled, disciplined, and reorganized until it was, in Stewart's words, in "a high state of efficiency." Part of the reorganization involved Stewart and his command. At Corinth, the brigade was joined by Colonel A. H. Bradford's 31st Tennessee. The 31st had been one of six regiments McCown had removed to Fort Pillow before Island No. 10's fall on April 7. The 31st had remained at Fort Pillow until after the retreat from Shiloh. Soon after the 31st joined the brigade, elections required under the conscript law turned Bradford out of his colonelcy and substituted Colonel Egbert E. Tansil, formerly captain of Company A.[4]

A further shake-up of the brigade occurred on July 8. The 13th Arkansas left the brigade and was replaced by the 24th Tennessee, veterans of Shiloh commanded by Lieutenant Colonel H. L. W. Bratton.[5] Just over two weeks before the 24th joined Stewart, its adjutant major, William H. Mott, wrote to his wife in Tennessee urging her not to despair despite the army's having abandoned Tennessee. Demonstrating that the morale of the

2. McWhiney, *Bragg*, 261–62; James Lee McDonough, *War in Kentucky: From Shiloh to Perryville* (Knoxville: University of Tennessee Press, 1994), 35–36.

3. McDonough, *War in Kentucky*, 37–38; Connelly, *Army of the Heartland*, 189; *OR* 16(2):715; McWhiney, *Bragg*, 267–68; APS to D. H. Hill, July 21, 1862, Daniel Harvey Hill Papers, SHC.

4. Lindsley, ed., *Military Annals*, 96, 460; TCWCC, *Tennesseans*, 1:240–41.

5. TCWCC, *Tennesseans*, 1:224–25.

army was improving as well, Mott wrote: "Our independence is as certain to be accomplished as the morrow is to dawn. . . . Our prospects are better of success than ever and the army of Lincolndom will fall of its own weight ere the lapse of many more; therefore bear up a while longer, and then all will be right."[6]

On the same July 8 the confident Mott and the 24th joined Stewart, the brigade was transferred to Major General Benjamin Franklin Cheatham's division of Polk's Corps. A year older than Stewart, Cheatham was from a prominent family of Tennessee politicians on his father's side, and descended from General James Robertson, a founder of Nashville, on his mother's. A veteran of the Mexican War, Cheatham was a political ally of Isham G. Harris. It is likely Stewart and Cheatham had become acquainted in Nashville before the war. Considered incompetent by Bragg, Cheatham had important political allies in addition to Harris, including Senator Gustavus A. Henry and Congressman Henry S. Foote. Unlike Bragg, Cheatham was genuinely liked by the Tennessee troops in the army, who formed a significant portion of its numbers, including all but one regiment of Cheatham's own division.[7]

Popular or not, Bragg was capable of sound strategic thinking. His decision to move four divisions of the Army of the Mississippi to Chattanooga in July put the army in a position to defend Chattanooga and operate on the Federal lines of communication in Middle Tennessee. Furthermore, Halleck's "hold the line" strategy in north Mississippi made it possible for Major General Sterling Price to face the Federals there with 16,000 men and for Van Dorn to hold Vicksburg on the Mississippi River with another 16,000. Bragg intended to combine with Kirby Smith and move into Middle Tennessee to isolate Buell while Price and Van Dorn moved toward West Tennessee.[8]

On July 21, while camped at Tupelo, Stewart wrote his West Point classmate Major General Daniel Harvey Hill, who commanded a division in the Army of Northern Virginia. Stewart expressed his gratification at

6. Charles R. Mott, Jr., ed., "War Journal of a Confederate Officer," *Tennessee Historical Quarterly* 5 (September 1946): 246–47.

7. *OR* 17(2):643; Christopher Losson, *Tennessee's Forgotten Warriors* (Knoxville: University of Tennessee Press, 1989), 1–27, 55–59; Warner, *Generals in Gray*, 47.

8. McWhiney, *Bragg*, 268–71.

the successes of Hill and others in their class, such as James Longstreet, and asked Hill to pass along his greetings to Longstreet, G. W. Smith, and any other of their classmates in the Virginia army. Interrupted, Stewart resumed his letter the next day, writing that the troops at Tupelo had been ordered to be ready to move on July 23, presumably to Chattanooga. Displaying a spirit similar to that of Major Mott of the 24th Tennessee, Stewart fervently wrote: "My earnest hope is that the day of redemption for Tenn. and the whole South is at hand—& that you & I may long live to witness the growth & prosperity of our beloved country, free, independent, & giving to all the nations such an example of Christian enlightenment as the world has not yet seen."[9]

The move from Tupelo to Chattanooga was remarkable. On July 23, the date the infantry began rolling out of Tupelo, elements of Buell's army were at Stevenson, Alabama, about twenty-five miles southwest of Chattanooga. The artillery, wagons, and cavalry traveled 432 miles by road to Chattanooga. The distance by the circuitous rail route from Tupelo, down to Mobile, back up to Atlanta and then to Chattanooga, was 776 miles. The long trip by rail was faster than Buell's overland march, which was delayed by Confederate cavalry operating in the Federal rear. When Bragg's first infantry units began rolling into Chattanooga, Buell had moved no farther.[10]

Bragg and Kirby Smith met in Chattanooga on July 31 and formulated a plan. Kirby Smith would move against Cumberland Gap while Bragg awaited his artillery and wagons. Then, the two would combine to march into Middle Tennessee, defeat Buell, recapture Nashville, and move into Kentucky. This plan soon went awry, however, primarily on account of the cumbersome Confederate command system. While Bragg ranked Kirby Smith, Kirby Smith had autonomy as a separate department commander, which he soon exercised to negate Bragg's plan to engage Buell in Middle Tennessee.[11]

By the time Bragg moved out of Chattanooga on August 28, Kirby Smith was so deep into Kentucky as to make it impractical for Bragg to en-

9. APS to D. H. Hill, July 21, 1862, Hill Papers; Warner, *Generals in Gray*, 126–37.

10. McWhiney, *Bragg*, 268–71; McDonough, *War in Kentucky*, 74–76.

11. McWhiney, *Bragg*, 272–74; Woodworth, *Jefferson Davis and His Generals*, 136–39; Connelly, *Army of the Heartland*, 209–13.

gage Buell in Tennessee. Bragg's 27,000 infantry were insufficient for that task. Out of necessity, Bragg had to follow Kirby Smith into Kentucky, to stay within supporting distance and to prevent Buell from getting between the two Confederate armies.

The army that Bragg marched north from Chattanooga consisted of four divisions divided into two wings. Polk's wing consisted of the divisions of Cheatham and Major General Jones M. Withers, an Alabama-born 1835 graduate of West Point who was a veteran of the Mexican War and the fight at Shiloh. The divisions of Brigadier General James Patton Anderson of Florida and Major General Simon Bolivar Buckner of Kentucky made up Bragg's other wing, under Major General William J. Hardee. Known as "Old Reliable," Hardee was famous in the prewar United States Army for his adaptation of a French infantry tactics manual, which he published in 1855 with the title *Rifle and Light Infantry Tactics.* Hardee served well at Shiloh and was considered by Bragg to be his only "suitable" major general.[12]

Stewart's Brigade and the rest of Polk's wing moved up the east side of Walden's Ridge from Chattanooga, crossing into the Sequatchie Valley above Pikeville. The wing moved northwest to Sparta, then north to Gainesboro on the Cumberland River, then across the Kentucky line to Glasgow. On the march, Stewart summoned the commissioned officers of his brigade and admonished them on the importance of discipline in the enemy's country. Stewart stated that pillage and plunder not only damaged noncombatants, but demoralized the perpetrators. Stewart expressed the hope that when the army left Kentucky, no one could say that personal property had been stolen or damaged by a member of his brigade.[13]

Buell moved his army north in response to the Confederate advance, with the initial goal of covering Nashville. When Buell determined that Bragg was moving into Kentucky, the Federal general shifted his forces to Bowling Green. Bragg captured the Federal garrison at Munfordville on

---

12. McWhiney, *Bragg,* 262. For Hardee's background, see Nathaniel C. Hughes, Jr., *General William J. Hardee: Old Reliable* (Baton Rouge: Louisiana State University Press, 1965), 4–6, 12, 14–18, 23–36, 41–46, 51–67, 112, 119, 320; Warner, *Generals in Gray,* 7, 38, 342–43. During the coming campaign, both Polk and Hardee would be elevated to the newly created rank of lieutenant general. Hughes, *Hardee,* 137 n. 5.

13. Connelly, *Army of the Heartland,* 222–26; Lindsley, ed., *Military Annals,* 197.

September 17. After two days further delay, Bragg marched east, Polk's wing moving to Bardstown. While Bragg has been criticized for not using his position at Munfordville astride the Louisville and Nashville Railroad to force Buell to battle, Buell had other routes to Louisville, and remaining at Munfordville would have surrendered the initiative to Buell while confining the Army of the Mississippi to a barren area.[14]

At the first of October, Bragg left the army in the care of Polk at Bardstown and occupied himself with the political task of installing a Confederate governor at Frankfort, the state capital, fifty-three miles from Bardstown. On October 2, Bragg received the unexpected news that Buell's replenished and strongly reinforced army was in motion, and that a Federal force was at Shelbyville, Kentucky, twenty-one miles to the east of Frankfort. Bragg ordered Polk to move north with his "whole available force" and strike the Federal column heading toward Frankfort in the flank. Polk called a council of several of his generals and secured the consensus of all not to obey the order. Stewart was on outpost nine miles away on the Louisville Road and did not participate. While Polk has been criticized for this unorthodox (and insubordinate) move, he had information that indicated a Federal force of unknown size was advancing on Bardstown, which would place it on the flank of the move north ordered by Bragg. Polk retreated east rather than advancing north.[15]

In his history of the army, Stewart wrote that by this juncture it was clear that Bragg was not going to achieve either of the "two great objects" of the Kentucky invasion: "Nashville would not be evacuated, and Kentucky would not join the Confederacy. Bragg, therefore, desired only to gain time to effect a retreat with his spoils." Bragg remarked that "the people here have too many fat cattle and are too well off to fight." According to a member of his staff, Bragg was aware he had made a mistake moving into Kentucky instead of against Buell in Middle Tennessee. He "was de-

14. Don Carlos Buell, "East Tennessee and the Campaign of Perryville," *B&L* 3:40–41; Connelly, *Army of the Heartland*, 228–33; Losson, *Tennessee's Forgotten Warriors*, 62–63.

15. Connelly, *Army of the Heartland*, 243–50; B. Bragg to L. Polk, October 2, 1862, Polk Papers, LC. While admitting that Bragg's intelligence was incomplete at the time that the order was made, both McWhiney and Woodworth argue that the attack Bragg contemplated on Sill's flank had a good chance of success. McWhiney, *Bragg*, 301–306; Woodworth, *Jefferson Davis and His Generals*, 156–57. For Stewart's absence from Polk's council, see *OR* 16(1):1105.

termined, however, not to expose his army to disaster, nor to take any chances." But Bragg's biographer writes that he intended to hold as much of the state as possible, protecting the new government at Frankfort to legitimize his conscription efforts, and covering his supply depot at Danville.[16]

Regardless of whether Bragg was seeking an escape, Buell's army converged on the Army of the Mississippi in three columns. Bragg ordered Polk to take Cheatham's Division south to Perryville to join with Hardee, "give the enemy battle immediately; rout him, and then move to our support at Versailles." Bragg personally rode to Perryville after ordering Polk to attack "vigorously" at first light on October 8.[17]

At first light on October 8, Polk suspected that Buell's whole army might be in his front. In such circumstances, compliance with Bragg's attack order was unwise. Polk substituted a "defensive-offensive" strategy, whereby he would "await the movements of the enemy and be guided by events as they developed." Around 9:45 that morning, Bragg arrived, irritated that his attack order had not been obeyed. Rejecting the premise that the bulk of Buell's army was on the field, Bragg substituted the offensive for the "defensive-offensive." Cheatham's Division shifted north to the right flank to control a strategic bend in the river and to provide strength to that portion of the line so Bragg could launch an attack with it.[18]

Bragg's original plan had been to strike the left flank of Major General Charles Gilbert's corps with Cheatham's Division shortly after noon. But Polk received a report from cavalry scouts that a large column of Federal infantry was approaching Perryville from the northwest, along the Mackville Road. These troops were Major General Alexander McCook's First Corps. Polk delayed Cheatham's attack so he could make sure Cheatham would be hitting the Federal left flank. Bragg decided to shift Cheatham's men further north, assemble the division in line of battle on Walker's Bend, cross the Chaplin River, and strike McCook with Cheatham's three brigades *en echelon*. The task of moving Cheatham's Division across the river

---

16. Lindsley, ed., *Military Annals*, 77; David Urquhart, "Bragg's Advance and Retreat," *B&L* 3:601; McWhiney, *Bragg*, 298–300.

17. McWhiney, *Bragg*, 308–12.

18. Kenneth A. Hafendorfer, *Perryville: Battle for Kentucky* (Louisville: KH Press, 1991), 132–33, 136, 162–65; *OR* 16(1):1110.

and up the bluffs so occupied Bragg that he neglected to direct the cavalry to keep in touch with the Federal left flank, which so extended itself that Cheatham's attack would not overlap the Federal flank on the north, as originally planned.[19]

As Stewart's Brigade moved into position with the rest of the division, one of its components, Stanford's Battery, engaged in an artillery duel started by Captain William W. Carnes's Tennessee battery. Carnes's cannon being smoothbores, his battery was quickly outranged by an Indiana battery of rifled guns. Stanford moved forward to deploy his three-inch rifles, but was hit by Federal fire before a shot could be fired. Two men were killed and an ammunition chest exploded. Stanford kept up the fight until fire slackened around 1:30 P.M.[20]

The five brigades of McCook's corps were placed with artillery support along a series of mostly open, rolling hills 3,000 to 4,000 feet from Cheatham's crossing of the Chaplin River. A sweep by a brigade of Confederate cavalry cleared Federal skirmishers off the bluff in preparation for Cheatham's attack. Thinking the Federal left was over 300 yards to the south of its actual position, Cheatham ordered Brigadier General Daniel Donelson's brigade forward to the attack. Donelson was missing two of his five Tennessee regiments, and moved to the attack with something over half his brigade's strength.[21]

Donelson proceeded in a westerly fashion toward Captain Samuel J. Harris' Indiana battery, located on a hill just south of the current Perryville Battlefield Park boundary. During Donelson's advance, the true extent of the Federal left became apparent, as Captain Charles Parsons' Federal battery on an open hill to the north of Donelson's line of advance opened an enfilade fire on Donelson's three regiments. Cheatham met this unexpected threat by sending Brigadier General George Maney's brigade from the rear of the division's line up to deal with Parsons and his supporting infantry.[22]

Maney advanced to a "strong staked rail fence" about a hundred yards from Parsons' battery and its support, an Illinois regiment. The Federals

---

19. Hafendorfer, *Perryville*, 180–83.

20. Daniel, *Cannoneers*, 50; Hafendorfer, *Perryville*, 178–80.

21. Hafendorfer, *Perryville*, 178–201; Losson, *Tennessee's Forgotten Warriors*, 65. For Donelson's background, see Warner, *Generals in Gray*, 74–75.

22. Hafendorfer, *Perryville*, 201–207, 214.

charged down the hill to confront Maney, but were sent reeling back. Maney's troops slowly advanced up the steep hill toward Parsons' guns, supported by the guns of Lieutenant William B. Turner's Mississippi battery, and opposed by fresh Federal troops from an Ohio regiment.[23]

After passing the river bluff, Stewart deployed his brigade some four hundred yards to the rear of Donelson, forming behind a ridge swept by Federal fire. While there, Maney moved from behind Stewart to the right and forward against Parsons' position. Stewart received no further orders, but Donelson requested support. Stewart advanced three of his regiments—the 4th, 5th, and 24th—into the gap between Maney and Donelson, while keeping the 33rd and 31st in reserve.[24]

Stewart's Brigade, in filling the gap between Maney and Donelson, became involved in each of the other two brigades' fights. Initially, the 4th and 5th assisted Maney in routing the Federals on the hill occupied by Parsons' battery. The left regiment of the first line, the 24th, joined in the attack of Donelson's 16th Tennessee on the 24th Illinois, forcing the Federals up the ridge about two hundred yards to the south of Parsons. Stewart then committed the second line of the brigade, the 33rd going up the ridge to the left of the 5th, the 31st joining the attack of the 24th and Donelson's regiments.[25]

Stewart admiringly wrote that his brigade "pressed forward under a galling fire, with a coolness & yet impetuosity that could not be surpassed." The 4th and 5th continued to support Maney's attack on the extreme left, combining with Maney to eventually drive Brigadier General John Starkweather's brigade off the next ridge to the west of Parsons' now-overrun position, the area of the present-day park known as "Starkweather's Hill." Before this final assault, Captain Oscar Gilchrist of the 4th Tennessee ordered his men to lie down, making the practical remark: "If you don't, the Yankees will shoot you!" The 4th's color-bearer fell, so Lewis White picked up the standard and placed the broken staff in the muzzle of his gun. Colonel C. D. Venable of the 5th Tennessee was thrown from his

    23. Ibid., 215–17, 240–41; Benjamin F. Cheatham, "The Battle of Perryville," *Southern Bivouac* (April 1886): 705.
    24. APS Perryville Report, William P. Palmer Collection of Braxton Bragg Papers, Western Reserve Historical Society, Cleveland; Hafendorfer, *Perryville*, 242–45.
    25. Hafendorfer, *Perryville*, 244–45.

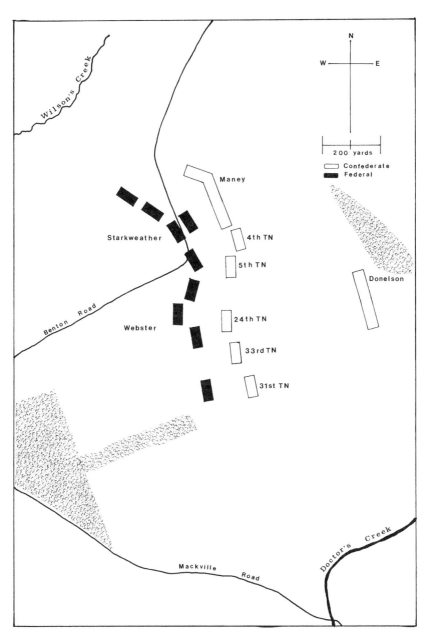

Perryville
Map by Blake Magner

horse and crippled early in the fight but continued on, carried by two of his men. The regiment's lieutenant colonel and major were both unhorsed, but continued the fight. Members of the 5th suffered unusual wounds: Private Haywood of Company B was shot with a ramrod, which he pulled out of his breast himself; Private Tip Allen of Company I was shot in the neck by a minié ball, which he soon coughed up. Private Joseph Riley of the 33rd Tennessee, following the 5th Tennessee in the second line, watched as the 5th swept forward and captured a battery at a dead run, swaths being cut from its ranks by the terrible Federal fire.[26]

From Stewart's description in his report, it appears that he stayed with the 24th, 31st, and 33rd in their attack on Colonel George Webster's brigade in the area of the southern boundary of the current park. Supported by Donelson's regrouped brigade and Brigadier General Sterling A. M. Wood's Brigade of Hardee's Corps, the 24th, 31st, and 33rd Tennessee moved forward. The combined assault resulted in the capture of Harris' Federal battery of four guns. In honor of the capture, all three brigades were later allowed to place crossed cannons on their colors. Pushing past Harris' guns to the cheers of the men of the 5th Tennessee, the line moved to the top of the next hill, an extension of Starkweather's Hill to the south of the Benton Road, where, after a struggle with the reorganizing Federals, the three regiments fell back to the bottom of the ridge for lack of ammunition.[27]

By the end of this fight, it was about 5:15, and close to sundown. Stewart and his brigade had been in action since about 3 P.M. and, like the rest of Cheatham's Division, were fought out. The brigade went into battle with an effective strength of about 1,750 and suffered 428 casualties, just under a quarter of its strength. Cheatham's attack was so fierce that McCook reported that he was assaulted by "at least three divisions." While elements of three divisions were employed, the bulk of the Confederate fighting was done by Cheatham's three brigades, totaling about 4,500 men, against a Federal corps of over double that number.[28]

26. APS Perryville Report; Hafendorfer, *Perryville*, 252–53, 262–63, 274–75; Lindsley, ed., *Military Annals*, 186–87, 197–98; Riley Diary, CCNMP.

27. APS Perryville Report; Hafendorfer, *Perryville*, 272–73, 299–304, 320; Riley Diary, CCNMP; *OR* 16(1):1111; General Order No. 1, November 23, 1862, Army of Tennessee, General Orders, 1862, RG 109, NA.

28. Hafendorfer, *Perryville*, 234, 321; *OR* 16(1):1043; 16(2):896.

Polk's report of the battle complimented Stewart, along with Cheatham's other brigadiers. While Stewart could be criticized for the separation of his brigade during the battle, such criticism would be unjust, as the Federal line was emplaced along a long ridge, where an attack on one area of the ridge would necessarily assist an attack on another. Stewart competently filled his role as support for the attack of Cheatham's Division on the Federal left. Maney largely succeeded in driving the Federal left flank back on its supports, capturing several guns in the process. That attack would not have been nearly so successful without the support of Stewart's 4th and 5th Tennessee. The attack of the remainder of the brigade, personally supervised by Stewart, drove the Federal line back several hundred yards, participated in the capture of four pieces of artillery, materially assisted Maney by engaging Federal troops that would have reinforced the far left, and relieved pressure on Hardee on the right.

Stewart was effusive in praise for his men. He wrote in his report of the battle that "throughout the entire day, the men & officers behaved as I thought as only veterans from the Volunteer State could do, all did their duty well and bravely." Veterans of the brigade remembered that October 8 as a "matchless fight" and "one of the bloodiest in which Bragg's army was engaged."[29]

Bragg, Polk, and Hardee learned from captured prisoners and headquarters documents that the great bulk of the Federal army was at Perryville. The three Confederate divisions at Perryville, victorious but battered and vastly outnumbered, retreated northeast to Harrodsburg, where they were rejoined by Withers' Division and Kirby Smith's troops on October 10. Bragg moved the combined force on to the advance base at Bryantsville. There, on October 12, news reached him that Price and Van Dorn had been defeated at Corinth on October 4. The Army of the Mississippi was the only strong Confederate force in the field between the Federals and the Deep South. Bragg called a council of war, and Polk, Hardee, Cheatham, and Kirby Smith all voted to retreat. Without delay, the Confederates started for Cumberland Gap on October 13, Kirby Smith moving on an eastern route and Bragg's army on a western route through Crab Orchard. Cheatham's Division composed part of the rear guard.[30]

29. APS Perryville Report; Lindsley, ed., *Military Annals*, 187, 197.

30. McWhiney, *Bragg*, 320–22; Connelly, *Army of the Heartland*, 266–68, 279–80; Cheatham, "Battle of Perryville."

Stewart's Brigade marched south into Tennessee through the Cumberland Gap, thence to Knoxville by way of the neighborhood of Rogersville, which must have brought memories of his boyhood and early education back to its commander. The column reached Knoxville on October 20. The men were "tired, foot-sore, and hungry, many . . . ragged and barefooted," and marched into camp in the midst of a "terrible snow-storm." Some of the barefoot men left bloody tracks in the snow.[31]

On October 23, Bragg was summoned to Richmond to report in person on the Kentucky campaign. Davis was delighted by the Army of the Mississippi's safe return to Tennessee. After interviews with Bragg, Polk, and Kirby Smith, Davis sustained Bragg in his command, notwithstanding Polk's and Kirby Smith's labeling the campaign a failure. Bragg must have been astonished, since Polk's and Kirby Smith's failures in the campaign had played a significant role in foiling Bragg's designs.[32]

Buell kept up something of a pursuit until the Army of the Mississippi reached London, Kentucky. He then began moving his army to Nashville, which the Federals had held throughout the campaign in Kentucky. A small Confederate force under Nathan Bedford Forrest, later augmented by Breckinridge's infantry division, lurked at Murfreesboro for the purpose of holding Middle Tennessee and threatening Nashville.[33]

From Knoxville, Stewart's Brigade, with the rest of the army, moved by rail to Tullahoma.[34] For the first time during the war, Stewart was home again in Middle Tennessee.

31. Lindsley, ed., *Military Annals*, 198.
32. McWhiney, *Bragg*, 326–27; Horn, *Army of Tennessee*, 190–91.
33. Horn, *Army of Tennessee*, 189.
34. Lindsley, ed., *Military Annals*, 187.

— 5 —

In a Manner That Is Beyond Praise

Murfreesboro

For over a year, the Confederate Army of the Mississippi had fought for the possession of Tennessee. Shiloh was an effort to recover the losses in West and Middle Tennessee occasioned by the fall of Forts Henry and Donelson. The Kentucky campaign started as an effort to protect Chattanooga and engage the Federals in Middle Tennessee. While the Kentucky campaign failed to rally the Bluegrass State to the Rebel cause, it did relieve the pressure on Chattanooga and accomplish the recovery of a great portion of Middle Tennessee. In July, 1862, the Federal army was thirty miles from Chattanooga. In December, the Confederate army was thirty miles from Nashville. As the army gathered around Murfreesboro in the late fall of 1862, its primary mission, as well as the largest portion of its regiments, was recognized by its new name, the Army of Tennessee.

Murfreesboro lay on the Nashville and Chattanooga Railroad thirty miles to the southeast of Nashville. It was a similar distance due south from Stewart's home in Lebanon, and about forty-five miles northwest of his father's home in Winchester. For the Confederates, the primary reason for occupying Murfreesboro was the political advantage and morale boost that being so close to Nashville provided. Substantial disadvantages included Murfreesboro's being much nearer to the Federal base in Nashville than to Bragg's base at Chattanooga and the position's susceptibility to a Federal move around either flank.[1]

---

1. Thomas L. Connelly, *Autumn of Glory* (Baton Rouge: Louisiana State University Press, 1971), 14, 23–25.

By the second week of December, the army was deployed in a thirty-mile arc around Murfreesboro, Hardee's Corps to the west, at Triune and Eagleville, Polk's Corps in the environs of Murfreesboro itself, and McCown's Division to the east, at Readyville. On November 22, the army was reorganized into three corps under Polk, Hardee, and Kirby Smith, but this arrangement soon evaporated when President Davis ordered Major General Carter Stevenson's division of 7,500 men to Vicksburg. Left with only one division, Kirby Smith returned to Knoxville. Kirby Smith's remaining division, McCown's, was attached to Hardee's Corps. Stevenson's Division, the army's largest, would be missed in the coming fight.[2]

A few days before Stevenson was detached, Bragg broke up Patton Anderson's division to achieve better balance between the corps of Hardee and Polk. In this process, the 19th Tennessee was added to Stewart's Brigade. The 19th had seen action at Mill Springs and Shiloh, had endured bombardment at Vicksburg, and had been part of Breckinridge's unsuccessful attempt to recapture Baton Rouge. The 19th was no doubt added to the brigade as a result of the consolidation of the 4th and 5th Tennessee and 31st and 33rd Tennessee into two regiments, part of an overall consolidation of eighteen understrength regiments into nine.[3]

The dissatisfaction with Bragg expressed to the authorities in Richmond by Polk, Kirby Smith, and others after the retreat from Kentucky occasioned a visit by President Davis himself in mid-December. Traveling incognito, Davis sought to ascertain the situation with the army and the morale of its men, and to gather information for planning the strategic defense of both Tennessee and Mississippi.[4] Davis found the army was well provisioned, well clothed, and in "fine spirits." Davis reviewed the troops and dined with the general officers at Bragg's headquarters. On December

2. Horn, *Army of Tennessee*, 193; Connelly, *Autumn of Glory*, 31–32; Lindsley, ed., *Military Annals*, 78.

3. Connelly, *Autumn of Glory*, 31–32; *OR* 20(2):448; Stewart Sifakis, *Compendium of the Confederate Armies: Tennessee* (New York: Facts on File, 1992), 120–21; TCWCC, *Tennesseans*, 1:183–84, 186, 214–16, 241, 245; McWhiney, *Bragg*, 343.

4. James Lee McDonough, *Stones River: Bloody Winter in Tennessee* (Knoxville: University of Tennessee Press, 1980), 33–35; Woodworth, *Jefferson Davis and His Generals*, 180–83; McWhiney, *Bragg*, 338–39.

13, the president reviewed Stewart's Brigade and others in "fine weather." Stewart likely met Davis for the first time on one of these occasions.[5]

That December at Murfreesboro was remembered for its festivities. In addition to the pomp of Davis' review of the army, there were Christmas parties, games, athletic contests, and the wedding of a local belle to the cavalry's brigadier general, John H. Morgan. But the season had to have been bittersweet for Stewart. Although it would have been possible, given his nearness to Winchester, for relatives to visit him, there is no indication that any did. While Lebanon was also close, Harriet had left the town some months prior to July, 1862, and had "refugeed" to Georgia with the couple's sons. Lebanon had, moreover, changed hands at least twice since the start of the war. There had been fighting in the town, as Morgan's cavalry had engaged Federal cavalry around the public square on May 5, 1862. Although Nathan Bedford Forrest had reported there were no Federals there on August 12, there had been another skirmish at Lebanon on November 9. Although Stewart's wife and sons had been gone from Lebanon at the time of these fights, many neighbors and friends had not, and he must have been concerned for them and for the university as well. He had spent most of his life in Middle Tennessee, and while it was doubtless good to be home, it must have been sad to see the country overrun with warring armies.[6]

For the second time in the war, Stewart faced one of his old West Point roommates in command of an opposing Federal force. Major General William S. Rosecrans had, at the end of October, 1862, replaced Buell at the command of the Federal troops that became the Army of the Cumberland. Rosecrans had resigned from the army in 1854 to pursue a career as an architect and civil engineer. Appointed a brigadier general in May, 1861, he had won the battle at Rich Mountain in western Virginia on July 11 of that

5. Woodworth, *Jefferson Davis and His Generals*, 183; Manigault, *A Carolinian Goes to War*, 52–53; Horn, *Army of Tennessee*, 194; McDonough, *Stones River*, 46–56; John Euclid Magee Diary, December 13, 1862, John Euclid Magee Papers, DU; William A. Brown Diary (typed copy), December 13, 1862, KNBP; Special Order No. 17, December 13, 1862, Polk's Corps, Army of Tennessee, Special Orders, RG 109, NA.

6. Wingfield, *Stewart*, 211; APS to D. H. Hill, July 21, 1862, Hill Papers, SHC; Burns, *Wilson County*, 43; N. B. Forrest to I. G. Harris, August 12, 1862, Harris letter book, Isham G. Harris Papers, LC.

year. He had faced Stewart at Corinth after Shiloh, and had commanded Federal troops at Iuka and Corinth in the fall of 1862. Now, Rosecrans was across the lines at Nashville, gathering supplies for a thrust at Bragg.[7]

Rosecrans had recognized the Army of Tennessee's disadvantage of being so close to his base and so far away from its own. He had resisted increasingly insistent demands from Washington to advance before he was ready. As Christmas came to an end, however, threats from Washington, coupled with the news of Stevenson's departure and the absence of a large portion of the Confederate cavalry on raids, prompted Rosecrans to advance on Murfreesboro. At the time of this move on December 26, Rosecrans' mobile force totaled 46,940 in three corps under Major Generals Alexander McCook, Thomas L. Crittenden, and George H. Thomas. Bragg's force totaled 37,719 men.[8]

As if a harbinger of the terrible fight to come, the temperature, which had been unseasonably warm through Christmas, began to plummet. The marching Federals plodded through roads "full of mud and slush," and the miserable Confederates awaited them in a cold drizzle, unable to build fires to warm themselves or cook their rations, as Bragg did not want his men to betray the location of their line. Stewart's men struck their tents and sent their wagons to the rear on Sunday night, December 28, in preparation for moving into line of battle.[9]

Bragg awaited Rosecrans' attack in front of Murfreesboro, Polk's Corps on the left, in front of the river, Hardee's on the right, behind it. Bragg selected his line to cover the many good roads leading into Murfreesboro, "until the real point of attack could be developed." One writer credits Bragg with utilizing the modern concept of a mobile defense in employing this plan. But another, Bragg's biographer Grady McWhiney, termed Bragg's failure to entrench his army "a serious tactical error."[10] After the war, Stewart agreed:

    7. Peter Cozzens, *No Better Place to Die* (Urbana: University of Illinois Press, 1990), 15–17; Herman Hattaway and Archer Jones, *How the North Won: A Military History of the Civil War* (Urbana: University of Illinois, 1983, 1991), 310.

    8. Hattaway and Jones, *How the North Won*, 310; Horn, *Army of Tennessee*, 196–98; Cozzens, *No Better Place to Die*, 45–46, 56–57.

    9. Cozzens, *No Better Place to Die*, 48; David R. Logsdon, ed., *Eyewitnesses at the Battle of Stones River* (Nashville: Kettle Mills Press, 1989), 8; *OR* 20(1):723.

    10. Richard J. Reid, *Stones River Ran Red* (Owensboro, Ky.: Commercial Printing, 1986), 45; *OR* 20(1):663, 672; McWhiney, *Bragg*, 348.

Some time before the battle of Murfreesboro General Bragg, while in conversation with an officer of his army, remarked that he would never again "use the spade;" that in the beginning of the war he had been compelled to resort to it, but he thought it did not suit the genius of the Southern people, and he would not use it again. Subsequent events made clear his error. In war there is no way of putting the weaker party on an equality with the stronger but by using the spade, or by superior strategy. Possibly by use of the spade he might have held Murfreesboro through the winter, and until his army could be sufficiently reinforced to enable it to take the offensive.[11]

Early on December 29, Stewart formed his brigade on the north bank of the Stones River, between Maney on the left and Donelson on the right, Cheatham's Division being in the second line behind Withers'. Stewart noted that nothing of great interest occurred that day. Stewart observed that an open country lay in front of his line; however, the field of conflict was generally wooded with dense cedar brakes, broken by open farmlands and cotton fields. Limestone outcroppings jutted out in both field and forest.[12]

On the afternoon of December 30, Colonel Arthur M. Manigault, commanding a brigade of Withers' Division, sent a request to Stewart for the rifled guns of Stanford's Battery. Manigault's one battery was involved in a contest with some Federal guns off to Stewart's left. Stewart dispatched two 3-inch rifles under Lieutenant A. A. Hardin. Manigault later wrote that the combined batteries had silenced one Federal battery and had fought to a draw with another. However, Stewart disgustedly reported that Manigault had not properly supported Hardin, "a most estimable and gallant young officer." Hardin had been killed, a rifled shell cutting him in two just after Manigault had relieved him. In Stewart's view, Hardin's longer-range rifles had not been employed to any "useful purpose." A member of Stanford's Battery observed that Hardin's rifles had been exposed to guns using shorter-range ammunition and to small-arms fire as well.[13]

11. Lindsley, ed., *Military Annals*, 79.
12. OR 20(1):723; Horn, *Army of Tennessee*, 197–98.
13. OR 20(1):723–24; Manigault, *A Carolinian Goes to War*, 56; Magee Diary, December 30, 1862, Magee Papers, DU; Brown Diary, December 30, 1862, KNBP.

That night, Bragg weakened his right to strengthen his left for the attack the next morning. Rosecrans also prepared for an attack on his left, which was Bragg's now weakened right. Rosecrans anticipated launching his attack at 7 A.M. on December 31, right after breakfast. McCown had his division of the Confederate left moving at dawn, however, so that it made contact with pickets on the extreme Union right at 6:22 A.M.[14]

Earlier that morning, Stewart received Bragg's order directing a wheeling attack against Rosecrans. He was also informed of Polk's decision that his brigade would be under Withers' command for the coming battle. Cheatham took command of Withers' two left brigades, Manigault's and Colonel J. Q. Loomis', along with his own two left brigades, those of Colonel A. J. Vaughn, Jr., and George Maney. Withers kept his two right brigades, Patton Anderson's and James R. Chalmers', and assumed direction of Stewart and Donelson. The logic behind this unusual move was to ensure that supports would be "thrown forward when necessary and with the least delay."[15]

Once again, Bragg's flanking attack fell upon the corps of the unfortunate Alexander McCook, whose two right divisions, those of Richard W. Johnson and Jefferson C. Davis, were pushed back some distance. McCook's third division, that of Philip Sheridan, proved to be of sterner stuff. Sheridan stubbornly fell back to the area between Harding's house and the Wilkinson Pike, posting a strong force of artillery to thwart Confederate attacks. Attacks by Manigault and Maney pushed Sheridan mostly across the Wilkinson Pike, into a dense cedar thicket on the southern edge of the present-day battlefield park. Sheridan later observed that his position was "strong," being "located in the edge of a dense cedar thicket and commanding a slight depression of open ground that lay in my front." Sheridan's left brigade, Colonel George W. Roberts', was at right angles to the rest of the division, facing roughly south, while the rest of the division faced roughly west. To Roberts' left were Colonel Timothy R. Stanley's and Colonel John F. Miller's brigades of James S. Negley's division.[16]

---

14. Horn, *Army of Tennessee*, 199–200; Cozzens, *No Better Place to Die*, 83–84.

15. *OR* 20(1):724, 754.

16. Alexander F. Stevenson, *The Battle of Stone's River* (Boston: James R. Osgood, 1884), 58–60; Philip H. Sheridan, *Personal Memoirs* (New York: Charles L. Webster, 1888), 1:226–27; Cozzens, *No Better Place to Die*, 122, 132; *OR* 20(1):345.

Stewart advanced his brigade into woods to the rear of Anderson's Brigade, arranging his line so that the brigade remained under the cover of the forest screened from the Federal artillery fire. Stanford's Battery went out of the fields onto the Wilkinson Pike, where it was intercepted by Polk and placed in a field along the pike to support a battery already placed there. While not at Stewart's immediate disposal during the battle, the position of the battery enabled it to support the brigade about as well as it possibly could, given the rough terrain on the field.[17]

It was now about 10 A.M. Previously, Patton Anderson had thrown his brigade against the Federal salient in the cedars on both sides of the Wilkinson Pike. Anderson's five regiments assaulted the south and east sides of the salient in succession, their goal to capture three batteries of Sheridan's and Negley's divisions on the north side of the pike. The Federals among the trees held their fire until the advancing Confederates in the open fields were but thirty yards away. Anderson's piecemeal attacks merely resulted in each of his regiments being shot to pieces.[18]

During these attacks by Anderson's Mississippians, Stewart moved his brigade up to some small breastworks thrown up by Anderson's men. There, the Federal batteries in front played upon the brigade, wounding several men. Anderson's right two regiments, the 30th and 29th Mississippi, fell back in disorder, but were rallied in the rear by Major Luke W. Finlay, a member of Stewart's staff since the consolidation of his 4th Tennessee with the 5th.[19]

Withers ordered Stewart to send two regiments to the assistance of Anderson's three left regiments, which were still assaulting Roberts even though the rest of Anderson's Brigade had fallen back. Stewart demurred, and suggested to Withers that his whole brigade be committed to the attack. With his experiences at Shiloh and Perryville no doubt on his mind, Stewart meant to keep his brigade together for this assault. Fortunately, Withers saw the logic of this proposal and agreed.[20]

The coordinated attack of the entire brigade spelled the end of the obsti-

17. *OR* 20(1):724, 732.

18. *OR* 20(1):728, 755–56; Cozzens, *No Better Place to Die*, 124–27; Logsdon, *Stones River*, 28.

19. *OR* 20(1):724, 727.

20. Ibid., 724–25.

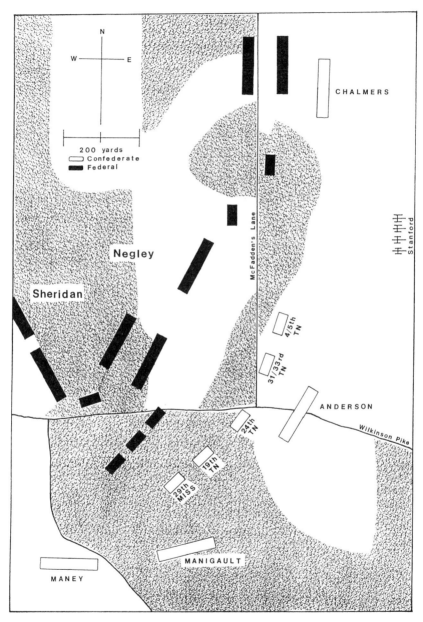

Murfreesboro
Map by Blake Magner

nate Federal position in the cedars. The Tennesseans advanced "in splendid order and with a cheer" with the 19th, 24th, 31st-33rd, and 4th-5th in line from left to right. Upon reaching the Wilkinson Pike, Stewart faced the brigade by the left flank and marched it down the pike about 300 yards, enabling the right of the brigade to form under the cover of "a dense cedar grove." By this maneuver, Stewart minimized casualties, although Anderson's regiments, still in close contact on the south side of the pike, must have drawn a great deal of fire. While the men were not subjected to a heavy fire during the greater portion of their advance, they did have to move through a portion of Anderson's retreating and demoralized troops, and over ground marked by Confederate casualties. A member of the 19th Tennessee later recalled seeing "a poor comrade's head in a small bushy tree."[21]

Stewart's attack struck the intersection of the Wilkinson Pike with McFadden's Lane, the 19th sweeping over the low rise upon which Captain Asahel K. Bush's 4th Indiana battery and a section of Battery G, 1st Missouri, was posted. Having exhausted their ammunition, both batteries were moving with some difficulty to the rear, hindered by the rockiness of the ground and the denseness of the cedars. Much of Roberts' brigade had also run low on ammunition, apparently just as the left of Stewart's Brigade burst into the dense cedars. Roberts' 42nd Illinois did not detect the Confederate advance until its troops "saw their glistening bayonets a few feet from them." The Federals delivered a "most galling fire" with their remaining ammunition, but Stewart's troops soon pushed the Federals back through the cedars. Out of ammunition, the Federals "fled in confusion."[22]

The 31st-33rd Tennessee came across two guns of Bush's battery which their crews were trying to drag out of the cedars. Doubtless these Federals were experiencing problems similar to those observed by a member of Miller's brigade, who, retreating from the woods, saw a lone artilleryman trying to remove his piece from the field with one horse, "the other five having been killed. One wheel of the gun carriage was fastened between

21. Cozzens, *No Better Place to Die*, 133; *OR* 20(1):724, 725, 728, 731, 756; Losson, *Tennessee's Forgotten Warriors*, 86; Lindsley, ed., *Military Annals*, 187; J. H. Warner, *Personal Glimpses of the Civil War* (Chattanooga: privately published, 1914), 6–7.

22. Cozzens, *No Better Place to Die*, 132; Stevenson, *Battle of Stone's River*, 68–69, 72–73; *OR* 20(1):725, 727–31.

two rocks, and the brave artilleryman was trying with a rail to pry it out." Members of the consolidated regiment dispersed the guns' crews with a "well aimed volley" and overran the guns, leaving them in their pursuit of the retreating Yankees. The Federals attempted several times to make a stand in the woods, but were unable to hold.[23]

The battle raged on either side of Stewart's Brigade. In keeping with Bragg's plan of a wheeling attack by brigades *en echelon,* on Stewart's right Chalmers' Brigade of Withers' Division rolled forward soon after Anderson's attack, striking the extreme right of the Federal line on the west side of the river, which was anchored in an area that became known as the "Round Forest." This area of the Federal line was so named because it consisted of a dense circular area of cedars on rocky, elevated ground along the railroad and the Nashville Pike. Packed into this area were the better part of John M. Palmer's division and a brigade of Thomas J. Wood's division, supported by over fifty cannon. Chalmers was hit with a whirlwind of fire from the massed guns and the rifles of the Federals jammed in the cedars. Chalmers himself was wounded, and his Mississippi regiments decimated.[24]

Donelson's Brigade constituted the last uncommitted Confederates west of Stones River. As Chalmers broke, Donelson led his cheering men forward against the brigades of Colonel William B. Hazen and Brigadier General Charles Cruft. Intending to disorganize the advancing Confederates, Cruft ordered the Federal 1st Kentucky of his brigade forward, which simply exposed it to the rifles of the oncoming Confederates. As this regiment came streaming back, Cruft experienced further troubles, as Stewart's advance had penetrated into the Federal rear. Stewart's attack forced Cruft back. Major General George H. Thomas then committed Lt. Colonel Oliver H. Shephard's regular brigade, which charged into the cedars to confront Stewart's oncoming Tennesseans. Stewart, aided by Donelson's left regiments, repulsed the regulars.[25]

At the height of the fighting, Stewart was observed but a few paces behind the firing line, leisurely smoking a pipe and quietly giving orders to his staff officers, "whilst ball, canister and grape were rattling around thick

23. *OR* 20(1):725, 731; Logsdon, *Stones River,* 28–29.

24. Cozzens, *No Better Place to Die,* 151–54.

25. Ibid., 154–56; *OR* 20(1):726, 729.

as hail." In the midst of this hot winter fight, Stewart added to his reputation for quiet courage among his men and competence among the officers of the army.[26]

Having driven the Federals out of the cedars, Stewart saw that they were rallying across an open field from the cedars on the somewhat higher ground in the area of the railroad. There, Union artillery was concentrated to hold off the Confederate pursuit of the routed Federals. Stewart sent staff officers out to summon Stanford's Battery to engage the Federal artillery. He also ordered up additional ammunition. Although the ammunition was soon procured, Polk notified Stewart that he had work for Stanford and he could not be spared.

At this point, a bizarre incident occurred, the record of which is sketchy. Colonel John A. Jaques of the 1st Louisiana appeared, presented himself to Colonel Tansil of the 31st-33rd, and said he was a member of Cheatham's staff with an order for the 31st-33rd to fall back. The 31st-33rd's retreat caused a short retreat of the entire brigade before Stewart could bring it to halt, upon which Jaques disappeared. It turned out that earlier in the battle Jaques had panicked and had disgracefully run away from his real regiment, which was in Loomis' Brigade on Stewart's left. It is not known whether Jaques meant well, had gone insane, or was actively attempting to sabotage Confederate operations. In any case, Stewart re-formed his line and moved it forward to the edge of the woods, where the brigade remained until after dark.[27]

During this unexpected retreat, the 24th lost its commander, Colonel Bratton. Bratton's left leg was shattered by a piece of shell or grape shot, which subsequently passed through his horse, killing it and wounding Bratton's right leg. Bratton's left leg was later amputated, and he remained in the hospital at Murfreesboro after the battle, where he soon died. Stewart lamented Bratton as "one of the best and bravest officers in the entire army."[28]

26. *Chattanooga Daily Rebel*, June 11, July 8, 1863.

27. *OR* 20(1):725; McWhiney, *Bragg*, 356; Arthur W. Bergeron, Jr., *Guide to Confederate Military Units, 1861–1865* (Baton Rouge: Louisiana State University Press, 1989), 69. Even if Jaques *had* been a member of Cheatham's staff, Stewart was under Withers' command that day. Stewart apparently did not know Jaques (whom he called "Jacquess") was a deserter.

28. Frank H. Smith, "'The Duck River Rifles,' the Twenty-fourth Tennessee Infantry,"

Donelson's Brigade joined Stewart's in driving the Federals out of the cedars south of the Round Forest. However, Donelson's right regiments, along with Chalmers' survivors, were unable to dent Hazen's salient in the Forest, which came to be known as "Hell's Half-Acre." On the extreme Confederate left, Hardee was calling for reinforcements to complete the victory on that side of the field. Bragg originally determined to use a portion of Breckinridge's uncommitted division east of the river to reinforce Hardee, but Breckinridge mistakenly thought the Federals were advancing on his front, and spent some time ascertaining that the Yankees were in fact quiet there. By the time Breckinridge moved four of his five brigades across the river, Bragg had determined to reinforce failure (Polk's attacks on the Round Forest) rather than success (Hardee's attack on the left). Furthermore, instead of concentrating Breckinridge's brigades for one massive assault, Bragg and Polk sent them forward one after the other to assault the Federal stronghold. In attacks eerily reminiscent of Bragg's assaults on the Hornets' Nest at Shiloh, Breckinridge's piecemeal attacks were repulsed. Meanwhile, Hardee's troops, unreinforced and worn out from a day's long fighting, stopped tantalizingly close to Rosecrans' escape route along the Nashville Pike.[29]

By nightfall, the Confederates had bent the Yankee line almost perpendicular to its location that morning. Only in the area of the Round Forest did Rosecrans hold his original line. Bragg justifiably telegraphed Richmond: "God has granted us a Happy New Year." As Bragg stated in his report of the battle, "Nearly the whole field with all its trophies—the enemy's dead and many of his wounded, his hospitals and stores—[was left] in our full possession." The Confederate commander fully expected that Rosecrans would fall back, and it seemed for a while that he would. After an inconclusive meeting with his corps commanders on the issue of retreat, Rosecrans actually rode to the rear with McCook to scout a fallback position. Seeing some troops moving by torchlight, Rosecrans mistakenly believed that the Rebels had moved to cut off his retreat, and returned to his

---

in *The Civil War in Maury County, Tennessee*, ed. Jill K. Garrett and Marise P. Lightfoot (Columbia, Tenn.: privately published, 1966), 87; *OR* 20(1):725–26, 730.

29. Cozzens, *No Better Place to Die*, 144–50, 156–66; McWhiney, *Bragg*, 357–61; Charles M. Spearman, "The Battle of Stones River: Tragic New Year's Eve in Tennessee," *Blue & Gray Magazine* 6 (February 1989): 8, 26.

headquarters resolved to "fight or die." Only at daylight was it determined that the torches had been carried by Federal cavalrymen. By an accident that Stewart would have no doubt ascribed to the will of God, the Army of the Cumberland stayed on the field.[30]

As night fell, Stewart withdrew the brigade "a few hundred yards" to bivouac, leaving a small picket guard. His troops removed a substantial amount of booty from the field as it withdrew.[31] Members of the brigade were among the thousands of both armies that suffered through that cold night. A member of the 19th wrote: "We lay all night with a feeling of loneliness as if all were dead but ourselves, knowing that although [*sic*] the cedars and rocks were lying thousands of friends and foes alike unconscious in that sleep from which the morning reveille will not awake them. There were many wounded too who had not been cared for, suffering not only from wounds but from cold."[32]

Corporal John Magee of Stanford's Battery rode out over the field after dark looking for some harness, tearful from hearing the groans of the suffering wounded. Sergeant William Brown of the battery noted the gloominess of resting that night with dead comrades lashed to the caissons.[33]

The first day of 1863 found both exhausted armies on the field, each waiting for the other to make a move. Stewart's Tennesseans held their position on the edge of the cedar brake facing the Union line along the railroad embankment, subject to "frequent shelling" by the batteries there. Rosecrans ordered the occupation of high ground above the river at McFadden's Ford, and consolidated his line among the railroad, giving up the Round Forest to Polk. Bragg continued to wait for the Federal withdrawal, which never came.

The next day, Bragg discovered the Federal force on the high ground above the ford. Bragg figured that he had two choices, drive the Federals off the hill or withdraw Polk's lines. The latter being deemed inappropriate, Breckinridge was ordered to drive the Federals off the heights. Even

---

30. Hattaway and Jones, *How the North Won*, 322; *OR* 20(1):666; Logsdon, *Stones River*, 46–47. For Stewart's conviction that the war's result was the will of God, see Ridley, *Battles and Sketches*, 624.

31. *OR* 20(1):725.

32. W. J. Worsham, *The Old Nineteenth Tennessee Regiment, C.S.A.: June, 1861–April, 1865* (Knoxville: Paragon Printing, 1902), 73.

33. Logsdon, *Stones River*, 48.

the nonprofessional soldier Breckinridge could see what Bragg could not: that the proposed attack was a potential disaster. Breckinridge turned out to be right, as a good portion of his fine division was massacred by the massed Federal artillery.[34]

Both armies were worn out. The Confederate infantry had been in line of battle for five days and nights, had no reserves, were subject to severe weather, and in some places could not have any fires. Due to rain, Stones River was rising, threatening to isolate one part of the army from the other. Reduced by over 10,000 casualties, the Army of Tennessee could put only about 20,000 infantry in line. To compound these problems, late on the morning of January 3 Bragg learned from McCook's captured papers that Rosecrans had 70,000 men under his command, and cavalry reported Rosecrans was being reinforced from Nashville. After a consultation with Hardee and Polk, both of whom counseled withdrawal, Bragg ordered a retreat, which started at 11 P.M. that night.[35]

Stewart and his brigade left the field for Shelbyville early on the morning of January 4, 1863. During the three days after the hard fighting on December 31, the brigade had been under intermittent artillery fire. Stewart had spent the time trying to police the battlefield in his sector, and getting both Federal and Confederate dead buried. Despite the Rebel soldiers' need for clothing, Stewart deplored "the plundering and stripping of the dead." Among those Federals buried on the field was Colonel George Roberts, killed on the north side of the Wilkinson Pike trying to resist Stewart's attack. Major Finlay wrapped Roberts in his own military cloak and gave him a military funeral. Soldiers of another Tennessee regiment placed a stone over the grave and scratched an inscription with a bayonet.[36]

Murfreesboro was Stewart's best performance to date. Colonel Francis M. Walker of the 19th made mention in his report of Stewart's skill in maneuvering and keeping the brigade together. The brigade accomplished as much as any other Confederate unit at Murfreesboro, as its devastating assault routed the Federals out of the cedars northwest of the Wilkinson

34. *OR* 20(1):667–68, 725; Cozzens, *No Better Place to Die*, 177–98.

35. McWhiney, *Bragg*, 370–73; Woodworth, *Jefferson Davis and His Generals*, 194. For the condition of the Army of the Cumberland, see Cozzens, *No Better Place to Die*, 202.

36. *OR* 20(1):726; Smith, " 'The Duck River Rifles,' " 88.

Pike. Stewart had resisted the temptation to blindly obey Withers' order to throw his brigade piecemeal into the fight. His insistence on a concerted attack doomed the hitherto successful defense of Sheridan and Negley. Like any good officer, Stewart recognized the valuable services of the regimental officers and his own staff, and noted the price in blood that his men paid for their success: 399 out of 1,635 killed, wounded, or missing. Stewart paid special tribute in his report to the conduct of his men, who "throughout the week . . . behaved in a manner that is beyond praise."[37]

37. *OR* 20(1):726, 709.

— 6 —

Old Straight

Interlude in Middle Tennessee

Bragg's retreat from Murfreesboro after announcing a hard-won victory set off a storm of criticism in portions of the press, the army, and the government. In response, Bragg embarked upon a clumsy campaign to confront his critics and gain reassurance, seeing himself as a martyr for the Cause. The net result of his efforts in that regard was the expression of opinions on the part of his staff and such officers as Hardee, Cleburne, and Breckinridge that he no longer had the army's confidence.

When this unseemly episode came to Davis' attention, the president sent his western theater commander, General Joseph E. Johnston, to Tullahoma to determine just what was transpiring within the army's command. Johnston was uncomfortable with the task and thwarted Davis' intention that he supplant Bragg. Johnston spent two periods with the army in the late winter and early spring of 1863, both of which ended in reports favorable to Bragg. Johnston's first endorsement emboldened Bragg to strike at certain of his critics in the army.[1]

One of the first officers to feel Bragg's wrath was McCown, who commanded a small division of three brigades nominally in "Smith's Corps," although that entity, as such, had not existed in the Army of Tennessee for some weeks. With some justification, Bragg blamed McCown for bungling

---

1. McWhiney, *Bragg*, 375–88; Connelly, *Autumn of Glory*, 77–86; Woodworth, *Jefferson Davis and his Generals*, 196–98.

the initial attack on McCook on December 31, 1862. Bragg had for some time considered McCown incompetent. McCown compounded matters by openly making anti-Bragg remarks, and by terming the Confederacy "a damned stinking cotton oligarchy." McCown was arrested, relieved of his command, and court-martialed on technical grounds.[2]

McCown's arrest order of February 27, 1863, appointed Stewart to the temporary command of the division, and assigned it to Polk's Corps. Stewart was placed at the head of the division instead of its sole surviving brigadier, Matthew D. Ector, and instead of other brigadiers in the army at that time, including such well-known officers as S. A. M. Wood, Bushrod Johnson, St. John R. Liddell, George Maney, William Preston, and Patton Anderson (who had commanded a division at Perryville). The advancement was indicative of Stewart's solid record, but doubtless also reflected such factors as his being a graduate of West Point (the only other was Johnson), his being the ranking Tennessee officer in the army on record as a Bragg supporter, and his having powerful support both within and outside the army.[3]

Indeed, several of Stewart's prominent friends had for some time been agitating for his promotion. Just before the Battle of Murfreesboro, Stewart wrote Jefferson Davis, enclosing recommendations for his promotion from Andrew Ewing, a former congressman, Governor Isham Harris, and Chancellor Bromfield Ridley, a Tennessee judge and a fellow faculty member of Stewart's at Cumberland. Stewart, who must have felt some awkwardness in writing the president directly on such a subject, forwarded the recommendations out of respect to his friends, "and because the promotion they ask for me would be very gratifying to me, if in the judgment of my military superiors, & especially your own, I am worthy of it. I would not desire or accept promotion on any other grounds." Efforts on Stewart's behalf continued into the new year, as Senator Gustavus A. Henry of Tennessee wrote letters to both Davis and Secretary of War James A. Seddon, stating that officers in the army and citizens of Tennessee felt Stewart

2. Connelly, *Autumn of Glory*, 81.

3. *OR* 23(2):654; McWhiney, *Bragg*, 330–31. Bragg's favorite Tennessee brigadier at the time was old Daniel S. Donelson, whom he recommended for a major generalcy in November, 1862. Donelson had been assigned to duty in East Tennessee on January 30 and died of natural causes there in the spring. See *OR* 20(2):417–18, 23(2):621.

was deserving of promotion, and that both Bragg and Polk had expressed that sentiment to him. Both Polk, and, interestingly, McCown, also wrote recommendations. All of these recommendations in December, January, and February made Davis inquire if there was a vacancy—which, at least until McCown's permanent removal, or the creation of a new organization, there was not.[4]

Stewart's senior colonel, Otho French Strahl, assumed temporary command of Stewart's Brigade. Strahl had served with the 4th Tennessee since Columbus and New Madrid, and became acquainted with Stewart at Corinth. A native Ohioan, Strahl lived in Tennessee and had practiced law there for several years before the war. A man who spoke in "clear, silvery tones," Strahl was the officer at Shiloh who, when asked by Stewart whether the 4th could take a Federal battery, responded, "We will try." As Stewart had earlier recommended Strahl for promotion, he must have believed his beloved brigade of Tennesseans was left in good hands.[5]

At the time Stewart assumed command, McCown's Division, which during McCown's court-martial proceedings retained that name, was made up of Ector's Brigade of dismounted Texas cavalry, Evander McNair's Arkansas brigade, under the command of the colonel of the 1st Arkansas Mounted Rifles, R. W. Harper, and Rains' Brigade of Georgia and North Carolina infantry, temporarily commanded by Colonel Robert B. Vance. James E. Rains, a Tennessean, had been killed in the division's devastating attack on the Federal right at Murfreesboro. Soon after Stewart assumed command of the division, Shiloh veteran Brigadier General William B. Bate was appointed to command the brigade.[6]

---

4. APS to Jefferson Davis, December 28, 1863, Henry to Seddon, February 10, 1863, Henry to Seddon, February 12, 1863, Henry to Davis, February 12, 1863, Recommendation of McCown, January 13, 1863, endorsed by Polk and Cheatham, February 5, 1863, Officers File, RG 109, NA; Robert Ewing, "General Robert E. Lee's Inspiration to the Industrial Rehabilitation of the South, Exemplified in the Development of Southern Iron Interests," *Tennessee Historical Magazine* 9 (January 1926): 215–16. APS and McCown appear to have been on good terms, as Stewart had earlier recommended McCown's promotion. See APS to A. S. Johnston, January 24, 1862, APS/CSR, RG 109, NA.

5. *OR* 23(2):734, 10(1):409, 427; Lindsley, ed., *Military Annals*, 184–85; Warner, *Generals in Gray*, 295; Charles M. Cummings, "Otho French Strahl: Choicest Spirit to Embrace the South," *Tennessee Historical Quarterly* 24 (winter 1965): 341, 349.

6. *OR* 23(2):655, 688; Warner, *Generals in Gray*, 19; *OR* 10(1):429.

Stewart's assumption of divisional command, even temporarily, necessarily involved the expansion of his staff. Already, two members of his staff had died in battle. Captain Thomas W. Preston of Memphis had been killed by a shot through the head at Shiloh. Lieutenant Colonel W. B. Ross, an aide-de-camp, who had joined Stewart before Shiloh, served until he was wounded in the neck at Murfreesboro, where he died on January 2.[7]

At the time of Murfreesboro, Stewart's staff included Ross and aides Captain Robert A. Hatcher of New Madrid, Missouri, Captain John A. Lauderdale of the 5th Tennessee, Major Luke W. Finlay of the 4th, and Lieutenant Paul Jones, Jr., of the 33rd, all having lost their regimental positions by reason of the consolidation of their units, but who "preferred to be in the field." Major Joseph D. Cross of Nashville served as commissary, Lieutenant Colonel T. F. Sevier as assistant inspector general, Major John C. Thompson of Nashville as acting assistant inspector general, Lieutenant Nathan Green as assistant adjutant general, and Stewart's brother John as ordnance officer.[8]

In February, Stewart's eldest son, Caruthers, then sixteen, was placed on the staff as an aide. Another young man joined Stewart later that spring, Bromfield Ridley. Ridley was a native of Rutherford County who aided Confederate forces at Murfreesboro as a member of the "Seed Corn Contingent," boys under eighteen who helped with prisoners and other support roles. Young Ridley was the son of Stewart's friend and supporter, Chancellor Bromfield Ridley. Before joining Stewart, Ridley fought with Morgan's cavalry in several skirmishes in Kentucky and Tennessee. Ridley would come to write a valuable account of his experiences during the war as a member of Stewart's staff.[9]

---

7. *OR* 10(1):428, 20(1):725; Joseph E. Crute, Jr., *Confederate Staff Officers, 1861–1865* (Powhatan, Va.: Derwent Books, 1982), 185–86. Stewart lauded both men for their bravery and devotion.

8. Crute, *Confederate Staff Officers*, 185–86; Ridley, *Battles and Sketches*, 475; Special Order No. 43, May 17, 1862, Special Orders, Polk's Corps, Army of the Mississippi, RG 109, NA; J. W. Stewart, CSR, RG 109, NA. Hatcher eventually left Stewart's staff to join the Confederate Congress. Portions of Hatcher's diary are extant, but they are in private hands and the author was unsuccessful in gaining access to them.

9. R. C. Stewart, CSR, RG 109, NA; Crute, *Confederate Staff Officers*, 185–86; Ridley, *Battles and Sketches*, 148–58, 474; APS to Samuel Cooper, June 20, 1863, Special Order Book, Stewart's Division, Departmental Records, Army and Department of Tennessee, RG

Though Ridley had ample cause by reason of family connections and deference due to age to admire Stewart, there is no reason to doubt his description of Stewart's personality as a general, for Ridley would serve with Stewart for the remainder of the war. He described Stewart as

> Quiet, modest, but withal a positive soldier of high moral character[;] his command was properly managed yet scarcely did he give an order. . . . The only unnatural thing about General Stewart was that he never dodged a bullet—(any natural man was bound to do it). [He was] as kind as a father to his command, and possessing their confidence that he would not willingly sacrifice them, [thus] whatever he said to do they did, even to leap into the very jaws of death. His counsels were so much looked to that the soldiers nicknamed him "Old Straight," as significant of their respect.[10]

Ridley was not alone in his opinion. Later that year, a correspondent for the *Chattanooga Daily Rebel* wrote:

> Very few possess more of the essential qualities for a commanding officer than Gen. Stewart. Coolness and skill coupled with a thorough acquaintance of the art militaire, a firm disciplinarian, but with a thorough, even temper, that never suffers itself to be exerted or betrayed into any rash or intemperate expression, always the same calm, unmoved demeanor, whether by the camp or parlor fire, as well as amidst the clang and clash of arms. Three times he has led his brigade into the fight, successively at Shiloh, Perryville and Murfreesboro, and every time it has been with credit to himself, honor to the brigade and to the State.[11]

Although Stewart was noted for his abstention from army politics, his new position as the temporary holder of one of the army's major commands called for some political skill on the treacherous ground created by Bragg's struggle with his corps commanders, Polk and Hardee, and their supporters. Bragg was criticized from several quarters for the conduct of

---

109, NA. See Ridley's book's introduction, written by Stewart in 1905, as to Ridley's background.

    10. Ridley, *Battles and Sketches*, 474–75.

    11. *Chattanooga Daily Rebel*, July 8, 1863.

the Kentucky campaign the previous autumn. Polk and Hardee added fuel to the fire by submitting reports insinuating they were aware that the bulk of Buell's army was at Perryville, and that each had warned Bragg, though in fact they had not. In April, 1863, Bragg sent out another of his clumsy circular letters, inquiring as to Polk's council at Bardstown on October 3, 1862, which resulted in Polk's disobeying the order to attack Joshua Sill's advance on Frankfort, and Polk's dawn council on October 8, 1862, at Perryville, which resulted in the disobeying of Bragg's order to attack immediately.[12]

Stewart was among the fourteen officers who received Bragg's letter. Unlike Hardee or others in the army, Stewart does not seem to have considered Bragg the particular cause of the failure in Kentucky. The letter placed Stewart in the difficult position of siding with either Bragg, the army commander, or Polk, the corps commander under whom he had served since Columbus. Polk appears to have canvassed certain of the officers at Shelbyville about Bragg's inquiry, including Stewart, who was reluctant to mention it to Polk. Stewart was able to honestly reply to Bragg that he did not attend either council, and was not even aware of the October 8 meeting. He covered matters with Polk by providing a courtesy copy of his reply to Bragg, yet made a record by confirming to Polk that it was Polk who initiated the contact between the two on the subject, noting that otherwise he "had an honest doubt of the propriety of mentioning the matter to you myself." This episode was the first of several in which Stewart skillfully stayed in the good graces of both camps in the midst of the high command's internecine struggle.[13]

During this period, a lengthy article in "bitter spirit" appeared in a soldier's newspaper, the *Daily Rebel Banner*. The article complained about Stewart's being kept at the rank of brigadier general notwithstanding his divisional command and Strahl's remaining a colonel in spite of his commanding a brigade. There is no evidence that either Stewart or Strahl was behind the article, which in any event reflected the esteem in which both men were

---

12. *OR* 16(1):1097–98. For Stewart's abstention from army politics, see Pollard, *Lee and His Lieutenants*, 712–13.

13. Connelly, *Autumn of Glory*, 87–89; *OR* 16(1):1097, 1105. For Stewart's opinion of the Kentucky campaign, see Lindsley, ed., *Military Annals*, 76–77.

held. The article indicates the partisan aspects of promotions in the army, and was no doubt an effort by a more vociferous member of or supporter of the army's "Tennessee clique" to advance the careers of two deserving Tennesseans. Of course, the real reason neither man could be promoted was that at the time, no vacancy existed for either, as McCown's absence was deemed temporary.[14]

Stewart's (McCown's) Division was based at Shelbyville on the Confederate left, with the remainder of Polk's Corps. Stewart's men, as well as the rest of the army, enjoyed the plenty of the Duck River valley, the general respite from battle, and entertainments ranging from revivals to gambling and old-fashioned horse races. Strahl observed that the army was "in the finest condition I have known it," its men "hearty, fat and in fine spirits." Stewart no doubt approved of and probably participated in a revival meeting of over a thousand men from Ector's and Vance's brigades in a cedar grove. One hundred forty conversions were reported for the entire division. A spiritual lift of a different sort doubtless occurred when Harriet was able to join the general.[15]

Stewart later wrote that during this time, "there occurred numerous reconnoissances [sic] and affairs of outposts." Stewart's command spent some time on outpost, being ordered from Shelbyville out the Triune Road to a place called Hooker's shortly after Stewart assumed command. However, there is no indication that Stewart became involved in any sort of fighting while in command of McCown's Division. Stewart's command was the subject of an inspection by Colonel William Preston Johnston, President Davis' aide, on March 30. Curiously, Johnston singled out some troops in the division, observing that "some dismounted Arkansas and Texas troops showed marks of neglect in many important points." Stewart was not personally criticized for this problem, probably because he had

14. Note, *CV* 4 (October 1896): 344; Larry J. Daniel, *Soldiering in the Army of Tennessee* (Chapel Hill: University of North Carolina Press, 1991), 93.

15. Foote, *The Civil War*, 2:175; Horn, *Army of Tennessee*, 230–31; O. F. Strahl to Dr. Richardson, April 25, 1863, O. F. Strahl and W. A. Taylor Civil War Letters, GA; Daniel, *Soldiering*, 117, 122; G. Clinton Prim, Jr., "Born Again in the Trenches: Revivals in the Army of Tennessee," *Tennessee Historical Quarterly* 43 (fall 1984): 250, 254; W. M. Gentry, "Surgeons of the Confederacy," *CV* 40 (September–October 1932): 336–37.

been in command of the division for only a month. In the following weeks, however, "much attention was given to drilling."[16]

As the spring wore on, events in Mississippi began to affect the army. Ulysses S. Grant's pressure against Vicksburg occasioned Davis to look to the Army of Tennessee, as he had before Murfreesboro, for help in Mississippi. In May, the Army of Tennessee sent reinforcements to Mississippi, which involved considerable shuffling of units within the army, including Stewart's temporary command. Bate's Brigade was disrupted considerably. His two North Carolina regiments, the 29th and 39th, were detached on May 11, and his two Georgia battalions, the 3rd and 9th, were consolidated into a new regiment, the 37th Georgia. On May 24, Breckinridge's Division, excepting Brigadier General John C. Brown's Tennessee brigade, and a single Tennessee regiment from another brigade, the 20th, was placed on the train for Mississippi. The 20th was given to Bate, who also retained his Eufaula battery of Alabama artillery and the 37th Georgia.[17]

On May 26, Bragg reported to Adjutant General Samuel Cooper in Richmond that "all McCown's division except one Georgia regiment" had gone with Breckinridge to Mississippi. Stewart had relinquished command of the division a few days previously, and returned to his brigade of Tennesseans on May 15. He received a note from Polk's headquarters on May 23, telling him to support the cavalry in his front (at Guy's Gap) whenever required. Stewart's prompt reply suggested that he did not need to be told the obvious, as "I have supposed my business here on outpost was to afford prompt support to the cavalry in front, whenever such support seemed necessary or might be called for." Stewart took the opportunity to suggest the placement of a brigade at a key location.[18]

Stewart's reunion with his brigade would not last long. The departure of the substantial portion of two divisions left the army with only three organized divisions, those of Cheatham, Withers, and Cleburne, as well as

---

16. Lindsley, ed., *Military Annals*, 79; *OR* 23(2):683, 757–58; D. H. Reynolds Diary, April 1–12, 1863, Daniel H. Reynolds Papers, UAR.

17. *OR* 23(2):735, 829, 849, 851, 853; Stewart Sifakis, *Compendium of the Confederate Armies: South Carolina and Georgia* (New York: Facts on File, 1995), 187, 247.

18. *OR* 23(2):849–50, 853; John Euclid Magee Diary, May 15, 1863, Magee Papers, DU.

Bate's reorganized brigade, Brown's brigade of Tennesseans, and Henry Delamar Clayton's Alabama brigade, a unit from the defenses of Mobile that had been with the army for some weeks, independent of the two corps. Hardee, down to only Cleburne's Division, organized a new division from these unattached brigades. On May 27, he telegraphed President Davis directly, advising him as to Breckinridge's departure and stating: "Another division will be immediately organized to replace his and I desire you will appoint Brig. Gen. A. P. Stewart major-general, to command it." Davis asked for Adjutant General Cooper's advice, and Cooper telegraphed Bragg to inquire whether Stewart had gone to Mississippi with McCown's Division. Bragg replied on May 28, stating that Stewart had returned to his brigade when McCown's Division had departed.[19]

Hardee's telegram asking for Stewart's promotion was one of several efforts by Stewart's friends and fellow officers to secure him a promotion. These efforts had continued into the spring of 1863. In mid-April, theater commander Joseph E. Johnston requested that Stewart be promoted to major general and permanently made commander of McCown's Division. Johnston deemed it of "great importance to the army" that McCown not join it. Johnston stated that Stewart was "an educated & gallant soldier & Christian gentleman who has done much service." Davis replied to the effect that creating a vacancy by transferring an officer (i.e., McCown) thought incompetent in one army to a similar command elsewhere was not his practice. Governor Harris wrote Seddon on Stewart's behalf on April 18, and Cheatham wrote a lengthy recommendation that was endorsed by Polk and Johnston, the latter stating: "I have already recommended Brig. Gen'l Stewart's promotion. I regard him as an officer of great merit." Curiously, Bragg did not endorse the document, but did forward the recommendations of Polk and Cheatham to Richmond.[20]

Nothing seems to have happened until June 2, when Bragg telegraphed

19. Stewart Sifakis, *Compendium of the Confederate Armies: Alabama* (New York: Facts on File, 1992), 82, 105–108; *OR* 23(2):854.

20. J. Johnston to J. Davis, April 18, 1863, Jefferson Davis Papers, Howard-Tilton Memorial Library, Tulane University; Dunbar Rowland, ed., *Jefferson Davis—Constitutionalist: His Letters, Papers and Speeches* (Jackson, Miss: Mississippi Department of Archives and History, 1923), 5:475; I. Harris to J. Seddon, April 18, 1863, Recommendation of B. Cheatham, April, 1863, endorsed by L. Polk, April 27, 1863, J. Johnston, April 29, 1863, Officers File, RG 109, NA.

Cooper that the need for a commander for the new division in Hardee's Corps was "most pressing." Bragg felt constrained by a general order from Richmond issued that March, prohibiting the detachment of brigadier generals from their brigades or colonels from their regiments, "except on ordinary temporary duty, without the special authority of the War Department." Stewart's command of McCown's Division was such an "ordinary temporary duty." Command of a new division, a new permanent establishment, was a different matter. Fortunately, the next day, June 3, 1863, Cooper telegraphed Bragg: "Brig. Gen. A. P. Stewart is appointed major-general for the division in Hardee's corps, as mentioned in your dispatch of yesterday."[21]

Stewart's promotion clearly arose more from merit than from the influence in Richmond of his powerful friends in Tennessee politics. His solid performance and soldierly bearing had impressed the officers of the army, and they made that known in Richmond. Bragg's silence is hard to explain; nevertheless, he did nothing to sidetrack Stewart's promotion. Stewart's serendipitous absence from Polk's Kentucky councils and his ability to walk the tightrope in the controversy between Bragg and his detractors had served him well.

On the morning of June 4, Stewart was commanding a reconnaissance in force of his own brigade and Maney's in support of a probe out from Shelbyville by Rebel cavalry. About noon, Cheatham rode out to check the probe's progress. Major W. B. Richmond of Polk's staff rode out with the army's English visitor, Lieutenant Colonel Arthur Fremantle, to inform Old Straight of his promotion and orders to report to Hardee. Congratulations were extended, and Stewart rode to the rear, leaving Cheatham in command. On June 7, Stewart's farewell was read to the brigade, whose members had mixed feelings over Old Straight's departure. John Magee of Stanford's Battery wrote: "The boys are all sorry to part with their well-beloved General, who has commanded them so long, but are glad to see him promoted."[22]

21. *OR* 23(2):856, 860.

22. John Euclid Magee Diary, June 4, 1863, Magee Papers, DU; see James A. L. Fremantle, *The Fremantle Diary*, ed. Walter Lord (Boston: Little, Brown, 1954), 133–34; *Chattanooga Daily Rebel*, June 11, 1863. Fremantle's diary does not mention Stewart, but his entry for the day agrees in most other relevant particulars with Magee's account.

Stewart's formal orders to report to Hardee for duty were dated June 6. Stewart was assigned to command Hardee's new division, to be composed of Johnson's, Bate's, Brown's and Clayton's brigades. With the exception of Clayton's Brigade, the troops of the new division were veterans of at least one of the previous battles at Shiloh, Murfreesboro, or Perryville, and the 18th Alabama of Clayton's Brigade had fought at Shiloh. William Brimage Bate, Henry Delamar Clayton, John Calvin Brown, and Bushrod Rust Johnson were all veterans who had been wounded in previous fighting.[23]

Stewart spent the days after his appointment familiarizing himself with his new command. In vain he wrote Bragg's chief of staff, Brigadier General William W. Mackall, asking reconsideration of the assignment of the unknown Major J. W. Eldridge as his chief of artillery, preferring the proven Captain T. J. Stanford. Old Straight sought promotions for his staff officers as befitted their new duties at the divisional level, and solicited nominations from his brigadiers of men "distinguished for their bravery, intelligence, soldierly qualities and good marksmanship," each to be armed with one of the division's four new Whitworth rifles. Eleven of the seventeen regiments and battalions in the new division were Tennessee units. They and their commander would face Rosecrans during the summer to renew the struggle for their home state. As events would transpire, Stewart would be at the center of the opening moves of the renewed struggle.[24]

23. *OR* 23(2):867; Warner, *Generals in Gray*, 35–36, 52–53, 157–58; Cozzens, *No Better Place to Die*, 186; *OR* 20(2):498. Johnson appears to have expected the new command. Charles M. Cummings, *Yankee Quaker, Confederate General: The Curious Career of Bushrod Rust Johnson* (Teaneck, N.J.: Fairleigh Dickinson University Press, 1971), 245–47.

24. Special Orders No. 1, June 8, 1863, No. 4, June 10, 1863, APS to W. Mackall, June 15, 1863, APS to Samuel Cooper, June 20, 1863, Special Order No. 12, June 15, 1863, Special Orders, Stewart's Division, Departmental Records, Army and Department of Tennessee, RG 109, NA.

— 7 —

An Entire Failure

The Tullahoma Campaign

The possession of a large portion of Tennessee was a spiritual as well as a material source of strength to the army that bore the state's name. Yet in the space of less than two weeks, the Army of Tennessee abandoned Middle Tennessee almost without firing a shot—and what shots were fired, were fired mostly by Stewart's Division. The loss of Middle Tennessee constituted the last of three disasters suffered by the Confederacy on or about July 4, 1863, and was, in many ways, the most perplexing and demoralizing. Unlike Vicksburg and Gettysburg, the Tullahoma campaign lacks notoriety primarily because it accomplished a great result for the Union without massive effusion of blood.

Looking southward from Murfreesboro toward Tullahoma and Bragg's line of communications, Rosecrans observed six principal routes along which to advance. He regarded the easterly route via McMinnville as impractical. That left the Manchester Pike through Hoover's Gap, the Wartrace Road through Liberty Gap, which passed into the road along the railroad by Bell Buckle Gap, the Shelbyville Turnpike through Guy's Gap, the dirt Old Stage Road through Middleton, and the road by Versailles that intersected the Shelbyville-Triune turnpike. The last two routes avoided the "range of high, rough, rocky hills" that covered Bragg's position.[1]

1. *OR* 23(1):404.

Bragg recognized his exposure to a Federal advance down one or more of these routes. Yet covering each avenue required that he stretch his army over a front of seventy miles. Polk was concentrated in the left center at Shelbyville and Hardee in the right center at Wartrace and Tullahoma. Van Dorn's cavalry corps extended the line to the left to the Columbia and Spring Hill area, and Joseph Wheeler's cavalry covered the right to Mc-Minnville. Bragg had to man this line with about a third fewer troops than Rosecrans and with mobility limited by the exhaustion of supplies and lack of transportation.[2]

Hoover's Gap is a narrow passage in the range of hills behind which Bragg retreated after the Battle of Murfreesboro, with its northern end about fourteen miles to Murfreesboro's southeast. The gap is approximately three miles long, flanked on either side by high hills. In June, 1863, the Confederates maintained fortifications in the narrow part of the gap, at a point about sixteen miles below Murfreesboro. On the lower end of the gap lies the town of Beech Grove, behind the Garrison Fork of the Duck River, which runs south about four or five miles to Fairfield.[3]

As of June 24, the 1st Kentucky Cavalry of Wheeler's Division picketed by Hoover's Gap. Prior to Stewart's elevation to command the new division, Bragg decided not to station any infantry in the gap. While Bate maintained pickets at the bridge over the Garrison Fork leading to Hoover's Gap, the main body of his brigade was a mile outside Fairfield, four miles from the gap. The next-closest infantry contingent was Bushrod Johnson's brigade, at Fairfield proper, where Stewart maintained his headquarters.[4]

2. Connelly, *Autumn of Glory*, 112–16.

3. *OR* 23(1):458; see also William B. Feis, "The Deception of Braxton Bragg," *Blue & Gray Magazine* 10 (October 1992): 10–21, 46–53, for an interesting discussion of Hoover's Gap and the Tullahoma campaign.

4. Connelly, *Autumn of Glory*, 126; *OR* 23(1):602, 611; R. A. Hatcher to W. B. Bate, June 23, 1863, Special Orders, Stewart's Division, Departmental Records, Army and Department of Tennessee, RG 109, NA. Bragg's decision not to man the gap is suggested in *OR* 23(2):862. See also Connelly, *Autumn of Glory*, 126. Oddly, Connelly suggests that the decision was Bate's or Stewart's as to how heavily to picket the gap. Connelly, *Autumn of Glory*, 118. "Stewart received no order to place troops at the Gap, or to hold the position." "Huntsville," in *Chattanooga Daily Rebel*, July 26, 1863. The author of a popular guidebook of the campaign states that the Confederates believed Hoover's Gap unsuitable for passage by a

June 24, 1863, was a dark and rainy day. Elements of Thomas' Fourteenth Corps were up and about early in their positions around Murfreesboro, departing down the Manchester Pike about 4 A.M. Thomas' lead formation was the 4th Division of Major General Joseph J. Reynolds. Reynolds commanded three brigades, his lead unit being Colonel John T. Wilder's brigade of "mounted infantry" outfitted with new Spencer repeating rifles.[5]

At Big Spring Branch, seven miles out of Murfreesboro, Wilder's troops were close to contact with Confederate pickets. Wilder held up to allow the remainder of Reynolds' Division to close up. Then, Wilder's men rolled forward, scattering the 1st Kentucky before it could deploy behind the works in the narrow part of Hoover's Gap. Wilder, sensing a *coup de main*, forged forward and took possession of the entire gap, capturing the colors of the overwhelmed 1st Kentucky. While one of Wilder's companies pushed on two miles past the gap toward Manchester, the remainder of the command occupied the hills on the southern end of the gap, awaiting the inevitable Confederate response.[6]

The routed cavalrymen of the 1st Kentucky struggled through the rain to the Rebel infantry camps around Fairfield. About 1 P.M., those who had survived showed up at Bushrod Johnson's headquarters and reported that the Federals had captured Hoover's Gap. Stewart must have received information of Wilder's advance at about the same time, because he soon ordered Johnson to have his brigade ready to move at a moment's notice. The surviving cavalrymen spread the story that the Federals advancing toward Manchester consisted of at least three regiments.[7]

---

large army and therefore picketed the gap with only cavalry. Jim Miles, *Paths to Victory* (Nashville: Rutledge Hill Press, 1991), 37.

5. *OR* 23(1):454, 602; Glenn Tucker, *Chickamauga: Bloody Battle in the West* (1961; reprint, Dayton: Morningside, 1981), 115–17; Roy Morris, Jr., "The Steadiest Body of Men I Ever Saw: John T. Wilder and the Lightning Brigade," *Blue & Gray Magazine* 10 (October 1992): 32–36.

6. *OR* 23(1):457–58; Glenn W. Sunderland, *Lightning at Hoover's Gap: The Story of Wilder's Brigade* (New York: Yoseloff, 1969), 36–39. Historian Steven Woodworth is critical of the Confederate cavalry's defense of the gap and the quality of the information it supplied about the situation at Hoover's Gap. Steven E. Woodworth, "Braxton Bragg and the Tullahoma Campaign," in *The Art of Command*, ed. Woodward (forthcoming).

7. *OR* 23(1):602, 611.

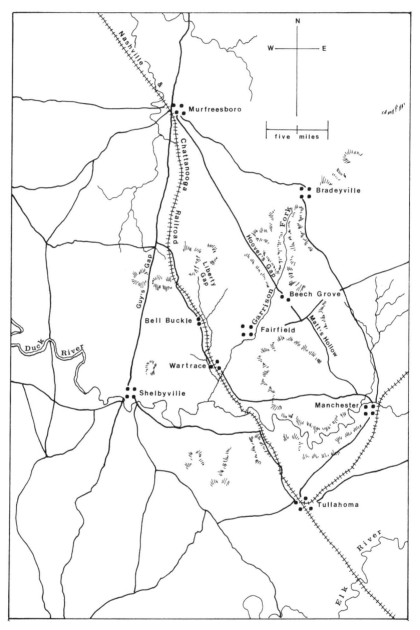

The Tullahoma-Shelbyville line
Map by Blake Magner

At the time of the attack, Stewart was enjoying a meal with his wife, Dr. Watson M. Gentry, a divisional surgeon, and Gentry's wife, Martha. Mrs. Gentry recalled the merry conversation during the meal being interrupted when a boy in a slouch hat brought Stewart some dispatches. Stewart's expression visibly changed, but he continued the conversation. Before the meal could continue, another courier came in with a furrow from a bullet in his scalp. Stewart and the doctor immediately went to camp, which was in something of an uproar.[8]

Stewart moved those elements of his division nearest Hoover's Gap into action. Although Bate was at least a mile closer to Hoover's Gap than Stewart at Fairfield, his first news of Wilder's attack came at about 2 P.M., when a courier from Stewart arrived with orders to dispatch a regiment and battery up to Beech Grove at the southern end of the gap. More news of the size of the Federal force soon reached Stewart, who dispatched a second courier to Bate ordering him to increase the size of his force to two regiments, and to have the rest of his brigade on alert. Bate accompanied the detachment directed to the gap, and soon encountered more cavalry-men, who falsely informed him that the Federals were advancing down some roads that would place them in Bate's rear. Bate directed the remainder of his brigade to advance along these approaches, and advised Stewart of these dispositions. Bate's men marched through the rain past the demoralized cavalrymen, chiding the horsemen for sending them on a wild-goose chase.[9]

At 3:45 P.M. Stewart sent a dispatch to Hardee, evidently transmitting whatever information he had on the situation at the gap, including the inflated report about the force of Federal cavalry moving toward Manchester. Hardee replied at 4:30 P.M., directing Stewart to send the scattered cavalry to intercept the Federal column driving to Manchester, leaving enough cavalry to cover his front. Stewart was advised that the Federals were demonstrating at Liberty Gap and other points. By the time of Hardee's response, Stewart had already given Bushrod Johnson instructions to send out some of the cavalry to scout the Federal position. Accompanied by Stewart, Johnson's Brigade had already been on the road to the gap for a half hour at that time.[10]

---

8. Gentry, "Surgeons of the Confederacy," 337.
9. *OR* 23(1):611; Sunderland, *Lightning at Hoover's Gap*, 39.
10. *OR* 23(2):884; 23(1):602.

Wilder's troops at Hoover's Gap could hear the long roll of the drums in Bate's camps. The advance company of Federals that had caused so much consternation was barely back in position before Bate arrived, probably between 3:30 and 4 P.M. Bate drove the Federal skirmishers into the gap and placed his two advance regiments, the 20th Tennessee and the 37th Georgia, in position to block any further Federal advance out of the gap toward Manchester.[11]

Bate next deployed troops to drive Wilder out of the gap. He moved a portion of his brigade across Garrison's Fork to the left of his position, sending the 20th Tennessee and the 4th Georgia Sharpshooter Battalion to occupy a high wooded hill held by the Federals. Bate pressed the bluecoats back on their second line, the 20th and the 4th charging up the hill cheering loudly. They soon got into a fight that Bate described as "sanguinary" and "desperate."[12]

A soldier of the 20th Tennessee described this contest in his diary: "The undergrowth was very thick and we were unable to see the Yankees until we came within thirty yards of them. Their first line was driven back in great disorder, but the woods were full of them. Here I think I killed my first yankee, and maybe my last one. We ran against a line of Yanks that was too strong for us and falling back, in no confusion, but with considerable swiftness, was then the order."[13]

The 20th had been presented a beautiful battle flag made from the wedding dress of Mrs. John C. Breckinridge for being the most gallant regiment in his division. In this fight, the staff of this new flag was shot in two and the eagle on the staff shot off its top, which is not surprising, considering the substantial firepower of the Spencer repeaters.[14]

Bate then threw the 37th Georgia into the fight on the left flank, which made some headway due to a Federal shortage of ammunition. Wilder claimed this assault involved "five regiments," yet he dispatched only a single fresh regiment, the 98th Illinois, as reinforcements. The 98th drove the

11. *OR* 23(1):455, 610.

12. Ibid., 458, 612.

13. William T. Alderson, ed., "The Civil War Diary of Captain James Litton Cooper, September 30, 1861, to January, 1865," *Tennessee Historical Quarterly* 15 (June 1956): 156.

14. W. J. McMurray, *History of the Twentieth Tennessee Regiment Volunteer Infantry C.S.A.* (Nashville: Publications Committee, 1904), 261.

37th Georgia's attack back in a "bloody engagement." Bate withdrew his troops into a defensive position, no doubt deceived by the firepower of Wilder's brigade into feeling he was greatly outnumbered, and covered by his artillery, awaited Stewart and reinforcements.[15]

Not for the first time, and certainly not for the last, the influence of technological innovation was felt in the course of the war. Wilder's force was small enough to be mounted and mobile, yet large enough, when equipped with the repeating rifles, to seize and hold Hoover's Gap against Bate and doubtless Stewart's entire division, had such been the attacking force. Given the firepower of the repeaters, the advantage of position, and the inherent advantage of defense, once Wilder seized the gap, probably no reasonably sized force of Confederates could have dislodged him from the gap.

That half of Bate's Brigade that was actively engaged, approximately 650 men, suffered 146 casualties, while Wilder lost 63 killed and wounded. Bate himself was painfully wounded, but remained on the field without attention until nightfall. At nightfall, the remainder of Reynolds' Division along with Rousseau's Division arrived on the field to reinforce Wilder. About the same time, Stewart came up to Bate's relief with Bush-rod Johnson's brigade. At 10 P.M., Clayton's Brigade arrived and occupied the Confederate right. As Stewart made these dispositions through the night, the rain continued to fall. A member of the 20th Tennessee later recalled standing picket in a freshly plowed field the whole night in mud up to his knees.[16]

Back at Stewart's headquarters, Harriet Stewart and Martha Gentry stayed up all night rolling bandages for the wounded. Mrs. Gentry was horrified to see a man who had been shot through the foot placed in her bed. Another man was brought in shot above the hips. Mrs. Gentry later learned that because this man was so thin, the bullet did not cut any vital organs. Mrs. Gentry, and most likely Harriet Stewart, too, left the next day.[17]

Stewart appears to have kept Hardee apprised of developments on his front. Hardee had to determine whether the Federal main effort was falling

15. Sunderland, *Lightning at Hoover's Gap*, 40–42; *OR* 23(1):459, 612.
16. *OR* 23(1):459, 602–603, 612; McMurray, *Twentieth Tennessee*, 261.
17. Gentry, "Surgeons of the Confederacy," 337.

on Cleburne's front at Liberty Gap or Stewart's at Hoover's Gap. At 10:30 P.M. on the night of June 24, Stewart received a message from one of Hardee's staff: "General Hardee desires that you will continue to furnish him information as speedily as possible, and directs that, if hard pressed tomorrow, you will fall back gradually toward Wartrace." Until he could determine the focus of Rosecrans' efforts, Hardee wanted to adhere to the fundamental Confederate plan (as he understood it) of fighting the Federals in the entrenchments at Tullahoma.[18]

At Hoover's Gap, June 25 was a day of skirmishes and long-range artillery duels. Stewart directed artillery fire at Federal skirmishers and a Federal battery. At Liberty Gap, Cleburne advanced Liddell's Brigade against the Federals holding the gap, which turned out to be Richard W. Johnson's division of the Federal Twentieth Corps, supported by a brigade of Jefferson C. Davis' division. After Liddell's attack failed, Cleburne correctly discerned the strength of his opponent, and made dispositions to defend his position south of the gap.[19]

Curiously, Bragg seems to have been unaware of what was happening at Hoover's Gap. This lack of information appears to have been Bragg's own fault. He had ordered Wheeler south toward Shelbyville just before the Federal advance. Hardee, too, bears some responsibility, as correspondence from his own headquarters reflects that Stewart was keeping Hardee informed. Not knowing the true state of affairs at Hoover's Gap, Bragg believed on June 25 that the main Federal force was at Liberty Gap. The next day, he ordered Polk, against Polk's wishes, to make a flanking attack through Guy's Gap against the Federals supposedly concentrated at Liberty Gap.[20]

With Brown's Brigade at Tullahoma, Stewart had only Johnson, Clayton, and Bate's battered brigade at Hoover's Gap on the morning of June 26. George H. Thomas, on the other hand, had three divisions, all of which commenced an advance on Stewart's positions around the gap late in the morning of yet another rainy day. For four hours, Stewart and his

18. *OR* 23(2):884; see also 23(2):862.
19. *OR* 23(1):406, 456, 586–87, 603–604.
20. Connelly, *Autumn of Glory*, 127–28. Steven E. Woodworth deems Bragg's plans for Polk to have been quite feasible. Woodworth, "Braxton Bragg."

outnumbered brigades resisted the heavy, overlapping lines of the Fourteenth Corps. The bulk of the fighting fell on Bushrod Johnson's Brigade,
Stewart taking care to judiciously post his artillery to break up the Federal
assaults. It was soon apparent that Stewart's Division was too weak to hold
its position on the south end of Hoover's Gap. Mindful of Hardee's injunc-
tion thirty-six hours earlier to fall back toward Wartrace if "hard pressed,"
Stewart began to move the division back toward Fairfield. As the division
retired, Stewart stayed with the rear guard.[21]

As he left the field, whatever thoughts Stewart may have had relative to
leaving the road to Manchester open must have been tempered by the
thought that he had no real choice in the matter. Between Hardee's orders
to retreat if "hard pressed" and the odds facing him, it was Stewart's duty
to withdraw once his three brigades could no longer effectively resist. The
only way the division could have defeated Thomas' Corps was by occupying the fortifications constructed for that purpose in the gap, an option no
longer available after Wilder's *coup* on June 24. Even if Stewart had had the
luxury of fortifications, it would probably have taken Hardee's whole corps
to resist Thomas and protect the road to Manchester, as there were ways
available for a patient general like Thomas to flank Hoover's Gap.[22]

Stewart must have been aware of Hardee's impression that Bragg intended to fight at Tullahoma. On the other hand, it cannot have escaped
Stewart's notice that a Federal force of any size at Manchester was ideally
placed on the flank of any defensive position centered on Tullahoma. In
fact, once Stewart began his retreat toward Fairfield, the bulk of Thomas'
Corps marched on toward Manchester, leaving enough troops to screen
the Manchester Pike from a renewed Confederate advance. At eight-thirty
that evening, Hardee dispatched a message castigating Stewart for the
number of stragglers from his division, and the fact that Clayton had not
struck some tents in his camp. Once again, Stewart was ordered to withdraw to Wartrace in preparation for a retreat to Tullahoma "if the enemy

21. *OR* 23(1):406, 604–605, 23(2):884, 886; Ridley, *Battles and Sketches*, 187.

22. "Huntsville," in *Chattanooga Daily Rebel*, July 26, 1863. If Bragg or Hardee had chosen to detach a small force, Thomas' advance to Manchester might possibly have been delayed
in the narrow defiles of Matt's Hollow, east of Hoover's Gap on the Manchester Pike.
Woodworth, "Braxton Bragg."

shows any disposition to press." Hardee further advised Stewart that the Confederate move against Liberty Gap planned for the next day was "given up."[23]

The reason for the cancellation was that Bragg finally realized Stewart's plight during the late afternoon of June 26. Bragg was given the impression that Stewart was being driven through Fairfield on to Wartrace, when actually Stewart was retiring under no real pressure from a Federal force much more interested in going to Manchester. Whether the threat to Wartrace was false or not, a retreat to Tullahoma was called for, in accordance with the plan Hardee understood existed all along. June 27 and 28 were spent concentrating the army at Tullahoma, Stewart receiving detailed instructions from Hardee on moving the division from Fairfield to Tullahoma. At Tullahoma, the division was placed on the army's right in the area of the Manchester Road.[24]

On June 30, Federal pressure on Stewart's flank resulted in orders for the division to press forward its fortification work. Later that day, Bushrod Johnson's brigade was moved southeast of Tullahoma to guard against Federal moves down the Hillsboro Road. Meanwhile, Bragg was even more confounded by the threat on his right. The heavy rains were both a blessing and a curse, as they swelled the rivers Rosecrans had to cross to get in Bragg's rear, but reduced to quagmires the roads by which the Army of Tennessee would march to meet the Federals. Late on June 30, Bragg determined to retreat across the Elk River, recognizing even as he made the decision that he would probably have to retreat even farther, as Rosecrans held a bridgehead across the Elk at Pelham, beyond Hardee's right.[25]

In addition to the rapid Federal movements and the horrible weather, another factor once again hampered the Confederate army: its high command. Bragg had been sick since June 29. On July 1, Hardee communicated to Polk his concern about Bragg's feeble health, and suggested that the corps commanders meet in secret to discuss the situation. Worried about the defensibility of the Elk River line, Bragg queried Polk the evening of July 1 whether the army should try to hold the line of the Elk or retreat to Cowan, at the foot of Sewanee Mountain, the last major defensible

23. *OR* 23(1):406, 23(2):886.
24. Connelly, *Autumn of Glory*, 128–29; *OR* 23(1):608, 23(2):888.
25. *OR* 23(1):608, 23(2):892–93; Connelly, *Autumn of Glory*, 130–32.

point short of the Tennessee River. Both Polk and Hardee preferred moving to Cowan—probably, as historian Thomas Connelly notes, because they did not want to fight under Bragg in the physical and mental state he was in at the time.

Early in the morning of July 2, orders went out for Polk to retreat to Cowan, while Stewart and the rest of Hardee's Corps moved to the area of Brakefield Point, at the foot of the mountain just west of Polk's beloved University Place. By the end of the day, Bragg determined to withdraw from Middle Tennessee, ordering the army across the mountain toward Chattanooga. Early on the morning of July 3, Stewart received orders to move his division up to University Place. Johnson's reinforced brigade moving in the rear of the corps, the division marched through University Place down the mountain to Battle Creek, where it bivouacked the night of July 4. On July 6, Stewart's Division crossed the Tennessee at Kelly's Ferry, camping at Wauhatchie in the shadow of Lookout Mountain. In Bragg's own words, the Army of Tennessee had suffered "a great disaster."[26]

In his history of the army in the *Military Annals*, Stewart was critical of Bragg, without mentioning his own understandable failure at Hoover's Gap:

> On the 24th the Federal army was in motion. On the 26th, after various skirmishes along the entire line, Bragg's right was passed, and he fell back to Tullahoma, where battle was offered but declined. As his communications were continually endangered by the enemy's movements, and his force was not sufficient to guard them without too much weakening his main body, he withdrew from Tullahoma to the most defensible line of Elk River, and finally, with but trifling loss of men and materials, crossed the Cumberland Mountains to the line of the Tennessee. . . . Thus a second time the Tennesseans, who composed so large a part of the Army of Tennessee, abandoned their homes to the tender mercies of the invader, and followed the fortunes of the Confederate flag. It would seem that with the aid of "the spade," the rivers, and the mountains, Middle Tennessee might have

26. Judith Lee Hallock, *Braxton Bragg and Confederate Defeat* (Tuscaloosa: University of Alabama Press, 1991), 2:20–24; Connelly, *Autumn of Glory*, 132–34; *OR* 23(1):609–10, 23(2):897, 901.

been held against a largely superior force. So far Bragg's operations had proved an entire failure although his army had performed all his demands.[27]

Stewart is correct, especially regarding the ultimate results of Bragg's tenure in command. At Hoover's Gap, however, the Confederates had both "the spade" and the mountains, or their equivalent, yet failed to defeat the Federal flanking movement. Tullahoma was well fortified, but the Army of the Cumberland's superior numbers enabled the Federals to flank even the most elaborate fortifications.

Stewart was closer to the mark when he wrote Bragg months later, in March, 1864, as to the true reason Middle Tennessee was lost: "Where by weakening you last summer we were forced out of Middle Tenn., I thought the Gov'mt ought to have sent you every man from Mississippi, every man that could be spared from Charleston, Mobile, and other points, and made you strong enough to meet Rosecrans beyond or at the Tennessee."[28] That opportunity was lost, and Stewart and the bulk of the Tennesseans in the army faced the third autumn of the war with their homes once again behind Federal lines.

27. Lindsley, ed., *Military Annals*, 80.
28. APS to B. Bragg, March 19, 1864, Palmer Collection of Bragg Papers, Western Reserve Historical Society.

A. P. Stewart about 1860
Courtesy Stockton Archives,
Cumberland University, Lebanon, Tennessee

Wartime photograph of Stewart
Courtesy Valentine Museum, Richmond, Virginia

Albert Sidney Johnston
Courtesy Library of Congress

Braxton Bragg
Courtesy Library of Congress

Leonidas Polk
Courtesy Library of Congress

William J. Hardee
Courtesy Library of Congress

Benjamin F. Cheatham
Courtesy Library of Congress

William B. Bate
Courtesy Library of Congress

Otho F. Strahl
Courtesy Library of Congress

Henry D. Clayton
Courtesy Library of Congress

Battlefield of Missionary Ridge
Courtesy Library of Congress

John B. Hood
Massachusetts Commandery,
Military Order of the Loyal Legion, USAMHI

Joseph E. Johnston
Courtesy Library of Congress

William W. Loring
Courtesy Library of Congress

Samuel G. French
Courtesy Library of Congress

Edward C. Walthall
Courtesy Library of Congress

Battlefield of New Hope Church
Courtesy Library of Congress

Battlefield of Peachtree Creek
Courtesy Library of Congress

Stewart about 1905
Chattanooga–Hamilton County Bicentennial Library,
United Daughters of the Confederacy, General A. P. Stewart Papers

— 8 —

Strong Arms and Stout Hearts

The Chickamauga Campaign

In July, 1862, the Army of Tennessee had moved into Chattanooga on its way into Kentucky. During the next year, the strategic little town on the Tennessee had, with its network of railroads, served as the army's base for the foray into Kentucky and the subsequent occupation of Middle Tennessee. July, 1863, found the army once again at Chattanooga, with the Federals again at the gates. The main difference between the two Julys was in the commanders: the Federals now had a triumphant Rosecrans instead of a hesitant Buell, and the Confederates had a broken-down Bragg, subverted by his closest lieutenants, rather than the imaginative, determined, and hopeful officer Bragg had been the year before.

The next phase of the struggle would center on Chattanooga, a location that seemed ideally situated to defend against Rosecrans. Immediately to the north of the town, the Tennessee River runs northeast for approximately seventy miles to Kingston, Tennessee. The Tennessee served as a moat behind the rampart of Walden's Ridge, a long mountain ridge extending northeast, paralleling the Tennessee as an arm of the larger Cumberland Plateau.

To the west and south of Chattanooga, the Tennessee flows around steep Raccoon Mountain, and then turns south into Alabama, past the two small towns of Stevenson, where in 1863 the Memphis and Charleston Railroad joined the Nashville and Chattanooga Railroad, and Bridgeport. East of these towns, Sand Mountain extends to the southwest of Chattanooga paralleling the Tennessee River on the west. East of Sand Mountain is the long ridge of Lookout Mountain, which extends from its spectacular point at Chattanooga ninety miles southwest to Gadsden, Alabama.

Notwithstanding this formidable combination of the mountains and the Tennessee River, Bragg viewed the country between himself and Rosecrans not as a help, but as a hindrance. At one point, Bragg "petulantly" observed to D. H. Hill: "It is said to be easy to defend a mountainous country, but mountains hide your foe from you, while they are full of gaps through which he can pounce upon you at any time."[1]

D. H. Hill was the first of a number of new officers transferred into the already volatile command mix of the Army of Tennessee. Unwisely, Jefferson Davis had once again robbed the army of an asset for the defense of Mississippi, in this case its most competent corps commander, Hardee. Hill was his replacement, and reported to Bragg at Chattanooga on July 19. In Hill's postwar account of his appointment to command Hardee's Corps, he stated that Davis made him a lieutenant general so that he could properly command the corps, "as General Stewart ranks me." While Stewart eventually did rank his classmate, this portion of Hill's account is curious, as Hill at the time ranked both Cleburne and Stewart, the corps' two divisional commanders. Either Hill's memory was faulty or he was making a case with a faulty premise to Davis that he needed to be a lieutenant general.[2]

During the interlude between the close of the Tullahoma campaign and the opening moves of the new struggle, Stewart began measures to reestablish discipline in his division. At Tyner's Station near Chattanooga on July 15, he issued orders regarding establishing and policing camps, and resuming drill. Two days later, he gave orders not to disturb growing tim-

---

1. Daniel H. Hill, "Chickamauga—The Great Battle of the West," *B&L*, 3:641, note; Connelly, *Autumn of Glory*, 163–65.

2. Hill, "Chickamauga," *B&L* 3:638–39. Hill's commission as a major general dated from March, 1862, Cleburne's from December, 1862, and Stewart's from June, 1863. Warner, *Generals in Gray*, 54, 219, 294. For Hill's background, see Warner, *Generals in Gray*, 136–37. See also Hal Bridges, *Lee's Maverick General: Daniel Harvey Hill* (New York: McGraw-Hill, 1961). While Hill had a fine combat record with the Army of Northern Virginia, he had a history of command quarrels, and seems to have been one of the few officers to have had a squabble with Robert E. Lee, the consummate handler of contentious officers. Hill was therefore about the last person Braxton Bragg needed.

ber unless fallen timber was not sufficient. On July 23, Stewart's brigade commanders were asked to explain the large loss of equipment within their commands during the retreat from Middle Tennessee. Stewart also joined Bragg, Polk, Hill, Withers, and several brigadiers, including Bate, Clayton, and Brown, in writing a letter dated July 25 to Confederate adjutant general Samuel Cooper to protest various detachments from the army for non-combat purposes and the exemptions to the conscription laws that were sapping the Confederacy's armed strength.[3]

The tired and footsore soldiers of the Army of Tennessee spent the weeks after their arrival at Chattanooga fortifying their position and grumbling about food. More fighting was in store and the army was in desperate condition. The dire consequences of defeat were painfully apparent. From Clayton's Brigade, Private A. M. Glazener of the 18th Alabama wrote a friend on August 17: "This army is in a bad condition. The men all think we are whipt all out of heart they don't put much confidence in this general, Bragg."[4]

In light of that summer's Confederate disasters, President Davis had designated August 21 as a day of fasting and prayer. Officers and civilians attended church in Chattanooga that morning, petitioning the Almighty "who rules in the armies of heaven and among the inhabitants of the earth." Suddenly, shells began crashing into the town from Stringer's Ridge, a height directly across the Tennessee River. They were fired by Captain Eli Lilly's 18th Indiana battery, attached to the brigade of the ubiquitous Colonel Wilder. D. H. Hill dryly observed: "Our pickets and scouts had given no notice of the approach of the enemy."[5]

Bragg received reports that the Federals were moving all along the lengthy front from northeast Alabama to Kingston, Tennessee. While

3. Circular, July 23, 1863, Special Orders, Stewart's Division, 1863, Army and Department of Tennessee; Issuances Received, 32nd Tennessee, July 13, 17, 1863, RG 109, NA; *OR* Series IV, 2:670–71. Stewart appears to have been away from the army for a period during this interlude. See *OR* 23(2):954, 958; 30(4):532, 535.

4. A. M. Glazener to T. M. Shuford, August 17, 1863 (typed copy), A. M. Glazener Letters, CCNMP; see Glazener to wife, August 20, 26, 1863, Glazener Letters; Jno. A. Kirby to "Pa," August 26, 1863, Confederate States Archives, Officers and Soldiers' Miscellaneous Letters, DU.

5. Circular, August 18, 1863, Issuances Received, 32nd Tennessee, RG 109, NA; Hill, "Chickamauga," *B&L* 3:638–39; Connelly, *Autumn of Glory*, 165–66.

there were substantial reports of Federal activity downriver to the west and southwest of Chattanooga, the bulk of Bragg's infantry was concentrated about ten miles upriver, at Harrison's Landing. Stewart seems to have believed that the Federals would cross the Tennessee just above Chattanooga at the mouth of Chickamauga Creek. A portion of Brown's Brigade was dispatched to that point, with Bate's Brigade in support. The remainder of the division covered other likely crossing points northeast of Chattanooga, with Clayton as far north as Birchwood, near the point where the Hiwassee River flows into the Tennessee from the east. Clayton reported Federals across the Tennessee at Washington's Ferry on August 22, and felt the great danger was a crossing above the Hiwassee, where the Confederates had no troops.[6]

It seemed logical that Rosecrans would cross north of Chattanooga. At the same time, Union major general Ambrose E. Burnside was advancing out of Kentucky toward Knoxville. The Confederate Department of East Tennessee was commanded by Major General Simon Bolivar Buckner, who had been placed under Bragg's direction in July. Among Buckner's scattered troops was only one organized division, Brigadier General William Preston's. In light of Burnside's and Rosecrans' apparently coordinated advances, Buckner moved Preston and a brigade of cavalry toward Kingston, where Bragg had posted Forrest as the northernmost of the Army of Tennessee's pickets on the Tennessee River. By August 24, Buckner had determined upon a concentration at Loudon, on the south side of the Tennessee, where the railroad from Chattanooga traversed the river to Knoxville.[7]

The crisis that began on August 21 caused Bragg to call for reinforcements from General Joseph E. Johnston in Mississippi, imploring: "If able to assist us do so promptly." Richmond authorized Johnston to give help "as far as you are able to do so." On August 22, Johnston advised Bragg that he would send two divisions numbering 9,000 infantry, under Major Generals William H. T. Walker and John C. Breckinridge. Upon reaching Chattanooga, Breckinridge's Division was assigned to D. H. Hill's Corps.

---

6. Connelly, *Autumn of Glory*, 168; *OR* 30(4):532–35.

7. *OR* 30(4):526–29, 536–37, 547–48. For Buckner's background, see Warner, *Generals in Gray*, 38. See also Arndt M. Stickles, *Simon Bolivar Buckner: Borderland Knight* (1940; reprint, Wilmington, N.C.: Broadfoot Publishing, 1987).

Doubtless because of its position on the northern flank of the army, Stewart's Division was transferred to Buckner's Corps as of September 1, thus giving both Hill and Buckner two divisions. Even before his division was officially assigned to Buckner, Stewart received orders on August 30 to join him at Charleston, where the East Tennessee and Georgia Railroad crossed the Hiwassee.[8]

Rosecrans had maneuvered Bragg out of Tullahoma by hard marching and bold flank moves, and in the Federal commander's mind there was no reason why he could not do so again. While one of his corps maneuvered on the north side of the Tennessee River opposite Chattanooga, Rosecrans sent the bulk of his army south into northeast Alabama and northwest Georgia, under the false belief that the Army of Tennessee was in headlong retreat into Georgia.[9]

Unlike his situation in Middle Tennessee in June, in September Bragg was not in befuddled retreat. In contrast to the outnumbered army of four divisions that had defended the Tullahoma-Shelbyville line, the army that marched south from Chattanooga under Bragg's orders of September 6 to "meet" and "strike" the scattered Federal corps on its flank constituted almost four corps, with more troops coming.[10] The authorities at Richmond, after considerable debate, had determined to reinforce Bragg with two divisions from the Army of Northern Virginia, under Robert E. Lee's "War Horse" and Stewart's old roommate, James Longstreet. Unfortunately for the Confederates, Longstreet's progress to north Georgia was hindered by the loss of Knoxville, which severed the direct rail route from Virginia to Chattanooga. Only time would tell whether Longstreet's veterans would reach Bragg's army in time to participate in the contemplated destruction of the Army of the Cumberland.

Stewart's Division joined the rest of Buckner's Corps in its strategic withdrawal into north Georgia. As Stewart later noted, Rosecrans' pursuit of what he perceived to be a Confederate retreat caused him to spread his corps out beyond the point where they could support one another. The situation presented Bragg with what Stewart termed "the finest opportunity

8. *OR* 30(4):538, 540–41, 547, 570, 578; Hill, "Chickamauga," *B&L* 3:641, note.

9. Woodworth, *Jefferson Davis and His Generals*, 230; Hattaway and Jones, *How the North Won*, 446–48.

10. *OR* 30(4):610–11.

of the war . . . to strike a decisive blow."[11] As Stewart wrote Bragg in March, 1864: "It always seemed to me that had our business been accomplished there—the business I understood we were sent there to accomplish—Rosecrans' army would have been destroyed at but little cost to us."[12]

Notwithstanding this friendly correspondence, Stewart wrote in 1886 that the real cause of the Confederate failure was Bragg, or perhaps more accurately, the lack of confidence in Bragg and his designs within the army's high command:

> Bragg was in a position to crush the enemy's center and interpose his army between the wings, which could not have escaped. . . . Whatever apologies may have been offered for this failure, the real cause of it was the lack of confidence on the part of the superior officers of the Army of Tennessee in its commander. If Robert E. Lee or either of the Johnstons had been in command, the blow would have been struck, and in all human probability Rosecrans' army would have been destroyed. One man, sometimes, is of as much value as an army. His followers said truly to King David: "But now thou art worth ten thousand of us."[13]

On September 8, Major General James S. Negley's division of Thomas' Fourteenth Corps pushed aside a Confederate cavalry screen and moved into McLemore's Cove between Lookout and Pigeon Mountains in northwest Georgia. Bombarded by messages, Bragg finally woke up to the fact that Negley's unsupported division was the first from Thomas' Corps to cross Lookout Mountain into the cove. Bragg swiftly formulated a plan to destroy Negley. Unfortunately, the senior Confederate officer of the troops within striking distance of Negley was Major General Thomas C. Hindman, who Stewart later observed "was not . . . the right man there in command."[14]

11. Lindsley, ed., *Military Annals*, 81.

12. APS to B. Bragg, March 19, 1864, in Palmer Collection of Bragg Papers, Western Reserve.

13. Lindsley, ed., *Military Annals*, 81. D. H. Hill also fixed a large portion of the blame on Bragg and his methods of command. Hill, "Chickamauga," *B&L* 3:641–42.

14. "Gen. Stewart Passes Away," *Chattanooga News*, August 31, 1908; Peter Cozzens, *This Terrible Sound: The Battle of Chickamauga* (Urbana: University of Illinois Press, 1992),

Four gaps provided routes across Pigeon Mountain from the east into McLemore's Cove. Bragg planned to strike the Federals through two of these: Dug Gap, on the road from Bragg's headquarters at La Fayette, Georgia, to Thomas' debouchment point off Lookout Mountain at Stevens' Gap, and Catlett's Gap, about three or four miles to the north. Hindman was to move through Catlett's Gap toward Davis' Crossroads, while Cleburne was to be detached from Hill to move through Dug Gap. Hindman initially moved quickly toward Davis' Crossroads, but Hill found excuses not to send Cleburne. Not wanting to waste time, at 8:00 A.M. on September 10 Bragg ordered Buckner to move his corps to Hindman's support.[15]

While Buckner and his "wearied" infantry marched into the cove, Hindman spent September 10 worrying about his lines of retreat, overwhelmed by the various dispatches and reports he received as to the locations of friend and foe. At nine o'clock that evening, he called a council of his division and brigade commanders that included Stewart. Bragg had sent two messages to Hindman earlier in the evening, urging him to "finish his movement . . . as rapidly as possible" and "to move vigorously and crush" the Federals in the cove. Hindman laid before his officers these instructions and the information he had gathered. Fearing from one of Bragg's two messages that Union general Thomas Crittenden's corps was a threat on his northern flank, and that there would be no support from Hill, Hindman claimed that his subordinates unanimously agreed not to advance pending further information. He sent a message to Bragg indicating that if Hill could not cooperate, or if the Federal force at Stevens' Gap was too great, his command should turn and destroy Crittenden, who was reported by Bragg to be advancing rapidly from the north.[16]

We do not have Stewart's version of this meeting or its result, but Hindman's account is supported to a degree in the report of Patton Anderson, the senior brigadier of Hindman's Division. Significantly, Anderson does

---

65–66. For Hindman's background, see Warner, *Generals in Gray*, 127–38; see also Diane Neal and Thomas W. Kremm, *The Lion of the South: General Thomas C. Hindman* (Macon, Ga.: Mercer University Press, 1993).

15. Cozzens, *This Terrible Sound*, 66–67.

16. *OR* 30(2):293–94, 301–302, 315; James Patton Anderson Account, n.d., James Patton Anderson Papers, North Carolina State Archives. Anderson indicates that no formal vote was taken whether to defer the attack and that it was tacitly agreed an attack would be made.

not mention Bragg's communications urging Hindman to move rapidly to attack, but he does state that an attack was intended, although the hour not fixed at the meeting. The time of the attack would not be decided until further information, including D. H. Hill's intentions, arrived. Three possibilities exist. First, Stewart was unaware of Bragg's positive orders, which his March, 1864, letter to Bragg and Patton Anderson's official report suggest. Anderson's undated account seems to refute this first possibility. The second possibility is suggested by Anderson's undated account: the council was aware of Bragg's orders, that most of the officers present felt that the orders were not discretionary, that an attack would be made, and yet that Hindman felt he did have discretion in the matter of the attack. Finally, it is also possible that Stewart and the others at the council were aware of the same information as Hindman and concluded, as suggested in Stewart's history of the army, that Bragg's orders were no longer worth obeying. This latter possibility seems entirely outside Stewart's character, regardless of any loss of confidence in Bragg he may have experienced.[17]

When advised of Hindman's decision, Bragg wasted no time in ordering an immediate attack on the Federal force in the cove, although his written orders were just ambiguous enough for Hindman to deem himself in danger rather than a danger to his adversary. Bragg unequivocally stated his orders to one of Hindman's staff officers, who was sent back to Hindman early on September 11. Amazingly, Hindman still claimed he was given "discretion" not to make the attack. On the Federal side, Negley had advanced toward Dug Gap on September 10 and encountered men from S. A. M. Wood's Brigade of Cleburne's Division. George H. Thomas smelled a rat, and unlike Rosecrans, was well aware of the tenuous and exposed position of the Army of the Cumberland.[18]

Thus, September 11, 1863, dawned with Hindman having clear orders to attack Thomas as soon as possible, and Thomas having realized that his corps, or a substantial portion thereof, was in grave danger. Even though Hindman's own division, commanded by Patton Anderson, was closest to the enemy, Hindman as senior officer ordered Buckner's Corps to lead the

    17. *OR* 30(2):315; James Patton Anderson Account, North Carolina State Archives; Manigault, *A Carolinian Goes to War*, 93; APS to B. Bragg, March 19, 1864, Palmer Collection, Western Reserve; Lindsley, ed., *Military Annals*, 81.
    18. *OR* 30(2):294–95; Cozzens, *This Terrible Sound*, 68–72.

advance on Davis' Crossroads. Stewart's Division was in the van of Buck-ner's Corps. Buckner's instructions from Hindman were to "move with caution and not to hazard an engagement until some reliable information was obtained of the strength and position of the [enemy]." Accordingly, Buckner cautiously felt his way toward Davis' Crossroads. About two and a half miles from that point, Buckner deployed Stewart's Division, which struggled through dense overgrowth to get into line. Preston's Division deployed to support Stewart to his rear and left, and Buckner awaited Hindman's Division to deploy on his right. Buckner was ready to continue his advance early in the afternoon, when he received an order from Hind-man to delay pending "further information." One soldier attached to Buckner's headquarters recalled that Buckner and Hindman joined in ask-ing for clarification of their orders.[19]

Elsewhere, Cleburne had deployed two of his brigades at Dug Gap, where he, Bragg, and Hill awaited the sounds of Hindman's attack. At Davis' Crossroads the Federal troops began their withdrawal westward to Bailey's Crossroads near Stevens' Gap. As the day wore on, Bragg's impa-tience understandably grew at an exponential rate. Hindman eventually discovered that the enemy was in retreat, and therefore ordered his troops forward, the advance beginning just before 5:00 P.M. When Stewart and his division pursued the Federals across a deep stream known as Chicka-mauga Creek, they encountered only enough of Thomas' men to bring about some skirmishing before dark. One of Buckner's staff officers aptly remarked that "a great blunder had been made."[20]

Overcoming what must have been the bitterest frustration, Bragg or-dered Polk on September 12 to concentrate a force to destroy Crittenden. True to his usual practice of ignoring Bragg's orders when it suited him, Polk delayed his advance to the point where Crittenden finally sensed the danger to his corps, and safely withdrew his troops before Polk sent men forward on the morning of September 13. The day before, Rosecrans fi-nally realized his danger and began concentrating his army. For his part, Bragg abandoned his efforts to defeat the Federals in detail, and devised a

19. OR 30(2):307–308; 30(4):632; Reminiscences of Milton P. Jarnigan, 20th Tennes-see File, CCNMP.
20. Cozzens, This Terrible Sound, 72–75; Hallock, Bragg, 58–60; OR 30(2):308; Jarni-gan Reminiscences, CCNMP.

plan to interpose his army between Rosecrans and Chattanooga. While
this was a good plan, Bragg delayed the move for two days, perhaps anticipating the arrival of the last two brigades of the Mississippi reinforcements
and the first of Longstreet's troops, which were en route from Virginia to
Atlanta.[21]

On September 17, the Confederate army marched north from La Fayette toward Lee and Gordon's Mill. On the west side of Chickamauga
Creek, Rosecrans was pulling together the scattered portions of the Army
of the Cumberland. Bragg moved north along the east side of the Chickamauga, with the immediate goal of seizing control of a number of fords
and bridges.

As Stewart and his troops prepared to march on September 16, Captain
John T. Humphreys of the 1st Arkansas battery attached to Clayton's Brigade mentioned to members of Stewart's staff that he dreamed the night
before of a battle with the Federals and a brilliant victory. Of the same
mind, Private Glazener of the 18th Alabama wrote his wife: "I think we
will whip them when we fight." The division moved out in the lead of the
corps as the northernmost contingent of Confederate infantry and
marched on September 17 to the area of Pea Vine Creek, deploying north
of Pea Vine Church.[22]

Early on September 19, Stewart's Division (less Johnson's Brigade) resumed its march, heading toward Thedford's Ford on the Chickamauga
with Bate leading Clayton and Brown in the march. Ridley recalled the determined looks on the faces of the division's men as they marched toward
the sound of booming cannon, and their exhortations to one another such
as "Boys, we have retreated far enough; we will whip 'em this time or
die."[23]

By this time Stewart's command may have gained the name of "the Lit-

21. Cozzens, *This Terrible Sound*, 81–90; Hallock, *Bragg*, 62–65.
22. Tucker, *Chickamauga*, 104–105; *OR* 30(2):657–58; Ridley, *Battles and Sketches*,
207; A. M. Glazener to wife, September 17, 1863, Glazener Letters, CCNMP.
23. Ridley, *Battles and Sketches*, 208–209. By September 18, Bushrod Johnson and his
brigade had been detached from Stewart's Division and combined with two brigades from
Mississippi and the famed Texas Brigade of the Army of Northern Virginia to form a provisional division under Johnson. Less the Texans, who would rejoin their division as more of its
brigades arrived from Virginia, Johnson's provisional division would fight separate from
Stewart in the upcoming battle. *OR* 30(2):17.

tle Giant Division." There is no explanation in any wartime or postwar writings as to how the division gained this epithet or if it was commonly known as such. A veteran of the division, Dr. W. J. McMurray, wrote an article published in *Confederate Veteran* in 1894 on the need for a monument to Stewart at the place on the field where "the Little Giant Division" fought. Historian Glenn Tucker dedicates a substantial part of one chapter in his book on Chickamauga to the efforts of "the Little Giant Division," but does not explain the origin of the name. It is certainly possible that the nickname indicated an *esprit* this relatively new organization developed under Stewart's command.[24]

The Confederates spent September 18 trying to gain control of several fords and bridges crossing the Chickamauga. Arriving that afternoon within a mile of Thedford's Ford, southwest of Alexander's Bridge, Stewart was instructed by Buckner to support Brigadier General John Pegram's cavalry at the ford. Bate was placed above the ford and Clayton below. While Pegram and Stewart were conferring, a cannonball struck about five paces from them before careening onward and nearly killing a member of Brown's staff. When several solid shot struck in Clayton's ranks, Stewart's staff worried that it might cause a panic among the untried soldiers of that brigade. Although Clayton's soldiers remained calm, at least one officer felt it necessary to steady his nerves with whiskey, to the extent that he suffered a disabling fall from his horse. About 5:00 P.M., both Bate and Clayton advanced troops across the ford.[25]

Early on September 19, George H. Thomas sent forward his 3rd Division, under Brigadier General John M. Brannan, to attack what Thomas thought was an isolated Confederate brigade on the west side of the Chickamauga at Jay's Mill, just south of Reed's Bridge. Brannan instead encountered W. H. T. Walker's Reserve Corps and a good portion of Nathan Bedford Forrest's cavalry. A vicious battle developed that drew additional Federal and Confederate divisions into its maelstrom. Cheatham's Division came into line to Walker's left, and battled the division of Brigadier

24. W. J. McMurray, "The Gap of Death at Chickamauga," *CV* 2 (November 1894): 329.

25. Tucker, *Chickamauga*, 112–15, 148–63; Ridley, *Battles and Sketches*, 209–12; Edgar W. Jones, *History of the 18th Alabama Regiment*, ed. Zane Geier (Mountain Brook, Ala.: privately published, 1994), 7; *OR* 30(2):361.

General Richard W. Johnson, which was soon joined by the divisions of Major Generals John M. Palmer and Joseph J. Reynolds and Brigadier General Horatio P. Van Cleve. Cheatham's line began to give way, and his left brigade, Brigadier General Marcus J. Wright's, soon lost its attached battery, that of Captain W. W. Carnes.[26]

Stewart passed the morning of September 19 getting his entire division across Thedford's Ford. The division was placed in an orderly line between Preston on the left and Bushrod Johnson's provisional division on the right. The Eufaula Battery was advanced to the front in response to Buckner's orders to fire on the Federals to the west. Retaliatory Yankee artillery fire fell among Stewart's Division and wounded a few men.

Near noon, Major Pollock Lee of Bragg's staff ordered Stewart farther to the right, where firing could be heard. Stewart found these orders too vague, and went to Bragg, who happened to be nearby, for clarification. Bragg's orders to Stewart reflected the commanding general's confusion and lack of a cohesive tactical plan. Stewart wrote that Bragg "informed me that Walker was engaged on the right, was much cut up, and the enemy threatening to turn his flank; that General Polk was in command on that wing, and that I must be governed by circumstances." Stewart then marched his division off to the right, Clayton's Brigade followed by those of Brown and Bate. Incredibly, Old Straight would not receive orders from any superior officer for the balance of the day.[27]

Bromfield Ridley described the division's harrowing march to action:

> Wounded men and mangled horses were soon met. Field surgeons and litter forces were becoming busy; but the spirit of none flagged but increased with the raging torrents of shot and shell. One man, as he was borne off on a litter, passed us with bowels protruding yet with animated fervor waved his hat and cried: "Boys, when I left we were driving 'em!" Cheatham's left was being flanked, the sweep of the battle was becoming more terrific; limbs were falling and the sound was like the roar of the river and the roll of the thunder.[28]

Stewart's march ended near a cornfield, where, in the spirit of Bragg's instructions, he sent out messengers to locate Polk. Across the field, heavy

26. Tucker, *Chickamauga*, 126–47.
27. *OR* 30(2):361, 363.
28. Ridley, *Battles and Sketches*, 219.

firing could be heard. As the roar of battle increased, it became clear that the division would be needed in action before Polk was found. Therefore, in accordance with Bragg's instruction that he be governed by circumstances, Stewart moved the division across the cornfield into action. A member of Polk's staff in search of the bishop rode up and advised Stewart that "a better place to attack could not be found."[29]

Stewart ordered Clayton forward and advised the Alabama brigadier that until he made contact with the enemy, he must be governed by circumstances—orders, of course, similar to those Bragg had given Stewart. Unlike Bragg, however, Stewart had no intention of dispatching a unit into battle without knowing where it was going or what it would encounter, especially a relatively untried unit such as Clayton's Brigade. Clayton moved forward accompanied by R. A. Hatcher of Stewart's staff, now a major, followed close behind by Stewart. As Clayton advanced, he came to the edge of the Brock field, where Cheatham was locked in mortal combat with increasing numbers of Federals. When Clayton halted before entering the clearing to correct his alignment, Colonel John C. Carter of the 38th Tennessee of Wright's Brigade ran up and told him that he was about to be enfiladed from the woods to the west, on Clayton's left. Clayton skillfully changed his front obliquely to the left, preparing to meet the Federal threat from that quarter. Meanwhile Stewart encountered General Wright, who stated that his brigade had fallen back, leaving its battery (Carnes's) in Federal hands.[30]

Having changed front, Clayton's regiments gave three cheers for Alabama and advanced about one hundred yards to a point just short of Carnes's abandoned guns. Moving forward against the Union brigades of Colonel George E. Dick and Brigadier General Samuel Beatty, Clayton encountered a fire Ridley later likened to "raindrops in a tempest," "hail stones to a growing cornfield," and "driftwood in a squall." Clayton ordered his men to lie down and return fire. After about a half hour, Clayton ordered his men not to fire unless they could see their targets. Few of the Alabamians could do so, so most of the brigade quit firing altogether. The brigade endured this state of affairs for another half hour, and then its commander determined to break the stalemate with a charge. Before mak-

29. *OR* 30(2):361.
30. Ibid., 362, 401.

ing the charge, Clayton wisely checked the state of his ammunition and found it nearly exhausted. He accordingly withdrew his men without much loss and in good order, the Federals having coincidentally ceased fire.[31]

At the time General Wright advised him of the near collapse of his brigade and the danger on his left, Stewart ordered Brown to advance to Clayton's support. Brown followed so closely that his brigade suffered casualties from fire directed at Clayton. As Clayton withdrew to replenish ammunition, Stewart personally ordered Brown to recapture Carnes's guns. Brown's four Tennessee regiments plunged into the dense undergrowth, their vision obscured by the smoke of battle and the burning woods. When Brown's skirmishers made contact, Beatty's and Dick's Federals opened "with a most terrific fire from all arms." The Federal first line was soon flanked on the right by Brown's infantry. Brown steadily moved his brigade forward toward the second Federal line, which was supported by guns on a "slight acclivity" about 250 yards from the vitally important La Fayette Road.[32]

Again, Brown's lines lapped the Federals on their right. The Tennesseans poured a fire upon the horses and gunners of the battery firing from the acclivity, immobilizing and then overrunning five pieces. Brown's men remained in line engaging the Federals, leaving it to Major J. W. Dawson's battalion following to the rear to draw off most of the captured guns. The Confederates drove the Federals from three other pieces but were unable to draw them off. In the course of this struggle, Brown's men recaptured the lost guns of Carnes's battery.[33]

Having advanced by flanking successive Federal lines on *their* right, Brown was now threatened by Federal troops on *his* right. The Federals forced Brown's two right regiments, the 18th and 45th Tennessee, to fall back "in some confusion under a heavy enfilading fire." With his right threatened in this manner, Brown had no choice but to withdraw the whole brigade to conform with his right two regiments. Although un-

31. Ibid., 400–401, 404–405, 407, 409; Cozzens, *This Terrible Sound*, 183; Ridley, *Battles and Sketches*, 219–20.
32. *OR* 30(1):823, 30(2):362, 370–71; T. I. Corn, "Brown's Brigade at Chickamauga," *CV* 21 (March 1913): 124.
33. *OR* 30(2):370–71.

horsed during the attack, Brown quickly re-formed his brigade in the rear and replenished his ammunition.[34]

Two of Stewart's brigades had gone in, and while neither achieved a breakthrough, they had both relieved Cheatham's left flank and driven the Federals to a point just east of the La Fayette Road. Despite the terrible punishment Clayton and Brown had taken, a further attack was needed. Stewart sent Bate forward with his brigade of Tennesseans, Alabamians, and Georgians. Brown had been driven back by pressure on his right, so Bate was ordered to advance toward the right of Brown's line of attack. Bate moved to the northeast, toward the area where the dirt Brotherton Road intersected the La Fayette Road, which was defended by the Federals of Colonel William Grose's brigade of Palmer's Division, assisted by the untried 75th Indiana.[35]

The flamboyant Bate rode up to the commander of the 20th Tennessee, Colonel Thomas Benton Smith, and cried: "Now Smith, now Smith, I want you to sail on those fellows like you were a wildcat." Smith and his 20th Tennessee were on the brigade's right, along with the 4th Georgia Battalion of sharpshooters and the 37th Georgia Regiment. These units forced Grose back. Eventually, Bate personally led these three units to the northwest into the Poe field, where they encountered twenty Union cannon, which quickly and bloodily broke up Bate's attack.[36]

W. J. McMurray, a member of the 20th Tennessee of Bate's Brigade, observed that his regiment had 98 killed and wounded out of 140 engaged, and the entire brigade lost more than half its strength in the battle. Despite the losses, McMurray was proud of his division's accomplishments that day. His 1894 call for a monument to Stewart's memory pronounced the site "the ground where this 'Little Giant Division' broke the Federal center."[37]

Clayton's Alabamians had withdrawn from the line of battle to replen-

34. Ibid., 371; Corn, "Brown's Brigade," 124.

35. Cozzens, *This Terrible Sound*, 244–48.

36. *OR* 30(2):383–84; Cozzens, *This Terrible Sound*, 244–48. On the fame of this attack, Bate rose from the status of a junior brigadier to a major generalcy, as about two weeks later Jefferson Davis was guided across the battlefield and observed three successive dead horses belonging to Bate. McMurray, "The Gap of Death at Chickamauga," 329–30.

37. McMurray, "The Gap of Death at Chickamauga," 330. Stewart's feelings toward a monument to his memory at a time he was still living (in 1894) are unknown.

ish their ammunition after their hour on the firing line. About 4:00 P.M., Clayton moved into the area to the left of Bate, whose left two regiments, the 58th Alabama and the consolidated 15th-37th Tennessee, moved more due west than northwest. These five regiments, along with a lost detachment of forty or fifty men from the 4th Alabama of Brigadier General Evander M. Law's brigade, made their way toward the Brotherton farm on the west side of the La Fayette Road, although Bate's regiments do not seem to have coordinated with Clayton.[38]

These five regiments of the Little Giant Division faced a favorable situation. The troops of Brigadier General Horatio P. Van Cleve's battered division, supported by twenty cannon, held the ridge that ran parallel to the La Fayette Road through the Brotherton farm. Most of these Union troops were exhausted from their previous fighting and were silhouetted targets for the Rebels in the woods across the La Fayette Road. In the woods south of the Brotherton farm, Bushrod Johnson's brigade, under the command of its senior colonel, John S. Fulton, was flanking the right of Van Cleve's position. To the north, Bate was driving Grose and putting pressure on Van Cleve's left. Fulton's attack proved more effective than Bate's, turning the Federals off the imposing Brotherton ridge before Stewart's men struck Van Cleve's position with any force.[39]

Stewart's five regiments poured unhindered over the Brotherton ridge. Colonel R. C. Tyler's 15th-37th Tennessee shouted three times for Old Tennessee and charged, chasing some Federal remnants off the ridge's top. Mingled with the 36th Alabama of Clayton's Brigade, the men of Colonel Bushrod Jones's 58th Alabama "charged with a run with loud and enthusiastic cheers." Stewart's men swept across the Brotherton farm and through the fringe of woods that separated the Brotherton place from the tanyard of their neighbors, the Dyers, a distance of about a half mile. Unfortunately, the almost complete lack of resistance and the incredible noise and confusion all over the field caused some of the regiments to break up in pursuing the scattering Federals. Clayton, supported by Bate's two regiments, had become dangerously exposed.[40]

---

38. *OR* 30(2):389, 395, 402.

39. Cozzens, *This Terrible Sound*, 244–56.

40. Ibid., 254–57; *OR* 30(2):362, 388, 395, 400–11. On the Chickamauga battlefield, the marker for Clayton's Brigade sits alone in the middle of the Dyer tanyard.

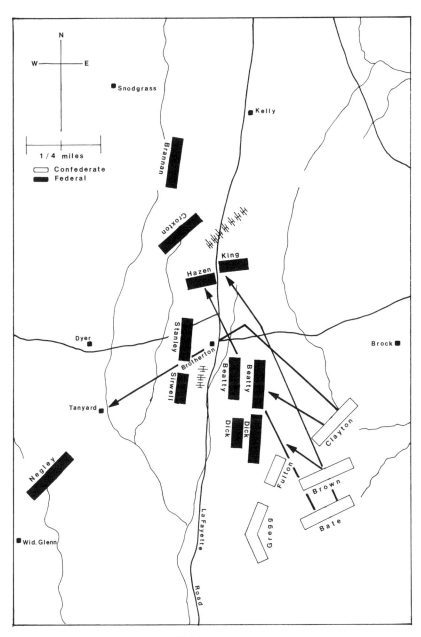

Chickamauga

Map by Blake Magner

Federal help was on the way. Major General Joseph Reynolds established a line of guns that began to fire canister at Clayton. From the south, Major General James S. Negley's veteran division was marching to repair the breach in the Union line. From the north, Thomas directed Brigadier General John M. Brannan to lend the support of his division. Clayton recognized the gathering storm that could transform his brigade's triumph into a disaster, and withdrew. Tyler likewise pulled his Tennesseans back in good order, taking captured artillery with them. While the Confederate withdrawal was termed "leisurely," a solid afternoon's fighting had worn the entire division to a frazzle.[41]

Battlefield markers erected in the 1890s indicate that Stewart was in personal supervision of Clayton's penetrating column. Ridley described the many hazards Stewart and his staff encountered that bloody afternoon:

> Stewart here penetrated the enemy's center, threatening to cut that army in two and drove Vancleve [*sic*] beyond the Lafayette road to the tanyard and the Poe house and carried dismay to Rosecrans, at the widow Glenn's. Later, Hood and Johnson on our left followed it up until from the Brotherton to the Poe field we pierced his line. Added to the horror of the galling fire, the generals and staffs encountered a number of yellow jackets' nests and the kicking of the horses and their ungovernable actions came near breaking up one of the lines. Blue jackets in front of us, yellow jackets upon us, and death missiles around and about us—oh, the fury of the battle, the fierceness of the struggle over Carnes' battery! From 2 o'clock until an hour after dark "it was *war to the knife and a fight to the finish* [Ridley's emphasis]."[42]

In his report, Stewart tabulated the results of the day's fighting: the recapture of Carnes's Battery and the flag of the 51st Tennessee; twelve pieces of artillery captured; 200 to 300 prisoners taken; several hundred stand of

41. *OR* 30(2):396, 402; Cozzens, *This Terrible Sound*, 254–57; Tucker, *Chickamauga*, 160–63.

42. Stewart's Division Marker, Monument map, B-4, 223; Ridley, *Battles and Sketches*, 220; see also "General A. P. Stewart, Ranking Confederate Officer," *New Orleans Times-Democrat*, May 10, 1908.

small arms secured and sent to the rear; "and the enemy's line pierced near its center and driven back beyond the Chattanooga road."[43]

As the guns fell silent on September 19 after a late Confederate attack by Cheatham and Cleburne, no Union or Confederate division had achieved results as great as those of Stewart's Little Giants. Launched in a column of brigades in accordance with the tactical doctrine of the day, Stewart's early-afternoon attack had arrested the collapse of Cheatham's left. Having restored Cheatham's line, Stewart gained a tactical advantage that he and his brigadiers skillfully exploited. The continuous pressure of one fresh Confederate brigade at a time resulted in the successful attack across the La Fayette Road and through the Brotherton fields to the Dyer tanyard. Remarkably, Stewart achieved success in spite of getting no direction from his corps or army commander, excepting Bragg's vague order to proceed to where the fight was hottest. As at Perryville and Murfreesboro, Stewart had directed an attack with telling success. The valor of his troops and the growing experience of his officers notwithstanding, it was Stewart's cool competence, initiative, and leadership that led to the success of his three brigades.[44]

During the night, Stewart's men occupied an area fronting the La Fayette Road across from the Brotherton farm. Stewart discerned that the Federals were constructing defenses and moving artillery to their left, indicating that Rosecrans meant to put his strength between Bragg and the roads back to Chattanooga. This work went on all night long, making Lieutenant Terry Cahal of Stewart's staff anticipate "a hot day's work" the next day.[45]

As dawn broke on September 20, Stewart's men saw a lone officer in an overcoat ride up and converse with their general. Stewart's old roommate, Longstreet, with whom the Tennessean had had no direct contact for many years, was at last on the field. Upon arriving late the previous night, Lee's "War Horse" met with Bragg, who divided his army into two wings, re-

43. *OR* 30(2):362–63.

44. Luke J. Barnett III, "Alexander P. Stewart and the Tactical Employment of His Division at Chickamauga" (Master's thesis, U.S. Army Command and General Staff College, 1989), 108–11.

45. *OR* 30(2):363; Terry Cahal to Colonel Atkinson, September 30, 1863, TSLA; Corn, "Brown's Brigade," 124.

spectively commanded by his senior lieutenant generals, Polk on the right and Longstreet on the left. As events transpired, Stewart would be under Longstreet's command as the right-flank division of the Left Wing. The Left Wing included the five brigades then present of Longstreet's Corps of the Army of Northern Virginia, Buckner's Corps of Stewart's and Preston's divisions, Hindman's Division of Polk's Corps, and Bushrod Johnson's provisional division. The remainder of the army constituted the Right Wing under Polk.[46]

Bragg's plan remained the same for September 20. An effort would be made to turn Rosecrans' left and push the Army of the Cumberland into McLemore's Cove, where it could be destroyed. The Confederate attack on the right did not occur until 9:30 A.M. on a clear, crisp Sunday morning, when Breckinridge's Division swept forward in a single line of three brigades against the extreme Federal right.[47]

When Longstreet came to confer with Stewart, he advised his old classmate that the attack was to start on the army's extreme right, then on the left, and move successively to the center. Stewart was to move when the division on his right or left moved. Stewart advised Longstreet that there was no division in touch on his right, which occasioned "Old Peter" to order him to move to the right to establish contact with Cleburne's Division. This move had the effect of masking a portion of that division, primarily Brigadier General James Deshler's brigade, which was somewhat behind and to the left of the rest of the division. Stewart's Division was now north of the Brotherton Road, in the woods east of the Poe field. Across the La Fayette Road, elements of Brigadier General John M. Brannan's and Reynolds' divisions waited behind the breastworks Stewart had heard being constructed the night before.[48]

Two of Breckinridge's attacking brigades, Marcellus A. Stovall's and Daniel W. Adams', flanked the Federal line and drove south toward the northern Kelly field. Breckinridge's third brigade, Benjamin Hardin

46. Ridley, *Battles and Sketches*, 222; APS to D. H. Hill, July 21, 1862, Hill Papers, SHC; Connelly, *Autumn of Glory*, 208–209.

47. For a good discussion of the army's command problems early on September 20, see Connelly, *Autumn of Glory*, 208–221. For weather conditions, see Ridley, *Battles and Sketches*, 222.

48. *OR* 30(2):153–56, 363; Cozzens, *This Terrible Sound*, 316; Matt Spruill, ed., *Guide to the Battle of Chickamauga* (Lawrence: University Press of Kansas, 1993), 151.

Helm's, crashed into a line of Federal breastworks occupied by the major portion of three Federal divisions, which projected to some degree as a salient on the east side of the La Fayette Road. Lucius A. Polk's Brigade, somewhat detached from the remainder of Cleburne's Division, continued this futile attack to the south. Cleburne's next brigade, S. A. M. Wood's, advanced through the prone soldiers of Bate's Brigade toward the point where the Federal breastworks bent back across the La Fayette Road in the northern portion of the Poe field. Repulsed, they retreated to a ravine in the open forest to the east, awaiting developments.[49]

After moving to the right in accordance with Longstreet's instructions, Stewart had his division behind breastworks on a slight ridge in the woods to the east of the Poe field, Brown on the left and Bate on the right, with Clayton behind Brown. This movement was made under a heavy fire from Union batteries in the division's immediate front, causing some loss. As Stewart awaited events that would justify an attack in accordance with Longstreet's orders, he received direct orders from a member of Bragg's staff to attack. Bragg was fed up with the slow progress of his planned daybreak attack, and sent an order for all divisions to attack. Stewart related to Bragg's officer that he was awaiting orders from Longstreet, but was told that Bragg wanted every unit to move. Stewart prepared to move toward Poe field and wisely secured flank support for Brown from Wood. Clayton was moved up behind Brown, and Bate moved up behind Wood, in close support.[50]

Brown threw out skirmishers and advanced at the double quick, driving Federal skirmishers through the woods and across the La Fayette Road, where the Federals north of the Poe farm poured a crossfire upon his troops. Stewart termed it "the most terrible fire it has ever been my fortune to witness." Wood's Brigade faltered, but Brown moved forward another few yards before his right regiments, the 18th and 45th Tennessee, broke and retreated to the brigade's breastworks. In the understated words of the colonel of the 45th Tennessee, "The grape and canister coming from [the right] was not at all agreeable."[51]

Brown and Wood having been repulsed, Clayton and Bate moved

49. Cozzens, *This Terrible Sound*, 322, 338–43.

50. *OR* 30(2):363–64.

51. Ibid., 364, 371–72, 376–80.

through their retreating lines and advanced on the blazing Federal position. Bate, being on the right, was subject to the same galling fire that had stymied Wood. Bate personally supervised his right units, the 20th Tennessee, the 37th Georgia, and the 4th Georgia sharpshooters, as casualties from the day before had left them in command of junior officers. Without support, Bate's right was punished fearfully. Bate "was compelled to retire that wing of my brigade, or sacrifice it uselessly fighting thrice its numbers, with the advantage of the hill and the breastworks against it."[52]

Only Bate's left regiments, the 58th Alabama and the 15th-37th Tennessee, were able to go forward. The 58th's Colonel Bushrod Jones, perceiving a lack of support, halted his line at the edge of the woods and dug in, exchanging musketry with the Federals until past 12:30 P.M. The 15th-37th moved forward at the double quick through the woods into the Poe field, where its acting commander, Lieutenant Colonel Dudley Frayser, was wounded. Captain R. M. Tankesley led the regiments to the point where he saw they were all alone. He then ordered them to fall back to the breastworks, with some of the retreating men bringing off Colonel Frayser. Frayser later ordered men back into Poe field to rescue wounded compatriots who were endangered by burning grass and bushes.[53]

Clayton, the left of the second line, moved forward through Brown's brigade and struck the Federals around the Poe house. The tornado of fire from the Federal breastworks and artillery stopped him, but his regiments succeeded in driving the Federals from some guns posted near the La Fayette Road. No doubt because they were shielded from the worst of the enfilade fire coming from the Federal right, Clayton's men felt they could have prevailed in their assault with a little more support.[54]

As Stewart's Division re-formed behind its breastworks, Stewart, Clayton, and members of their staffs received contusions from spent fragments of grape and canister. Bromfield Ridley observed James D. Richardson, the adjutant of the 45th Tennessee of Brown's Brigade, moving slowly out of the exposed area in front of the breastworks, coolly observing, "This is hot, isn't it?" When Richardson asked a passing soldier to which command he belonged, the man replied: "Thirty-eighth Ala—," being cut short

---

52. Ibid., 385–86; Spruill, *Guide to the Battle of Chickamauga*, 158–60.
53. *OR* 30(2):395–99; Spruill, *Guide to the Battle of Chickamauga*, 161–62.
54. *OR* 30(2):402–11.

when a cannonball removed half his head and splattered Richardson and others with his blood.[55]

The pounding that Stewart administered the Federal lines was the last of the uncoordinated Confederate attacks that fateful morning. Except for Breckinridge's assault into the northern edge of the Kelly field, the morning had gone fairly well for Rosecrans. Under a misapprehension, however, Rosecrans issued an order to division commander Thomas J. Wood to close on a division down the line. Wood took the order literally, marched his division around the division next in line, opening a gap just as Longstreet launched an attack out of the woods to the east of the Brotherton farm with most of the uncommitted troops of his wing.[56]

Longstreet's attack caught Wood in motion with great results. As the day moved past high noon, Longstreet recognized that the best chance for a great Confederate victory was to wheel right and strike the rear of the troops resisting Polk. Longstreet directed Stewart to act as a pivot, and except for realigning for that purpose, the division remained stationary during the afternoon assaults on Snodgrass Hill. Stewart watched heavy fighting on the right and left of the Kelly field, but on Buckner's orders did not move, awaiting further word from Longstreet.[57]

Rosecrans and about a third of his army were swept from the field by Longstreet's attack. As the afternoon wore on, Federals under Thomas held on in two locations, Snodgrass Hill and the salient to the east of the Kelly field. Thomas faced the problem of extricating his outnumbered troops without further disaster. Withdrawal orders went to the Federal commanders in the Kelly field salient. Failing to coordinate with the others, Union general Joseph Reynolds set his troops in motion about 4:45 P.M. Reynolds' column presented a tantalizing target to Stewart.[58]

55. Ridley, *Battles and Sketches*, 225.

56. Spruill, *Guide to the Battle of Chickamauga*, 162–63; Cozzens, *This Terrible Sound*, 357–68. D. H. Hill and Longstreet give Stewart's attack credit for creating confusion in the Federal lines, but from the timing of events as described in Peter Cozzen's extensive study, it seems unlikely that they are correct. However, Stewart's attack certainly had some value in drawing Rosecrans' attention just before Longstreet's assault. See Hill, "Chickamauga," *B&L* 3:657; James Longstreet, *From Manassas to Appomattox* (1896; reprint, Secaucus, N.J.: Blue & Gray Press, 1984), 447.

57. Tucker, *Chickamauga*, 260–78; Longstreet, *From Manassas to Appomattox*, 447–49; Ridley, *Battles and Sketches*, 225; OR 30(2):364.

58. Cozzens, *This Terrible Sound*, 495.

Lieutenant Colonel G. Moxley Sorrel of Longstreet's staff saw Reynolds' move and ordered Stewart to attack, but was rebuffed. Stewart, no doubt remembering the confusion caused by Colonel Jaques at Murfreesboro, courteously told Sorrel that he needed assurance that the order was Longstreet's. Recognizing the need for action, Stewart prepared his division to attack while Sorrel obtained Longstreet's written order. When Sorrel returned with Old Peter's order, Stewart sent Clayton and Bate forward. The two brigades swept over the abandoned breastworks, routing Reynolds' column and capturing 300 to 400 prisoners in the area of the Kelly house. Stewart's staff, led by Major Hatcher, impulsively swept forward in a scene of "thrilling animation, impetuosity and dash," splitting up a body of regulars and aiding in their capture. Bate brought up the Eufaula Battery, whose shots chased the retreating bluecoats in the gathering twilight.[59]

On the Confederate left, Longstreet finally drove the retreating Federals off the ridge at and to the west of the Snodgrass cabin. As the Army of Tennessee's two wings came together, picking up the last of the Federals on the field as prisoners, its veterans, joined by their compatriots from Virginia and Mississippi, shouted "loud huzzas" of victory. As Buckner stated: "The continued cheers of the army announced at dark that every point of the field had been gained." Stewart camped within the captured breastworks, and had his division spend most of the night gathering the arms and supplies left on the field.[60]

After the war, Stewart observed that "if practicable, [the enemy] should have been closely and hotly pursued, and the victory rendered decisive." Both Longstreet and Hill argued that Bragg failed in his pursuit, and thereby frittered away the Confederacy's best chance for decisive victory in the West. Bragg argued that the army's heavy losses forestalled a close pursuit. Thomas Connelly has detailed the arguments for both sides, and it seems reasonable to conclude that Bragg was not exclusively at fault, as both Polk and Longstreet appear to have been unsure whether the Federals were entirely off the field on September 21.[61]

59. G. Moxley Sorrel, *Recollections of a Confederate Staff Officer* (1905; reprint, New York: Bantam Books, 1992), 168; *OR* 30(2):364; Bromfield L. Ridley, "Daring Deeds of Staff and Escort," *CV* 4 (October 1896), 358.

60. Longstreet, *From Manassas to Appomattox*, 456; *OR* 30(2):359, 364–65.

61. Lindsley, ed., *Military Annals*, 82; Hill, "Chickamauga," *B&L* 3:662; Longstreet, *From Manassas to Appomattox*, 461–63; Connelly, *Autumn of Glory*, 226–33.

At the dedication of the Tennessee monument on Horseshoe Ridge in the 1890s, James D. Porter observed that Chickamauga would not have been a barren victory if Stewart had commanded the army. This could very well be dismissed as complimentary hyperbole, but there can be no question that Stewart performed well on Chickamauga's bloody field. As noted earlier, Old Straight's leadership contributed significantly to the army's partial success on September 19. Stewart's primary role on September 20 was to hold the pivot for Longstreet. Buckner's report of the battle commended Stewart and his brigadiers. Bate and Clayton also expressed appreciation for Stewart's generalship, Clayton observing that Stewart "was everywhere and under all circumstances present with his command." There can be no question that the men of the Little Giant Division were likewise due the appreciation of their commander. Certainly, they paid the price of victory. Of the 4,400 men of Stewart's Division who crossed the Chickamauga at Thedford's Ford, 205 were killed, 1,499 were wounded, and 29 were missing.[62]

In the end, Stewart credited the Being he deemed to be the true source of victory: "I desire to express my humble but most grateful acknowledgments to Almighty God for the signal success that crowned our arms. Greatly outnumbered as we were by a skillful and determined foe, our own strong arms and stout hearts could never have secured to us the victory without the divine favor. Let all the praise be ascribed to His holy name."[63]

62. *OR* 30(2):359, 365, 387, 403; Barnett, *Alexander P. Stewart and the Tactical Deployment*, 138–39. Among the dead was Private Glazener of the 18th Alabama, who, with two other members of his Shelby County, Alabama, Baptist congregation, died in the fighting on September 19. Resolution of the Tallassee Baptist Church, November 22, 1863, CCNMP.

63. *OR* 30(2):366.

— 9 —

My Line Was Too Long and Weak

Missionary Ridge

As September became October, the Army of Tennessee settled into a siege of Chattanooga, effectively by default. Bragg felt he lacked the transportation, especially for the troops acquired from Mississippi and Virginia, to cross the Tennessee and flank Rosecrans out of Chattanooga, although such was the plan he proposed to Richmond. He also ruled out a direct assault, as the Army of the Cumberland was strongly entrenched in Chattanooga within a few days after its defeat at Chickamauga. Bragg hoped that his lines on Missionary Ridge, to the east of Chattanooga, extending to Lookout Mountain on the south, as well as the rugged terrain to the west, would cut Rosecrans off from both supplies and reinforcements.[1]

The siege resulted in an uneasy *status quo* between the armies, during which the discontent that had been building between Bragg and his officers since Perryville reached its peak. In the last week of September, 1863, Bragg seized upon Hindman's failure in McLemore's Cove and Polk's slowness on the morning of September 20, 1863, at Chickamauga to move against them. At the same time, Polk and Longstreet, among others, engaged in an unsavory letter-writing campaign behind Bragg's back to urge his dismissal from command. The resulting furor ended in the removal or transfer of four of the six men who were corps

---

1. Connelly, *Autumn of Glory*, 232–34.

and wing commanders at Chickamauga, with a fifth, Hood, recovering from the loss of a leg.[2]

By the time the Confederates filed into positions around Chattanooga, Bragg had reached a state of near isolation within the command structure of his army. His West Point classmate and chief of staff, Brigadier General William W. Mackall, tried to warn Bragg that his proposed changes would cause "great dissatisfaction." Flushed with his victory at Chickamauga, Bragg was hard to persuade. He continued to put his heart and soul into his work, though Mackall thought he did so in a "repulsive" manner. Mackall wrote his wife on September 29, 1863, that Bragg was "as much influenced by his enemies as his friends and does not know how to control the one or preserve the other."[3]

The byzantine maneuvers by Bragg and his opponents, which together were one of the major factors in the dissipation of the advantage gained by Chickamauga, are outside the scope of this book. An outline is necessary, however, to analyze Stewart's position in the dispute. Concerning the two officers removed in late September, Stewart had favorable feelings toward Leonidas Polk, who was popular among the Tennesseans in the army and who had recommended Stewart for promotion. Nonetheless, Stewart wrote in the *Military Annals* that Polk commanded the right wing at Chickamauga and that the orders for the daylight attack on September 20 "were not obeyed." Having been present in McLemore's Cove under Hindman, Stewart was of the opinion that the "right man was not there in command."[4]

The initial anti-Bragg moves were made by Polk, Longstreet, Hill, and Buckner, who met in the week after Chickamauga and agreed that Longstreet and Polk would write influential friends in Richmond and advise them of Bragg's inadequacies. Polk's removal by Bragg on September 30 did nothing to quiet Longstreet and the others. Another meeting of the corps commanders on October 4 resulted in the preparation of a petition to Davis calling for Bragg's removal, a document which caused Bragg

---

2. See ibid., 235–78, for the most extensive discussion of this dismal episode and its effect on the army.

3. Warner, *Generals in Gray*, 203–204; W. W. Mackall to wife, September 29, 1863, W. W. Mackall Papers, SHC.

4. "Gen. Stewart Passes Away," *Chattanooga News*, August 31, 1908.

"much distress & mortification." Twelve officers eventually signed the petition, including Longstreet, Hill, Buckner, and Cleburne, as well as Brigadier Generals William Preston, Archibald Gracie, James A. Smith, Marcellus Stovall, Lucius Polk, Bushrod Johnson, and John C. Brown, and Colonel Randall Gibson, who commanded the brigade of Daniel Adams, who had been wounded and captured at Chickamauga.[5]

Stewart did not sign the petition. It is noteworthy, however, that a copy of the petition is among a collection of Stewart's official papers at the Georgia Historical Society. This copy of the petition bears the names of Buckner, Preston, Gracie, Hill, and Brown.[6] If in fact this was Stewart's copy of the document, it is interesting to speculate how and when it came into his possession. Since Stewart's corps commander, Buckner, two of his brigadiers, Johnson and Brown, and his old roommate, Longstreet, were among the signers, there are any number of possibilities. Stewart's being a Tennessean, and Tennesseans being a group known for their antipathy to Bragg, might also explain his possession of a copy of the petition. Even if the document is not Stewart's, there can be no question that he had the chance to sign it and did not. The absence of his signature from the petition is in itself not conclusive evidence of Stewart's being a Bragg supporter, as strong Bragg opponents such as Breckinridge and Cheatham did not sign the document either.[7]

Davis came to the army once more in October, 1863, to try to settle matters. In meetings with Bragg and his malcontent corps commanders, Davis ultimately sustained Bragg. In the process, Bragg endured the obviously mortifying ordeal of having Longstreet, Buckner, Hill, and Cheatham all express to Davis in his presence their view that it was in the best interest of the army that Bragg be removed.[8]

---

5. Connelly, *Autumn of Glory*, 235–38; Bridges, *Lee's Maverick General*, 237; W. W. Mackall to wife, October 5, 1863, Mackall Papers, SHC. Even Mackall was "afraid of [Bragg's] generalship." W. W. Mackall to wife, September 29, 1863, Mackall Papers.

6. Petition to Davis, October 4, 1863, Item 3172, Collection 169, Confederate States Army Papers, GHS. The copy retained by Buckner, the supposed author of the petition, does not indicate to whom the petition was circulated. Petition to Davis, October 4, 1863, Simon Bolivar Buckner Collection, Huntington Library, San Marino, Calif.; see also Stickles, *Buckner*, 233–36.

7. APS to Marcus J. Wright, October 30, 1880, Wright Papers, SHC; Connelly, *Autumn of Glory*, 240.

8. Connelly, *Autumn of Glory,* 245–46.

Once Bragg was sustained, all but one of his opponents were left to his not-so-tender mercies. Polk's friendship with Davis resulted in the dismissal of the charges against the bishop. Polk went to Mississippi, trading places with Hardee. Bragg had already run off Forrest by stripping him of all but a single regiment of his command. He next moved against Hill, who was removed for his alleged failure to launch the early attack on the right on the second day of the Chickamauga battle. Buckner was reduced to divisional command following the elimination of his Department of East Tennessee, and Preston to brigade command for the same reason. On October 31, Cheatham, stripped of the support of Bishop Polk, requested reassignment.[9]

It was much harder for Bragg to dispose of James Longstreet, the Confederacy's senior lieutenant general, Lee's "War Horse" and a substantial contributor to the army's victory at Chickamauga. Whatever good Longstreet had accomplished at Chickamauga he largely dissipated by the end of October by arguably his worst performance in the war, first failing to seal off Lookout Valley, the obvious route of Federal resupply and reinforcement west of Lookout Mountain, and then launching a woefully inadequate night attack at Wauhatchie, in a failed effort to reclose that route. Eventually, at the first of November, Bragg dispatched Longstreet and his two divisions north into East Tennessee, ostensibly to deal with Major General Ambrose E. Burnside's Union force at Knoxville, but primarily to rid himself of Old Peter.[10]

While the members of the Confederate high command were fighting each other as zealously as they would any Yankees, their counterparts in blue were not idle. Rosecrans, deemed too befuddled by his defeat at Chickamauga to continue commanding the Army of the Cumberland, was replaced by Thomas. Major General William T. Sherman, with elements of two corps totaling over 20,000 men, moved across north Alabama along the line of the Memphis and Charleston Railroad, and Major General Joseph Hooker, former commander of the Army of the Potomac, was placed in command of the Eleventh and Twelfth Corps of that army and went

9. Ibid., 240, 246, 248, 252–53; Losson, *Tennessee's Forgotten Warriors*, 116.

10. Connelly, *Autumn of Glory*, 255–64; Wiley Sword, *Mountains Touched with Fire* (New York: St. Martin's Press, 1995), 123–44.

with them to Bridgeport. Most important, Ulysses S. Grant took command of the whole theater between the Appalachians and the Mississippi River. The Army of Tennessee would soon face the Union's three most competent commanders, Grant, Sherman, and Thomas, at a time when it was weakened by dissension and the detachment of troops to Knoxville.[11]

What little chance the army had to resist the formidable combination building against it was further reduced by the final spasms of Bragg's moves against his opponents. With the return of Johnson's Brigade two days after its brilliant attack at Chickamauga, Stewart's Division resumed the organization it had maintained since its creation in June. However, on November 12, Bragg ordered a major reorganization of the army, formalizing a move that had been in effect for four or five days. The ostensible reason of the reorganization was to spread out brigades among the various divisions and thereby prevent hardship on one particular community or state. The real reason was to break up the old Tennessee and Kentucky blocs, which had supported Polk, Cheatham, Buckner, and Breckinridge in their opposition to Bragg. Like Cheatham's Division, the Little Giant Division was composed primarily of Tennessee troops. The Tennessee brigades in both divisions were dispersed throughout the army. Brown's Brigade went to the newly arrived division of Major General Carter L. Stevenson, where Brown, a signer of the petition, and his troops could be watched by a Bragg supporter. Bate, a Bragg supporter, went with his brigade to Breckinridge's Division. Bushrod Johnson and his brigade, along with the brigade of anti-Bragg man Archibald Gracie, were dispatched north to Knoxville with fellow petition signer Buckner to assist Longstreet.[12]

While Stewart did not sign the petition, the reorganization of his division has led some writers to conclude that he was a member of the anti-Bragg faction. There is, in fact, reason to think that Stewart by this time felt Bragg needed to go. In the *Military Annals,* written in the mid-1880s, Stewart said that although Bragg was an "able officer . . . [h]is greatest de-

11. Connelly, *Autumn of Glory,* 261–62.

12. *OR* 30(4):689; Edwin H. Rennolds Diary, November 8, 1863, typescript copy, CCNMP; Connelly, *Autumn of Glory,* 250–51; Losson, *Tennessee's Forgotten Warriors,* 118–19; *OR* 31(2):659, 31(3):618, 685–86; Longstreet, *From Manassas to Appomattox,* 501, 503.

fect was that he did not win the love and confidence of either the officers or men." In the same work Stewart stated that this fault was the "*real* cause" of the failure in McLemore's Cove.[13] Thomas Connelly has characterized Stewart as a Bragg "opponent" and Steven Woodworth has written that Stewart had criticized Bragg in a "relatively restrained and unobtrusive" manner. Neither refers to Stewart's writings in placing him in the anti-Bragg camp. Connelly's primary reason for putting Stewart there was the dispersal of Stewart's Tennessee brigades in the November 12 reorganization.[14]

Yet while the dispersal of his division was no doubt a blow to Old Straight, it need not be viewed as a slight to Stewart so much as a necessary move in Bragg's overall plan to break up the Tennessee troops. Several factors support this conclusion, and the concomitant conclusion that Stewart was not among Bragg's opponents.

First, the transfer was made as painless to Stewart as possible. In scattering the Tennesseans in Cheatham's Division, Bragg moved Stewart's old brigade, under Strahl, back to Old Straight's command. If Bragg wanted to punish Stewart, it does not seem likely that he would have regained his old brigade. Stewart also retained Clayton's Alabama brigade, which had fought well at Chickamauga. Adams' Brigade, formerly of Breckinridge's Division, was also assigned to Stewart. The Louisianans were under the command of their veteran senior colonel, Randall Gibson, a bitter Bragg enemy who signed the petition. Finally, Stewart received a Georgia brigade of exchanged Vicksburg prisoners that was assigned to the veteran Brigadier General Marcellus A. Stovall, another petition signer. Obviously, Stewart was given Gibson and Stovall to watch.[15]

A stronger indication that Stewart did not oppose Bragg is his letter to

13. Lindsley, ed., *Military Annals*, 81, 85.

14. Connelly, *Autumn of Glory*, 251; Woodworth, *Jefferson Davis and His Generals*, 265. James D. Porter wrote that Stewart participated in the famous meeting with Davis and Bragg with the corps commanders and expressed with the others "that the officers and men of the army could not and would not trust General Bragg, and the necessity for another commander was imperative." James D. Porter, "Criticisms by Friends of General Johnston" *CV* 4 (August 1896): 369. The preponderance of the evidence, however, is that Stewart was not a participant in that meeting. See Woodworth, *Jefferson Davis and His Generals*, 242–43.

15. *OR* 31(3):685–86; Warner, *Generals in Gray*, 104, 294–95. Sifakis, *Compendium: South Carolina and Georgia*, 251–55, 266–67.

Bragg dated March 19, 1864, "prompted by a feeling of respect and kindness." The missive emphasized that Bragg still had friends in the Army of Tennessee and intimated that Stewart was one of them. Considered "an ardent lover of the truth," Old Straight was no hypocrite. While Stewart wrote after the war that Bragg's effectiveness as a commander was at an end by this time, that sentiment is not inconsistent with friendship toward Bragg. (This is especially so since Stewart did not define Bragg's problem as one of competence, but as a lack of confidence of the officers and men of his army.) By the time Stewart wrote his March, 1864, letter, Bragg was in a position to influence promotions even more than he had been as commander of the Army of Tennessee. Stewart's promotion in 1864 demonstrates that Bragg's baleful influence was not directed against him, as perhaps it was against Cleburne.[16]

While Stewart may have been glad to see his Tennessee brigade again, its troops were unhappy to leave Cheatham's Tennessee division. Furthermore, the move was made against a backdrop of widespread privation that increased disgruntlement. A member of the 5th Tennessee wrote in his diary on November 9: "After 12 we moved to Gen. Stewart's Div. . . . I entered Chattanooga Valley with just such feelings as I would Camp Chase. The wind blew cold. Most of the trees were cut and we were set down in an open place without shelter or wood. To add to this we heard that no more meat would be issued, but that an ounce of sugar per day in lieu. The Rebels freely vented their feelings and made their threats. I fear this will be the Valley Forge of the war."[17]

Its men happy or not, Stewart's reorganized division remained in Hill's Corps, which became Breckinridge's upon Hill's removal on October 15. Bragg's various reorganizations that fall resulted in the army being divided into two corps. (This excluded Longstreet's, which though nominally under Bragg, for all practical purposes was on its way back to Lee and Virginia.) Joining Stewart's Division in Breckinridge's Corps were Cleburne's Division, Breckinridge's Division, now under Bate, and Stevenson's Division. Breckinridge, one of Bragg's bitterest enemies, was not a West

---

16. APS to B. Bragg, March 19, 1864, Palmer Collection of Bragg Papers, Western Reserve Historical Society; Pollard, *Lee and His Lieutenants*, 717; Lindsley, ed., *Military Annals*, 85; Woodworth, *Jefferson Davis and His Generals*, 260–64.

17. Rennolds Diary, November 9, 1863, CCNMP.

Pointer and did not inspire confidence in some of his officers. He had, however, commanded a corps at Shiloh, had fought well at Chickamauga, and had not signed the anti-Bragg petition. In the middle of November, the corps' line stretched from Lookout Mountain to the middle of Missionary Ridge, Stewart's Division being positioned in Chattanooga Valley, a low-lying area between Lookout Mountain and Missionary Ridge to the southeast of Chattanooga. Stewart's lines extended from the east bank of Chattanooga Creek to the base of Missionary Ridge.[18]

Bragg continued to slide toward disaster, just as Grant planned to employ Sherman to crush the extreme Confederate right on Missionary Ridge and seize the main Confederate railhead east of the ridge at Chickamauga Station. This would place Grant's forces in position to succor Burnside in Knoxville, a subject of much concern in Washington. With two of Buckner's three brigades gone to join Longstreet just that morning, on November 23 Bragg ordered Cleburne to take his division to Chickamauga Station and proceed by rail to Longstreet, thereby ridding himself of the last of the petition-signing divisional commanders. Grant, fearing that the Confederate movements portended a plan to capture Burnside and then bring Longstreet back to Chattanooga, ordered Thomas to capture Orchard Knob, a small knoll about two-thirds of the way between the Union lines around Chattanooga and Missionary Ridge. The Federal move had the desired effect of retaining Cleburne and the last of Buckner's brigades at Chattanooga, but put Cleburne and his battle-toughened veterans in position to defend the north end of Missionary Ridge when Sherman assaulted two days later.[19]

On November 24, Bragg observed Sherman's five divisions moving across the Tennessee to advance against the northern end of Missionary Ridge. Bragg also saw the advanced echelons of the Army of the Cumberland around Orchard Knob. Bragg hurried to make dispositions, including moving Cleburne, less one brigade, into line on the extreme right. As he

18. *OR* 30(4):752, 31(2):660–62; Liddell, *Liddell's Record*, 154; Peter Cozzens, *The Shipwreck of Their Hopes: The Battles for Chattanooga* (Urbana: University of Illinois Press, 1994), 25, 118–19.

19. James Lee McDonough, *Chattanooga: A Death Grip on the Confederacy* (Knoxville: University of Tennessee Press, 1984), 108–14; Irving A. Buck, *Cleburne and His Command* (1908; reprint, Wilmington, N.C.: Broadfoot, 1987), 162–63; U. S. Grant, "Chattanooga," *B&L* 3:696–99.

was returning southward down his line, he heard "a heavy cannonading" by the Federal batteries on the Confederate left. Hooker was moving to assault Bragg's defenses on Lookout Mountain.[20]

Stewart watched the "Battle Above the Clouds" from his own extreme left at the Watkins house, near Chattanooga Creek. He had a good view of the slopes of Lookout Mountain, except to the extent it was obscured by the rolling mists and clouds. Occasionally, the troops around Stewart, of Clayton's Brigade, could see the breastworks and the lines of blue infantry moving against them. That afternoon, Stewart, Colonel James T. Holtzclaw, who was the brigade commander in Clayton's temporary absence, and some of their officers stood "watching with deep interest and astonishment this evident attack in heavy force along a line deemed so nearly impregnable that earthworks there seemed almost unnecessary." "Suddenly," a witness wrote, "as a cloud rolled away, we saw our line of breastworks swarming with men for nearly a half mile and flags waving there. 'What flag is that?' was asked. 'Try the field-glass. There, it is plain enough: It is the Stars and Stripes!' "[21]

Breckinridge ordered Stewart to furnish a brigade for the corps commander to take across Chattanooga Creek and communicate with and facilitate the withdrawal of the Lookout Mountain defenders. Stewart dispatched his nearest brigade, Clayton's, which reported to Breckinridge at the foot of Lookout Mountain. Holtzclaw was instructed to take his Alabamians and relieve the two brigades holding the shelf east of the Cravens house. About 6 P.M., under a full moon, Holtzclaw engaged the Federals in a "sharp fight . . . which lasted with but short intervals until 11 o'clock." At one point, Holtzclaw launched a counterattack to straighten out an area of the line. About 2 A.M., Holtzclaw was ordered to withdraw. A total eclipse of the moon obscured Holtzclaw's march to rejoin the division on Missionary Ridge.[22]

Bragg arrived on the left about sunset on November 24 and determined

---

20. *OR* 31(2):664; Connelly, *Autumn of Glory*, 272.

21. J. W. A. Wright, "Bragg's Campaign Around Chattanooga," *Southern Bivouac* 2 (1886/87): 467; William Stanley Hoole, *A Historical Sketch of the Thirty-sixth Alabama Regiment, 1862–1865* (University, Ala.: Confederate Publishing, 1986), 22.

22. APS Chattanooga report, Item 3172, J. T. Holtzclaw Chattanooga report, Item 3180, CSA Papers, GHS; C. L. Willoughby, "Eclipse of the Moon at Missionary Ridge," *CV* 21 (December 1913): 590; Sword, *Mountains Touched with Fire*, 227.

the Confederates "had lost all advantages of position." He therefore ordered the evacuation of Lookout Mountain. Later, at army headquarters
on Missionary Ridge near the Moore Road, Bragg met with corps commanders Hardee and Breckinridge. Hooker now threatened the Confederate left flank at the south end of Missionary Ridge, and Sherman's main effort against the north end was likely the next day. Hardee was for moving
across the Chickamauga, which was swollen with rain and impaired the
army's line of retreat. Breckinridge, his blood up after the fight on Lookout
Mountain, argued that Missionary Ridge was as favorable ground as the
army would have. Bragg agreed with Breckinridge, and Hardee eventually
acquiesced, once it was decided to put the bulk of the army on the northern end of the ridge to contest Sherman. This left Breckinridge holding the
southern two-thirds of the ridge with three divisions, Hindman's under
Patton Anderson, Breckinridge's under Bate, and Stewart's. Stewart later
expressed disapproval of the decision to stay: "This line was a very long
one, and, although the position was naturally strong, it *seemed* like folly to
hold it in the face of the immense force concentrated in its front."[23]

Missionary Ridge must indeed have seemed like a strong position to defend. Viewed from Chattanooga, it looms like a great rampart to the east.
The ridge runs southward from near the point where Chickamauga Creek
empties into the Tennessee River and extends fifteen or twenty miles down
into Georgia. Just below the Tennessee-Georgia state line, a narrow gap
exists at Rossville, through which ran one of the roads utilized by the
Army of the Cumberland in its retreat from Chickamauga. From Rossville
Gap northward to the point where Missionary Ridge ends in a jumble of
hills overlooking Chickamauga Creek and the Tennessee River is approximately seven miles.

From his position in the center of the ridge, Brigadier General Arthur
M. Manigault, promoted from colonel earlier in the year to command one
of the brigades in Anderson's (Hindman's) division, observed that from
the crest of the ridge one had a full view of Chattanooga and the surrounding country. Most of the timber had been cut off the ridge, the presence of
the armies necessitating its use for breastworks, building purposes, and

---

23. *OR* 31(2):664; William C. Davis, *Breckinridge: Statesman, Soldier, Symbol* (Baton
Rouge: Louisiana State University Press, 1974), 386–88; Cozzens, *Shipwreck of Their Hopes*,
195–96; Sword, *Mountains Touched with Fire*, 236–37; Lindsley, ed., *Military Annals*, 83.

fuel. Between Chattanooga and the ridge lies a plain with two small elevations, Orchard Knob and the hill around which the current National Cemetery is situated.[24]

Even as Holtzclaw covered the withdrawal from Lookout Mountain in the early hours of November 25, Breckinridge, in accordance with the decision made in his meeting earlier that night with Bragg and Hardee, ordered Stewart to move out of Chattanooga Valley and onto Missionary Ridge, prolonging Bate's line there. Stewart was to withdraw his pickets before daylight, use them to prolong Bate's line of skirmishers, and leave a reserve at the foot of the ridge. Stewart was to place his division's artillery behind the ridge, and detail a battery and two regiments to guard Rossville Gap. The division's ordnance trains were moved to the east side of the ridge. A mix-up in orders from corps headquarters caused the division's wagons to depart before they were able to load, causing some loss of tents and quartermaster stores.[25]

Stewart complied with Breckinridge's instructions by dispatching to Rossville the two largest regiments of Stovall's Brigade, the 42nd and 43rd Georgia, under the command of the 42nd's Colonel Robert J. Henderson, and Dawson's Georgia battery, under Lieutenant R. W. Anderson. Henderson selected a position about 300 yards in front of Rossville Gap, where his two regiments were placed in line of battle with the battery between them on a slight eminence a few yards in advance of the infantry line. Henderson posted a line of skirmishers about 150 yards in front, "with orders to hold the position at all hazards."[26]

Farther north, the 31st and 33rd Tennessee of Strahl's Brigade were placed in the skirmish line out from the foot of the ridge, with the 4th and 5th Tennessee in reserve in the rifle pits about one-third of the way up the ridge. The 19th and 24th Tennessee formed on the ridge, along with the three remaining regiments of Stovall's Brigade, Clayton's (Holtzclaw's) Brigade, and Adams' (Gibson's) Brigade.[27] Stewart's command, half of

24. Manigault, *A Carolinian Goes to War*, 128–29.
25. *OR* 31(2):679; APS Chattanooga report, CSA Papers, GHS.
26. APS Chattanooga report, CSA Papers, GHS; Henderson Chattanooga report, Item 3188, CSA Papers, GHS.
27. APS Chattanooga report, CSA Papers, GHS; Strahl Chattanooga report, Item 3189, CSA Papers, GHS.

which was completely unfamiliar to him, moved into a new position in the line after a march that probably involved most of the night. The fragmentation occasioned by Breckinridge's orders must have increased the confusion. The division was dangerously extended, and it would get worse.

The Confederate lines on Missionary Ridge were in terrible disorder, especially in Breckinridge's sector. Although the army had had two months to fortify the ridge, Breckinridge did not order the fortification of the crest until November 23, while Stewart had still held his lines in Chattanooga Valley. Breckinridge's engineer officer, Captain John Green, claiming he was acting under instructions, had laid the line out on the natural crest of the ridge rather than on the military crest. This resulted in the line being at the ridge's highest point rather than at the point where the ridge's height could be used to maximum tactical advantage. General Manigault, holding a position to the right of Stewart in the center, noticed this defect, observing that "at many points, an intervening projection or irregularity of the downward slope prevented the fire of the defenders from playing on the enemy, after their reaching the foot of the ridge and when they ascended. The same obstacle protected them until within 15, 20, or 30 yards of our works." The Confederates also lacked proper implements to dig in the rocky ground, and there was a dearth of timber for fortification.[28]

Stewart's troops at the top of the ridge had little benefit of even the inadequate entrenchments Breckinridge had ordered, although there were apparently some fortifications constructed by troops who had previously occupied the position. The 19th Tennessee's front was "partially covered by incomplete and hastily formed breast-works composed of logs and a little dirt" on the right of its position. Elsewhere, the rifle pits the 4th and 5th Tennessee were occupying had been prepared earlier by men of Bushrod Johnson's brigade and were better situated than those on Anderson's and Bate's fronts at the foot of the ridge. The 31st and 33rd Tennessee also had access to some rifle pits at the base of the ridge.[29]

28. Manigault, *A Carolinian Goes to War*, 134–35; Report of Colonel William F. Tucker, December 4, 1863, in *The Confederate Collapse at the Battle of Missionary Ridge*, ed. John Hoffman (Dayton: Morningside, 1985), 71; Horn, *Army of Tennessee*, 300; Cozzens, *Shipwreck of Their Hopes*, 250–54.

29. See reports of Stewart's division, CSA Papers, GHS. For example, Captain Stanford, temporarily commanding the division's artillery battalion, was of the opinion that given enough time to deploy, the artillery could have come into action earlier in the engagement,

As the clear and cold day wore on, Stewart received a flurry of orders to shuffle his division back and forth across the ridge. Before noon, word was sent to dispatch a brigade to a vacant spot in the line to the north of Bragg's headquarters. Stewart sent Adams' Brigade to report to Patton Anderson. Later, about 2:00 P.M., Stewart was told to move the whole division toward the right, and reassume command of Gibson's men. In the course of this latter movement, Breckinridge asked for a brigade and a battery to make a "reconnaissance towards Rossville." Stewart dispatched Holtzclaw with Clayton's Brigade, along with the 1st Arkansas Battery under Lieutenant John W. Rivers.[30]

On the Confederate right, Sherman kicked off the day's events by sending his skirmishers forward to engage Cleburne. Sherman's main assault, which was supposed to be the Union army's primary effort of the day, went forward at about 10:00 or 10:30 that morning, and lasted, with some intermissions, well into the afternoon. While elements of Walker's and Stevenson's divisions were available to reinforce Cleburne, most of the credit for the repulse of Sherman went to the veterans of Cleburne's Division and the ever-vigilant Irishman who commanded them.[31]

Hooker's move across Chattanooga Creek on the Confederate left constituted the second prong of the Federal attack. Hooker had under his command Brigadier General Charles Cruft's division of the Fourth Corps of the Army of the Cumberland, Brigadier General John Geary's division of the Twelfth Corps of the Army of the Potomac, and Brigadier General Peter J. Osterhaus' division of the Seventeenth Corps of the Army of the Tennessee. At 10:00 that morning, Hooker set his column marching for Rossville with Osterhaus in the lead. Arriving at the bridge over Chattanooga Creek, Hooker found that the retreating Confederates had destroyed it, which delayed the crossing of the bulk of his column about three hours. Osterhaus pushed his lead regiment across on a footbridge and ordered it forward to attack the Henderson's infantry and artillery in the gap. Osterhaus' skirmishers traded fire with the Georgians for approximately two hours, from 11:00 A.M. to 1:00 P.M. or later.[32]

"and in position better calculated to inflict damage on the foe." T. J. Stanford Chattanooga report, Item 3184, CSA Papers, GHS.

30. APS Chattanooga report, CSA Papers, GHS.
31. McDonough, *Chattanooga*, 143–59; Horn, *Army of Tennessee*, 299–300.
32. *OR* 31(2):318, 600; Henderson Chattanooga report, CSA Papers, GHS.

Back at Confederate headquarters on the ridge, Bragg and Breckinridge made dispositions to prepare the Confederate center and left for attack. They determined that Breckinridge would go to Rossville in person to deal with the looming crisis there, while Bragg would direct the defense of the center should the Army of the Cumberland move against the rifle pits at the foot of the ridge. It was at this point, sometime in the early afternoon, that Breckinridge detached Holtzclaw from Stewart and moved down the ridge toward Rossville.[33]

As Breckinridge departed, he directed Stewart to form the remainder of his division along the crest of the ridge in one rank, from the left of Bate's division to the area of Breckinridge's own headquarters, a distance that Stewart determined was at least a mile. Stewart later analyzed how the various detachments from the division impaired the strength of his command on the crest of the ridge:

> This left me with three regts of Stovall's Brigade the 40th, 41st and 52d Ga., two of Strahls, the 19th & 24th Tenn. (the 4th 5th 31st & 33d being as already stated, at the foot of the Ridge as skirmishers) Adams' small Brigade under Gibson, and Stanford and Oliver's Batteries . . . with which to hold the space designated a distance I should think of at least a mile. The total number of muskets, from report of Brigade Commanders was just 1774: viz. in Adams' Brigade, 684; in 19th & 24th Tenn, Strahls' Brigade 349, in 40th 41st & 52d Ga, Stovall's Brigade 741—total 1774. The balance of Strahl's Brigade numbering 484 muskets at the beginning of the fight, subsequently came up the ridge, but they had previously been hotly engaged with the enemy, were nearly or quite out of ammunition, and many of them had been killed, wounded or captured.[34]

As Holtzclaw placed the time he reported to Breckinridge at 3:00 P.M., it must have been almost 3:30 before Stewart got his division in line as finally directed, moving by the right flank north along the ridge. Stewart

33. Davis, *Breckinridge*, 388–89; APS Chattanooga report, CSA Papers, GHS.

34. APS Chattanooga report, CSA Papers, GHS. See also APS to W. F. Smith, February 15, 1894, in "Correspondence Relating to Chickamauga and Chattanooga," *Papers of the Military Historical Society of Massachusetts*, vol. 8, *The Mississippi Valley, Tennessee, Georgia, Alabama, 1861–1864* (Boston: Military Historical Society of Massachusetts, 1910), 252–53.

was unable to see any troops on the division's right, or determine what troops were supposed to be there. Stovall was told to place his reduced brigade in line in a single rank and place his left, the division's left, at a suitable point beyond the location of Breckinridge's headquarters. Strahl's two regiments were placed on Stovall's right, also in one rank, with a section of Stanford's artillery between them. Stanford's other section, along with the Eufaula artillery and Dawson's (Oliver's) Georgia battery, were left in the road to the right of Strahl, waiting for Stewart to post them along the line.[35]

While Stewart posted his division, Ulysses S. Grant ordered the four divisions of the Army of the Cumberland holding the Federal center to move forward and take the rifle pits at the foot of the ridge. Grant hoped that an attack against the Confederate center would force Bragg to weaken his lines confronting Sherman. At about 3:40 P.M. six Federal signal guns on Orchard Knob fired to unleash the divisions of Absalom Baird, Thomas J. Wood, Philip H. Sheridan, and Richard W. Johnson against the rifle pits at the base of the ridge. A wave of 23,000 men moved against the imposing heights defended by a veteran army.[36]

Just beforehand, Stewart had given Gibson instructions relative to the disposition of his brigade. Stewart told Gibson to place his men in a single rank, "owing to the great space to be covered by [the] division." Stewart then rode off to the left to oversee the posting of the artillery. Gibson turned to post Major John E. "Ned" Austin's 14th Louisiana Battalion of sharpshooters on the division's extreme right, but some excitement from men on top of the ridge interrupted him. Riding to the crest, Gibson observed the right of Sheridan's division "moving in heavy lines proceeded [sic] by a great cloud of skirmishers, against our position." At this point, Austin's battalion was about 200 yards to the left of Bragg's headquarters. Gibson moved his brigade forward immediately, but in deploying, noticed his two right regiments veering off on a right oblique. Tennessee governor Isham G. Harris, acting under Bragg's instructions as a volunteer aide, deployed these troops into the space immediately before army headquarters,

35. Holtzclaw Chattanooga Report, CSA Papers, GHS; APS Chattanooga Report, CSA Papers, GHS; APS to W. F. Smith, February 15, 1894, "Correspondence Relating to Chickamauga and Chattanooga."

36. Cozzens, *Shipwreck of Their Hopes*, 246–48, 262.

which was uncovered. Gibson's line accordingly ran from a point just a few yards from the Moore Road to the right of Bragg's headquarters to the elevation to the left of the headquarters, where a battery was posted. There was some irony in the petition-signer Gibson covering Bragg's headquarters. The enmity between Gibson and Bragg dated back to a bitter confrontation at Shiloh.[37]

After leaving Gibson, Stewart rode toward the left to start putting what little artillery the division had left into position. Just beyond Gibson's left, Stewart came upon the guns waiting in the road for deployment. At that moment, Stewart became aware of the Federal advance, which was rapidly approaching the ridge and driving in the advanced Confederate skirmishers. As the batteries were on or near the elevation noted by Gibson, Stewart determined their position to be good enough and the emergency imminent enough to order them to unlimber and open fire immediately. Stewart thought that these two and a half batteries covered space between Gibson and Strahl. As events transpired, Gibson's move to the right directed by General Bragg through Governor Harris opened up something of an interval. Being unaware of Gibson's shift, Stewart moved down the line toward the left, after spending some minutes watching his massed cannon fire on the advancing bluecoats.[38]

At the foot of the ridge, the 31st and 33rd Tennessee became the first of Stewart's remaining troops to closely engage the enemy. Like the rest of the division, these regiments marched to the right and then to the left in an effort to deploy properly in front of the division. Both units fell back to the second line of entrenchments at the foot of the ridge after the 31st had burned some cabins in its front on orders from Breckinridge earlier in the afternoon. This activity attracted Union artillery fire that actually assisted in destroying the cabins. The two veteran regiments initially held firm

37. Gibson Chattanooga Report, Item 3179, CSA Papers, GHS; Sword, *Shiloh: Bloody April*, 252–56, 440.

38. APS Chattanooga Report, CSA Papers, GHS; APS to W. F. Smith, February 15, 1894, "Correspondence Relating to Chickamauga and Chattanooga." Cozzens, writing without the benefit of Stewart's report or those of his subordinates, criticizes the deployment of the batteries "in a clump." While Cozzens recognizes that Dawson's Georgia battery did not get deployed until late, he indicates "little attention" was given to the batteries' deployment. In fact, the emergency was upon Stewart before the batteries or his right brigade were fully deployed. See Cozzens, *Shipwreck of Their Hopes*, 253.

against the Federal onslaught. The collapse of the skirmishers on the Tennesseans' right, likely from Brigadier General Jesse J. Finley's Florida brigade, "without firing a gun," necessitated the evacuation of the rifle pits at the base of the ridge.[39]

As the 31st and 33rd fell back to the lines of the 4th and 5th a third of the way up the ridge, Lieutenant Colonel H. C. McNeill of the 33rd shouted to the officer of the 4th commanding that portion of the reserve line, "Why don't you open fire?" The reply was that the 4th would, "as soon as you uncover our front." As soon as their front was clear of friendly troops, the 4th and 5th opened up with "deliberate and well aimed fire." A brave Federal subaltern bearing his regiment's colors was rallying the bluecoats thrown into confusion by the storm of Confederate lead when the 4th's Private W. C. King, a crack shot, brought him down. The 4th and 5th "completely checked" the Federals in their front. The 4th then turned and broke up a group of Yankees to its right.[40]

By the time Stewart rode from the massed batteries on Gibson's left to Strahl's right, the whole line was engaged. Strahl's two regiments on the crest, the 19th and the 24th Tennessee, were "hurried forward to the brow of the hill" to get a better line of fire on the enemy. As the fire got hotter, Stewart got calls for more ammunition. Old Straight sent messengers to his ordnance officer and brother, Captain John Stewart, to bring ammunition forward. Captain Stewart had the ordnance train on the east side of the ridge, to the left and rear of Stovall's line. Riding to the top of the ridge to get a view of the fight, he saw "a column of the enemy coming from towards Lookout directly upon him." He therefore moved the ordnance train northward. There, two of General Stewart's three messengers found the train and brought up ammunition in the nick of time, as the troops in the front line were nearly out.[41]

At Rossville Gap, Hooker's lead division, under Osterhaus, pushed Colonel Henderson's two Georgia regiments and battery out of their position in the gap by flanking them on the ridge on both the right and the left of

39. Chattanooga Reports of F. E. P. Stafford, 31st Tennessee, Item 3182; H. C. McNeill, 33rd Tennessee, Item 3183; L. W. Finlay, 4th Tennessee, Item 3178; O. F. Strahl, Item 3189, all in CSA Papers, GHS.
40. Lindsley, ed., *Military Annals*, 188, 198.
41. APS Chattanooga report, Strahl Chattanooga report, CSA Papers, GHS.

the gap. Henderson resisted this attack and the Federal enfilade fire for about an hour, but eventually was compelled to withdraw from the gap to the east, apparently getting lost in the process. Osterhaus then occupied the gap "with but little resistance" and captured artillery, ammunition, wagons, ambulances, and "large amounts of subsistence stores." By this time, Hooker had completed the bridge across Chattanooga Creek and had all three of his divisions across and in possession of Rossville and the gap. Hooker ordered Osterhaus to move north along the eastern slopes of Missionary Ridge, Cruft to move directly up the crest of the ridge, and Geary to advance north, parallel to the ridge on the west side.[42]

Colonel Holtzclaw came under Breckinridge's direct command at about 3:00 P.M., and marched his brigade down the narrow crest of the ridge toward Rossville after that time. It must have been almost 4:00, possibly even later, before Holtzclaw reached the end of the ridge, expecting to find Henderson's two regiments in possession of the gap. To Holtzclaw's "great surprise," his skirmishers, accompanied by Breckinridge, looked down into the gap and saw the head of a "long column" of Hooker's command. These Federals quickly drove in the Alabama brigade's skirmishers. Two of Holtzclaw's regiments, the 36th and 38th Alabama, were hastily pressed into line. The Federals soon threw the 38th into confusion, so Holtzclaw deployed the 18th Alabama in its place. Holtzclaw stabilized his front line facing Cruft, but experienced great difficulty in containing Osterhaus on the left.[43]

While Cruft drew Holtzclaw's attention, Osterhaus disposed his line to flank the Confederates on the ridge crest and cut off their retreat on the east side. Holtzclaw was unable to resist Osterhaus. The fight went on for thirty to forty-five minutes, the Alabamians fighting stubbornly under the eye of their commanding colonel and their corps commander.

Holtzclaw felt that he could stabilize the line on the left, and called on Breckinridge for some assistance "to check the column that had enveloped my left flank." By this time, Breckinridge had learned that the main line in the center of the ridge had been broken, so he sent back to Holtzclaw to withdraw his brigade. Holtzclaw tried to bring the brigade off in order, covered by his own 18th Alabama. Breckinridge soon sent a "preemptory

42. Henderson Chattanooga report, CSA Papers, GHS; *OR* 31(2):318, 600–601.
43. Holtzclaw Chattanooga report, CSA Papers, GHS; Hoole, *Historical Sketch*, 32–33.

order to withdraw the command and make the best of my way to Chickamauga." By this time, Cruft was in Holtzclaw's front, Geary moving on his
right, and Osterhaus and the troops that had carried the ridge to the north
in his rear. The better part of Holtzclaw's brigade ran for the only small
opening left, retreating "like a mob."[44]

The temporary commander of the division's artillery battalion, the reliable Captain T. J. Stanford, had accompanied Breckinridge, Holtzclaw,
and the Army of Tennessee's chief of artillery, Lieutenant Colonel James
H. Hallonquist, on their initial march to the south of the ridge with Rivers' Arkansas battery. Stanford reached the point where it was "impractica-
ble" to take the battery any farther south and deployed it about 600 yards
to the left of the end of Stovall's line, to impede a flanking movement. Rivers apparently fired on Geary's men for some time until the Federals gained
the ridge between the battery's position and Stovall, necessitating the battery's removal. Osterhaus' men moving north up the east side fired on the
battery as it retreated, causing it to lose one piece.[45]

Back on the main line of Stewart's Division, the 4th and 5th Tennessee,
assisted by the men of the 31st and 33rd, cleared their fronts of Federal
troops. The bluecoats, meeting no resistance at the foot of the ridge on either the right or the left of the Tennesseans, soon began lapping around
them. The Yankees on the Tennesseans' right flank began pouring an enfilade fire into the regiments, necessitating their withdrawal up the ridge.
The four Rebel regiments had not been too badly hurt while in the fortifications below, but took substantial casualties as they made a fighting withdrawal up the ridge. The 5th gamely launched a counterattack on a Federal
force firing on the regiment from a ravine on its right. Those men that
made it up the ridge, in Strahl's words, "rallied at once" and took their
place in the brigade's line to resist the Federal advance.[46]

Stewart passed on down the left to the remnants of Stovall's Brigade,

44. Cozzens, *Shipwreck of Their Hopes*, 314–18; Holtzclaw Chattanooga report, APS
Chattanooga report, CSA Papers, GHS.

45. T. J. Stanford Chattanooga report, APS Chattanooga report, CSA Papers, GHS.

46. Lindsley, ed., *Military Annals*, 189, 198; Strahl Chattanooga report, Lamb Chattanooga report, Finlay Chattanooga report, CSA Papers, GHS; N. C. Howard, "An Incident
of Missionary Ridge," *CV* 21 (June 1913): 283; Riley Diary, CCNMP.

which held the extreme left of infantry on the ridge. The men of Stovall's three remaining regiments, the 40th, 41st, and 52nd Georgia, were holding well. Stovall's regimental commanders noticed that their position on the crest did not put them in an adequate position to fire on the Federals ascending the hill. They moved their men forward several yards to the military crest of the ridge, where the Federals of Carlin's brigade advanced. Lieutenant Colonel R. M. Young of the 40th Georgia ordered his men to move the seventy-five to one hundred yards to a point where they could engage the Federals. Young's thin, single-ranked line advanced at the double quick, "with a yell that seemed to send terror to [the Yankees'] soles [sic]." After repeated volleys from Young's Georgians, the Federals "soon gave way and fled promptly towards Chattanooga perfectly demoralized a large number of them throwing down their arms & two stands of colors was left near our breastworks, but for fear of being cut off by the enemy on our right, we could not get at them." It appears that Carlin also received some artillery fire on his right from either Rivers' Battery or more likely the section of Stanford's Battery on Stovall's front. Once the Federals got to the bottom of the ridge, the Rebel cannon could not be depressed enough to reach them. Stewart passed the word to Stovall and his men to use ammunition sparingly, and, if necessary, resist with the bayonet.[47]

An hour into the battle, the first breach of the Confederate line occurred on the left of Anderson's Division. The collapse of Anderson's Division and the penetration of the Federals on the ridge to the right of his headquarters made Bragg desperately seek troops to repair the break. As Stewart was moving back toward the right from Stovall's line, he encountered one of Bragg's staff officers, who reported a break somewhere on the right and that he had been sent to Stewart for men to repair the breach. Stewart must have given him a look of incredulity, given the fact that his whole line was in a single rank, a brigade and a half were in limbo on the left, and what looked like the whole Yankee army was in his front at the bottom of the ridge. Stewart noted in his report: "As the only men, *if any,* that *could*

47. Chattanooga Reports of R. M. Young, 40th Georgia, William E. Curtis, 41st Georgia, Capt. A. R. Asbury, 52nd Georgia, collectively Item 3188, CSA Papers, GHS; Cozzens, *Shipwreck of Their Hopes*, 310–13; APS Chattanooga report, CSA Papers, GHS; Brown Diary, November 25, 1863, KNBP.

be spared were on the left, an officer of my own staff was sent with him, with directions to take any men not needed there."[48]

To this point, the division had successfully resisted the Federal assault on its main line along the crest of the ridge. Gibson's Louisianans were stoutly holding their line in front of Bragg's headquarters, though their ammunition situation was becoming perilous. Morale was high in this veteran unit, the men actually clapping their hands in anticipation as they saw the Federals about to charge their position. The Yankee first and second lines were driven down the ridge in disorder, and some of Gibson's men ventured out of line and captured a few prisoners. Gibson thought that a charge was called for, but could not do so because his line was in one rank, the men about ten or fifteen feet apart. As their ammunition ran out, Gibson's men threw rocks at the advancing Federals. Eventually, more ammunition came up, and the brigade drove back the third line of advancing bluecoats.

Gibson's right unit, and therefore that of the division, was Austin's battalion of sharpshooters. Austin began to notice the troops on his right, Finley's Floridians, wavering from the Federal onslaught in their front and doubtless from concern over the penetration on their own right. Gibson made what dispositions he could to strengthen his right, ordering a section of artillery in his lines, probably from Cobb's Kentucky battery, to play to the right. He also deployed a company from the 13th-20th Louisiana, the regiment next to Austin, to further extend the brigade's right. Gibson then traveled to the left and conferred with Colonel Daniel Gober, the commander of his left regiment, the 16th-25th Louisiana, who was quite uneasy about his left.[49]

When Stewart placed artillery in the gap between Gibson and Strahl on the eminence to the south of Bragg's headquarters, he was unaware of Bragg's redeployment of Gibson's brigade to cover army headquarters.

48. Cozzens, *Shipwreck of Their Hopes*, 289–99; Sword, *Mountains Touched with Fire*, 282–89; Manigault, *A Carolinian Goes to War*, 139–40; *OR* 31(2):73–74; APS Chattanooga report, CSA Papers, GHS, emphasis in original; see also APS to W. F. Smith, February 15, 1894, "Correspondence Relating to Chickamauga and Chattanooga."

49. Gibson Chattanooga report, CSA Papers, GHS; Chattanooga Reports of J. E. Austin, 14th Louisiana Battalion, Daniel Gober, 16th-25th Louisiana, collectively part of Item 3179, CSA Papers, GHS; Douglas John Cater, *As It Was: Reminiscences of a Soldier of the Third Texas Cavalry and the Nineteenth Louisiana Infantry* (1981; reprint, Austin, Texas: State House Press, 1990), 167.

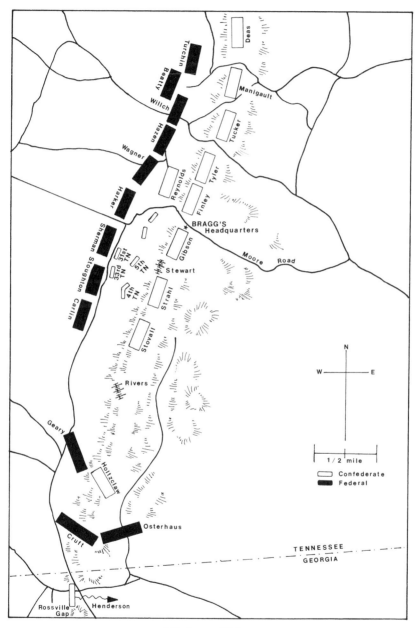

Missionary Ridge
Map by Blake Magner

This placed Gibson's center where Stewart supposed his right to be. Like Colonel Gober, the commander of Strahl's right regiment, Colonel Francis M. Walker of the 19th Tennessee, discerned the gap, which he deemed to extend about a hundred yards. The 19th Tennessee was partially constituted of men from the Chattanooga area, and, ironically, the home of its lieutenant colonel, B. F. Moore, was at the foot of the ridge near Bragg's headquarters. As Stewart passed by on his return to the division's right, Walker informed Stewart of the gap. Stewart, believing that Gibson was where he was supposed to be, and knowing where he posted the artillery, did not believe there was much of a problem to Walker's right. In any event, he told Walker, he did not have any men to fill the interval.

As Stewart rode on to the right, he discovered that the guns in the massed battery posted there had exhausted their ammunition and retired from the ridge. A chance existed to fill the interval, as the 6th Florida Regiment of Finley's Brigade, which had retreated up the ridge from the trenches at its foot, was in position for members of Stewart's staff to rally it and place it into the gap. Despite the best efforts of Stewart and his staff, the Floridians were too shaken to put up much resistance, and the makeshift line gave way to a brigade of Sheridan's division. A captain of the 16th-25th Louisiana found Stewart on the left of his position and informed the general of the Florida unit's collapse. Stewart could not give the Louisianans any assistance, but admonished the captain to tell Colonel Gober to "hold his position at all hazards—even with the bayonet."[50]

While Stewart was rallying men in the area of the interval, "entreating them to return" to the line of battle, someone called his attention to the top of the ridge to his left, where he saw several Federal flags flying and his own line beginning to retire. The Federals had penetrated the interval between Gibson and Strahl. Gibson watched the Federals occupy the ridge on his right when a section of Cobb's Kentucky battery on his front limbered up and began to move off. Gibson rallied the 13th-20th Louisiana, which was unsettled by this withdrawal, when he received word that the Federals on his right were moving down the ridge and firing on his position. As if this were not bad enough, one of his men tapped him on his

50. Chattanooga Report of F. M. Walker, 19th Tennessee, Item 3190, APS Chattanooga report, Gober Chattanooga report, CSA Papers, GHS; Worsham, *Old Nineteenth Tennessee*, 100–101.

shoulder and pointed out a Federal line of battle advancing from his left. Perceiving that his position was hopeless, Gibson ordered a retreat off the ridge.[51]

The Federal penetration between Gibson and the 19th Tennessee also spelled the doom of Strahl's position on the ridge. The Federals moved down the ridge on Walker's Tennesseans, subjecting them to a "terrible and destructive enfilade fire." Strahl found it necessary to withdraw his men to avoid "being entirely cut off from the army and surrounded by the enemy." During Strahl's withdrawal, Stewart fell in with his old brigade, which formed in line of battle on the smaller ridge about three hundred yards to the east, and, replenishing its ammunition, engaged the advancing Federals. In re-forming the line, Stewart seized the colors of the 5th Tennessee and exhorted the regiment to rally and protect the army's rear. The 5th did an about-face and charged the pursuing bluecoats, Stewart leading them for a short distance. Strahl held this ridge for a period of time until being flanked, and then conducted a fighting retreat to the Chickamauga. Tragically, Lieutenant Colonel Moore of the 19th received a mortal wound within a few hundred yards of his home.[52]

Assured that Strahl and his old brigade were withdrawing in good order, Stewart tried to go northward and ascertain the status of Gibson's brigade. Stewart was fired on by Federal troops descending Missionary Ridge and was unable to locate Gibson, some of whose regiments were making a fighting withdrawal to the Chickamauga. Stewart then turned southward to find Stovall and Holtzclaw. Stovall's regiments had successfully resisted the Federals in their front, and were therefore surprised to see Strahl give way. Although Stovall tried to extend his right, he found the Federals on the ridge in force and eventually withdrew from the ridge without any serious loss. In making good his escape from the Federal envelopment that gobbled up over half his brigade, Holzclaw's horse had

51. APS Chattanooga report, Gibson Chattanooga report, CSA Papers, GHS. Austin's battalion assisted the 5th Company of the New Orleans Washington Artillery (Slocomb's Battery) in resisting the Federal breakthrough toward the more northerly of the bridges across the Chickamauga. Nathaniel C. Hughes, Jr., *The Pride of the Confederate Artillery: The Washington Artillery in the Army of Tennessee* (Baton Rouge: Louisiana State University Press, 1997), 164–68.

52. Strahl Chattanooga report, APS Chattanooga report, CSA Papers, GHS; Worsham, *Old Nineteenth Tennessee*, 100–101; Lindsley, ed., *Military Annals*, 198–99.

been shot, causing him to career down the side of the ridge and injure his leg. He directed the next-senior colonel, L. T. Woodruff of the 36th Alabama, to move the brigade to the crossing of Chickamauga Creek at Bird's Mill.[53]

As Stewart attempted to locate his two left brigades, he encountered Breckinridge, who was shaken by his ordeal on the left. The corps commander informed him that Hooker had passed Rossville Gap and turned his flank, that Holtzclaw's brigade had been cut to pieces and captured, and that he had lost his son, Cabell, who, unknown to him at that time, had been captured. Breckinridge ordered Stewart to proceed to the crossing of the Chickamauga at Bird's Mill and assume command. Stewart returned for Strahl's Brigade, and found that it had already moved away. He therefore moved in the gathering darkness to the pontoon bridge at the crossing and found a number of disorganized brigades and a crowd of stragglers from several different commands. Gibson and his regrouped brigade were posted to defend the approaches to the crossing, and Strahl and his Tennesseans passed across the bridge and formed a line to defend the crossing itself. Stewart dispersed the crowd of stragglers, reorganized the milling troops into ranks, and passed the wagons and artillery across the bridge. Bate, who like Strahl had conducted a fighting retreat from Missionary Ridge, also moved his troops across the bridge, under Bragg's orders to report to the army commander at Chickamauga Station.[54]

After all other troops had crossed, Stewart ordered the rest of his command across the pontoon bridge and on to Chickamauga Station. Strahl covered the division's rear, and at about 2:00 A.M. on the morning of November 26, destroyed the bridge over Chickamauga Creek. Soon thereafter, a "considerable force" of the enemy arrived on the other side of the creek, but did not attempt a crossing in the face of Strahl's battle line. Strahl remained in line at the crossing until about 10:00 A.M., when Breckinridge ordered him to take the brigade on to Chickamauga Station.

53. APS Chattanooga report, Gibson Chattanooga report, Young Chattanooga report, Holtzclaw Chattanooga report, CSA Papers, GHS.

54. APS to W. F. Smith, February 15, 1894, "Correspondence Relating to Chickamauga and Chattanooga," 252–53; Cozzens, *Shipwreck of Their Hopes*, 341; APS Chattanooga report, CSA Papers, GHS; Pollard, *Lee and His Lieutenants*, 714; Gibson Chattanooga report, Strahl Chattanooga report, CSA Papers, GHS; *OR* 31(2):742–43.

Strahl remained separated from the division for the rest of November 26 as part of the army's rear guard, repulsing a pursuing column of Federals during the day. The brigade halted at Ringgold, Georgia, for some well-deserved rest that night, but was roused between 4:00 and 5:00 A.M. on the morning of November 27, when Hooker's pursuing column pressed upon Ringgold. Strahl put his men in line of battle, but was soon relieved by Cleburne's Division. The brigade marched through Ringgold Gap, but halted around Tunnel Hill under orders from Bragg to provide support for Cleburne. Cleburne and his division fought an epic battle at Ringgold Gap that morning, delaying Hooker long enough for the Army of Tennessee to withdraw to Dalton, Georgia. There, Strahl rejoined the division.[55]

The casualty figures for Missionary Ridge set forth in Stewart's battle report dated December 14, 1863, reflected the separate ordeals of each of his four brigades. Stovall's Brigade, including the two regiments at Rossville, suffered only 69 killed, wounded, or missing from the 1,411 engaged. Gibson's small brigade, numbering 764, lost 363, having been flanked on both its right and left. Strahl's Brigade, numbering 947, lost 259, the greater proportion doubtless occurring when the 4th-5th and 31st-33d had to retreat up the side of the ridge under fire from the Federals at the bottom. Holtzclaw's Brigade, 1,531 strong, was hit in its front, rear, and on both flanks. The Alabamians' loss totaled 810, more than the rest of the division combined. Only 10 out of the 326 officers and men in the division's artillery battalion were lost, and, incredibly, only two guns, one from the Eufaula Battery and one from Rivers' Battery. All told, casualties at Missionary Ridge numbered over one-third of the division's strength.[56]

55. APS Chattanooga report, Strahl Chattanooga report, CSA Papers, GHS. For a good description of Cleburne's fight at Ringgold Gap, see Cozzens, *Shipwreck of Their Hopes*, 370–84.

56. APS Chattanooga report, CSA Papers, GHS. The numbers set forth in Stewart's Chattanooga report do not match up with the comparative abstract from the returns of the army for October 31 and December 10, 1863, published in *OR* 31(2):656–57. The numbers from the *Official Records* seem untrustworthy, as the division is indicated to have only a difference of 161 enlisted men and a *gain* in officer strength. Although doubtless several men of the division deemed missing in Stewart's report eventually returned, the disaster that befell Holtzclaw's Brigade alone would seem to belie the numbers from the *Official Records*.

Bragg's report of the disaster, prepared on November 30, did not acknowledge that his amateurish disposition of his veteran army was largely to blame for its rout. Bragg blamed the troops on the left for allowing the Federal penetration. Having been present all along his line, Stewart could not fault his men or their courage for the defeat, expressing in his report his admiration for their "heroism and unflinching firmness." While the Federals did enjoy an overall numerical advantage of over two to one, the disparity in numbers in the area of the breakthrough was somewhat less. Yet the double line at the foot and crest of the ridge in Bate's and Anderson's sectors caused great confusion. Bragg reported that "the position was one that ought to have been held by a line of skirmishers," which is exactly what Stewart had in line due to the "undue concentration" on the army's right, something he wrote of in his own history of the army, perhaps with a touch of bitterness.[57]

The breakthrough in the center on Anderson's and later Bate's front seems to defy logic, except for the incomprehensible disposition of the troops of those two divisions. There was a simple reason, Stewart explained, why his division was unable to hold its line: "My misfortune was that my line was too long and weak, and time was not afforded me to form it properly before the attack was made. The change of the . . . right of Gibson's Brigade, during my absence from it, and without my knowledge, proved fatal to my whole line, which had however been flanked on its extreme right and left. The enemy, in strong force, having gained our left and rear, it would seem to be providential that the entire division was not captured."[58] Other causes for the retreat of Stewart's Division included the open flank to the left, which resulted in the detachment of a brigade and a half to Rossville Gap, the further fragmentation of the division by sending detachments to the bottom of the ridge, and the unarticulated but likely unfamiliarity of Stewart with at least two of his four brigades caused by the November 12 reorganization.[59]

---

57. *OR* 31(2):664–66; APS Chattanooga report, CSA Papers, GHS; Lindsley, ed., *Military Annals*, 83. For numbers engaged, see Horn, *Army of Tennessee*, 301. Stewart no doubt availed himself of the opportunity to write history as commissioner of the Chickamauga-Chattanooga National Military Park. Descriptions of the battle on battlefield markers emphasize the attenuated line on the Confederate left.

58. APS Chattanooga report, CSA Papers, GHS.

59. An example of this last factor was Gibson's failure to advise Stewart of the move to

Given these disadvantages, it is to the division's credit that it held as long as it did. Stewart was not alone in recognizing that he was lucky that the whole division was not captured, given the Federal breakthroughs on both flanks. Stewart's retreat in the face of Johnson's and Sheridan's attacks no doubt saved his force from the much more devastating defeat that would have occurred had Osterhaus' advance up the east side of the ridge gotten into the rear of the division's main line on the crest. William Brown of Stanford's Battery felt that if his unit had held its position a half hour longer, the Federals "would have had us between two fires." A volunteer member of Breckinridge's staff wrote just over a week after the battle that *"it was fortunate our line gave way where it did or else our left if not the whole Army would have been cut off by Hooker and his corps."* The disproportionate losses in Holtzclaw's Brigade are an indication of that possibility.[60]

Ultimately, the defeat at Missionary Ridge was the result of the cancer in the Army of Tennessee's high command that had been growing for over a year. Notwithstanding his fixing the blame for the disaster on the men of the army, Bragg for the first time realized that his ability to continue commanding the army was compromised. He submitted an offer of resignation that President Davis quickly accepted.[61] After a tenure of about a year and a half, Braxton Bragg's command of, but not influence on, the army came to an end. In his history of the army, Stewart summed up the state of its morale at this critical juncture:

> The Army of Tennessee had retreated across the Cumberland Mountains, had fought and gained the great battle of Chickamauga, and, as at Shiloh and Murfreesboro, lost the fruits of victory, and suffered the disaster of Missionary Ridge. It was not disheartened. It knew there were brave men in vastly superior numbers opposed to it,

---

the right ordered by Bragg, although more properly Bragg should have advised Stewart that he had overridden Stewart's disposition of one of his brigades. Richard McMurry theorizes, with convincing logic, that the November 12 reorganization contributed to the army's defeat by separating the troops from their familiar leaders. Richard M. McMurry, *Two Great Rebel Armies* (Chapel Hill: University of North Carolina Press, 1989), 136.

60. Brown Diary, November 25, 1863, KNBP; Henry C. Day to Charles Day, December 5, 1863, in Charles A. Earp, ed., "A Confederate Aide-de-Camp's Letters from the Chattanooga Area, 1863," *Journal of East Tennessee History* 67 (1995): 106, 118 (emphasis in original).

61. Hallock, *Bragg*, 149.

but had confidence in itself and in its ability to cope with its adversaries, provided the odds were not *too* great and it were skillfully handled.[62]

Stewart still had hope in a cause that even then did not seem lost. Old Straight closed his report of the battle with praise to God for sparing the army and its Cause from "utter ruin," and expressed the hope that God "may yet have in store for us a triumph that will efface the recollection of this single disaster and prove the Yorktown of this revolution."[63]

62. Lindsley, ed., *Military Annals*, 84.
63. APS Chattanooga report, CSA Papers, GHS.

— 10 —

A Defensive Campaign

From Dalton to the Chattahoochee

In a sense, Joseph E. Johnston was Braxton Bragg's exact opposite. During Bragg's tenure as commanding general of the Army of Tennessee, he largely retained the confidence of Jefferson Davis, but lost the confidence of many of his officers and men. Jefferson Davis, on the other hand, reluctantly deemed Johnston the best of the poor choices available to replace Bragg, and Davis' confidence level in Johnston declined from that point. Unlike Bragg, Johnston gained the love and the trust of many of the army's officers and enlisted men, which in large part he never lost, even when the army had retreated to the very gates of Atlanta. Private Sam Watkins of the 1st Tennessee wrote that Johnston "was loved, respected, admired; yea, almost worshipped by his troops." Brigadier General Arthur M. Manigault observed that the ordinary soldiers had great confidence in Johnston, a feeling he obviously shared. And General Alexander Peter Stewart expressed his opinion when he wrote to Johnston after the war: "*You* were the only commander of that army whom *men* and *officers* were disposed to trust and confide in without reserve."[1]

---

1. Sam R. Watkins, *Co. Aytch* (1900; reprint, New York: Collier, 1962) 126; Manigault, *A Carolinian Goes to War*, 199–200; APS to J. E. Johnston, February 11, 1868, quoted in Lindsley, ed., *Military Annals*, 96; Joseph E. Johnston, *Narrative of Military Operations Directed During the Late War Between the States* (New York: D. Appleton, 1874), 367–68. These opinions have been challenged by subsequent scholarship. See Richard M. McMurry,

When Johnston received command of the Army of Tennessee in December, 1863, he was the Confederacy's third-ranking full general, behind Adjutant General Samuel Cooper and Robert E. Lee (Albert Sidney Johnston having been killed at Shiloh). This order of rank either caused a rift between Johnston and Davis, or exacerbated a previously existing one, because Johnston felt that Confederate law required that *he* be ranked the highest, since he had been the senior brigadier in the prewar United States Army—and Johnston had no qualms about telling Davis this. Their relations deteriorated in the spring of 1862 as Johnston, with the force soon to bear the name of the Army of Northern Virginia, retreated before George McClellan's Army of the Potomac to the very gates of Richmond without giving a pitched battle. Finally, Johnston struck the Federals at Seven Pines, where he was wounded and put out of action for several months. After his recovery, he was assigned a theater command over Bragg in Middle Tennessee and John Pemberton in Mississippi. Whether justly or not, Davis came to blame Johnston for his inability to relieve Pemberton and the subsequent fall of Vicksburg.[2]

To Davis, Johnston was the best of several disagreeable alternatives. Hardee, who held the interim command after Bragg's departure as the army's most senior corps commander and only lieutenant general, was Davis' initial choice. Hardee declined, believing Johnston was the better man for the assignment. Davis next considered the possibility of sending Robert E. Lee to the Army of Tennessee. That solution would have left the president with the problem of who should replace Lee in the vital front in front of Richmond. Lee at first urged Davis to appoint Beauregard, but to Davis, still angry over Beauregard's conduct as commander of the army in the spring of 1862, that choice was out of the question. Lee then recommended Johnston, which was soon seconded by Davis' old friend Polk, Johnston's second-in-command in Mississippi. With the greatest of reluctance, Davis gave Johnston the appointment.[3]

"Confederate Morale in the Atlanta Campaign of 1864," *Georgia Historical Quarterly* 54 (summer 1970): 226, 232–35; Connelly, *Autumn of Glory*, 406–15.

2. Woodworth, *Jefferson Davis and His Generals*, 258–59; Warner, *Generals in Gray*, 161–62; Richard M. McMurry, "'The *Enemy* at Richmond': Joseph E. Johnston and the Confederate Government," *Civil War History* 27 (March 1981): 5–16.

3. Woodworth, *Jefferson Davis and His Generals*, 256–59. For Hardee's motives, see Hughes, *Hardee*, 183–85.

When Johnston joined the army, he found it encamped around Dalton, where Bragg's retreat from Missionary Ridge had ended. Johnston did not think Dalton had any defensive advantages, and considered a retreat farther south to the Oostanaula River. He held off, however: a further retreat would, he determined, damage the fragile morale of the soldiers and the spirit of the people. Johnston was fortunate that the Federals had shown no sign of pursuit since Cleburne had dealt Hooker his sharp repulse at Ringgold Gap. Accordingly, the Rebel army spent the winter housed in rough cabins laid out in brigade-sized camps, while Stewart lodged in a "snug little house."[4]

Johnston had not been in Dalton a week when the factionalism in the officer corps that remained even after Bragg's departure erupted again. In the wake of his successful defense of the northern end of Missionary Ridge and Ringgold Gap, Patrick Cleburne turned his attention to the fundamental disadvantages the Confederacy faced as 1863 turned to 1864. As slavery gave the Federals a cause to fight for and a means to increase their strength, Cleburne felt that it had gone from being a Confederate strength to "one of our chief sources of weakness."[5] His solution was simple: arm the slaves and give them their freedom in return for their military service. This would eliminate the Confederacy's manpower problems as well as deprive the Federals of the moral high ground. Because the idea was so new and sensitive, Cleburne determined to present it to the army's corps and division commanders, which he did at a meeting at Johnston's headquarters in Dalton on January 2, 1864.[6]

Present at the meeting were Johnston, Hardee, Stewart, W. H. T. Walker, Carter Stevenson, Hindman, Bate, and Cleburne. The only infantry division commander absent was Cheatham, perhaps by design. Cleburne presented his proposal, but it met with little support. Only his close

---

4. Horn, *Army of Tennessee*, 311; Manigault, *A Carolinian Goes to War*, 159; diary entry, March 15, 1864, Catherine Barnes Whitehead Rowland Diary, GA. For an example of the low morale in Stewart's Division, see Oliver W. Strickland to "Mother," December 18, 1863, Oliver W. Strickland Papers, DU.

5. Buck, *Cleburne and His Command*, 192. Cleburne appears to have been influenced by his friend, Hindman, in making the proposal. See Neal and Kremm, *The Lion of the South*, 183–87.

6. Buck, *Cleburne and His Command*, 187–200.

friend Hindman spoke in favor, and one of Cleburne's staff officers actually read a paper against it. Among the assembled generals, Bate, Anderson, and, most vociferously, Walker spoke against it. Eventually, Cleburne withdrew his paper, but not before Walker announced he was going to submit it along with a report to President Davis. Within the week, Walker asked Cleburne for a copy of the paper, which the Irishman gladly provided. Walker also asked the assembled generals to provide a response to Cleburne's proposal, which he stated he would submit to Davis along with Cleburne's paper so as not to misrepresent each man's response.[7]

Walker wrote Stewart for his views on January 9, and Stewart replied that very day, expressing his disapproval of Cleburne's proposal as defeatist, and stating that the contradictory proposition of slaves fighting for the independence of the South was "at war with my social, moral and political principles." Anderson and Bate replied in a similar vein, although Stevenson was willing to consider using the slaves in some unarmed capacity. Hardee did not respond to the letter, Cheatham refused to do so, and Hindman replied to the effect that he did not recognize Walker's right to question him.[8]

Davis moved quickly to suppress the matter, ordering Johnston, and, through him, the officers involved, to no longer discuss Cleburne's proposal and to stifle the controversy surrounding it. Both Walker and Cleburne were lauded for patriotic motives, but the government felt that the country was not ready for such a revolutionary proposal.[9]

There is not enough extant primary source material to fully set forth Stewart's racial views. While neither he nor his family owned slaves, it would be unrealistic to expect that he did not view blacks as an inferior race. Like many other southerners, Stewart always spoke of the slavery

7. Ridley, *Battles and Sketches*, 291; Russell K. Brown, *To the Manner Born: The Life of General William H. T. Walker* (Athens: University of Georgia Press, 1994), 195–201; Buck, *Cleburne and His Command*, 187–200; W. H. T. Walker to APS, January 9, 1864, Item 3173, CSA Papers, GHS. Although on friendly terms with Walker, St. John Liddell termed the Georgian a "crackbrained fire-eater." Liddell, *Liddell's Record*, 137.

8. APS to W. H. T. Walker, January 9, 1864, Item 3174, CSA Papers, GHS; Brown, *To the Manner Born*, 200–203.

9. Ridley, *Battles and Sketches*, 290, 292–94; Buck, *Cleburne and His Command*, 188–91. Before his death, Cleburne was vindicated by the Confederate Congress's having entertained a similar proposal.

issue in terms of the recognition of constitutional property rights rather than the moral aspect of involuntary servitude. His reply to Walker clearly states that the proposal offended not only his political (constitutional) principles, but his social and moral principles as well. It is certainly reasonable to conclude that Stewart's view of blacks largely comported with the beliefs of his southern contemporaries.[10]

Two significant organizational changes affected Stewart and his men during the winter of 1863–64. The first was the appointment of Lieutenant General John Bell Hood to command the corps of which Stewart and his division was a part. Hood was a graduate of West Point who had earned an enviable combat record in the Army of Northern Virginia. Johnston was delighted to have Hood as a corps commander. Stewart's feelings about the appointment are not recorded. Certainly, Stewart was older than Hood by a decade, had been with the Army of Tennessee from its earliest antecedents at Columbus, and himself had a good combat history. His only chance to observe Hood in action would have been at Chickamauga, and to the degree Stewart could possibly have watched, Hood must have made a favorable impression. The factionalism in the army was such that bringing in an outsider with Hood's reputation as a fighter, someone who had the confidence of both Johnston and the government, must have appeared to make sense. Yet Hood's actual experience above brigade command was more limited than it appeared, and his record as an administrator was weak. Hood assumed command of the corps on the first of February, 1864. Only time would tell whether he would succeed at his new level of command.[11]

The second of the organizational changes affecting Stewart and his men was Johnston's move to reverse the worst of Bragg's November reorganization and reconstitute Cheatham's Tennessee division. The change once

---

10. In 1906, Stewart wrote to his nephew, Wharton S. Jones, of the approaching "end of the age," in which a time of great trouble would afflict the country and the whole world, "in which the Negro is to play a conspicuous part, here at least." APS to W. S. Jones, October 23, 1906, quoted in Wingfield, "Old Straight," 120.

11. Craig L. Symonds, *Joseph E. Johnston: A Civil War Biography* (New York: W. W. Norton, 1992), 251; Richard W. McMurry, *John Bell Hood and the War for Southern Independence* (Lexington: University Press of Kentucky, 1982), 74–78, 81–84, 87–88; Woodworth, *Jefferson Davis and His Generals*, 261, 266–71; McMurry, *Hood*, 93.

again separated Stewart from his old brigade when Strahl and his Tennessee regiments rejoined Cheatham. Brigadier General John C. Moore's Alabama brigade, made up of the 37th, 40th, and 42nd Alabama, soldiers who were exchanged Vicksburg prisoners that had joined the army on Missionary Ridge, was transferred to Stewart to replace his old brigade. A member of the 40th Alabama sourly noted in his diary that the cabins his regiment received from Strahl's men were not nearly as good as those they had left. But on the whole, and especially as far as the Tennesseans were concerned, the reorganization was a big morale boost.[12]

Morale in the army continued to rise, as some of the men received furloughs, the food got better, necessities such as shoes were provided, and the Federals in Chattanooga and its environs had yet to advance. The morale of Strahl's Brigade had risen so quickly that in January its men enlisted *en masse* for the war. The inspiring example of Strahl's Brigade did not sweep through Stewart's entire division, though. In Clayton's Brigade, few were willing to reenlist without first getting a chance to go home. As various exhortations and inducements failed to achieve the desired result, Clayton resorted to more devious means. On a stated day and hour, the brigade was paraded, and bad whiskey passed around. When many were half-drunk, it was announced that the colors would be presented and those who formed on them would be reenlisted. Clayton shouted "March!" echoed by the other officers of the brigade, and most of the men moved to the colors. Those few who did not were shamed into doing so. A veteran remembered: "We then marched back into our quarters, where the men whooped and yelled until the bad whiskey died out." Stewart's reaction to this unheroic episode is unrecorded.[13]

*   *   *

12. General Order No. 10, January 17, 1864, Army of Tennessee, General Orders and Circulars, 1863–1865, J. E. Johnston to Samuel Cooper, January 31, 1864, Army of Tennessee, Telegrams Sent, 1864, RG 109, NA; *OR* 38(3):642; Sifakis, *Compendium: Alabama*, 109–10, 112–13; Elbert D. Willett, *History of Company B (Originally Pickens Planters), 40th Alabama Regiment, Confederate States Army, 1862 to 1865* (Northport, Ala.: Colonial Press, 1963), 60–61.

13. Jones, *History of the 18th Alabama*, 13. It should be noted that in light of the Confederate Conscription Act, converting all enlistment periods to the duration of the war, these "reenlistments" were at best symbolic. See Bell I. Wiley, *The Life of Johnny Reb: The Common Soldier of the Confederacy* (1943; reprint, Baton Rouge: Louisiana State University Press, 1997), 132.

The steep ramparts of Rocky Face Ridge, covered, at least on the northwest, the Confederate position at Dalton. As they had since the end of the retreat from Missionary Ridge, Stewart and his division occupied Mill Creek Gap, which divided Rocky Face Ridge northwest of Dalton. On February 24–26, Union general George Thomas launched a series of probing attacks against Rocky Face, which Stewart's men helped repulse "handsomely." In the view of one of Stewart's Georgians, the limited nature of the Federal attack saved the Yankees "from a terrible whipping." Thomas' attacks made Johnston frantically call for the return of Hardee and three of his four divisions, on their way to resist a raid on Meridian, Mississippi. Thomas gained some intelligence about the Confederate defenses that would be utilized in the coming spring.[14]

During the winter interlude, Stewart thought an offensive was appropriate, but he deemed it necessary that the army be strengthened for that purpose. On March 19, he wrote Bragg a letter urging augmentation of the army by detachments of troops from other, less vital areas, reminding Bragg that the detachment of Stevenson to Mississippi in late 1862 and the failure to reinforce the army at that time made all the difference in the army's ability to hold Middle Tennessee. Relying upon a rumor that Sherman might be heading up the Red River in Louisiana, Stewart pointed out the opportunity afforded by the proposed concentration. Should Sherman rejoin Thomas, Stewart continued, "could there be a greater *necessity* for concentration here?" Old Straight invoked Bragg's link to the army as a means to urge his point of view: "We all flatter ourselves that through your instrumentality our army will be increased until it can take the initiative in the campaign and become aggressive—and that all our future operations will be on the offensive."[15]

14. Connelly, *Autumn of Glory*, 294–95; Albert Castel, *Decision in the West: The Atlanta Campaign of 1864* (Lawrence: University Press of Kansas, 1992), 54–55; APS to B. Bragg, March 19, 1864, Palmer Collection of Bragg Papers, Western Reserve; C. A. Rowland to K. B. Rowland, February 28, 1864, Charles A. Rowland Diary and Letters, GA.

15. APS to B. Bragg, March 19, 1864, Palmer Collection of Bragg Papers, Western Reserve. It has been suggested that Stewart violated military protocol by writing directly to Bragg. Castel, *Decision in the West*, 578 n. 17, Richard M. McMurry, "The Atlanta Campaign: December 23, 1863, to July 18, 1864" (Ph.D. diss., Emory University, 1967), 57. When read in its entirety, the letter makes clear that Stewart, like Johnston, thought reinforcements were needed before any offensive action could be taken. See Connelly, *Autumn of Glory*, 295–305, concerning Confederate offensive thought at this time.

Stewart's letter to Bragg makes clear that Stewart looked upon Bragg as a friend, and possibly a patron, to the extent that one historian terms "fulsome." Certainly, Stewart went out of his way to compliment Bragg on his new position at the seat of government, and also recalled what were two of the great might-have-beens of Bragg's career, Murfreesboro and McLemore's Cove. While a jaundiced view might consider the letter sheer ingratiation for the purpose of future promotion, on its face the letter does not seek favors for Stewart but for the Army of Tennessee as a whole, something consistent with what Johnston also sought. Furthermore, Hood's promotion left no vacant corps command in the army, Stewart's next logical step for promotion. While he had normal ambitions, Stewart was not known as a sycophant, and there is no reason to think he was so motivated in this instance.[16]

Johnston certainly wanted to consider Stewart's views as they related to command issues in his own division. Johnston one day came to Stewart's headquarters to inquire of Old Straight whom he wished promoted to command Moore's Alabamians—Confederate authorities in Richmond had asked Johnston for a recommendation. In Stewart's absence, a member of his staff, Colonel J. C. Thompson, confirmed Johnston's belief that Stewart's preference would be Colonel James T. Holtzclaw, who had commanded Clayton's Alabamians during their unequal struggle on Missionary Ridge. Johnston made the request for Holtzclaw, but a stranger to the Army of Tennessee, Colonel Alpheus Baker, received the appointment. Baker was known to Stewart, as he had commanded the 1st Alabama, Tennessee, and Mississippi Regiment at New Madrid and Island No. 10. Baker had been captured at Island No. 10 and was seriously wounded in the Vicksburg campaign. Notwithstanding Stewart's familiarity with Baker, he doubtless would have preferred Holtzclaw. This incident made it ominously clear to Johnston that the Richmond authorities cared little for his opinion.[17]

16. APS to Bragg, March 19, 1864, Palmer Collection of Bragg Papers, Western Reserve; Castel, *Decision in the West*, 338; as to lack of promotion seeking, see Pollard, *Lee and His Lieutenants*, 712–13.

17. Symonds, *Johnston*, 253; J. E. Johnston to Samuel Cooper, February 16, 1864, Army of Tennessee, Telegrams Sent, 1864, RG 109, NA; W. W. Mackall to wife, March 18, 1864, Mackall Papers, SHC; McMurry, "The *Enemy* at Richmond," 21–22; Warner, *Generals in Gray*, 14.

The Army of Tennessee stayed in Dalton through the early spring of 1864 while Sherman, the new Federal commander in the West, assembled an army group to advance against Johnston. Although Stewart hoped for an offensive, he recognized that the army needed reinforcements to move forward. Since none were forthcoming, he later wrote that "a defensive campaign was the only one possible in view of the overwhelming odds opposed to [Johnston]."[18]

As winter changed to spring, the Army of Tennessee spent its time drilling and reequipping. Hood's Corps engaged in a "drill and sham battle" on March 16, and in the aftermath of the freakish snowfall of March 22, Stewart's Division triumphed over Bate's in a snowball "battle." Many soldiers experienced a religious reawakening during that time, and the three churches in the camps were filled nightly. General William N. Pendleton, an Episcopalian priest and the Army of Northern Virginia's chief of artillery, visited the western army during this time on an artillery inspection. At one service, Pendleton preached and Stewart, as an elder in the Cumberland Presbyterian Church, assisted in the administration of the Lord's Supper. Stewart must have reflected on the pathetic scene that occurred in one of his old regiments, the 4th Tennessee, when several men were killed at prayer by a tree falling on them.[19]

Forms of discipline harsher than religion were sometimes necessary. Ridley recounted the bitter scene of the planned execution of fifteen deserters from the army, two from Stewart's Division. Early on the morning of the execution, a detail from the division's provost guard marched to headquarters and left their muskets. After they left, staff officers loaded the pieces, half with blank charges and half with buck and ball. Then, the guns were mixed so that no one knew which ones had live ammunition. One of the condemned men was a member of Colonel Henderson's 42nd Georgia, and the soldier's distraught father came to Stewart seeking a reprieve on the grounds that the man was an easily influenced half-wit. Stewart, Hen-

18. Symonds, *Johnston*, 267; Lindsley, ed., *Military Annals*, 85–86.

19. J. H. Curry, "A History of Company B, 40th Alabama Infantry, C.S.A., from the Diary of J. H. Curry," *Alabama Historical Quarterly* 17 (1955): 193; *Atlanta Southern Confederacy*, March 19, 1864; Brown Diary, March 22, 1864, KNBP; C. B. W. Rowland Diary, March 22, 1864, GA; Prim, "Born Again in the Trenches," 258; Losson, *Tennessee's Forgotten Warriors*, 135–37.

derson, and the father went to Johnston's headquarters and secured the reprieve, just in time. As it turned out, the "half-wit" bided his time and deserted at a later date.[20]

During these months, Catherine B. Rowland, a young relation of Stovall's who was visiting her soldier husband, encountered Stewart on several occasions. The general and his brother, Captain Stewart, visited one evening after church services, and Mrs. Rowland described Old Straight as "a very charming man in his manners, he is a perfect gentleman, & very entertaining & social, & one of the most modest and unassuming gentlemen I ever saw."[21]

Harriet Stewart was by this time in Savannah with her two youngest sons, joining her mother and some other relatives. Harriet's mother, Mrs. Alice Spalding Chase, died in Savannah on January 22, 1864. The Stewarts' second son, Alphonso, remained in school in Middle Tennessee even after the army withdrew from Murfreesboro. No doubt the separation from her husband and two sons was enough cause for concern, but, as a refugee, Harriet also worried about her home, now far behind the lines. A letter of hers dated April 26, 1864, to Stewart's brother in Auburn, Alabama, reported that "the general" had recently written her about a man who had been through Lebanon in the middle of March and reported all but two houses burned. Harriet feared the report was true because the town was a "negro depot." Her greatest regret was the loss of her pictures, including the best one of her mother.[22]

On May 1, 1864, the Army of Tennessee numbered about 55,000 "present for duty." Sherman's three armies—Thomas' Army of the Cumberland, 60,733 strong, Major General James B. McPherson's Army of the Tennessee, 24,465, and Major General John M. Schofield's Army of the Ohio, 13,559—totaled 98,797 men and 254 guns. Johnston was of course at a distinct disadvantage in numbers. Yet Stewart observed it was an army high in morale, its absentees returned, and with all its reasonable wants

20. Ridley, *Battles and Sketches*, 282–86.

21. C. B. W. Rowland Diary, April 10, 1864, GA; see also the C. B. W. Rowland Diary entries of March 17, 30, April 13, 17, 1864.

22. APS to Jefferson Davis, December 11, 1864, Confederate Citizens or Business Firms File, RG 109, NA; Wingfield, *Stewart*, 107. Fortunately, the Stewart home had been spared.

supplied. Old Straight later wrote: "Probably no army was ever in better condition to begin a campaign than that which took the field under Johnston early in May, 1864." Stewart had done his part, drilling and reviewing his division on a regular basis.[23]

Sherman termed the Confederate position on Rocky Face as a "terrible door of death." Stewart and his division were waiting for the Yankees on the right, or east, side of the railroad through Mill Creek Gap. Stewart fortified his position, and devised a new defensive tactic by constructing small advanced works for his skirmishers, a practice that the entire army soon adopted. Aided by Stevenson's pioneers, the division's pioneer company dammed Mill Creek at the two railroad bridges. The division also constructed roads to the top and along the summit of Rocky Face. Johnston directed Hood to have Stewart secure Wheeler's line of retreat across the creek. Stewart wrote Wheeler seeking to coordinate in accordance with these instructions, asking for notice in case of a heavy advance.[24]

On May 7, after several days of skirmishing, the Army of the Cumberland advanced toward Mill Creek Gap. Stewart occupied an advanced line in front of the gap, but after dark, fell back under Hood's orders to the main line on the Dalton side of the gap. In addition to his own division, Stewart was given the direction of Bate's Division of Hardee's Corps. On May 8, the Federals advanced into Stewart's abandoned line in front of the gap, and commenced heavy skirmishing that continued until May 12. The Federals made several attempts on Stewart's skirmish lines and were repulsed every time. A newspaper reporter observed that during these encounters, Stewart was "wide awake and constantly in the saddle." Within the main line, Stewart deployed Clayton on the side of Rocky Face Ridge, Baker and Stovall on the ridge to the right of the creek and the railroad,

23. Lindsley, ed., *Military Annals*, 85, 87; William T. Sherman, "The Grand Strategy of the Last Year of the War," *B&L* 4:252; Willett, *History of Company B*, 62; C. B. W. Rowland Diary, April 13, 21, 1864, GA. The difficulty of establishing Confederate strength is discussed in McMurry, "The Atlanta Campaign: December 23, 1863, to July 18, 1864," 39–40. McMurry's estimate of Johnston's strength is used here.

24. Foote, *The Civil War*, 3:321; Pollard, *Lee and His Lieutenants*, 714; *OR* 38(3):816, 38(4):665; Hiram Smith Williams, *This War So Horrible: The Civil War Diary of Hiram Smith Williams*, ed. Lewis N. Wynne and Robert A. Taylor (Tuscaloosa: University of Alabama Press, 1993), 40.

and Gibson on an advanced ridge to the left of the railroad. Gibson's Brigade suffered from being enfiladed by Federal artillery, but the loss was not heavy. The division's total loss in these encounters was small.[25]

True to his characterization of Buzzard's Roost as a "door of death," Sherman's main effort was not against Mill Creek Gap, or at Dug Gap to the south, where Hooker's "demonstration" with the Federal Twentieth Corps almost carried the Confederate position. It was Sherman's intention to send McPherson and the Army of the Tennessee eighteen miles to the south of Dalton, through Snake Creek Gap to the small village of Resaca, where the railroad crossed the Oostanaula. Most of Johnston's strength was deployed in an inverted L from Crow Valley on the north of Dalton to and along Rocky Face Ridge. Therefore, McPherson's move would place him in the virtually unguarded Confederate rear. To Stewart's credit, he stated to one of his staff while watching a moving Federal column from atop Rocky Face that Sherman might be making such a move, and made a telegraphic report to Johnston's headquarters that the Federals were moving toward the Confederate left with their wagon trains.[26]

While Stewart successfully held Mill Creek Gap, events to the south eventually rendered his position untenable. In accordance with Stewart's prediction, McPherson marched far into the Confederate rear to Resaca. Fortunately for Johnston, elements of Leonidas Polk's corps-sized Army of Mississippi arrived at Resaca in time to deter McPherson's far more numerous force. Once Johnston determined that the bulk of Sherman's army was concentrating at Resaca, he abandoned Dalton.[27]

25. *OR* 38(3):816, 823, 831, 844–45, 854; Henry D. Clayton Diary, Henry Delamar Clayton Papers, UAL; Williams, *This War So Horrible*, 57–63; Curry, "History of Company B," 194–95; Bate's Report of May 30, 1864, in "Lines of Battle: Major General William B. Bate's Partial Reports of the Atlanta Campaign," ed. Zack Waters, in *The Campaign for Atlanta and Sherman's March to the Sea*, vol. 1, ed. Theodore P. Savas and David A. Woodbury (Campbell, Calif.: Savas Woodbury, 1992), 176–77; *Memphis (Atlanta) Appeal*, May 12, 1864.

26. Sherman, "Grand Strategy," 252; Symonds, *Johnston*, 274–76; APS to W. W. Mackall, May 8, 1864, Joseph E. Johnston Collection, Huntington Library.

27. *OR* 38(4):661–63; Castel, *Decision in the West*, 136–50. At various points in the *Official Records,* Polk's force is known as either "the Army of Mississippi" or "Army of the Mississippi." To distinguish Polk's men from the Army of the Mississippi that fought at Shiloh and Perryville, I have chosen to use "the Army of Mississippi" here.

On May 12, Stewart withdrew his division from Dalton and headed south to Tilton, bringing up the rear of Hood's Corps. At nightfall on May 13, the division camped on the railroad above Resaca. The next morning, Stewart's men moved to a position astride the railroad facing north, their right resting on the Connesauga River, a north-south stream flowing into the east-west Oostanaula to the east of Resaca. The bulk of Hood's Corps faced north and northwest; the remainder of the army, including Polk, confronted the Federals to the west along Camp Creek. Johnston's position, with its rear to a good-sized river, was precarious. There is no doubt Sherman recognized it as such, as he launched a series of attacks against the Confederate line on May 14.[28]

During the skirmishing on May 14, Sherman's left flank was anchored by Major General David S. Stanley's division of Major General Oliver Otis Howard's Fourth Corps. Stanley's men were deployed to extend east of the Tilton-Resaca road. The lines of Hood's Corps overlapped Stanley's left flank, which Johnston looked to take advantage of by ordering Hood to launch a flank attack with Stevenson and Stewart, supported by a portion of Walker's Division. About 5 P.M., Stewart's men moved out along the railroad and formed in two lines parallel to the Tilton-Resaca road, Clayton on the left front and Baker on the right front. Stewart swept forward for almost two miles, but the few Union troops he encountered retired with little resistance. Stewart appears to have been in a position to deal the Federals a punishing blow on the flank. Unfortunately, Baker's Brigade, on the far right of the division, encountered problems. The thick undergrowth made it impossible for the brigade to maintain its alignment. Further, two regiments obliqued to the right, away from the Federals. Federal resistance seemed greater on Baker's front, which must have seemed disconcerting, as the division's right flank was in an exposed position. Stewart found it necessary to supervise Baker's advance personally. According to one soldier, Stewart found Baker drunk, and the brigade exposed to heavy Federal artillery fire. By the time these problems were resolved and the division re-formed, nightfall precluded any further advance.[29]

---

28. *OR* 38(3):816–17; Symonds, *Johnston*, 280–81.

29. Castel, *Decision in the West*, 163, 166; *OR* 38(3):817, 825–28, 845–54; Curry, "History of Company B," 195; Philip L. Secrist, "Resaca: For Sherman a Moment of Truth," *Atlanta Historical Bulletin* 22 (1978): 22. To be fair to Baker, it should be noted that neither

Advancing on Stewart's left, Stevenson crashed into Stanley's flank and managed to drive the Federals some distance before Union artillery fire and Brigadier General Alpheus Williams' division of the Twentieth Corps, which had moved up to reinforce Stanley, brought Stevenson to a halt. Despite the disappointing results, Johnston ordered the assault continued the next day, but subsequently canceled the order that night when he received a report that the Federals were across the Oostanaula toward Calhoun, to the south. Johnston sent W. H. T. Walker's Division to repulse the crossing, but the fiery Georgian found no Federals.[30]

On the morning of May 15, Stewart made an adjustment in his lines, deploying his right forward somewhat more than his left, and entrenching his new line. In the early afternoon, the Federals launched an attack on Stevenson and Hindman to Stewart's left, engendering a struggle for a small advanced redoubt where Captain Max Van Den Corput's Cherokee Battery had been placed by Hood to provide counterbattery fire in front of Brown's Brigade of Stevenson's Division. The Federals were eventually bloodily repulsed, but the Rebels were unable to rescue Van Den Corput's guns. Some skirmishing occurred along Clayton's lines during this struggle, which Stewart observed, according to a reporter, "with the utmost coolness."[31]

Having received word from Walker that the Federals were not crossing the Oostanaula to his south, Johnston resolved to resume the offensive on the right. Old Joe ordered Hood to prepare an attack. Hood in turn ordered Stewart at 3 P.M. to make a wheeling attack to the left at 4 P.M. should he not be attacked in the meantime. Stewart was advised that Stevenson would also move forward on his left. To lend weight to the charge, Johnston provided Stewart with Maney's Brigade of Tennesseans from Cheatham's Division.[32]

Shortly before his advance, Stewart received intelligence of a heavy movement of Federals to his front, which turned out to be Williams' Fed-

---

Stewart, Baker, nor Colonel Jonathan A. Higley, who purportedly relieved Baker, reported the drunkenness incident recounted by Curry. See *OR* 38(3):816–17, 845, 850.

30. Castel, *Decision in the West*, 164–66; *OR* 38(3):615.

31. Castel, *Decision in the West*, 173–75; *OR* 38(3):817; "St. Clair," *Atlanta Daily Intelligencer*, May 18, 1864.

32. Castel, *Decision in the West*, 176; *OR* 38(3):615, 817, 837, 839.

eral division. Stewart notified Hood of this movement, but received no word altering the attack orders. At precisely 4 P.M., the division moved forward, Clayton on the left and Stovall on the right, each making a half wheel to the left. The movement placed the brigades in echelon in order to keep the division from being flanked on the right. Stewart deployed Maney between Stovall and the river, along with a small body of cavalry, to cover the right. Gibson moved up into the second line to support Clayton, and Baker to support Stovall. As Stewart later reported: "The men moved forward with great spirit and determination and soon engaged the enemy." At this point, Hood's inspector general, Lieutenant Colonel Edward Cunningham, arrived with an order to suspend the attack, since the Federals had indeed crossed the Oostanaula to the south. Unfortunately, Stewart's attack had already commenced against Union infantry supported by artillery and covered by breastworks.[33]

Moving forward on the right of the division, Stovall's Brigade encountered a "thicket almost impenetrable," beyond which were Williams' entrenched troops. The rough country over which Stovall advanced, combined with the fact that the brigade's left was engaged to a much greater extent than the right, disrupted the Georgians' assault. After firing but one volley, the brigade broke. Despite its early exit, Stovall's Brigade suffered 270 casualties.[34]

Because all but one regiment of Stevenson's Division had gotten the word to suspend the attack, Clayton went in not only poorly supported by Stovall on his right, but virtually unsupported on his left. To make matters worse, Clayton had been watching the Federals mass in front of his position for several hours. Because of the difficult wheeling maneuver, Clayton personally moved out with his right regiment, Holtzclaw's 18th Alabama, and then supervised the movement of the next regiment in line, Colonel Bushrod Jones's 32nd-58th Alabama. Supporting Clayton's attack was the battery of Stewart's old artilleryman, Captain Thomas J. Stanford. Clayton ordered: "Forward, guide left, march!" and the Alabamians moved forward under an extremely heavy Federal fire. The key to the Federal position was a high knoll topped by the house of a Mr. Scales. Clayton appears

<hr />

33. *OR* 38(2):28–29; 38(3):615, 817.

34. *OR* 38(3):817, 823–24, 828; "St. Clair," *Atlanta Daily Intelligencer*, May 18, 1864; *Augusta Daily Chronicle and Sentinel*, May 18, 1864.

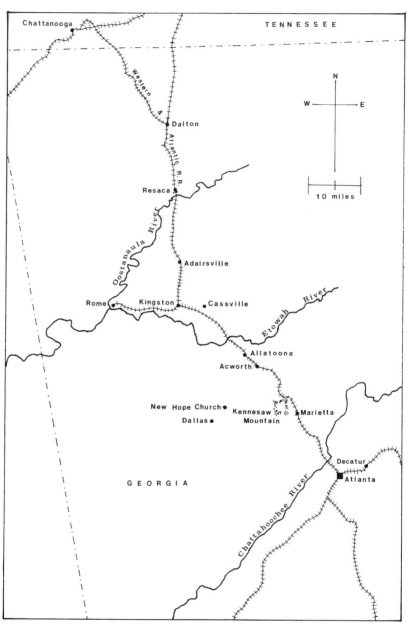

The Atlanta campaign
Map by Blake Magner

to have directed his attack toward that point, but the Federals resisted "with perfect steadiness." Clayton's two left units, the 36th and 38th Alabama regiments, joined the attack, making the left wheel just after they came out of their own breastworks. By this time, it was clear to the Alabamians that they had little hope of success. They nonetheless surged forward toward the Federal lines, enduring a "fatal and scathing fire" for almost a half hour with "praiseworthy firmness." Three successive color-bearers of the 38th Alabama were cut down before the regiment's colonel, A. R. Lankford, took the flag so far forward that he was captured. The Federals were so impressed with Lankford's bravery that they refused to shoot him as he approached. Captain Stanford watched the attack from behind a tree. One of his men asked him to get back behind the breastworks, but Stanford replied, "I reckon not." Within seconds, he was dead, a bullet in his brain. Clayton suffered over 350 casualties.[35]

Baker, being behind Stovall on the extreme right, also went forward before he could be stopped. His Alabama men, like Stovall's Georgians before them, encountered dense undergrowth in the line of advance. Baker's men moved through Stovall's retreating men and advanced to within thirty yards of the Federal lines, where the withering blasts of the Yankee guns eventually forced them back. Sergeant Preston S. Gilder, the color-bearer of the 40th Alabama, bore his colors in front of the command, but was cut down by the Federals. Three brave young officers of the 40th returned under a heavy fire to retrieve the colors. In this "hard battle," Baker's casualties exceeded 150.[36]

Fortunately for Gibson's Louisianans, Stewart stopped their attack before they followed Clayton into the sights of Alpheus Williams' guns. When Stewart learned of Hood's order to cancel the attack, he desperately dispatched several members of his staff to recall the attacking brigades. Ridley dramatically described his own ride to the far right, characterizing the battle as "an unintermittent roar of the most deafening and appalling thunder." Ridley found Maney's Brigade working to cover the Confeder-

---

35. *OR* 38(2):28–29, 59–60, 64; 38(3):833–44; Clayton Diary, UAL; "St. Clair," *Atlanta Daily Intelligencer*, May 18, 1864; Brown Diary, May 15, 1864, KNBP. Stanford was succeeded by Lieutenant James S. McCall, a veteran of the battery's many battles. Rowland, *Official Register of Mississippi*, 876, 878.

36. *OR* 38(3):818, 844–54; Curry, "History of Company B," 196.

ate far right against Federal cavalry. Eventually, the Federal cavalry was driven off, but not before harassing one of the division's hospitals. When Ridley returned, he found that in the short time he had been gone, Stewart had had three horses shot from under him. Most of the other members of the staff were dismounted. Lieutenant Terry Cahal, who had ridden to try to stop Stovall, came back from his errand on foot. Another staff officer dispatched to Clayton had his horse fall on him when it was shot, almost paralyzing him.[37]

Whether the order countermanding the assault could have reached Old Straight in time to prevent a useless and costly assault later became a controversy between Johnston and Hood. Johnston asserted after the war that the cancellation order had not been promptly relayed to Stewart. Hood responded that he had not had time to relay the order, a logical statement in light of the fact that Stewart's Division was on the end of the line and therefore farthest from headquarters. Stewart's feelings relating to the controversy are unrecorded.[38]

The Army of Tennessee was in a tight spot the evening of May 15, 1864—in Ridley's opinion, the tightest of the campaign. Not only was it backed against the Oostanaula River, but Sherman had troops across the river to the south and had captured a hill on the Confederate left that put Federal artillery in range to interdict the permanent bridges across the Oostanaula. This latter event occasioned the erection of a pontoon bridge up the Oostanaula from the other bridges, out of artillery range. Johnston determined to withdraw to the south to look for better ground around Calhoun, and gave orders for a withdrawal. No doubt because of his position on the far right, Stewart received orders to deploy his men as rear guard. Hardee and Polk's infantry crossed the threatened bridges, their wagons and artillery using the pontoon bridge. Stevenson's and Hindman's divisions crossed by the pontoon bridge, leaving Stewart and his men in line of battle across the railroad and the Dalton and Resaca road.

37. OR 38(3):854; Ridley, *Battles and Sketches*, 299–301; Watkins, *Co. Aytch*, 147–48; Williams, *This War So Horrible*, 69.

38. Joseph E. Johnston, "Opposing Sherman's Advance to Atlanta," *B&L* 4:266. Ridley pointed out that the other units of Hood's Corps (except Hindman's 54th Virginia) got the word in time, yet Stewart did not. If Stewart expressed this opinion to Ridley at the time, the record is silent. Ridley, *Battles and Sketches*, 298–99; Lindsley, ed., *Military Annals*, 88.

The nerve-racking experience may have contributed to some confusion in Stovall's Brigade, which was under the command of the 40th Georgia's Colonel Abda Johnson, owing to Stovall's having become sick that evening. The Federals began attacking the division's pickets and shelling its position, so Stewart directed Gibson, commanding his other front-line brigade, to assume command of both units. In Stewart's words, "the situation was perilous, and calculated to try the endurance of the men." Gibson threw forward a heavy line of skirmishers, and was pleased with the steadiness of both brigades. Eventually, at about 3 A.M., the rear of the army was sufficiently en route for Hood to order Stewart to withdraw, apparently across the railroad bridge, which gave the engineers time to disassemble the pontoon bridge. Austin's Louisiana sharpshooters brought up the division's rear, which the Federals shelled as it retreated the morning of May 16.[39]

The country around Calhoun, being somewhat open, was unsuitable for defense. After resting the army for most of a day in that area, Johnston moved south to Adairsville, where he hoped to use a valley to present a line of battle to Sherman. The valley proved too wide to defend, so he determined to move on to Cassville. At Cassville, the army deployed to bring Sherman to battle. The army gave up two successive positions without fighting a significant engagement.[40]

The Army of Tennessee again moved south, crossing the Etowah River to Allatoona and occupying a strong position where the Western and Atlantic Railroad went through a narrow defile in the Allatoona Mountains. The ability to rest here for two or three days did much to restore the men's strength, but allowed Sherman to move across the Etowah to the west of Allatoona, his first move away from the railroad.[41]

39. Ridley, *Battles and Sketches*, 300–301; *OR* 38(3):818, 823, 825, 854, 860, 862, 866–67; Symonds, *Johnston*, 283–84.

40. Symonds, *Johnston*, 291–96; Johnston, "Opposing Sherman," 267–69; Horn, *Army of Tennessee*, 327–29; McMurry, *Hood*, 108–109; *OR* 38(3):818, 862, 899. For Stewart's views, see Lindsley, ed., *Military Annals*, 90, 97. The Cassville episode was the subject of bitter controversy between Johnston and Hood after the war. See Connelly, *Autumn of Glory*, 345–54. On May 17 and 18, the last of Polk's reinforcements, the cavalry division of Brigadier General William H. Jackson and the infantry division of Major General Samuel G. French, joined the army.

41. Castel, *Decision in the West*, 209, 216.

Sherman's intention was to maneuver Johnston behind the Chattahoochee, the last river barrier between the three Federal armies and Atlanta. On May 23, Sherman sent his troops swarming across the Etowah at three locations, heading for Dallas, fourteen miles south of his Etowah crossings, fourteen miles to the southwest of Johnston's position at Allatoona, and about sixteen miles to the west of Marietta, the point where he intended to rejoin the railroad. Sherman did not expect heavy resistance from the Confederates until he moved through Dallas toward Marietta.[42]

Johnston responded by setting the Army of Tennessee in motion on May 23, moving Hardee and Polk toward Dallas, but leaving Hood to watch for Federal movements across the Etowah at the point where it was crossed by the railroad. The next day, Johnston received information from his cavalry that Sherman's main body was moving on Dallas. Johnston ordered Hood to move early on May 25 to New Hope Church, a "plain wooden meeting house" at a crossroads on the Allatoona and Dallas road northeast of Dallas. Hood's line prolonged that of Polk, who occupied a line between Hood near New Hope Church and Hardee directly east of Dallas.[43]

Before noon on May 25, Stewart and his division arrived at New Hope Church, and deployed on a ridge around the crossroads. Johnston rode up and called for Stewart, advising him that the Yankees were "out there" and that a breakthrough would imperil Stevenson's Division, to Stewart's rear. Stewart deployed Baker's Brigade on the right, Clayton's in the center, and Stovall's on the left. Baker's and Clayton's men erected some crude breastworks, but Stovall's did not, as the Georgians' line went through a cemetery across the road from the church building. Gibson remained in reserve, except for Austin's Battalion and the 16th Louisiana, which deployed as skirmishers. Sixteen pieces of Eldridge's artillery battalion, from Oliver's, Fenner's, and Stanford's batteries, unlimbered on Stewart's line, and Brown's and Pettus' brigades of Stevenson's Division extended Stewart's line to the right.[44]

42. Ibid., 213, 217–18.

43. *OR* 38(3):986–87; Philip Daingerfield Stephenson, *The Civil War Memoir of Philip Daingerfield Stephenson, D.D.*, ed. Nathaniel Cheairs Hughes, Jr. (Conway, Ark.: UCA Press, 1995), 187; Castel, *Decision in the West*, 221.

44. *OR* 38(3):813, 818, 833, 848; Ridley, *Battles and Sketches*, 303. Only a "small portion" of Brown's Brigade was engaged. *OR* 38(3):813.

Hood determined to conduct a reconnaissance to develop the Federals massing to the west. Colonel Bushrod Jones and the 32nd-58th Alabama moved out the road to the west. Lieutenant Colonel Edward Cunningham of Hood's staff, who had belatedly delivered the attack cancellation order to Stewart at Resaca, told Jones that Hood desired him to advance and drive the Yankees down the road—they were few in number. A small cavalry unit accompanied Jones to cover his flanks, and Austin's Battalion deployed as skirmishers on his left flank. Jones and Austin found the Federals in heavy force, and Jones sent an officer to inform Stewart he had gone as far as was practicable. At this time, one of Hood's staff officers rode up and read a written order to press forward and develop the enemy's strength. The two units moved forward and charged a line of Federal troops. A captured Unionist stated that the force in front was Hooker's corps, and Austin ordered him escorted to Hood and Stewart. Jones's Alabamians and Austin's Louisianans executed a stubborn withdrawal to the division's main line before a massive line of Federals.[45]

The Federals in Stewart's front were indeed Hooker's Twentieth Corps, Williams', Geary's, and Daniel Butterfield's divisions, totaling approximately 16,000 men. To the west of New Hope Church ran Pumpkinvine Creek, a tributary of the Etowah River. Geary's division deployed in the center, and moved across the creek at Owen's Mill. Geary then advanced two brigades, which engaged Austin's and Jones's skirmishers. From Confederate prisoners, Geary learned that Hood's entire corps was in his front. Hooker was present, and ordered a temporary halt pending the arrival of the corps' other two divisions. Geary overestimated the force of Confederate skirmishers in his front, terming Jones's consolidated regiments and Austin's Battalion a "brigade." As the day wore on, the other two Federal divisions arrived, so that by 5 P.M. Hooker had all three divisions on the field, and prepared them for attack. All three divisions formed in columns of brigades, on a single brigade front. Under the gathering clouds of a thunderstorm, Williams' division went forward, driving in the Confederate skirmishers. Colonel John Coburn's brigade of Butterfield's division followed Williams, while Colonel James Wood, Jr.'s brigade moved out of the column to the left and Brigadier General William T.

45. *OR* 38(3):843, 862.

Ward's brigade moved out of the column to the right. Geary's division followed Coburn in the main column of assault.[46]

The Federal attack struck all along Stewart's line, but most heavily on Stovall and Clayton. As soon as the skirmish line of Louisianans cleared the division's front, Stewart's men opened fire on the Federals, who by that time were a hundred yards away. Thereafter, as Ridley termed it, Stewart's Division stood in line "for three hours and whipped Hooker's entire corps." Stewart later reported that his "entire line received the attack with great steadiness and firmness, every man standing at his post." As Williams' division approached the foot of Stewart's slight ridge, it was almost dark, and Stewart's sixteen pieces of artillery threw "shot, shell and canister in murderous volleys."[47]

The heavy fire soon enveloped the scene of the conflict in smoke. In the Confederate rear, one of the division's pioneer corps heard volleys so continuous that the reports of single muskets could not be heard. A newspaperman later reported that the roar of musketry was the loudest heard in the army since Chickamauga. Geary felt that "the discharges of canister and shell from the enemy were heavier than in any other battle of the campaign in which my command were engaged." A Louisiana soldier of Gibson's Brigade watched the Confederate artillery blast down the timber through which the Twentieth Corps advanced, while one of Stovall's men watched the artillery mow the Yankees down "by the hundreds." As they fought, the thunderstorm broke and drenched the combatants with a "cold, pelting rain."[48]

Hooker's lines of battle resolutely came forward into this infernal scene where the forces of heaven and earth seemed arrayed against them. So relentless was the Federal attack that one observer thought the advancing bluecoats were drunk. Stewart's position was such that the heavy Federal fire passed over his line to a great extent, accounting for low casualties throughout the division. An artilleryman in reserve behind Stewart's main

46. *OR* 38(1):115; 38(2):30, 123, 342–43, 382, 438.
47. Ridley, *Battles and Sketches*, 303; *OR* 38(2):30; 38(3):818, 825, 833, 846.
48. "J.B.D.," *Memphis (Atlanta) Appeal*, May 27, 1864; Williams, *This War So Horrible*, 81; *Macon Daily Telegraph*, May 31, 1864; *OR* 38(2):123–24, 38(3):818, 825, 833, 846; H. J. Lea, "In the Battle of New Hope Church," *CV* 31 (February 1923): 60–61; C. A. Rowland to C. B. Rowland, May 27, 1864, C. A. Rowland Diary and Letters, GA.

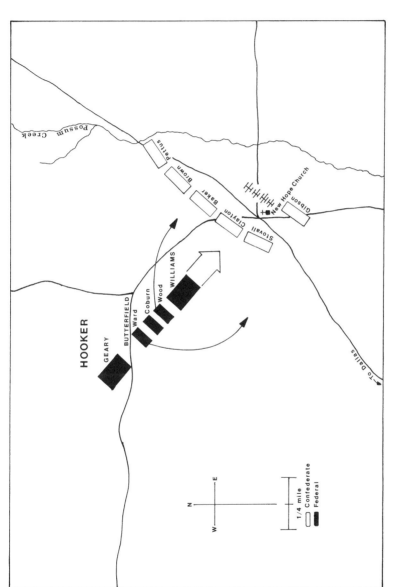

The battle at New Hope Church

Map by Blake Magner

line later wrote that the "bullets were thick in the bushes over our heads." Common sense also played a part in keeping casualties down, at least in Stovall's Brigade, where the men lay down to load their rifles and waited for the oncoming Federals to come into range. Nonetheless, the storm of Yankee bullets occasionally found the unfortunate. A man on Baker's front was hit by a ball that passed *under* the log he was using for cover.[49]

Eldridge's artillerymen, being exposed as they necessarily were, suffered forty-three killed and wounded, and another forty-four horses became casualties. In Stanford's Battery, William Brown watched as the yelling Yankees surged through undergrowth so heavy it was hard to see them. In Fenner's Battery, three brothers manned one gun. The oldest, the rammer, was killed, and his place taken by another brother, who was shot in the thigh. The third brother took their place and survived unhurt.[50]

Stewart encouraged his men by leaping upon his old roan and riding up and down the line. The men called on him to get back, fearing he would be wounded or killed. However, Old Straight rode on, telling the men he was there to die with them. As he passed his son, Caruthers, the young man called out: "Now, father, you know you promised mother that you would not expose yourself today." This generated mimicking cries from the men up and down the line. Admiring the steadiness of his men and the courageous attacks of the Federals, Stewart later wrote: "No more persistent attack or determined resistance has anywhere been made." At one point during the battle, Johnston sent a messenger inquiring whether reinforcements were needed, and Stewart replied: "My own troops will hold the position." The battle continued in the cold rain without interruption until long after dark.

When the engagement finally ended, some of Stewart's troops, including many in Clayton's Brigade, were down to their last rounds of ammunition. Ridley wrote that the outcome so gratified Joe Johnston that he promised Stewart an eventual promotion to lieutenant general. Stewart

---

49. *OR* 38(3):818; *Atlanta Daily Intelligencer*, May 28, 1864; William Ralston Talley, "An Autobiography of Rev. William Raulston Talley, with a Condensed History of the Talley Family," 37, MS at KNBP; William Stanley Hoole and Martha DuBose Hoole, eds., *Historical Sketches of Barton's (Later Stovall's) Georgia Brigade, Army of Tennessee, C.S.A.* (University, Ala.: Confederate Publishing, 1984), 19; Curry, "History of Company B," 197.

50. Brown Diary, May 25, 1864, KNBP; Ridley, *Battles and Sketches*, 304; Robert Howe, "Dead at New Hope Church," *CV* 5 (October 1897): 534.

was likely more pleased by the message sent by the men of his command that he should take care of himself, as they wanted no other commander.[51]

Stewart and his division had gained a good measure of revenge against Hooker and his men for their repulse of the Tennessean's division at Resaca. Hooker reported casualties of only 1,665 out of the engagement at New Hope Church, but the Confederates believed that the Federal loss was much higher. Stewart reported a loss of between 300 and 400 men. Even if Hooker's report of his losses was correct, Stewart and his division had given the Army of Tennessee its first victory of the campaign in the space of three hours. Ridley called it an "epoch" in the division's history, comparable to Cleburne's stand at Ringgold Gap the previous November and Cheatham's at the Dead Angle at Kennesaw in June, 1864.[52]

New Hope Church had been Stewart's most intensive defensive battle since November 25, 1863, and, in the words of the *Augusta Daily Chronicle and Sentinel*, the outcome was "no Missionary Ridge affair." Stewart had built a sense of cohesion in the division, the majority of the men having been together as a unit since only the previous November. Stewart's conspicuous presence along his front on horseback, where the Yankees were shooting high, inspired his men, and his calm attitude steadied them. A few days after the battle, Stewart proudly wrote Colonel A. J. Keller, soon to be commander of the 5th Tennessee, that he had heard it said that his example had inspired his men. The *Memphis Appeal* reported that Stewart, "by his constant presence, set an example which we take pleasure in saying was nobly emulated by all." Years later, a correspondent inquired of Stewart what was his most notable achievement in the war. Stewart replied that the repulse of Hooker at New Hope Church was "one, at least, of the most noteworthy incidents in my war career."[53]

The Federals dug in near Stewart's lines and maintained a harassing skirmish fire, causing some casualties over the next two days. For a time

51. Ridley, *Battles and Sketches*, 304, 474; Wharton S. Jones, "Glory Enough for All," *CV* 38 (June 1930): 216; *OR* 38(3):818, 833; Johnston, *Narrative*, 327; Pollard, *Lee and His Lieutenants*, 714.

52. *OR* 38(2):14, 38(3):818; Ridley, *Battles and Sketches*, 303, 305.

53. "Georgia," *Augusta Daily Chronicle and Sentinel*, July 2, 1864; APS to A. J. Kellar, May 31, 1864, Alexander P. Stewart Letter, Hargett Library, University of Georgia; "J.B.D.," *Memphis (Atlanta) Appeal*, May 27, 1864; APS to William B. Dupree, May 14, 1895, William B. Dupree Papers, DU.

during May 27, some troops of Baker's Brigade were subjected to a particularly effective fire from a Federal battery. Meanwhile, Sherman still believed that he did not face the entire Confederate army, but merely Hood's
Corps. Sherman accordingly ordered Howard to move his Fourth Corps
of the Army of the Cumberland to strike the extreme Rebel right flank
north of New Hope Church. Johnston responded by shifting more of his
troops northwest of Stewart's line, Cleburne's veterans taking position on
the far right at Pickett's Mill.[54]

On May 27, the Federals made an attack on Cleburne at Pickett's Mill.
Cleburne's men inflicted yet another defeat upon the advancing Yankees,
similar in scope and loss to that inflicted at New Hope Church. The next
evening, Bromfield Ridley and Caruthers Stewart went to marvel at the appalling piles of Federal dead.[55]

Sherman, stymied at his attempt on Marietta through Dallas, moved his
armies back toward the Western and Atlantic Railroad around the Army of
Tennessee's right. About June 4, the Federals regained the railroad between Allatoona and Acworth. Johnston responded by moving his army
east to cover the railroad north of Kennesaw Mountain and west of Marietta. Johnston's engineers marked out a line with its left on Lost Mountain,
to the west of Kennesaw, and its right across the railroad behind Noonday
Creek. When Sherman sidestepped to Acworth, Johnston contracted his
line to cover the roads to Atlanta, posting Hardee on the left at Gilgal
Church, Polk in the center extending to the Marietta and Acworth road,
and Hood to the east of Polk. Pine Mountain, in front of Hardee's line,
was held as a salient by Bate's Division.[56]

Bate's position left his division exposed, so on June 14, Johnston, accompanied by Polk, Hardee, and cavalryman W. H. "Red" Jackson, climbed up
to the low summit of Pine Mountain. By chance, Sherman saw the group
of Confederate officers scrutinizing his lines from the top of the hill, and
ordered Federal guns to scatter the unknown Rebels. The Federals fired,

54. *OR* 38(3):818; Castel, *Decision in the West*, 228–30; McMurry, "The Atlanta Campaign: December 23, 1863, to July 18, 1864," 161–62.

55. Castel, *Decision in the West*, 229–41, 243–46; McMurry, "The Atlanta Campaign:
December 23, 1863, to July 18, 1864," 161–69; Ridley, *Battles and Sketches*, 305.

56. Horn, *Army of Tennessee*, 331; Johnston, "Opposing Sherman," 270; McMurry,
"The Atlanta Campaign: December 23, 1863 to July 18, 1864," 170–78.

making the Confederate generals and their staffs seek cover. Polk moved "off by himself, walking thoughtfully along" when the next Yankee shot went straight through him.[57]

Although Polk had been involved in some past Confederate failures, he was loved throughout the army. Stewart mourned him as "a brave soldier, of knightly courtesy and honor, and a true Christian gentleman." Polk's death left a vacancy in the command of the Army of Mississippi. Its senior major general, William Wing Loring, temporarily assumed command.[58]

On June 19, Johnston fell back to another strong line anchored upon Kennesaw Mountain, four miles west of Marietta. Hood's Corps initially held the Confederate right, but the weakness of the army's left flank led Johnston to shift it south to the area of Zion Church and Kolb's farm, on the Powder Springs Road. Hood placed Hindman on his right and Stevenson on his left, with Stewart in reserve. In the early afternoon of June 22, Federal troops moved onto Kolb's farm, a short distance west of Hood's lines. Sensing an opportunity to strike the bluecoats a blow, Hood launched an attack on his own initiative with Hindman and Stevenson, which the Federals repulsed with heavy loss.[59]

Hood's Corps remained in the area of the Powder Springs Road until July 2. During that interlude, on June 27, Sherman shed his predilection for flanking maneuvers, and launched a violent but unsuccessful attack on Johnston's Kennesaw Mountain line at two points. On the army's extreme left during the battle, Stewart's Division came under some artillery fire, but was otherwise unengaged.[60]

Polk's death precipitated a search for a successor both inside and outside the Army of Tennessee. On June 14, the day Polk was killed, Johnston wired President Davis: "It is essential to have a Lt. Genl immediately to succeed Lt. Genl Polk. I regard Maj. Genl Stewart as the best qualified of the Maj. Genls of this army. Time is important." An analysis of the eligible officers with the army demonstrates the logic of Johnston's statement re-

57. Johnston, "Opposing Sherman," 270–71; Horn, *Army of Tennessee*, 331–32; Stephenson, *Civil War Memoir*, 189–90.

58. Lindsley, ed., *Military Annals*, 92; James W. Raab, *W. W. Loring: Florida's Forgotten General* (Manhattan, Kans.: Sunflower University Press, 1996), 151.

59. McMurry, *Hood*, 112–13; Manigault, *A Carolinian Goes to War*, 192–94.

60. Manigault, *A Carolinian Goes to War*, 194; Losson, *Tennessee's Forgotten Warriors*, 154–65; Ridley, *Battles and Sketches*, 313–20.

garding Stewart. At the time of Polk's death, the army had nine infantry major generals. In order of seniority by date of commission, they were Loring, Cheatham, Hindman, French, Stevenson, Cleburne, Walker, Stewart, and Bate. Stewart's combat record was equal to, and in most cases superior to, the combat records of the other eight. Only Cheatham, Cleburne, and Bate had nearly as much service with the Army of Tennessee as Stewart. Unlike Old Straight, none of these men, able as at least Cleburne and Cheatham may have been, had a West Point education, a factor that weighed heavily with President Davis. In fact, of the fourteen men elevated to the rank of lieutenant general to that point in the war, only Richard Taylor, Davis' brother-in-law, was not a USMA graduate.[61]

The issue of Polk's replacement was of considerable concern to Davis, who turned to his most trustworthy officer, Robert E. Lee, for advice. On June 15, Lee stated he could not recommend a successor. He declined to recommend his own chief of artillery, Brigadier General William N. Pendleton, as Lee did not deem him able to command a corps in the Army of Northern Virginia. Davis had listed other officers as candidates (who were unidentified in Lee's response), but Lee knew little of them, except to say that to the extent he did know them, he thought them not equal to the job. The one officer whom Lee mentioned by name, Major General Stewart, he simply did not know.[62]

The fact that Johnston suggested Stewart may initially have worked against Old Straight, as Davis had not been inclined to promote other officers recommended by Johnston. In a second letter from Lee dated June 21, Lee reiterated that he could not recommend Pendleton and indicated that Lieutenant General Richard S. Ewell, recently relieved from corps command in the Army of Northern Virginia, would not be equal to the job on account of his poor health. In response to a now-lost comment by Davis, Lee agreed that Stewart might be the best choice to replace Polk.

61. J. E. Johnston to Jefferson Davis, June 14, 1864, Officers File, RG 109, NA; see also Pollard, *Lee and His Lieutenants*, 715. Johnston's telegram appears to have been previously unknown. See discussions in McMurry, "The Atlanta Campaign: December 23, 1863, to July 18, 1864," 255–57, Castel, *Decision in the West*, 338; Brown, *To the Manner Born*, 252; Woodworth, *Jefferson Davis and His Generals*, 262.

62. Clifford Dowdy, ed., *The Wartime Papers of R. E. Lee* (New York: Bramhall House, 1961), 783.

Lee thought Johnston needed a replacement immediately, since he understood Loring was in command—an indication that he did not regard Loring highly. Since moving quickly was important, and the government had been slow to act upon his initial suggestion of Stewart, on June 26 Johnston asked that Ewell, already a lieutenant general, be sent to him. Behind Ewell's back, and to his great embarrassment, Ewell's wife went to Bragg to urge his appointment. Bragg told her that Ewell would not be considered because of his health.[63]

There is evidence that the opinions of the surviving two corps commanders were also solicited. W. H. T. Walker wrote that he had heard that Hardee recommended Cleburne, certainly a natural choice on account of their great friendship and Cleburne's unmistakable competence. Hood later wrote that he recommended Stewart, whom he doubtlessly considered his best division commander. Hood's (and Johnston's) reliance on Stewart throughout the campaign was readily apparent. Stewart held Mill Creek Gap with a quasi–corps command at the campaign's inception. Old Straight and his division held the critical right flank of Hood's Corps at Resaca, and the point of danger at New Hope Church. In light of Hood's influence in Richmond, manifested by a private and secret correspondence he had kept up with Davis and Bragg since his arrival with the army, his recommendation must have carried some weight. Bragg, too, must have expressed his opinion, and he undoubtedly preferred Stewart to Cleburne, who signed the petition against Bragg the previous October.[64]

63. D. S. Freeman and Grady McWhiney, eds., *Lee's Dispatches to Jefferson Davis* (New York: Putnam, 1957), 242–43, 255–57; W. W. Mackall to wife, March 18, June 22, 1864, Mackall Papers, SHC; *OR* 38(4):785; D. S. Freeman, *Lee's Lieutenants* (New York: Charles Scribner's Sons, 1944), 3:552.

64. Brown, *To the Manner Born*, 253–54; John B. Hood, *Advance and Retreat* (New Orleans: G. T. Beauregard, 1880), 126. One reason to question what W. H. T. Walker heard is the theory set forth in a recent Cleburne biography that Hardee may have felt Cleburne was best left a major general. Craig L. Symonds, *Stonewall of the West: Patrick Cleburne and the Civil War* (Lawrence: University Press of Kansas, 1997), 222–23. Symonds' theory is plausibly based on Hardee's representing to Hood that Cheatham was the "best man at [Hood's] disposal" for temporary corps command on July 19, 1864. See *OR* 38(5):892. This is extremely telling in light of Liddell's observation that Hardee was "very partial" to Cleburne. Liddell, *Liddell's Record*, 103. Cleburne, the one major general whose combat record was perhaps superior to Stewart's, appears to have been undisturbed by Stewart's promotion.

Others in the army seem to have believed that Stewart would receive the post. Major General Samuel G. French noted in his diary that he had predicted from the start that Stewart would be the man promoted. W. H. T. Walker, who himself expected the promotion, termed Stewart a "very worthy, modest gentleman." Stewart was known to the rank and file of the army as an officer who had served with them since Columbus, who had grown with them, in whom they had gained confidence. Old Straight was an officer they were "used to." Stewart's promotion, when it became a fact, would meet with the approval of the press as well. An article quoted in the *Chattanooga Daily Rebel*, published from exile in Griffin, Georgia, praised the "fitness and justice" of the promotion.[65]

On June 25, 1864, Johnston received a communication from Confederate adjutant general Samuel Cooper indicating that Stewart had been appointed to command Polk's troops, to date from June 23. Stewart did not assume command until July 7. This two-week hiatus is explained by Johnston's request that Stewart remain with his division an extra few days, as its position was on the exposed left of the army. Ridley believed that Stewart won his promotion at New Hope Church, where a grateful Johnston exclaimed: "If I can make you a Lieutenant-General for your management, you shall have it."

Johnston rode out to the segment of the line occupied by Stewart and his division, and found Old Straight superintending the construction of a redoubt. Johnston informed Stewart of his promotion. Stewart thus learned that he had become the highest-ranking officer in the Confederate service from the state of Tennessee. As Stewart had earlier recommended, Clayton was promoted to major general and was given command of Stewart's Division.[66]

Symonds, *Stonewall of the West*, 215–16. The conclusion that Bragg was in favor of Stewart is supported by a telegram Bragg sent Davis the next month that the army's reaction to Stewart's elevation was "most gratifying." *OR* 39(2):713–14.

65. Ridley, *Battles and Sketches*, 474; French, *Two Wars*, 215; Brown, *To the Manner Born*, 253; Stephenson, *Civil War Memoir*, 212; *Chattanooga Daily Rebel*, July 1, 1864; see also *Macon Daily Telegraph*, July 2, 1864. Earlier newspaper articles advocated the promotion of Carter Stevenson and G. W. Smith. *Atlanta Daily Intelligencer*, June 18, 1864, *Macon Daily Telegraph*, June 24, 1864.

66. Ridley, *Battles and Sketches*, 311–12, 474; Willett, *History of Company B*, 72; H. D. Clayton to wife, June 7, 1864, Clayton Papers, UAL. Stewart's promotion was to the temporary rank of lieutenant general in accordance with the Act of May 31, 1864. The Confederate

At the time Stewart assumed command, the Army of Mississippi numbered about 14,000 officers and men. It consisted of nine brigades organized into three divisions, and three artillery battalions. Major General William Wing Loring's Division was made up of Brigadier General John Adams' and Brigadier General Winfield S. Featherston's Mississippi brigades, and Brigadier General Thomas M. Scott's Alabama brigade. Major General Samuel G. French's Division consisted of Brigadier General Francis Marion Cockrell's famed Missouri brigade, Brigadier General Claudius M. Sears's Mississippi brigade, and Brigadier General Matthew D. Ector's brigade of dismounted Texas cavalrymen and North Carolina infantry. (Stewart, of course, had commanded Ector and his veterans in the spring of 1863, when they were part of McCown's Division.)

The Army of Mississippi's newest division commander was Major General Edward Cary Walthall, promoted to that grade to rank from July 6. Walthall's command included Brigadier General James Cantey's Brigade of one Mississippi and three Alabama regiments, led by its senior colonel, Edward A. O'Neal; Brigadier General Daniel H. Reynolds' Arkansas brigade; and Brigadier General William A. Quarles's Brigade of one Alabama, two Louisiana, and six skeletal Tennessee regiments. Ironically, Quarles's two Louisiana regiments would soon be transferred to Gibson's Brigade.[67]

Several officers of the Army of Mississippi petitioned Davis to elevate Loring to its permanent command. Stewart's appointment, however, seems to have been favorably received by the officers of the corps. On July 8, Lieutenant Colonel Columbus Sykes of the 43rd Mississippi wrote to his wife concerning the pro-Loring petition, doubting that it reached Davis in time, or that it would have made any difference, as "I doubt not that the present appointee is a far superior officer." Noting that Stewart

---

Congress confirmed the promotion on February 20, 1865. APS/CSR, RG 109, NA; *Journal of the Congress of the Confederate States of America, 1861–1865* (Washington, D.C.: Government Printing Office, 1904), 4:350, 581. For a discussion of the Act, see Freeman, *Lee's Lieutenants*, vol. 3, 509. Stewart's fellow Tennessean Nathan Bedford Forrest was promoted to lieutenant general on February 28, 1865, without the "temporary" qualification. It would appear that Stewart would still be ranking officer by date of commission. Bruce S. Allardice to author, September 23, 1997.

67. *OR* 38(3):659–60, 664, 678, 679; Mary Virginia Duval, "The Chevalier Bayard of Mississippi: Edward Cary Walthall," *Publications of the Mississippi Historical Society* 4(1901): 401, 410; Cummings, "Strahl," 342.

was "supposed to be an excellent officer," Sykes was "very much pleased at [Stewart's] assignment to the command of the 'Army of Mississippi.' "[68]

The Tennessee troops of Quarles's Brigade were especially pleased by the appointment of a fellow son of the Volunteer State as their corps commander. Their chaplain, James H. McNeilly, wrote that Stewart was a friend to the chaplains "and was ever ready to promote their work." Mc-Neilly wrote of his own observation of Stewart in battle, as he rode along encouraging his men, "as calm and composed as if he were in his room at home." McNeilly also was impressed with Stewart's consideration for his men, having watched Old Straight ride carefully through a column of men at rest during a march, politely asking them to make room. McNeilly contrasted this with officers of a lesser grade dashing through and making the men dive out of the way.[69]

Men unfamiliar with Stewart noted his respect for the feelings of the common soldiers. In the latter part of June, there was a prayer meeting near the line of battle, and about 3,000 soldiers gathered to worship within the sound of the guns. As the men prepared to sing the opening hymn, they noticed a general, unattended by any staff or escort, ride up to the rear of the assembly and hitch his horse. Sitting on the ground in the midst of the worshipers, the general took a deep interest in the service. When it concluded, he mounted his horse and rode away, every man present saluting him in silence by the raising of his hat. Though no one knew at the time who the general was, they quickly found out that it was Old Straight, whose attendance in such an unpretentious and pious manner "did more good than many eloquent sermons."[70]

When Stewart assumed command of his new corps, Johnston's army had fallen back to a position covering the Chattahoochee, the last great natural barrier between Sherman and Atlanta. About this time, Johnston received his last substantial reinforcement, a "division" of Georgia militia commanded by Stewart's old friend after whom his son was named, Major General Gustavus Woodson Smith.[71]

68. Raab, *Loring*, 159–60; Columbus Sykes to wife, July 8, 1864, Columbus Sykes Letters, KNBP; see also Sykes to wife, June 15, 29, 1864, Sykes Letters, KNBP.

69. James H. McNeilly, "A Great Game of Strategy," *CV* 27 (October 1919): 377, 380–81.

70. James W. Lee, Letter, *CV* 17 (October 1909): 485.

71. Gustavus Woodson Smith, "The Georgia Militia About Atlanta," *B&L* 3:331–32.

Facing Johnston's formidable works in front of the Chattahoochee River, Sherman reverted to using his superior numbers to flank the Confederates out of a well-prepared defensive position. On July 9, Lieutenant General Stewart and the Army of Mississippi joined the Army of Tennessee's other two corps in their retreat across the Chattahoochee, only a few miles from Atlanta. While he had faith in Johnston, Stewart must have wondered, as did the authorities in Richmond, how Old Joe planned to handle the imminent threat to the city just in his rear.[72]

72. Horn, *Army of Tennessee*, 339–40.

— 11 —

After a Desperate Fight and Heavy Loss

The Fall of Atlanta

For over two months, for over one hundred miles, Joe Johnston had re-treated. Even though the army continually moved backward in the face of Sherman's inevitable flanking moves, Stewart and the Army of Tennessee's weary men continued to believe that Old Joe somehow, some way, would decisively defeat Sherman. Unfortunately for Johnston, the authorities in Richmond did not share the view or the confidence of his men.[1]

By the time Johnston crossed the Chattahoochee in the second week of July, the campaign had been under way for over two months. There had been no Confederate attempts at the outset to disrupt Sherman by an offensive strike, like Lee had done in the Wilderness. The Army of Tennessee had punished Sherman at New Hope Church, Pickett's Mill, and Kennesaw Mountain, but these defensive victories did not convince an offensive-minded administration that enough was being done to defend Atlanta.

In addition to the obvious disadvantage of simply being outnumbered by a better-equipped enemy, by the second week of July, Johnston had two other significant problems. The Virginian did not indicate to Richmond a design to defend Atlanta for any significant length of time. He may not have even had a comprehensive plan. He did not convince Jefferson Davis

---

1. Lindsley, ed., *Military Annals*, 95–99. The issue of the army's morale at this time seems to have been more complex than Stewart imagined. See McMurry, "Confederate Morale in the Atlanta Campaign of 1864," 226, 232–35.

or Braxton Bragg that he did, and the results of his campaign no doubt fu-eled suspicions of the president and his military adviser that Old Joe would not fight for Atlanta.[2]

Johnston's second problem was the unethical and unprofessional con-duct of John Bell Hood, aided and abetted by Braxton Bragg and, to a lesser extent, Jefferson Davis. Almost within a week from his arrival with the army, Hood opened a correspondence with Richmond. Hood often laced his letters with criticisms of Johnston and his lack of offensive spirit. By the second week of July, Sherman's presence at the gates of Atlanta forced Davis to consider replacing Johnston. Bragg went to Atlanta on July 13 to get a firsthand view of the situation. Hood took advantage of the visit to deliver a letter dated July 14 to Bragg critical of the army's having missed "several chances to strike the enemy a decisive blow."[3]

Bragg also visited Hardee and Stewart, the army's other two lieutenant generals, to get their views of the situation. These discussions, in addition to Bragg's visits to Johnston, resulted in a report to Davis. Bragg felt John-ston was opposed to seeking battle, and that Hardee (Bragg's old enemy) favored the "retiring policy." Bragg portrayed Hood as the best choice to replace Johnston, although he did have a favorable word for Stewart, who Bragg stated was in favor of an "aggressive policy." Bragg further re-ported: "It affords me great pleasure to report to you the entire and perfect satisfaction which has been given by your recent appointments in the army. I have not heard of a complaint, and in General Stewart's case the feeling is most gratifying." Notwithstanding the favorable report concern-ing Stewart, having been in command of his corps less than ten days, Old Straight obviously did not have sufficient experience for army command.[4]

2. For a painstaking analysis of Johnston's planning (or lack thereof) and his lack of com-munication with Richmond, see Connelly, *Autumn of Glory*, 361–68; 403–405. See also McMurry, "The Atlanta Campaign: December 23, 1863, to July 18, 1864," 332–36.

3. Woodworth, *Jefferson Davis and His Generals*, 284; Hallock, Bragg, 192; *OR* 38(5):879; McMurry, *Hood*, 95–98, 118. An older biography of Hood does not make a judgment as to Hood's ambition. See John P. Dyer, *The Gallant Hood* (Indianapolis: Bobbs-Merrill, 1950), 245.

4. McMurry, *Hood*, 117–18; D. H. Reynolds Diary, July 14, 1864, UAR; Steven Davis, "Hood and the Battles for Atlanta," in *The Campaign for Atlanta and Sherman's March to the Sea*, ed. Savas and Woodbury, 1:56–57; *OR* 39(2):713–14. While Bragg portrayed Stewart as favoring the "aggressive policy," Stewart's postwar writings do not criticize Johnston's pol-icies in the least. See Robert D. Little, "General Hardee and the Atlanta Campaign," *Georgia*

Bragg's influence turned the tide for Hood, who was given command of the Army of Tennessee in Johnston's place on July 17. That day, Stewart learned that the Federals were across Peachtree Creek and driving in his outposts. As Adams' Brigade of Loring's Division was in an exposed position in the angle between the Chattahoochee and the creek, Stewart found it necessary to withdraw it to the Atlanta side of the creek. After deploying his troops, he rode to Johnston's headquarters to report and receive any further orders. Old Straight arrived there after dark, and Johnston showed him Cooper's order directing Johnston to turn command of the army over to Hood.

Astounded by the order, Stewart asked Johnston to suspend its execution until the army made the planned attack, but Johnston refused. Stewart then rode to Hardee's headquarters. Old Straight found Hardee primarily interested in seeing if he was mentioned in the change order. When Stewart said he was not, Hardee suggested Stewart find Hood. Stewart agreed, but asked Hardee not to publish the existence of the order, perhaps hoping that it could be reversed before the word got out to the troops. Hardee agreed, but subsequently leaked word.

Stewart addressed a note to Hood, who agreed to meet with Old Straight early on July 18. About sunrise, Stewart and Hood met on the road near Johnston's headquarters. Hood was genuinely interested in Stewart's proposal to suspend the order, probably because he would assume command at a critical time when there was little hope of success. Stewart and Hood went together to Johnston's quarters. While there, Hood and Johnston had a conversation out of Stewart's presence. At the close of this conversation, Hood, with Hardee and Stewart, composed and sent a telegram to Richmond asking suspension of the order, at least until Atlanta's fate was determined. Davis refused.[5]

Historical Quarterly 29 (March 1945): 12–15, for a repudiation of Hardee's favoring a "retiring policy." Johnston later asserted that if either Hardee or Stewart had been promoted, Atlanta would have been held. Johnston, "Opposing Sherman," *B&L* 4:277.

5. *OR* 38(5):885, 888; Lindsley, ed., *Military Annals*, 97; Hood, *Advance and Retreat*, 126–27; APS to Hood, August 7, 1872, typewritten copy in Davis Papers, Tulane; Hood, Hardee, and APS to Jefferson Davis, July 18, 1864, Davis to Hood, Hardee, and APS, July 18, 1864, Davis Papers, Tulane; Woodworth, *Jefferson Davis and His Generals*, 285–86; T. G. Dabney, "Gen. A. P. Stewart on Strong Topics," *CV* 17 (January 1909): 31–32. Though Stewart wrote Hood in 1872 that Hood, Stewart, and Hardee sent a joint telegram to Davis

Over forty years later, Stewart characterized Johnston's replacement as a "stupendous blunder" that "was the coup de grace of the Confederate cause." Stewart opposed Johnston's relief primarily because he had confidence in the latter's ability and because he believed Johnston careful of the blood of his soldiers. Stewart had seen Hood in action as a corps commander since the end of February. Nowhere does Stewart indicate that Hood's abilities impressed him, either as an administrator or as a tactician.

Stewart's true feelings about Hood were no doubt reflected by what he wrote in the *Military Annals* over fifteen years later: "Hood was a brave soldier, a man of many excellent qualities, and a good subordinate. There were many who thought he was not fitted, either by capacity or temperament, to command an army and conduct a campaign." The *Military Annals* reflect Stewart's postwar view that Hood had defamed the Army of Tennessee, and to a lesser degree Johnston, by his claim that the army had been demoralized by Johnston's method of conducting the campaign to that point. He quoted portions of Johnston's memoirs that in turn quoted letters both Hardee and Stewart wrote Johnston in 1868. These postwar documents made clear that both corps commanders thought their men were in good spirits and had confidence in Johnston. As Stewart observed, the fighting that soon took place disproved the notion that the Army of Tennessee was demoralized.[6]

At the time Hood took command, Sherman's largest force, Thomas' Army of the Cumberland, was preparing to cross Peachtree Creek, a stream that flowed generally in a westerly direction between Atlanta and the Chattahoochee. Hood, either on his own initiative or because Johnston shared his plans with him, recognized an opportunity to strike Thomas while he crossed his troops over Peachtree Creek, and the Army of the Tennessee and the Army of the Ohio moved to the east of Atlanta to Decatur to break the Georgia Railroad. Hood put the army in line of battle facing Peachtree Creek on the night of July 18 and the morning of the 19th. Stewart and the Army of Mississippi deployed on the left, Hardee in the

---

asking the order be suspended, in old age Stewart erroneously recalled that it was only he that sent a telegram. Compare 1872 letter at Tulane in Hood, *Advance and Retreat*, 127, to Dabney, "Gen. A. P. Stewart on Strong Topics," 32.

6. Stewart, foreword in Ridley, *Battles and Sketches*, xii; Lindsley, ed., *Military Annals*, 95–99, 100.

center, and Hood's old corps (with Cheatham temporarily in command) with Smith's militia on the right.[7]

On the morning of Wednesday, July 20, Hood determined to attack at 1 P.M. that afternoon. Stewart, along with Hardee, Cheatham, and G. W. Smith, met with Hood at army headquarters to receive Hood's "specific" orders. With Cheatham on the right, Hood intended to strike Thomas with Stewart's and Hardee's corps, each with one division in reserve. Hood determined to make the attack *en echelon,* from right to left—in other words, an attack down the line by successive divisional advances, a tactic seen at both Gettysburg and Chickamauga. Hardee was to commence the assault, the attack progressing through his three front divisions—Bate's, Walker's, and Maney's (Cheatham's). After Maney attacked, Loring and then Walthall were to attack on Stewart's front. Hood anticipated finding the Federals mostly unfortified and in an unsettled condition as they crossed the creek. Hood later wrote that he asked each corps commander if he understood his orders, and each answered in the affirmative.[8]

As the morning of July 20 broke, beginning another hot Georgia summer day, Thomas resumed his movement across Peachtree Creek. He had most of his men across by noon, although not in a continuous line. This was especially the case in his center corps, Hooker's Twentieth. Although Hood would not catch the Army of the Cumberland straddling the creek, conditions were promising for Hood's and Stewart's first attack in their respective new roles. Unfortunately, Schofield and McPherson were reported moving on Atlanta from Decatur, forcing Hood to order Cheatham to move a one-mile division front to cover the Decatur Road. Hood compensated in part by ordering both Hardee and Stewart to move a half mile to the right. As this move only started at 1 P.M., Stewart feared that the most favorable time for an attack would slip away during the time it took to make the shift. The Tennessean sent an officer to Hood to urge an immediate attack.[9]

---

7. Errol M. Clauss, "The Atlanta Campaign, 18 July–2 September, 1864" (Ph.D. diss., Emory University, 1965), 68; *OR* 38(5):885, 38(1):71; Hood, *Advance and Retreat,* 161–66; Lindsley, ed., *Military Annals,* 98.

8. *OR* 38(3):630, 871; Hood, *Advance and Retreat,* 167–68; Lindsley, ed., *Military Annals,* 98–99; Davis, "Hood and the Battles for Atlanta," 61–62.

9. Castel, *Decision in the West,* 371–73; *OR* 38(3):871.

While waiting for the attack to commence, Stewart personally addressed some of his men, exhorting them to carry everything on the south bank of Peachtree Creek, and that mere temporary breastworks should not halt their attack. These instructions also passed through Loring and Walthall down the chain of command. Hood was present and listened with approval. As one historian of the campaign has pointed out, Hood, like Robert E. Lee, gave his corps commanders their orders and sat back to watch them and their men execute his commands. Stewart disapproved of this method of command, at least in the circumstances then confronting the army. In light of the changes required by the shift to the left, Hood should have kept in closer touch and made adjustments where necessary. Stewart felt Johnston would have kept a tighter rein on his troops.[10]

Eventually, Hardee's shift to the right halted. Loring, in command of Stewart's right division, had maintained contact with Hardee and finally encountered a staff officer Hardee had posted to monitor the shift in accordance with Hood's instructions. Loring was belatedly told that it was not intended for him to make any more than the half-mile shift. It was roughly 3 P.M. when Stewart learned of this error and much too late, in Old Straight's opinion, to countermarch to where the corps should be.[11]

As it turned out, Stewart was right that the attack should have been launched from his previous location. The Twentieth Corps divisions of Williams and Geary were not yet fully deployed after crossing the creek. At that point Hardee was on the flank of John Newton's division of the Fourth Corps, which was linked to Hooker's main body by William T. Ward's division of the Twentieth Corps. The Federals in Stewart's front were on a ridge, in a generally wooded area broken by cleared fields, small streams, fences covered with briars, and "deep ravines and thickets, while here and there were isolated hills and spurs." It was questionable whether

---

10. Hood, *Advance and Retreat*, 168–69; *OR* 38(3):871, 876, 894, 896, 898; J. P. Cannon, *Bloody Banners and Barefoot Boys: A History of the 27th Regiment Alabama Infantry, C.S.A.*, ed. Neil Crowson and John V. Brogden (Shippensburg, Pa.: Burd Street Press, 1996), 84; Castel, *Decision in the West*, 372; Lindsley, ed., *Military Annals*, 100. Hood wrote that Stewart doubtless thought a direct appeal to the troops was necessary because of a "long-continued use of entrenchments." Hood, *Advance and Retreat*, 168–69. Though Stewart did not mention his appeal, the *Military Annals* make it clear that Stewart did not consider his soldiers too timid to attack breastworks. See Lindsley, ed., *Military Annals*, 96–100.

11. *OR* 38(3):878.

Stewart and his men could sufficiently overcome the difficulties of the terrain, the "almost impenetrable jungle" and the "oppressive heat" to take
advantage of the somewhat disorganized situation of Hooker's force.[12]

Stewart's first action as a corps commander forced him to employ only
four brigades, a force no larger than his division had been a year before.
Brigadier General John Adams' brigade of Loring's Division and Brigadier
General William A. Quarles's brigade of Walthall's Division were each detached on picket duty, although both would be in position to support a
successful attack. French's Division was kept in reserve to cover the army's
left.[13]

A few minutes before 4 P.M., Featherston, commanding Loring's right
brigade, watched Maney's (Cheatham's) Division move toward the front
in what Featherston supposed was the opening of the attack on his immediate right. This was Featherston's cue in Hood's *en echelon* plan to move
forward himself. The order to advance was received with the "wildest enthusiasm." The Mississippians swept forward with "eagerness and rapid-
ity," crossing a small stream in their front, Tanyard Branch, and advanced
"under a very heavy and destructive fire from the enemy's batteries and
small-arms." Featherston's five regiments and battalion of sharpshooters
seized what he observed to be "incomplete" Union works in his front,
which were held by a thin line from Ward's division. Maney had not attacked, however, and thus the Federals were able to direct a fire on Featherston from his right and front that was too much for his exposed brigade
to bear. Reluctantly, Featherston retired 250 to 300 yards to a strip of timber, convinced that Maney's delay had ruined a promising attack.[14]

Geary's line was advanced on its right flank to a high, narrow, timbered
hill where Geary positioned the 33rd New Jersey. Geary went forward
with the regiment and interrogated three Rebel prisoners, who informed
him that there were no large bodies of Confederate troops within two
miles. Suddenly, Federal skirmishers came scurrying back to the hill,
closely followed by masses of Rebels, who forced the 33rd New Jersey off
the hill with heavy casualties. Moving forward with Stewart's orders to let

---

12. Castel, *Decision in the West*, 375; *OR* 38(2):138, 38(3):881, 886.

13. *OR* 38(3):871, 876, 930–31.

14. Ibid., 871, 881–82, 887; Castel, *Decision in the West*, 377; *Augusta Daily Chronicle
and Sentinel*, July 23, 1864.

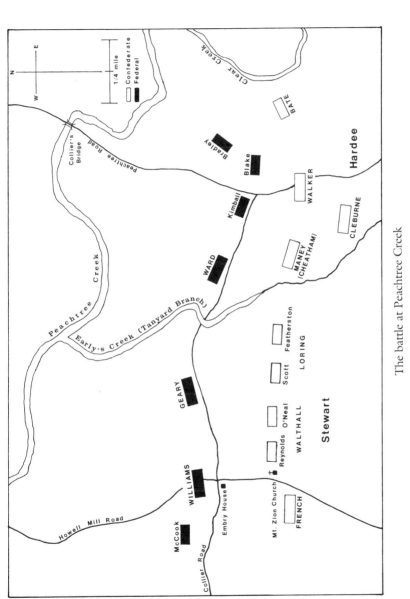

The battle at Peachtree Creek
Map by Blake Magner

nothing stop them, Scott's Brigade swept across the Federal position. The consolidated 27th-35th-49th Alabama Regiments captured the 33rd's colors. Pressing on, a mix-up in orders stalled the consolidated regiments' attack, bringing them to what appeared to be a "sudden standstill." Once the confusion was sorted out, the Alabamians captured a redoubt with three cannon. Scott's two right regiments assaulted the main Federal line along with Featherston and succeeded in capturing a portion of the Yankee works. Facing pressure from Geary's reserve brigade as well as the brigades the Rebels had initially forced back, Scott retreated when Featherston withdrew, abandoning the captured pieces. Scott took position about 150 yards to the rear of the Federal works, where Loring assured him that he had done all he could, lacking support on the right.[15]

Posted in the area of the Howell Mill (Pace's Ferry) Road, Hooker's right division, under Alpheus Williams, deployed with two brigades forward and one in reserve. While deploying a battery to engage a Confederate outpost near the Embry house, Williams heard the roar of battle off to his left. Hurrying his men into line, Williams observed that a dense area of woods and thickets covered his entire front. Under Stewart's watchful eye, Walthall's two assault brigades were advancing through the woods toward Williams' line. Walthall's right brigade, Cantey's under Colonel Edward A. O'Neal, initially advanced in good order. In his first battle as a brigade commander, O'Neal soon encountered difficulties as his left unit, the 29th Alabama, mistakenly guided to the left, necessitating the left center and center units in line to cover the gap thus created, "attenuating their line to almost a skirmish line." At about the same time, the brigade passed on its right a crescent-shaped Federal line. O'Neal's right regiment, the 37th Mississippi, along with three companies of the 17th Alabama, swung around to engage this line, but were in danger of being flanked themselves. The brigade fell back in a disorganized fashion, and O'Neal appealed for reinforcements. Walthall recognized the need for support on his right, and

---

15. *OR* 38(2):138, 38(3):894–95, 896; Harry V. Barnard, *Tattered Volunteers: The Twenty-seventh Alabama Infantry Regiment, C.S.A.* (Northport, Ala.: Hermitage Press, 1965), 64; Joel Murphree, "Autobiography and Civil War Letters of Joel Murphree of Troy, Alabama, 1864–1865," *Alabama Historical Quarterly* 19 (1957): 185–87; Cannon, *Bloody Banners and Barefoot Boys*, 84–85; Castel, *Decision in the West*, 370, 377; *Augusta Daily Chronicle and Sentinel*, July 26, 1864.

Stewart sent forward the 24th South Carolina. When O'Neal's call came, Walthall released the Palmetto State men to O'Neal, who also received help from the division's skirmishers. O'Neal charged again and made some progress, but being unsupported again fell back.[16]

On Walthall's left, Reynolds moved his brigade out to the right obliquely across the Howell Mill Road, keeping in contact with O'Neal. Notwithstanding their exhaustion from hours of battle on the picket line the day before, Reynolds' men overran some Yankee entrenchments on the brigade's left, but were unable to do so on their right because of the need to dress on O'Neal. Reynolds' left came under a heavy enfilading fire from elements of Palmer's Fourteenth Corps posted on Williams' right. The Federal fire from the left forced Reynolds back 75 or 100 yards. To counteract the heavy flanking fire on the left, Captain Joseph Selden's Battery hurried forward, under the supervision of Walthall's artillery chief, Major William Preston. Selden's fire alleviated the threat to Reynolds' left, which enabled the Arkansas brigade to engage the Federals for some time in a fierce firefight. During this interlude, a cannon shot killed Preston. When Selden's Battery exhausted its ammunition, Reynolds temporarily fell back, but eventually regained the lost ground and held it to the end of the engagement.[17]

Probably because Walthall was new in his divisional command and O'Neal inexperienced in brigade command, Stewart spent the afternoon of the attack on the left. Too, with French's Division in reserve on the left to guard that quarter and to exploit any large breakthrough, Stewart must have wanted to be near to deploy French should the situation require it. Late in the afternoon, Stewart received a message from Loring requesting a fresh brigade in place of his third brigade, Adams', which had been out on picket duty. Stewart and Loring sought help from Hardee, who had no troops to spare. The advancing Federals to the east of Atlanta necessitated Cleburne's dispatch to that quarter, weakening Hardee's attack. Stewart's role in the battle ended when he received an order from Hood requiring him to pull his corps back into the entrenchments from which it had advanced.[18]

16. *OR* 38(2):33–34, 38(3):925–26, 943.

17. *OR* 38(3):925–26, 935–43; D. H. Reynolds Diary, July 19, 20, 1864, Reynolds Papers, UAR.

18. *OR* 38(3):871, 877, 926.

On the Confederate right, Hardee's attack stalled. Overall, it was one of Hardee's poorer performances, and Stewart wrote in his report of the action some months later: "I cannot but think, had the plan of the battle, as I understood it, been carried out fully, we would have achieved a great success." Hood commended Stewart and his command for having done all that was asked of them, Stewart being held to have "carried out his instructions to the letter." Hood later wrote that the troops of Hardee's Corps, "although composed of the best troops in the army, virtually accomplished nothing." Hood ascribed the failure of these troops to a reluctance to assault breastworks, his favorite complaint. A writer for the *Augusta Daily Chronicle and Sentinel* disagreed, reporting that the troops were disappointed they were not allowed to go on by their "overly prudent" officers. Stewart had a simpler explanation: that Hardee was disturbed at being passed over by a junior officer for command of the army, and for some reason did not relay Hood's orders to his command. Stewart also believed Hood had to bear some of the blame, as he was not on the field to spur Hardee on, as Old Straight believed Johnston would have done.[19]

The Army of Mississippi experienced some success on July 20, but Hardee's Corps had not, causing one newspaper writer to curiously characterize the Battle of Peachtree Creek as "a negative victory plainly won." As pointed out recently by one historian, contrary to the standard view of this engagement, Hood's plan had not been one of headlong attack, but rather of oblique assaults on the exposed flank of the Army of the Cumberland. Because of the lack of execution by Hardee's Corps, Loring and Walthall went forward virtually unsupported, allowing elements of three Federal corps to absorb their fierce attacks and defeat the assault. Loring took a severe beating, as his losses totaled 1,062. Walthall's casualty distribution was somewhat unequal, O'Neal losing 279 and Reynolds 67. On the other hand, their two principal antagonists, Geary and Williams, had suffered a total of 1,056 of Thomas' approximately 1,750 casualties.[20]

19. Castel, *Decision in the West*, 375–76; Hughes, *Hardee*, 225; *OR* 38(3):871; Hood, *Advance and Retreat*, 168–71; *Augusta Daily Chronicle and Sentinel*, July 26, 1864; Lindsley, ed., *Military Annals*, 99–100.

20. *Augusta Daily Chronicle and Sentinel*, July 26, 1864; *Savannah Republican*, July 25, 1864; Davis, "Hood and the Battles for Atlanta," 62; Stephen Davis, "Hood Fights Desperately: The Battles for Atlanta—Events from July 10 to September 2, 1864," *Blue & Gray Magazine* 6 (August 1989): 17; *OR* 38(2):34, 141, 38(3):877, 938, 942. For a more gener-

In Stewart's first major engagement as a corps commander, his men had fought well. Stewart had the advantage of attacking over more favorable ground than Hardee and against troops not particularly well-disposed to receive that attack. Stewart's attack was not coordinated with Hardee's in the manner Hood intended, but within the Army of Mississippi the *en echelon* attack progressed in a relatively smooth fashion. Stewart had been Hood's most reliable general while Hood was his corps commander. Peachtree Creek proved that Old Straight could be counted on in his larger role.

Even as the dead and wounded lay in the waning heat of the night of July 20, Hood perceived an opportunity in the Federal advance from the east that had affected his assault on Thomas that afternoon. Intelligence reports indicated that McPherson and his Army of the Tennessee had an exposed flank on the southern end of their north-south line about three miles southeast of Atlanta. Sensing an opportunity for another Chancellorsville, Hood resolved to throw Hardee's Corps on this exposed flank. July 22 was another day of blood, costing the army over 5,000 casualties and W. H. T. Walker, while the Federals lost 3,722 men, including James B. McPherson, Sherman's young friend and the commander of the Army of the Tennessee. Stewart and his men held the Atlanta entrenchments against Thomas, no more than 13,000 Rebels nervously protecting the city from over 40,000 Yankees.[21]

Hood blamed Hardee for the failure of July 22. Furthermore, he attributed the defeat of one of his well-conceived attacks to the timidity of the soldiers of the Army of Tennessee, who he believed had been imbued with the "timid defensive" policy of his predecessor. Years later, Stewart wrote in rebuttal: "There was never a single occasion during the entire campaign . . . that the 'rank and file' of the Army of Tennessee failed in its duty." Hood had convinced himself that the army wouldn't fight, even after the two sanguinary conflicts of July 20 and 22, and soon passed that sentiment on to his newest corps commander, Lieutenant General Stephen D. Lee,

---

ous view of Hardee's performance, see Clauss, "The Atlanta Campaign, 18 July–2 September, 1864," 98–101.

21. Horn, *Army of Tennessee*, 354–58; Davis, "Hood Fights Desperately," 20–25; Clauss, "The Atlanta Campaign, 18 July–2 September, 1864," 105–67; *OR* 38(1):116.

who within a few days involved Stewart and a substantial portion of his corps in a fiasco.[22]

Lee's arrival from outside the army was yet another sign of the depleted nature of the army's officer corps. Hindman's departure with an eye injury had been the occasion for the elevation of one of Stewart's old brigadiers, John C. Brown, to temporary divisional command. As a more permanent solution, Patton Anderson was brought up from Florida to command that division. Meanwhile, Walker's death left his division without a commander, and there being no appropriate officer for that command, it was broken up and its three brigades were distributed to the other three divisions of Hardee's Corps. Hardee himself continued to be unhappy with Hood's elevation over him, and requested a transfer, which, for the time being, was denied. All the while, the Federal grip around Atlanta was tightening.[23]

Having been foiled on the east side of Atlanta, Sherman turned his attention to the west side. He moved the Army of the Tennessee, now under eastern veteran Major General Oliver Otis Howard, to the Federal right, seeking to cut the railroads leading south and west out of Atlanta. Rebel cavalry had provided Hood with information of this move, and he saw yet another opportunity to strike a blow. The southeast-to-northwest Lick Skillet Road intersected near two north-south roads in the area of Ezra Church, almost due west of the works on the north side of Atlanta. Hood planned for Lee and his corps to gain control of the intersection on July 28, stack the Federals up there, and then to strike them on the flank the next day with Old Straight and the Army of Mississippi, newly designated as "Stewart's Corps." Stewart being given the difficult flank attack seems to have been affirmation of Hood's continuing reliance on the Tennessean, especially in light of Hood's dim view of Hardee's recent performances.[24]

---

22. Hood, *Advance and Retreat*, 183; Lindsley, ed., *Military Annals*, 100–101; *OR* 38(5):910–12. For Stephen D. Lee's background, see Herman Hattaway, *General Stephen D. Lee* (Jackson: University Press of Mississippi, 1976), 3, 9, 47–59, 78–125, 133–34; Warner, *Generals in Gray*, 183. Lee had incurred the ire of Nathan Bedford Forrest only days before with a botched attack at Tupelo. See Brian Steel Wills, *A Battle from the Start: The Life of Nathan Bedford Forrest* (New York: HarperCollins, 1992), 220–33.

23. *OR* 38(5):904, 907; Connelly, *Autumn of Glory*, 451.

24. Horn, *Army of Tennessee*, 359–60; *OR* 38(3):763, 872, 38(5):912; Castel, *Decision in the West*, 426.

Unfortunately for Hood and the Confederates slated to occupy the crossroads, Howard and the three corps of the Army of the Tennessee already occupied breastworks there on the morning of July 28, holding the area of the church and two ridges to either side of it. As Lee advanced out toward the Lick Skillet Road, he found Federal troops already in control of the area. Rather than applying to Hood for new orders in light of this unanticipated development, Lee pitched in, launching Stewart's old division, now commanded by Henry D. Clayton, and Hindman's old division, at this point still commanded by John C. Brown, against the Federals. In Lee's words, "the enemy's works were slight, and besides they had barely gotten into position when we made the attack."[25]

Brown, and then Clayton, threw their divisions against the Federal works. Their men suffered severely in attacking the fortified Federal veterans. While Lee felt the enemy could have been driven away by coordinated attacks, the well-tried Clayton, veteran of assaults at Chickamauga and Resaca, "found the enemy in strong works and upon ground well chosen." Such was Lee's first attack with the Army of Tennessee.[26]

In his memoirs, Hood stated that Lee "promptly obeyed orders" at Ezra Church. Yet a communiqué from army headquarters that morning to Hardee stated, "General Lee . . . is directed not to attack unless the enemy exposes himself in attacking us." A message to Stewart at 3:25 P.M. that day, which possibly he never read, ordered him "not to do more fighting than necessary, unless you can get a decided advantage." Stewart had previously been required, however, to "support [Lee] fully." It appears that since Lee told Hood he saw a "lack of spirit" in the troops, Hood conveniently ignored the fact that Lee disregarded orders not to attack.[27]

The spirit of his corps had been on Stewart's mind a few days earlier. On July 24, he issued a message exhorting his men to prepare for the final struggle for Atlanta. As the following passage reflects, the long retreat from Dalton had not lessened Stewart's conviction in his Cause:

> To succeed we must work hard and fight hard, and many of us must die. You, at least, who have faced him a hundred times, do not

25. Castel, *Decision in the West*, 424–29; *OR* 38(1):77, 38(3):763.

26. *OR* 38(3):763, 767–68, 821; Clauss, "The Atlanta Campaign, 18 July–2 September, 1864," 203–205.

27. Hood, *Advance and Retreat*, 194–95; *OR* 38(5):919–20; Castel, *Decision in the West*, 131.

fear death. I believe, and so do you, in an overruling, Special Providence, that in some mysterious way guides the course of events and shapes the destinies of nations. Our cause is just. Heaven favors it, and will give us success if we do our duty. Let us put our trust in God, using the means He has given us, and we cannot fail.[28]

With orders to "support Lee fully," Stewart found Lee heavily engaged at Ezra Church and "in need of assistance," and therefore sent for his lead division under Walthall. Having just arrived on the field himself, Stewart deferred to Lee, who suggested that Walthall assault the area that Brown had attacked. Lee must have relayed to Stewart his belief that the Federals "would yield to a vigorous attack." With Loring in support, Walthall moved against the enemy works at about 2 P.M. Walthall was particularly concerned about his left, and expressed that concern to both Stewart and Lee. Stewart advised Walthall that Lee would cover his left with a brigade, but Lee failed to do so, exposing Walthall's men to "a damaging flank fire." Walthall later wrote that he "found [the enemy] in strong position and large force on a hill a short distance in front, and failed to dislodge him after a vigorous and persistent effort, in which I lost 152 officers and nearly 1,000 men, considerably over one-third my force." Walthall felt that a force twice the size of his division could not have successfully assaulted the Federal line.[29]

Stewart watched Walthall's attack, which failed only "after a desperate fight and heavy loss." Walthall sent an officer advising Stewart that the attack desired by Lee had hit Federal works too strong to be carried. Rather than launching Loring's Division against the same works, Stewart sent orders to Walthall to hold his position until Loring could be deployed to cover his withdrawal. Loring was wounded before his division was fully deployed. Stewart then went forward to ascertain whether the Federals might launch a countercharge. Passing the Confederate line, Stewart rode into an open field in full view of the Yankees and was struck in the forehead by a nearly spent ball, knocking him senseless and leaving a wound in the shape of a V. With Stewart incapacitated, Walthall assumed command as

28. *Macon Daily Telegraph,* August 2, 1864.
29. *OR* 38(3):763, 872, 926–27; D. H. Reynolds Diary, July 28, 1864, Reynolds Papers, UAR.

the senior officer of the corps on the field about 4 P.M., and supervised its withdrawal back into the Atlanta works that night.[30]

In the *Military Annals*, Stewart challenged the assertions of Hood and Lee that the failure at Ezra Church was the fault of the common soldier of the Army of Tennessee. For the first time in that work, he quoted his own report of the action, which to him made it clear that the men did their duty. Without naming names, it seems clear that Stewart laid the blame of the day on Lee, who did not properly adapt to the changed situation he found at Ezra Church and "to the inaccuracy of [Hood's] information. The enemy was found to be in far greater numbers and occupying a far stronger position at the point to be attacked than had been supposed." Lee's biographer notes that as at Tupelo, the young and inexperienced lieutenant general had made the mistake of making continued unprofitable attacks against entrenched defenders. Thomas Connelly criticized Stewart for not sticking to his orders to hit the Federals in their flank and rear, but this criticism ignores the fact that that assault was scheduled for the next day, once Lee had control of the crossroads and the Federals were bunched up, ripe for a flank movement. Given the time of Stewart's wounding, just before 4 P.M., the only order he probably received from Hood that day was to support Lee fully.[31]

There is room to criticize Stewart for his part of the Ezra Church defeat, primarily because he failed to exercise the discretion called for by the tactical situation. It should have been obvious to Old Straight that Lee was attacking because the situation envisioned by Hood had changed. While Lee had asked for support, there was no indication that he needed a covering force to withdraw his own battered troops from the field. Lee remained convinced that determined attacks could still drive the Federals away, and wanted to employ Stewart's men to prove that point. If Stewart had been on the field long enough to review the situation, he probably would have realized the Federals were too strong to attack with success. If he had not been on the field long enough to make that determination, he should not have deployed Walthall before seeing for himself. Stewart's position as senior officer on the field conferred discretion that should have been exer-

30. *OR* 38(3):872, 927–28; Ridley, *Battles and Sketches*, 475; Wingfield, *Stewart*, 179.

31. Lindsley, ed., *Military Annals*, 101–102; Hattaway, *General Stephen D. Lee*, 128–30; Connelly, *Autumn of Glory*, 454.

cised so as not to compound Lee's mistake. In Stewart's defense, however, the young corps commander on the field had asked for help. Stewart gave it, but in a different context than Hood had originally anticipated.[32]

When wounded, Stewart was carried from the field by a member of his staff, Aristide Hopkins. As Harriet Stewart was at Savannah, and communications to that city still existed from Atlanta, Stewart went there to recover. Stewart and Loring barely missed capture when the train bearing them from Atlanta had to turn back to avoid encountering Federal raiders. Old Straight's wounding illustrated the deepening problem of command within the army. With Stewart down, and Loring wounded, Walthall, himself in divisional command for only a period of weeks, was the corps' senior officer on the field, and completed its battle on July 28.[33]

With Lee so new to command and Stewart gone, Hood took the unusual step of ordering Hardee to the scene to assess the situation and assume command if necessary. Within Stewart's Corps, Loring's absence made French the senior officer present in the corps, although French was not on the field. Upon hearing of Stewart's incapacity, Hood sent for Cheatham and placed him in command of the corps. French, who had no problem in Stewart's elevation over him to command the corps, was indignant that Cheatham, a major general from another corps, should be placed over him. French angrily wrote Hood and then Davis in protest. Hood also asked for the temporary rank of major general for John C. Brown so that he could command Loring's Division until Loring returned.[34]

There is little record of Stewart's stay in Savannah, which lasted approximately two weeks. Probably in hopes that Stewart would soon be in a position to return, Ridley went to Forsyth, Georgia, with Stewart's baggage wagon on July 30 to await Stewart's orders. In the interlude before the general resumed command on August 15, Stewart's Corps resumed its po-

32. As to Stewart's outranking Lee, see "Note," *CV* 12 (February 1904): 85; APS to Robert Alonzo Brock, June 2, 1891, Alonzo Brock Collection, Huntington Library.

33. Aristide Hopkins, Y. R. Le Moncier, and J. A. Chalaron, "Tributes to Gen. A. P. Stewart," *CV* 16 (November 1908): 594–95; *Augusta Daily Chronicle and Sentinel*, August 2, 1864; *Savannah Republican*, August 2, 1864; Ridley, *Battles and Sketches*, 479.

34. *OR* 38(3):699–700, 38(5):920, 924–25; French, *Two Wars*, 219–20. Hardee's being ordered to the field raises two issues: Lee's competence and the validity of Hood's criticisms of Hardee as to July 20 and 22.

sition within the Atlanta works, occasionally skirmishing and making demonstrations, and being subjected to Federal artillery fire.[35]

When Stewart returned to the lines around Atlanta, he had a few new staff members there to greet him, including Polk's son-in-law, Captain William D. Gale, as assistant adjutant general. Gale, who had served on Polk's staff as well, had just returned to the army after escorting the bishop's body to Augusta for burial. Writing to his wife on August 19, 1864, Gale offered his first impressions of Stewart: "Genl Stewart has returned and assumed command. We all like him very much indeed. He has a son about 18 with him as A. D. C. The Genl is one of the most natural men I ever saw. Perfectly well bred and highly educated, very quiet and sedate, a thorough soldier and in all his actions precise & military."[36]

At the time of Stewart's return, his corps occupied the northwestern sector of the Confederate line, from the Marietta Road to a point just west of the Lick Skillet Road. His men constantly skirmished with the Federals and occasionally endured severe bombardments. Early on August 17, two days after his return, Stewart rode out to French's headquarters, and the two generals rode along the line and then returned for breakfast. French's headquarters was behind a Confederate redoubt which was a favorite target of Sherman's gunners. While Stewart and French were finishing breakfast, the nearly daily bombardment of the redoubt began. Shells fell on either side of French's headquarters, requiring Stewart to stay with French

---

35. *OR* 38(3):872; Special Order, July 30, 1864, Army of Tennessee, Special Orders, 1864–1865, RG 109, NA; French, *Two Wars*, 220; Davis, "Hood Fights Desperately," 36, 38–39, 45; Horn, *Army of Tennessee*, 362–63.

36. W. D. Gale to wife, August 19, 1864, Gale-Polk Papers, SHC. Among officers inherited from Polk were Lieutenant Aristide Hopkins, a member of the escort whom Polk had used as an aide, and Major Douglas West, assistant adjutant general. The staff also included Major John Lauderdale of Chattanooga, assistant quartermaster; Major William F. Foster, chief engineer; Lieutenant Colonel T. F. Sevier, inspector general; Major J. J. Murphy, chief commissary; and Captain Charles A. Vanderford, chief ordnance officer. Crute, *Confederate Staff Officers*, 185–86; United States War Department, *List of Staff Officers of the Confederate States Army*, ed. John M. Carroll (Mattitucky, N.Y.: John M. Carroll, 1983), 56, 58; "Last Roll Call," *CV* 10 (March 1902): 125; "Last Roll Call," *CV* 33 (September 1925): 346; Field Returns, September 20, 1864, Army of Tennessee Records, Joseph Jones Collection, Tulane.

an hour longer than anticipated. French's diary reflects that the firing on his portion of the line continued through August 25.[37]

Having tried cavalry raids to no avail, Sherman became convinced by the middle of August that disrupting Atlanta's remaining rail connections would require the bulk of his army. He devised a plan whereby the Twentieth Corps would withdraw to hold the bridgehead over the Chattahoochee and the remaining six corps would move around the Confederate left, first to Fairburn, about eighteen miles to the southwest of Atlanta, to disrupt the West Point Railroad, and then to Jonesboro, to cut the Macon Railroad. Sherman began his move on the night of August 25 by pulling back from his lines close to Atlanta.[38]

The next morning, elements of both Lee's and Stewart's corps advanced into the abandoned Federal works. On his front, French observed that the works were both strong and incredibly filthy. A soldier of Sears' Brigade noted that the thick undergrowth between the lines had been cut away by bullets at an even height like stubble in a grain field. On August 27, French sent a reconnaissance force of two brigades accompanied by artillery to the Twentieth Corps' lines at Turner's Ferry on the Chattahoochee. French's diary shows that even on August 26, however, the Confederates knew that Sherman was moving to their left.[39]

Although it appears that Hood believed that the Rebel cavalry raids on Sherman's rail connection had some effect on the Federal supply situation, Hardee's contention that Hood was completely taken in by Sherman's move appears untrue. By August 28, Hood's scouts had located Sherman's new line stretching from the lower reaches of the Chattahoochee west of Atlanta to a point near the West Point Railroad. Hood began shifting elements of his army to the south, to cover Jonesboro and Rough and Ready, both on the Macon rail line.[40]

On August 30, it became clear that the Federals were going to strike the railroad at Jonesboro, and Hood dispatched Hardee's and Lee's corps to

37. *OR* 38(3):872; French, *Two Wars*, 220–21.

38. *OR* 38(1):79–80.

39. French, *Two Wars*, 221; William Pitt Chambers, *Blood and Sacrifice: The Civil War Journal of a Confederate Soldier*, ed. Richard A. Baumgardner (Huntington, W.Va.: Blue Acorn Press, 1994), 163.

40. Connelly, *Autumn of Glory*, 458–61.

that point to deal with the threat. Once more, Hardee would command. Hood remained in Atlanta, with Stewart's Corps and the Georgia militia. What occurred next is laconically described by Stewart in the *Military Annals*: "Hardee was dispatched to [Jonesboro], with orders to attack the enemy at an early hour on the 31st, and to drive them, 'at all hazards, into the river in their rear.' The corps commanded by General S. D. Lee was to cooperate. The attack was not made until two in the afternoon. It failed; the enemy had possession of the railroad, and during the afternoon of September 1st Atlanta was evacuated." Stewart marched south out of Atlanta toward McDonough, and then to Lovejoy's Station, south of Jonesboro, his corps reduced to 11,457 men. Sherman, content with the prize he had sought so long, left the Confederates in peace and withdrew into Atlanta.[41]

The loss of Atlanta ended the campaign that started outside of Dalton in May. At the beginning of the campaign, and for a time thereafter, the Army of Tennessee had been in remarkably good spirits, reinforced to an extent never before seen, and materially in as good shape as was possible. Four months later, after thousands of casualties and great material loss, it had lost thousands of square miles of territory and Atlanta. Although Hood telegraphed Richmond that the officers and men of his army were not discouraged, since they felt that every effort had been made to hold Atlanta to the last, Hood secretly did not agree. In his opinion, "according to all human calculations we should have saved Atlanta had the officers and men of the army done what was expected of them." This analysis, which Alexander P. Stewart most emphatically denied, would cause the army grief in the months ahead.[42]

Hood spent the days after the fall of Atlanta seeking to rejuvenate his army. He appealed to Richmond for reinforcements, and prevailed upon Hardee to write Davis personally with a similar request. He sought pay for the men, which by then was ten months in arrears. He asked Davis to visit the army or to at least send Bragg. On September 7, he sent orders to his corps commanders to "use all diligence in reorganizing and recuperating your commands," and to make recommendations relative to officer vacan-

41. Horn, *Army of Tennessee*, 365–68; Lindsley, ed., *Military Annals*, 103; *OR* 38(3):683, 872.

42. *OR* 38(5):1018, 1023. Stewart's opinion is made perfectly clear in the *Military Annals*.

cies in their various commands. The army remained at Lovejoy's for another ten days or so, eventually moving to the northwest to Palmetto, on
the railroad to Montgomery, Alabama. There, on September 25, Jefferson
Davis made his third visit to the army.[43]

Davis once more faced problems with the high command of the Army
of Tennessee. Even as he reviewed the troops, he heard cries from the ranks
for Johnston. When a call came for three cheers for the president from
some Tennesseans of Quarles's Brigade, the men were silent. Hardee, in
light of his own bruised feelings for being passed over and Hood's blaming
him for the loss of Atlanta, essentially told Davis that either he or Hood
must go. Sensibly, and especially in light of the tension between Hood and
Hardee, Davis included in his visit a meeting with Stewart and Lee on September 27. Old Straight forthrightly told the president the army preferred
Johnston as its commander.[44]

Davis' solution did little to remedy the army's problem of a commander
that believed it too timid to engage the enemy. Hood would be retained,
yet Beauregard received a theater command similar to that held by Johnston in 1862–63, with authority over Hood and the Army of Tennessee
and over Lieutenant General Richard Taylor and his troops in Mississippi
and the Gulf coast. Since Hood stayed, Hardee left, and was placed in
Beauregard's old command along the South Carolina and Georgia coast.
Cheatham, by now accustomed to temporary corps command, assumed
command of Hardee's Corps as its senior major general.[45]

The army crossed the Chattahoochee on September 29, moving north

---

43. *OR* 38(5):1021, 1023, 1027, 1028; Lindsley, ed., *Military Annals*, 103; Horn,
Army of Tennessee, 371–72.

44. Woodworth, *Jefferson Davis and His Generals*, 290–93; Cannon, *Bloody Banners and
Barefoot Boys*, 96; Chambers, *Blood and Sacrifice*, 170; Robert Patrick, *Reluctant Rebel: The Secret Diary of Robert Patrick, 1861–1865*, ed. F. Jay Taylor (1959; reprint, Baton Rouge: Louisiana State University Press, 1996), 230; McNeilly, "A Great Game of Strategy," 382; Connelly, *Autumn of Glory*, 470–72; Hood, *Advance and Retreat*, 253–55; Lindsley, ed., *Military
Annals*, 97, 103.

45. Woodworth, *Jefferson Davis and His Generals*, 292–93; Lindsley, ed., *Military Annals*,
103; Connelly, *Autumn of Glory*, 478; Hood, *Advance and Retreat*, 254–55. Davis later inquired of Stewart whether he recalled that the plans for invading Tennessee were made at Palmetto at the president's insistence. Stewart replied he was not aware of it, nor had he heard it
since. APS to Jefferson Davis, September 6, 1873, Davis Papers, Tulane.

to fall upon the Western and Atlantic Railroad from the Chattahoochee north to the Etowah. On the morning of October 3, Stewart was detailed to attack the Federal garrisons at Big Shanty and Acworth. Early on October 4, Featherston's Brigade captured Big Shanty with about a hundred prisoners. Loring, back with the army after his wound at Ezra Church, captured Acworth and a few hundred bluecoats. Reynolds' Brigade captured Moon's Station between Big Shanty and Acworth, with another hundred prisoners. By the afternoon of October 4, Stewart's Corps had destroyed ten or twelve miles of railroad and captured 600 prisoners, all at a loss of 12 to 15 casualties, mostly wounded.[46]

While at Big Shanty, Stewart received orders from Hood directing him to concentrate two of his divisions in the area between Lost Mountain and New Hope Church, while a third, French's, was to advance to the railroad cut at Allatoona and fill it with dirt, logs, brush, rails, and other fill material. Then, if possible, French was to see if he could destroy the railroad bridge over the Etowah. A later dispatch emphasized Hood's desire to destroy the railroad bridge and indicated that Sherman was then in pursuit. Hood believed that Stewart would be back near the remainder of the army by the time Sherman got close enough to be a threat. In following Hood's orders, Stewart determined from prisoners the presence of a garrison at Allatoona, something apparently unknown to Hood. French marched his division to Allatoona, where he arrived about 3 A.M. on October 5. Because of the Federal presence at Allatoona, Stewart increased French's artillery by one 4-gun battery.[47]

After what French described as a "beautiful and bright" dawning of an Indian summer day, the Federal pickets were driven in and French's artillery opened up on two Federal forts on either side of the railroad. Following the shelling, French demanded the surrender of the Federal post, which the Federal commander refused by not replying. French launched an attack from the north with Sears's Brigade, and from the west with Cockrell's Missourians and Ector's Brigade, under Brigadier General William H. Young.

---

46. Hood, *Advance and Retreat*, 256–57; *OR* 39(1):812.

47. Ridley, *Battles and Sketches*, 396–401; Phil Gottshalk, " 'Is It Surrender or Fight?': The Battle of Allatoona, October 5, 1864," in *The Campaign for Atlanta*, ed. Savas and Woodbury, 1:105.

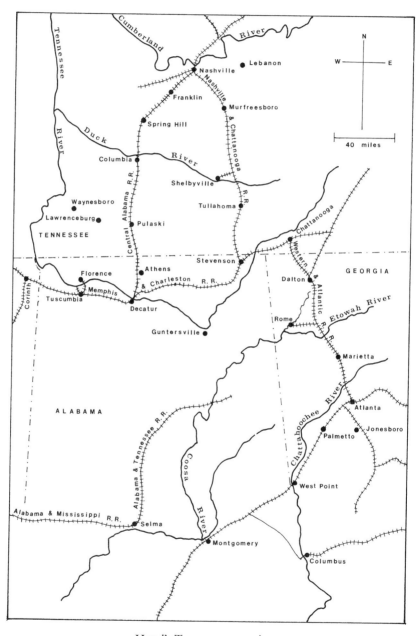

Hood's Tennessee campaign
Map by Blake Magner

The Confederate onslaughts overran an advanced redoubt, resulting in the capture of 950 Federals. Eventually, most of the Federals fell back into their main fortification, a star-shaped fort on the heights just west of the railroad. A small redoubt to the east of the railroad also remained in Federal possession, and materially impeded Sears's attack from the north. The other two Confederate brigades, however, so closely invested the star fort that no Yankee dared show his head over its ramparts. The bloodied Rebel veterans were ready to finish the job.

At this point, shortly after noon, French received word that a strong Union column was coming to relieve the defenders of Allatoona. The relief force's line of advance would soon place it in position to cut French off from the rest of the army. Properly deeming the safety of his division more important than the capture of an isolated outpost, French withdrew, having suffered 799 casualties in what Stewart later termed "a heroic but fruitless attack."[48]

To this point, Hood's strategy of falling on the railroads and making Sherman chase him had worked. On October 9, the army was near the Alabama line at Cave Springs, Georgia, where Hood conferred with Beauregard, his new theater commander. Hood told Beauregard that he would once more fall on the Western and Atlantic, this time in the area between Dalton and Resaca. Hood left Beauregard with the impression that he would stick to the strategy discussed with Davis only two weeks before of hanging near Sherman, looking for an advantageous place to give battle. But Hood was already thinking of an alternative move north across the Tennessee River.[49]

Consistent with Hood's plan to disrupt the railroad, Stewart struck the railroad about two miles north of Resaca late in the evening on October 12. By the next evening, the Confederates had destroyed the railroad to within a few miles of Dalton, along with a great quantity of railroad ties and bridge timbers. Concerned that his men might get overzealous on

---

48. *OR* 39(1):813–20; French, *Two Wars*, 222–84; Gottshalk, "Is It Surrender or Fight?" 113–25. Gottshalk's piece is an excellent account of this bloody but little-known battle. In his autobiography, *Two Wars*, French wrote a lengthy justification for his failure to win at Allatoona, in part to respond to Hood's comments in *Advance and Retreat*, 257. Stewart believed French's account accurate. See *Two Wars*, 284.

49. Connelly, *Autumn of Glory*, 481–82.

their mission of destruction, Stewart issued a strict order against the destruction of private property and made his brigade commanders personally responsible for its enforcement. The corps captured a Yankee work party of 70 or 80 men and reduced a blockhouse at Tilton, capturing about 300 men. Also on October 13, other units of the army forced the surrender of the Federal garrison at Dalton. Sherman's pursuit reached Resaca the same day, so Hood moved northwest to the area south of La Fayette, in the general area of where the army had faced Rosecrans' columns crossing the mountains prior to the Battle of Chickamauga.[50]

On October 15 or 16, Hood inquired of several officers, one of which must have been Stewart, as to whether the army should give battle to Sherman at this point. The opinion was apparently unanimous that although the army's spirits had improved, it was not in shape to do battle with Sherman's main body. Such being the case, and because the army's interdiction of Sherman's supply line had not worked, it appears Hood's mind was made up. The army would move into Alabama, with the purpose of crossing the Tennessee River at Guntersville, disrupting Sherman's communications in the Stevenson and Bridgeport areas, and then marching on the great supply base at Nashville.[51]

While Sherman's larger and slower-moving army doggedly followed the Army of Tennessee into Alabama, its commander tried to convince his superior and friend, Ulysses S. Grant, to allow him to detach enough men for the defense of Tennessee and to take the rest on a raid through Georgia to a point on the Atlantic coast, preferably Savannah. Even as Hood made his proposal to Beauregard on October 21 to authorize a move by the Army of Tennessee across the Tennessee River, Sherman called off his pursuit in preparation for his march to the Atlantic, creating the rare scenario of opposing armies advancing in opposite directions.[52]

At Gadsden, Alabama, Beauregard caught up to Hood and for the first time heard of the bold plan to march the army into Middle Tennessee. In

50. *OR* 39(1):812; General Order, Headquarters, Loring's Division, October 9, 1864, in W. S. Featherson Papers, UM; Connelly, *Autumn of Glory*, 482.

51. Connelly, *Autumn of Glory*, 483; Hood, *Advance and Retreat*, 263–68; Lindsley, ed., *Military Annals*, 103–104.

52. Lindsley, ed., *Military Annals*, 104; Hood, *Advance and Retreat*, 267–69; Hattaway and Jones, *How the North Won*, 638–42.

view of the consensus among the army's officers that Sherman was too strong to be confronted, and the obvious fact that the Confederacy needed some hope of great results, Beauregard was convinced. In Stewart's own words, "the condition of the army and other considerations rendered it necessary, in my judgment, that an offensive campaign should be made in the enemy's rear and on his line of communications." Beauregard did insist that Wheeler and his cavalry shadow Sherman. In return, and to Hood's great gain, Forrest would be ordered to join the army on the north side of the Tennessee.[53]

The proposed move to the Tennessee River in eastern Alabama being impractical, the Army of Tennessee turned west toward Decatur, Alabama. The men toiled through bleak mountain country that gave way to a muddy prairie. Phil Stephenson of the Washington Artillery later wrote of the profound suffering of the men: "[We were] cut off from our rations, ragged, shoeless, hatless, and many even without blankets[;] the pangs of hunger and physical exhaustion were now added to our sufferings."[54]

Fortunately, conditions began to improve. Aristide Hopkins of Stewart's staff observed that once the Rebels marched back into the Tennessee Valley, the farms were larger and the houses neater. A young single man, Hopkins was glad "to see that we are gradually getting into a country where the women are more patriotic, prettier, & use less snuff than in certain portions of N. Ga."[55]

On October 26, the corps marched to within three miles of the Yankee forts at Decatur, in cold temperatures and a nonstop drizzle. Hopkins was miserable enough, but was moved to pity by the sight of the foot soldiers marching through the mud, soaked to the skin. Riding forward on a reconnaissance, Hopkins became involved in a skirmish, chasing a new member of the 10th Indiana on horseback, neither man able to hit the other in a running pistol duel. Eventually, Hopkins captured his foe, grateful that neither had found the mark. Stewart's men skirmished with the bluecoats at Decatur until October 29, losing 135 killed and wounded, but made no serious attempt on the strong Federal position. The army moved west again, to Tuscumbia, and established a bridgehead across the Tennessee at Florence.

53. McMurry, *Hood*, 163–64; Hood, *Advance and Retreat*, 268–69; *OR* 39(1):812–13.

54. Stephenson, *Civil War Memoir*, 263.

55. Aristide Hopkins Diary (typescript), October 23, 1864, SHC.

By the first of November, the Army of Tennessee was finally in position to return to Tennessee, eleven months after it had been driven therefrom, and two months after it had been forced to abandon Atlanta. Even as Hood gathered provisions and made other preparations for advance, Abraham Lincoln's reelection ensured that the war would progress to the bitter end. Nonetheless, the Army of Tennessee was on the brink of its last great offensive movement, in Hopkins' view "preparing to cross the Rubicorn [*sic*]," into the state from which it derived its name. The hardy remnants of the native sons of the Volunteer State who remained with its standards, Alexander Peter Stewart among them, were ready to return home to whatever fate Providence might have in store.[56]

56. Ibid., October 26, November 4, 1864, SHC.

— 12 —

The Disastrous Campaign into Tennessee

Spring Hill, Franklin, and Nashville

On November 16, 1864, the headquarters of the Army of Tennessee was relatively quiet, as all but the most absolutely necessary military duties were suspended for the day of fasting and prayer proclaimed by Jefferson Davis. Hood had been on the Tennessee River at Florence, Alabama, for three days. Forrest and his cavalry were a few days from a rendezvous, Lee's Corps had finished its passage across the Tennessee River, with Cheatham and Stewart expected to follow, and work continued on the railroad from Corinth to establish a supply line for the army's anticipated advance into Middle Tennessee. Over 150 miles to the southeast, William T. Sherman watched from a hill overlooking the battlefield of July 22 as his four corps of 62,000 veterans abandoned a smoldering Atlanta and set out for Savannah and the sea.[1]

The difference between the two antagonists on that day of prayer was that there were very few Confederates left in Georgia, primarily the thin ranks of the Georgia Militia under Stewart's friend G. W. Smith, and a few brigades around Savannah under Hardee, while there were many thousand Federals in Tennessee, scattered in garrisons across the state, guarding the railroads and other strategic points. No matter how slowly Sherman

---

1. *OR* 45(1):669; Hopkins Diary, November 16, 1864, SHC; Hood, *Advance and Retreat*, 275–78; Hattaway and Jones, *How the North Won*, 642; Joseph T. Glatthaar, *The March to the Sea and Beyond* (New York: New York University Press, 1985), 7.

moved, the Confederates could not mass any significant force in his path, especially with Hood so far away. On the other hand, if Hood moved fast enough, there was a chance he could get into Tennessee before the Federal commander there, George H. Thomas, could concentrate his forces sufficiently to defeat the Army of Tennessee. Thomas' primary force was the Federal Fourth and Twenty-third Corps, massed at Pulaski, Tennessee, between Hood and his main prize, Nashville.[2]

The delay of nearly three weeks was hard on the men. The first few days of November were spent waiting to make the advance into Tennessee. Aristide Hopkins of Stewart's staff wrote in his diary of plans to move on November 9, but rain on November 8 made the roads "almost impassable" and the streams "very much swollen." Hopkins recorded that the corps was reviewed by an "unenthusiastic" Beauregard on November 12, a beautiful but windy day. Stewart was to cross the river on November 19, but "horrid" weather and the slow progress of the supply trains delayed the crossing again until November 20. On that cold, rainy day, the corps crossed a makeshift bridge of pontoons, barges, and flatboats and moved several miles north on the road to Lawrenceburg, Tennessee. That same day, Hood received an order from Beauregard to go "on active offensive immediately." During the march north from the crossing of the Tennessee, Stewart endeared himself to some of his men by getting off his horse and down in the water and mud to assist them in getting unstuck a gun of Tarrant's battery. On November 21, the entire army moved north, Stewart's men marching on the road to Lawrenceburg. The next day, Stewart and the pitiful remnants of the Tennessee regiments in Quarles's Brigade crossed the state line into Tennessee, many barefoot and ragged, yet "buoyant and hopeful," no doubt in agreement with a sign that met Cheatham's men as they passed the line to the west: "Tennessee, a grave or a free home."[3]

2. Hattaway and Jones, *How the North Won*, 638–43; Henry Stone, "Repelling Hood's Invasion of Tennessee," *B&L* 4:441.

3. *OR* 45(1):669; Hood, *Advance and Retreat*, 281; Hopkins Diary, November 7, 8, 11, 12, 15, 19, 1864, SHC; Wiley Sword, *Embrace an Angry Wind: The Confederacy's Last Hurrah: Spring Hill, Franklin and Nashville* (1992; reprint, Lawrence: University Press of Kansas, 1992), 2; Joseph Boyce, "Missourians in the Battle of Franklin," *CV* 24 (March 1916): 101; United Daughters of the Confederacy, South Carolina Division, *Recollections and Reminiscences* (Columbia, S.C., 1990), 1:259–60; E. W. Tarrant, Letter, *CV* 17 (April 1909): 160;

Stewart's arrival at Lawrenceburg on November 22, along with the activity of Forrest's cavalry in that quarter, caused the Federal commander, Major General John M. Schofield, to withdraw north to Columbia, on the Duck River. Pressed by Forrest, the two Federal corps were in Columbia by November 24. Works were hastily thrown up to resist the oncoming Confederates, who were converging on Mount Pleasant, less than twenty miles to the south. Marching through snow, sleet, and mud, the army faced Schofield's works at Columbia on November 27, with Lee on the left, Stewart in the center, and Cheatham on the right. That night, the Federals, reinforced to number 23,000 infantry and 5,000 cavalry, retreated across the Duck River, burning the railroad bridge and sinking their pontoon boats.[4]

With Schofield across the river unmolested, Hood guessed that the Union commander would feel safe, and determined to cross the river about three miles above his left flank, and, in the manner of Stonewall Jackson, throw the bulk of the army on the Federal rear. Hood's engineers put a bridge across the Duck during the night of November 28, and at dawn the next day Hood led Cheatham's Corps across the river, followed by Stewart and Edward D. Johnson's (formerly Hindman's) division of Lee's Corps. Lee and his two other divisions remained at Columbia with the bulk of the artillery, with orders to "demonstrate heavily against Schofield and follow him if he retired."[5]

November 29, 1864, was a mellow, sunlit day. Cheatham's Corps was in the lead of Hood's seven-division flanking column of almost 20,000 men, preceded by Forrest and his cavalry. Stewart followed Cheatham with his three divisions—in order of march, Loring, Walthall, and French. Johnson's Division, also under Stewart's orders, followed French. The flanking force moved quickly on a country road toward Spring Hill, thirteen miles in the rear of Schofield's position at Columbia, each soldier understanding the purpose of the rapid march. Forrest took the Federal cav-

John M. Copely, "Battle of Franklin, with Reminiscences of Camp Douglas," *Journal of Confederate History* 2 (No. 1, 1989): 29.

4. *OR* 45(1):670; Hood, *Advance and Retreat*, 282; Stone, "Repelling Hood's Invasion of Tennessee," 444; W. L. Truman to Confederate Veteran, May 17, 1908, Confederate Veteran Papers, DU.

5. Hood, *Advance and Retreat*, 283.

alry out of the fight by deceiving its commander into thinking he was riding for Nashville. Reaching the neighborhood of Spring Hill about noon, Forrest dismounted a significant portion of his command and moved toward the town. Fortunately for the Federals, Schofield had started some of his troops north from Columbia. The first of his infantry divisions, Brigadier General George D. Wagner's, along with Fourth Corps commander General David S. Stanley, moved up in time to save Spring Hill and its massive wagon park from Forrest's clutches.[6]

Over the next twelve hours, the "best move in [Hood's] career as a soldier . . . [came] to naught." At around 3 P.M., Cheatham's lead division, Cleburne's, crossed Rutherford Creek, about a mile and a half south of Spring Hill. Cleburne was directed to move on to Spring Hill, communicate with Forrest, and attack immediately. While the accounts of Hood, Cheatham, Brown, and the survivors of Cleburne's Division differ as to the cause, Cleburne's Division did not occupy the town or block the pike.[7]

At about 5 P.M., Cheatham ordered Brown and Cleburne to connect their lines and attack. Hood promised Cheatham that Stewart and his corps would soon be on the field. Cleburne was to advance upon hearing the sound of Brown's guns. Cheatham then rode to give orders to Bate, and wondered aloud several times, "Why don't we hear Brown's guns?" Brown was alarmed by a small force of Federals on his flank, and never made the attack, claiming that he didn't have orders. Darkness came and Cheatham's Corps had not blocked the road.[8]

Cheatham later related that Hood told him that Stewart was being pushed forward to support him and would "be here in a few minutes." Cheatham noted the discrepancy between this representation of Hood and Stewart's own account, which left Old Straight at the crossing of Ruther-

6. W. O. Dodd, "Reminiscences of Hood's Tennessee Campaign," *Southern Historical Society Papers* 9 (1881): 520; J. P. Young, "Hood's Failure at Spring Hill," *CV* 17 (January 1908): 26, 28, 30; J. S. Collins, "W. W. Gist's Article Commended," *CV* 24 (February 1916): 89; Copely, "Franklin," 30.

7. Buck, *Cleburne and His Command*, 265–67, 272–73; Hood, *Advance and Retreat*, 290, 284–85; Benjamin F. Cheatham, "The Lost Opportunity at Spring Hill, Tenn.—General Cheatham's Reply to General Hood," *Southern Historical Society Papers* 9 (October, November, and December 1881): 525, 528–29.

8. Cheatham, "Lost Opportunity," 525–26; Young, "Hood's Failure," 33–35; see also Winston Groom, *Shrouds of Glory* (New York: Atlantic Monthly Press, 1995), 147–48, 157.

ford Creek until almost dark. Cheatham wrote of Stewart: "That he would have executed an order to make such disposition of his command no one who knows that officer will doubt; and he would have done it in the darkness of night as surely and as certainly as in the day."[9]

Stewart arrived at Rutherford Creek just as Brown's Tennesseans made their crossing. Instead of orders to advance to Cheatham's support, Stewart received orders from Hood to remain at the crossing and deploy on the south side of the creek, with his right near the crossing, so as to move down the creek if necessary. Eventually, Stewart was ordered to send a division across the creek, and, later, to cross the whole corps, leaving a division to cover the crossing. Stewart accordingly crossed, leaving Johnson on the south side of Rutherford Creek. Riding ahead about dusk, Stewart encountered Hood and a single orderly by a small fire on the roadside. Hood "complained bitterly" that Cheatham had not followed his orders to attack. Stewart held his tongue, but felt like saying "Why did you not see yourself that your order was obeyed and the attack made?"[10]

Stewart inquired why he had been halted at Rutherford Creek. The army commander replied that he fully expected Cheatham to attack and rout the enemy and that Stewart's deployment at Rutherford Creek would keep the Yankees from escaping in the direction of Murfreesboro. Stewart later reflected that either Johnson's Division alone, or with one of his, could have performed that function. The remainder of his corps should have been dispatched to reinforce Cheatham and Forrest.[11]

Hood then directed Stewart to deploy his corps so as to place its right across the pike beyond Spring Hill and his left "extending down this way." Hood said, "The men have had a hard day's march, and I do not wish you to march your whole corps up to the right. It will be too far for the men to march." Stewart perceived that this would place his left in Cheatham's rear. Hood provided a young native of the area as a guide for his march. At this juncture, Hood reported that Cheatham rode up in person, and that he

---

9. Cheatham, "Lost Opportunity," 527.

10. APS to W. O. Dodd, February 8, 1881, in Cheatham, "Lost Opportunity," 534–35; *OR* 45(1):712; Dabney, "Gen. A. P. Stewart on Strong Topics," 32; APS to S. G. French, May 11, 1897, S. G. French Papers, MDAH.

11. APS to W. O. Dodd, in Cheatham, "Lost Opportunity," 534–35; Dabney, "Gen. A. P. Stewart on Strong Topics," 32.

(Hood) detained Stewart, supposedly to witness his confrontation with Cheatham. Hood stated that he exclaimed, "General, why in the name of God have you not attacked the enemy, and taken possession of that pike?" Cheatham later wrote that this "dramatic scene . . . only occurred in the imagination of General Hood." Stewart had no recollection of Hood's "dramatic scene" either. However, Old Straight's account also con- tradicted Cheatham, who wrote that Hood informed him in Stewart's presence that he had concluded to wait until morning to attack. Stewart did not recall being together with Hood and Cheatham at the same time that day.[12]

Stewart rejoined his men in the gathering darkness and followed his young guide northward. The guide told Stewart that the road they were on would eventually make a sudden turn to the left that would lead into Spring Hill itself. At the turn there was a road that used to lead from this point to the tollgate a mile and a half past Spring Hill on the road to Franklin. Stewart said if the guide could find it, that was the road he wanted. Arriving at the bend, the column passed through a large gate, tak- ing an indistinct path in the darkness. After going a short distance, Stewart came upon Forrest's headquarters, and stopped to talk to his fellow Ten- nessean about the position of Forrest's pickets and the Federals. Forrest told Stewart that his men had discovered that the Federals were leaving the direct pike from Spring Hill to Franklin and going up one along Carter's Creek, to the west.[13]

While engaged in his conversation with the cavalryman, Stewart learned that a staff officer from Hood had halted his column. Stewart was just re- mounting his horse when this officer, who was actually on Cheatham's staff, told him that he had come to place the corps in position. It struck Stewart as odd that Hood would send one of Cheatham's officers rather

12. *OR* 45(1):712; Hood, *Advance and Retreat*, 286; APS to J. D. Porter, October 24, 1881, in Cheatham, "Lost Opportunity," 525–26; APS conversation with Young, April 1895, in Young, "Hood's Failure," 39. Hood's comment to Stewart that he wanted the corps' right across the pike above Spring Hill in Young's article seems to contradict Hood's com- ment to Stewart reported in the same source that moving the whole corps to the right would be too far for the men to march. The only way that they can be reconciled is Stewart's percep- tion that only his right would be across the pike, while his left would have been in Cheatham's rear.

13. *OR* 45(1):712; APS conversation with Young, in Young, "Hood's Failure," 39.

than one of his own. It further bothered Old Straight that he had recently seen Hood and received somewhat different orders. Stewart asked the officer if he had seen Hood since he had, and the man replied that he had just come from Hood. The officer stated that Hood wanted Stewart to go into line on Cheatham's right, which would keep him from blocking the pike to the north of Spring Hill. Stewart decided Hood had changed his orders because the army commander had received the same information that Forrest had given him, to the effect that the Federals were moving north on a road to the west. Stewart accordingly marched his men to Cheatham's right, which was occupied by Brown and his Tennesseans. Finding Brown, Stewart determined that if he formed on Brown's right, his line would oblique away from the pike. Convinced that these orders were a mistake, and his men having been on the march all day and into the night, he directed that they bivouac while he got clarification from Hood.[14]

At this point, it was near 11 P.M., and by the time Stewart made his way to headquarters, probably with Forrest, Hood was in bed. Stewart inquired as to whether Hood had sent Cheatham's officer to change his position. Hood indicated that he had. Stewart then asked if Hood had changed his mind as to what he wanted Stewart to do with his men. Hood replied he had not, but that Cheatham had represented to him that Brown needed support on his right. By now no doubt exasperated, although he probably did not betray it, Stewart explained that his men had been on the road since daylight and that he had ordered them into bivouac while he straightened out the situation. Hood said that Stewart's stopping the corps for the night was not material, that he should let his men rest and take the lead the next morning for the advance on Franklin.[15]

The ultimate result of this disastrous series of events was that, in the course of the night, with no Confederate infantry across the pike, Schofield marched across Hood's front and made his escape. Stewart, Hood, Cheatham, and a number of the other officers present that night were haunted by this incident for decades to come. When Stewart initially wrote his report of this incident on January 20, 1865, he simply commented that after he

14. *OR* 45(1):712–13; APS conversation with Young, in Young, "Hood's Failure," 39.
15. *OR* 45(1):712–13; APS conversation with Young, in Young, "Hood's Failure," 39–40; Thomas Robeson Hay, "The Battle of Spring Hill," *Tennessee Historical Magazine* 7 (July 1921): 81.

crossed Rutherford Creek, he went into line on Cheatham's right and bivouacked about 11 P.M.[16] Hood's report, dated February 15, 1865, stated:

> Though the golden opportunity had passed with daylight, I did not at dark abandon the hope of dealing the enemy a heavy blow. Accordingly, Lieutenant-General Stewart was furnished a guide and ordered to move his corps beyond Cheatham's and place it across the road beyond Spring Hill. Shortly after this General Cheatham came to my headquarters, and when I informed him of Stewart's movement, he said that Stewart ought to form on his right. I asked if that would throw Stewart across the pike. He replied that it would, and a mile beyond. Accordingly, one of Cheatham's staff officers was sent to show Stewart where his (Cheatham's) right rested. *In the dark and confusion he did not succeed in getting the position desired, but about 11 p.m. went into bivouac.* (Emphasis added.)[17]

Stewart felt compelled to supplement his report of the campaign, which he dated April 3, 1865, giving many of the details set forth above. Stewart quoted a statement of Hood's absolving him from all blame and attached a letter of Hood's dated April 9, 1865, expressing regret that his report "led to uncertainty as to yourself and troops." Hood went on to state that "you did all that I could say or claim that I would have done under similar circumstances myself."[18]

Notwithstanding Hood's having absolved Stewart of any blame for the episode, a charge was purportedly privately made by Isham Harris in 1868 that Stewart disobeyed orders at Spring Hill. In a conversation recorded by Major Campbell Brown (Richard S. Ewell's son-in-law and wartime aide), Harris claimed to have been a witness to events the afternoon and evening of November 29. Harris disclosed that he participated in Cheatham's interview with Hood about 5 P.M., and that Hood stated at that time that he had ordered Stewart to Cheatham's right so as to place Old

16. Hay, "Spring Hill," 81–82; W. B. Bate to B. F. Cheatham, November 29, 1881, I. G. Harris to J. D. Porter, May 20, 1877, in Cheatham, "Lost Opportunity," 540–41, 532; *OR* 45(1):708.

17. *OR* 45(1):652–53.

18. Ibid., 712–13. While Stewart's report was dated April 3, 1865, no doubt it was withheld because of the Confederate government's flight from Richmond.

Straight and his corps across the turnpike, and that he had provided Stewart with a guide for that purpose. According to Brown, Stewart at that time was told to "put yourself across the road if it costs you every man of your command."

As Brown recalled, Harris stated that nothing occurred until 8 P.M., when Stewart and Forrest showed up at Hood's headquarters. According to Harris, Stewart said he had dismissed Hood's guide because he found an officer who said he knew the country. Following the new officer's directions, however, had gotten Stewart lost. Stewart is reported to have said his men were worn out by long marching and he had thought it best to let them rest until morning and then cross the pike, as he was ignorant of the ground and Federal strength in his front. Brown recorded that Harris said: "Hood was annoyed by Stuart's [*sic*] report, and said with emphasis, 'Gen. Stuart [*sic*], it is of great importance that a brigade should be put on the road tonight. Can you send one?' 'Well, General,' began Stuart [*sic*], 'my men have had nothing to eat all day, and are very tired and—' " Hood supposedly cut Stewart off and asked Forrest to put one of his brigades on the road. In Brown's account of his conversation with Harris, Stewart was viewed to have failed to execute the initial order to block the pike, "and on reporting his failure was treated contemptuously almost by Hood, —Harris evidently thinks justly."[19]

The Brown-Harris account differs from Stewart's in several particulars. Stewart made no mention of Hood's dramatic order to sacrifice the whole corps to block the road, and no mention of Hood's contemptuous treatment. Stewart stated that he diverted from the path charted by Hood's guide only when Cheatham's staff officer arrived with orders from Hood, rather than on his own whim with an officer Stewart encountered on his own, as suggested by Harris. Harris recalled Stewart reporting a problem with his position at 8 P.M.; Stewart stated it was near 11 P.M. Hood's own subsequent accounts, which do not castigate Stewart, support Stewart as to the time of his reporting to Hood and the more important particular of Cheatham's officer being dispatched to change his orders.

Less easily dispelled is the charge that Hood wanted a brigade placed across the pike and that Stewart was reluctant to do so. On the one hand,

19. Campbell Brown record of conversation with Isham Harris, April 1868, typescript in Campbell Brown–Richard Stoddart Ewell Papers, TSLA.

it makes sense that Hood would have made such a request, and there is no question that Stewart was concerned that his men were exhausted by the time he met with Hood after dark. Yet on the other hand, no other eyewitness account, including any by Hood or Stewart, indicates that Hood made the request of Stewart or that Stewart demurred. Harris, who had other opportunities to comment on Spring Hill, never publicly mentioned the incident.[20] As Cheatham said, Stewart would obey orders, day or night. Too, Hood was never averse to casting blame. Therefore, if Hood had made the order Brown said Harris described, it is highly likely that one or both men would have later written of it, and that Stewart would have carried it out.[21]

The publication of Hood's memoirs in 1880 stirred up another round of interest in the subject, if it had ever died down. Stewart was once more called on to comment on what occurred from his standpoint. Stewart remarked, as he consistently would in later years, that as Hood was present on the field, he should have made sure that his orders were obeyed. The subject followed Stewart into extreme old age, as Longstreet's artillery chief, E. Porter Alexander, published a book entitled *Military Memoirs of a Confederate: A Critical Narrative*, which rather sloppily accused Stewart (and Cheatham) of not following explicit orders to attack the fleeing Federals and of being absent from their "divisions" that night. Characterizing Alexander's words as a "remarkable tissue of false statements," Stewart

---

20. For example, see I. G. Harris to J. D. Porter, May 20, 1877, in Cheatham, "Lost Opportunity," 532. Harris seems to have blamed Stewart and Cheatham to the end of his days. I. G. Harris to Charles Todd Quintard, December 29, 1894, Quintard Papers, DU.

21. No contemporary publicly blamed Stewart for the failure at Spring Hill. See, for example, Dodd, "Reminiscences of Hood's Tennessee Campaign," 521. There is scant use of the Brown document in recent historical treatment. With little analysis, Thomas Connelly gives credence to Brown's account. Connelly, *Autumn of Glory*, 499. A locally published account of the battle also gives credit to the Brown story. Alethea D. Sayres, *The Sound of Brown's Guns* (Spring Hill: Rosewood Publishing, 1995). James L. McDonough and Thomas Connelly, in *Five Tragic Hours: The Battle of Franklin* (Knoxville: University of Tennessee Press, 1983), 56, devote a sentence to Stewart's "lack of interest" in deploying his "relatively fresh" men that seems derivative of Connelly's *Autumn of Glory*. Other standard histories of this campaign do not mention Brown's account. See Thomas R. Hay, *Hood's Tennessee Campaign* (Dayton: Morningside Bookshop, 1975), 88–91, 100; Sword, *Embrace an Angry Wind*, 137–39, 147; W. T. Crawford, "The Mystery of Spring Hill," *Civil War History* 1 (June 1955): 118–19; see also Horn, *Army of Tennessee*, 388–89.

noted that the *Official Records* had been published thirteen years previously and disproved Alexander's account. Stewart stated yet more tellingly that since Hood was on the scene, it would have demonstrated Hood's incapacity for command if Stewart and Cheatham had disobeyed orders and Hood had let the insubordination go. After Stewart's death, members of his staff wrote in the *Confederate Veteran* that Alexander's report was "most positively . . . false," as Stewart "was most actively moving about enforcing General Hood's orders."[22]

Some modern writers have minimized the magnitude of the Confederate blunder at Spring Hill, observing that the Federals had other escape routes open to Nashville that night. A Federal officer on General Thomas' staff wrote, however, that a single Confederate infantry brigade would have been enough to bottle up Schofield's whole force. Whatever the truth, Spring Hill was fatal to the Army of Tennessee, because it seems to have convinced Hood that the army was still not broken from the "evil" Johnston had instilled to avoid a fight unless protected by breastworks. Whether intentionally or otherwise, the next day would prove to be Hood's ultimate effort to purge the Army of Tennessee of this "stumbling block."[23]

Hood was in a foul mood as he accompanied Stewart's column at the head of the army the morning of November 30. John C. Brown made the comment to a staff officer that Hood was "wrathy as a rattlesnake [that] morning, striking at everything." There is no record as to Stewart facing Hood's ire that day, but it appears that Cheatham and at least two of his division commanders, Cleburne and Brown, were criticized. As the corps advanced, one of Stewart's staff stopped retreating bluecoats from killing some mules with axes and destroying a bridge on the route to Franklin. Others saved some wagons that had just been set on fire. William D. Gale, Stewart's staff officer, later wrote his wife that the road was strewn with the articles of a flying army. Hood felt that his men had a new spirit,

22. See APS to W. O. Dodd, February 8, 1881, in Cheatham, "Lost Opportunity," 534–35; Young, "Hood's Failure," 36; Alexander P. Stewart, "A Critical Narrative," *CV* 16 (September 1908): 462–63 ; Dabney, "Gen. A. P. Stewart on Strong Topics," 32; Hopkins, Le Moncier, and Chalaron, "Tributes to Gen. A. P. Stewart," 594–95.

23. See Connelly, *Autumn of Glory*, 501–502; McMurry, *Hood*, 173–74 (relies heavily on Connelly). For the potential Federal disaster, see Stone, "Repelling Hood's Invasion," 446.

brought on by the previous day and night's "fearful blunder" which manifested itself in a determination to redeem themselves for missing the "rare
opportunity" at Spring Hill.[24]

At Franklin, John M. Schofield fully intended to get his small army
through the town, across the Harpeth River, and on to Nashville as
quickly as possible. The only bridge across the swollen Harpeth, however,
was a railroad bridge that had to be planked for foot and wagon traffic. The
pontoon train Schofield expected was nowhere to be found. For the time
being, the fleeing Federals would have to halt their retreat to Nashville.
The exhausted Yankees expanded on some old entrenchments south of the
town, which stretched in a semicircle from one bank of the Harpeth to the
other. As the day wore on, the Federal fortifications became more formidable, the bluecoats using timbers and boards from a cotton gin just south
of the town near the Columbia Pike. On the eastern end of the Federal
line, a thicket of thorny Osage orange, "which no man can touch with bare
hands," ran for some distance, forming a natural abatis. Where the thorny
obstruction ended, the Federals cut fence rails, sharpened the ends, and
stuck them in the ground pointing outwards at a forty-five-degree angle
and placed close together so as to form a three-foot-high fence.[25]

The last Federal unit marching north from Spring Hill was Wagner's
2nd Division of the Fourth Corps. The brigade of Chickamauga veteran
Colonel Emerson Opdycke was Wagner's rear guard. Opdycke occupied
the dual heights of Breezy Hill on the east side of the Columbia Pike, and
Winstead Hill on the west side. The two hills were about two miles due
south of Franklin, and looked down on a small plain of farmland interspersed with woods. Off to the east, the Harpeth ran generally southeast to
northwest just past the town on the north. About midday, Stewart's pursuing column approached Opdycke's line, and, after a conference with Hood
and other officers, Stewart was ordered to move around Breezy Hill to the
right toward the river. As Stewart formed into line of battle, Opdycke

---

24. Young, "Hood's Failure," 36; J. C. Brown to B. F. Cheatham, October 24, 1881, in
Cheatham, "Lost Opportunity," 539; Hopkins, Le Moncier, and Chalaron, "Tributes to Gen.
A. P. Stewart," 595; W. D. Gale to wife, January 14, 1865, in Ridley, *Battles and Sketches*,
409, original in Gale-Polk Papers, SHC, copy in TSLA; Hood, *Advance and Retreat*, 292.

25. Sword, *Embrace an Angry Wind*, 159–64; W. L. Truman to Confederate Veteran,
May 17, 1908, Confederate Veteran Papers, DU.

withdrew from the heights. Stewart marched the corps around Breezy Hill through woods and fields until it was within a mile and a quarter of the town. Stewart's men had an unobstructed view of Schofield's wagons hurrying across the Harpeth and of the Federal troops throwing up breastworks. Stewart encountered Hood on a hillside reconnoitering the Federal position, and was asked if he could move his corps north of Franklin. Stewart, knowing that there were several fords over the river, answered in the affirmative. Hood directed Stewart to send some cavalry and infantry to drive the Federals out of a bend in the Harpeth to the south of the town, and then wait for further word. When Hood left, Stewart expected to soon receive an order to move around the Federal flank to the right.[26]

In Cheatham's advance Cleburne and Brown moved on the pike between the two hills, while Bate marched around the left of Winstead Hill. Cheatham and Forrest both expressed doubts about any efforts to attack the entrenched Federals, but Hood stated that he would rather fight the Federals at Franklin, where they had had only eighteen hours to fortify, than at Nashville, where they had been fortifying for three years. There is no indication as to whether Stewart was consulted on the issue of whether to make the assault, although it does not seem likely that he was. After the battle, Hood sent for Stewart and explained his reasons for making the assault—captured Federal dispatches indicated to Hood that the Federals were preparing to evacuate the town and Hood hoped to catch them in a disorganized state. With this knowledge, Stewart termed the popular supposition that Hood ordered the charge at Franklin because of his chagrin over Schofield's escape at Spring Hill a "great injustice." Notwithstanding his effort to be fair with Hood, Stewart most certainly did not agree with the assault.[27]

The Federal position was strong, but had one serious tactical fault. Opdycke's division commander, George D. Wagner, selected a position straddling the Columbia Pike about a half mile in front of the main Federal

26. Sword, *Embrace an Angry Wind*, 177–79; Cannon, *Bloody Banners and Barefoot Boys*, 99; *OR* 45(1):708, 720; Dabney, "Gen. A. P. Stewart on Strong Topics," 32; APS to S. G. French, April 20, May 11, 1897, S. G. French Papers, MDAH; John P. Hickman, Letter, *CV* 22 (January 1914): 15.

27. Sword, *Embrace an Angry Wind*, 177–79; Dabney, "Gen. A. P. Stewart on Strong Topics," 32; Buck, *Cleburne and His Command*, 280; Ridley, *Battles and Sketches*, 416; Hickman letter, *CV* 22 (January 1914): 15; French, *Two Wars*, 299.

works. Wagner had only two brigades, as Opdycke refused to place his brigade in this foolishly exposed position. In the main Federal works, the three-brigade division of Brigadier General Jacob D. Cox occupied the line from the Harpeth to the Columbia Pike. To the west of the pike were Brigadier General Thomas H. Ruger's and Brigadier General Nathan Kimball's divisions. These troops were supported by twenty-six artillery pieces, with twelve more in reserve. They faced the forming Confederate lines across an almost entirely unobstructed and fenceless plain, stretching from the small hill on which sat the house of Fountain Branch Carter, a Virginia transplant with a son serving in Cheatham's Corps, back over two miles to Winstead Hill.[28]

As the warm, hazy day wore on, Stewart prepared his corps for attack. Loring's Division deployed on the corps' right, Walthall's Division in the center, and French's Division on the left. Stewart's entire corps (less Ector's Brigade, detached to guard the army's pontoon train on November 20) was drawn up on the army's right, between the Columbia Pike on the west and the Harpeth on the east. Brigadier General Abraham Buford's Division of cavalry covered the space between Loring's flank and the river. Less Ector's Brigade, the corps numbered about 8,000 effectives, reflecting its hard service since Old Straight took command on July 7. As the corps formed for battle, the men were aware of the formidable task that awaited them, and the likelihood that many of them would not survive the fight. This realization must have contributed to the uncanny near-silence that accompanied the preparation for advance. An incident that was probably unknown to Stewart indicated building tensions in the highest ranks of the corps. During the deployment of their divisions, Loring rode up to Walthall and "roughly" accused him of causing some confusion in the alignment of the two units. After some sharp words were exchanged, Walthall commented it was no time for a quarrel, and that Loring could find him after the attack. Apparently, the maelstrom both men plunged into purged all ill feelings, because there is no further record of any argument between the two.[29]

28. Stone, "Repelling Hood's Invasion," 449–52; Buck, *Cleburne and His Command*, 281–82; Sword, *Embrace an Angry Wind*, 173–76.

29. *OR* 45(1):678, 708, 720; David R. Logsdon, ed., *Eyewitnesses at the Battle of Franklin* (Nashville: Kettle Mills Press, 1991), 8–9; APS to S. G. French, November 20, 1864, Samuel G. French Papers, RG 109, NA; James H. McNeilly, "Franklin—Incidents of the

On Stewart's left, Cheatham also formed for the attack, with Brown on the left and Cleburne on the right, pointed straight down the Columbia Pike toward the Federal position on Carter House Hill. At 4 P.M., one of Hood's staff officers brought word to begin the advance. Orders rang down the Confederate lines: "Forward, march!" Funneled by the Harpeth on the right and Cheatham on the left, Stewart's divisions moved somewhat diagonally toward the Federal lines east of the Columbia Pike. The advance was accompanied for the first and only time in the experience of many with the music of the various bands in the corps, playing "Dixie," "Bonnie Blue Flag," and "The Girl I Left Behind Me." Unlike its other advances, at Shiloh, Perryville, Murfreesboro, Chickamauga, and the three terrible days in July around Atlanta, the army moved across mostly clear, flat ground, on a march at least twice as long as that taken by Pickett, Pettigrew, and Trimble at Gettysburg.[30]

Stewart observed that his men moved forward "in fine order . . . in high spirits." The line of the corps became somewhat disordered by some broken ground and some brush on its line of march, and, at one point, halted to re-form. Some disruption in Walthall's Division was remedied by the shifting of brigades. Shortly thereafter, the corps line was back in order, and the march resumed. As the corps moved forward, it began to take fire from both the Federal lines in its front and some batteries posted across the Harpeth, which swept its lines with an oblique fire.[31]

The Confederate attack was in effect a massive converging move on the Federal lines. French described the assault as having started, "as it were, from the circumference of a wagon wheel." Each division "marched in the direction of the spokes, and overlapped at the hub, which would represent the [Federal] works. Hence, Loring's left overlapped Walthall, Walthall over me, and I over Cleburne on the pike."[32]

The corps proceeded toward the lines of Colonel Joseph Conrad's brigade of Wagner's division in its advanced position on the east side of the Columbia Pike. Stewart's lines moved obliquely, French's and then Wal-

Battle," *CV* 25 (March 1918): 116–17. There is no mention of any bitterness toward Walthall in Loring's biography. See Raab, *Loring*, 182–88.

30. Logsdon, *Franklin*, 8–9; *OR* 45(1):708.
31. *OR* 45(1):708, 720.
32. French, *Two Wars*, 295.

thall's divisions crossing over the tracks of the Central Alabama Railroad. At the same time, Cleburne and his division were converging on the same portion of the advanced Federal line. French and Walthall approached Conrad obliquely from his left, and Cleburne from the center. The oncoming Rebels swarmed across Conrad's lines, scattering or capturing most of that brigade. On the Federal advanced right, the men of Colonel John Q. Lane's brigade, facing Brown's Division, saw the collapse of their support on the left and also broke for Schofield's main lines.[33]

Cheatham and Stewart's five divisions came on with a rush. Brown and Cleburne, following on the heels of and, in some cases, mixed in with Wagner's retreating brigades, swarmed toward and into the gap in the Federal lines where they were intersected by the Columbia Pike. Likewise, Stewart's divisions made the dash for the second, more extensive line of Federal works. On the corps' right, Loring advanced with Featherston and Scott forward, and Adams in reserve. Featherston's advance was significantly obstructed by the railroad cut of the Central Alabama Railroad and the Osage orange hedge. Furthermore, the brigade suffered terribly from enfilade fire from the Federal batteries on the other side of the Harpeth. Yet the Mississippians surged forward against the Federal works. The flags of the 3rd, 22nd, and 33rd Mississippi regiments were all placed on the Federal works, but the fire was too great. Each of the men who carried the colors onto the works was killed or wounded, and the flags of all three regiments fell into Yankee hands.[34]

Scott's Alabama brigade advanced with its right on the Harpeth. Scott urged his men to capture the Yankees before they could escape across the river. They had not gone far past the Randal McGavock house, Carnton, when the Federal artillery opened up on them. Scott's men, too, were raked with enfilade fire from across the river. The intention was for the brigade to move deliberately forward, so the whole line of the division could strike the works at the same time, but the Federal canister fire was too much. Accordingly, the Alabama men raised a shout and moved forward at a run. When they got to within fifty or seventy-five yards of the Federal works, the Unionists rose up in a "blue wave" and blasted the oncoming

33. OR 45(1):708, 720; Logsdon, Franklin, 14–19.

34. OR 45(1):708, 714; Logsdon, Franklin, 22–23, 46–47; Sword, Embrace an Angry Wind, 217–18.

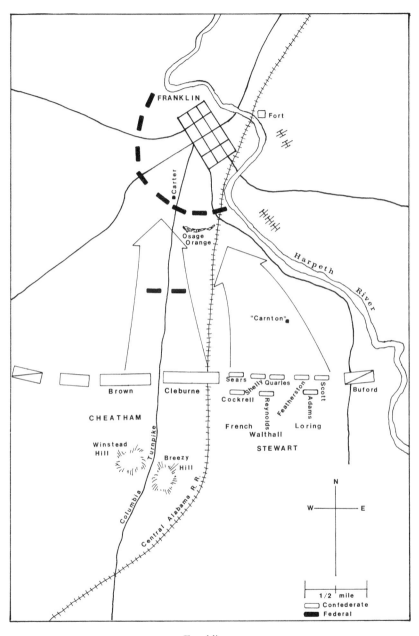

Franklin

Map by Blake Magner

Rebels. While many fell, others rushed up and tried to get into the works, but they were hampered by the Osage orange hedge. One officer of the 35th Alabama was cut down trying to hack his way through the hedge with his sword. Eventually, the Federal fire was too much, and Scott's men went streaming back into a railroad cut. Loring, impressive in full uniform and plumed hat, rode among them trying to rally them and Featherston's Mississippians. Being largely unsuccessful, Loring shouted "Great God! Do I command cowards?" and then galloped after his fleeing men.[35]

Walthall's forward brigades were Quarles's mostly Tennessee brigade on his right and Brigadier General Charles M. Shelly's mainly Alabama brigade on the left. After participating in overrunning Conrad's advanced line, Walthall's men advanced over the short, deadly space between the two lines. Walthall wrote in his report: "This was done under far the most deadly fire of both small-arms and artillery that I have ever seen troops subjected to. Terribly torn at every step by an oblique fire from a battery advantageously posted at the enemy's left, no less than by the destructive fire in front, the line moved on and did not falter till, just to the right of the pike, it reached the abatis fronting the works. Over this no organized force could go, and here the main body of my command, both front line and reserve, was repulsed in confusion."[36]

A portion of the Federal troops Walthall engaged were equipped with sixteen-shot Henry rifles, and gunned down virtually anything that moved in their front. Walthall struck in the area of the Carter cotton gin, where the Federal works formed a salient. Looking down the line of battle, a member of the 49th Tennessee of Quarles's Brigade could see fellow Rebels shot down by the platoon. In Walthall's second line, Reynolds' Arkansas men advanced steadily through the "retreating mass" of Quarles's and Shelly's men to within fifteen or twenty steps of the Federal line until they were forced to fall back from the terrific Yankee fire. Reynolds thought the struggle "the most terrible fighting I have seen during the war."[37]

With Ector's men detached, French attacked with two brigades, Cock-

35. Logsdon, *Franklin*, 45–47; Cannon, *Bloody Banners and Barefoot Boys*, 100; Sword, *Embrace an Angry Wind*, 216–17; McNeilly, "Franklin," 117.

36. *OR* 45(1):720–21.

37. Copely, "Franklin," 42–43; Reynolds Diary, November 30, 1864, Reynolds Papers, UAR.

rell's small brigade of veteran Missourians and Sears's Mississippians. Cheatham's delay with Wagner brought Cockrell's men into the range of the Federal guns in the main line first. Scores of men were shot down, and the brigade was near annihilation when Brown and Cleburne broke through the Federal center on the Columbia Pike. Cockrell's Brigade washed across the Federal line in the same area as Cleburne's men, near the Columbia Pike. The Missourians encountered the bluecoats of Opdycke's brigade, who rushed to fill the gap left by the panic of their compatriots of Wagner's division. In their advance on the Federal main line, Cockrell's men were so badly cut up that they did not have the strength to hold the fortifications they initially seized. They battled the bluecoats across the work with picks, shovels, muskets, and sabers. Cockrell's Brigade suffered immense casualties: of the 696 officers and men it took into the fight, 419 were killed, wounded, or missing. Courage in Sears's Brigade was measured by the number of men who managed to reach the Federal main works. One hundred seventy-eight men were "foremost among the forlorn hope"; of these, 57 were killed or wounded.[38]

Among the last of Stewart's brigades to assault the Federal works was Adams' Mississippi brigade. An officer in the 65th Indiana of Casement's brigade counted nine separate charges by the Rebels in his sector, the most desperate by Adams and his men. It took awesome courage for these men to march over the torn and bleeding bodies of their comrades and through the retreating remnants of earlier assaults toward the tangled Osage orange abatis. The Mississippians filed to the left around the hedge to an area without as many obstructions. Adams, a native Tennessean, rode back and forth and cheered his men on. Wounded severely in the right shoulder early in the fight, Adams declined to leave the field. As his men approached the Federal line, Adams spurred his horse forward toward the colors of the 65th Illinois. The 65th's colonel called out for his men to not fire on Adams, but he fell, pierced by nine bullets, his dead horse straddling the Federal works. Adams died soon thereafter, comforted by the Union sol-

38. Logsdon, *Franklin*, 35–38; Sword, *Embrace an Angry Wind*, 226–27; Phillip Thomas Tucker, "The First Missouri Brigade at the Battle of Franklin," *Tennessee Historical Quarterly* 46 (spring 1987): 21, 26–30; W. L. Truman to Confederate Veteran, May 17, 1908, Confederate Veteran Papers, DU; Boyce, "Missourians in the Battle of Franklin," 102–103; *OR* 45(1):716–19.

diers. The Federal brigade commander, Colonel John S. Casement, eventually returned Adams' saddle to his widow in 1891, with a chivalrous letter describing the general's last moments.[39]

In light of Stewart's position as corps commander, he doubtless went no farther forward than the vicinity of the McGavock house, Carnton. His report of the action reflects admiration for the "dauntless courage" with which his men assaulted the Federal works again and again, and pain at the terrible casualties the corps suffered, over 2,000, "many of our best officers and bravest men." Of the corps' 8 brigade commanders involved in the fight, Adams was killed, Cockrell wounded and captured, and Scott paralyzed by a shell exploding near him. Quarles was severely wounded just short of the Union inner line, and all of his staff officers were killed. Five regimental commanders were killed, 14 wounded, 4 wounded and captured, and 1 was missing. Furthermore, Walthall was severely bruised and had two horses killed out from under him, one while he conferred with French.[40]

Cheatham's three divisions and Johnson's Division of Lee's Corps, thrown into the fight late, were also decimated. Losses among the army's officers were terrible. In addition to Adams, Stewart's protégé Otho F. Strahl and his longtime compatriot in the army, Patrick R. Cleburne, were killed, along with three other generals. The army suffered approximately 7,000 casualties, compared to Federal casualties of about 2,600. At terrible cost, the Army of Tennessee had finally proven to its commander that it had the courage to assault the most formidable of breastworks.[41]

While Stewart's surviving officers were collecting their shattered units, Stewart and Gale went to Hood's headquarters and found the commanding general determined to renew the assault the next morning. Once all the artillery was up, it would open on the Federal works at daylight, and at 9:00 A.M. Hood planned to throw the army at Franklin once again. Gale

39. Sword, *Embrace an Angry Wind*, 226–27; Logsdon, *Franklin*, 48–49; Ridley, *Battles and Sketches*, 414–20; Bryan Lane, "The Familiar Road: The Life of Confederate Brigadier General John Adams," *Civil War Times Illustrated* 35 (October 1996): 40, 46.

40. *OR* 45(1):684–85, 708, 721; French, *Two Wars*, 299.

41. Buck, *Cleburne and His Command*, 284; Sword, *Embrace an Angry Wind*, 269–70; *OR* 45(1):684–86.

wryly wrote to his wife: "You might think it was a bitter prospect for our poor fellows." Through the night, Gale assisted in placing units in position for the renewed assault. Investigating a stillness in the Federal lines, Gale found that Schofield had cleared out. Just as day was dawning, he returned to the corps headquarters' campfire, "wet, weary, hungry and disheartened, telling General Stewart that Schofield was gone."[42]

As dawn broke on December 1, the winter daylight revealed a charnel house. The ditch before the Federal line, on either side of the pike, was filled with dead men, "lying across each other, in all unseemly deformity of violent death." The town was swamped with wounded, both Confederate and Union, and some residents, such as the Carter family itself, found that the terrible battle had killed or maimed a loved one. At Carnton, wounded were piled into every room, all the outbuildings, and finally the yard. The house's mistress, Mrs. John McGavock, assisted the surgeons as best she could with cloths for bandages, and moved from room to room nursing and ministering to the affected soldiers. At about 9 A.M., she found the time and energy to give Stewart and his staff "a nice, warm breakfast, and a warmer welcome."[43]

The next day, December 2, 1864, Stewart's Corps moved out for Nashville, "in mourning," marching past the piled-up dead around the ginhouse. A soldier in one of Stewart's Alabama regiments thought this route of march very bad for morale. Although he could have chosen his route better, Hood in truth had few options. Unless he had reinforcements—which he had a faint hope of getting from the Trans-Mississippi—his only chance of turning the tide in the West was to lurk outside Nashville and hope for a mistake by George H. Thomas, a rare occurrence. Its thin lines spread out in a pseudo-siege of the Tennessee capital, the ruined Army of Tennessee could no longer shape events, only react and hope for the best when Thomas' inevitable assault came. As Gale wrote his wife, although the army was close enough to see the spires of the city, "between us and them[,] there bristles on every hill a fort and . . . long lines of rifle pits con-

42. W. D. Gale to wife, January 14, 1865, in Ridley, *Battles and Sketches*, 410–11.

43. Ridley, *Battles and Sketches*, 411–12. A good compilation of personal experiences of the terrible scene at Franklin on December 1, 1864, may be found in Logsdon, *Franklin*, 64–81.

necting them, with the dark blue lines of armed men, [which] tells us too plainly that our way is not open."[44]

The Federal army in Nashville consisted of the Fourth Corps, now under Brigadier General Thomas J. Wood of Chickamauga notoriety, the Twenty-third Corps, under Schofield, Major General A. J. Smith's Sixteenth Corps, Major General James B. Steedman's corps-sized detachment of occupation troops from Chattanooga and the surrounding areas, the Nashville garrison under Brigadier General John F. Miller, and Major General James Wilson's cavalry corps, a total of 70,272 "present for duty, equipped." As Gale had observed, these men were protected by some of the most elaborate fortifications on the continent, with an outer line, inner line, and the Tennessee capitol itself manned with a regiment of infantry and fifteen guns. The only problem Thomas had was from his superiors in Washington, who found it outrageous that Hood was on the outskirts of Nashville that late in the war. Urged again and again to attack, Thomas recognized that Hood was not going to cross the Cumberland River under the frowning cannon of the Federal gunboats. This gave him time to properly outfit his cavalry to face Forrest. Thomas' prudence almost got him relieved, but he was able to launch his attack before Grant could act.[45]

The good weather that followed the army's advance north broke on December 8, a mixture of sleet, rain, and snow falling during the night. In addition to the obvious suffering that the cold and ice caused, the adverse weather affected what little transportation was available. It also made it difficult to dig entrenchments. During the first week of December, Sears's Brigade was detached with Bate's Division to provide infantry support to an abortive effort by Forrest to take Murfreesboro. Although by December 9 the brigade was back with the corps, Hood wanted Stewart to finish fortifying his flank so that if conditions at Murfreesboro merited it, Stewart could march with two of his divisions and another from one of the other corps to prevent its reinforcement or the Federal force there from with-

44. Logsdon, *Franklin*, 80; W. D. Gale to wife, January 19, 1865, in Ridley, *Battles and Sketches*, 412; Hood, *Advance and Retreat*, 299–300; W. D. Gale to wife, December 9, 1984, Gale-Polk Papers, SHC.

45. Stanley F. Horn, *The Decisive Battle of Nashville* (1956; reprint, Baton Rouge: Louisiana State University Press, 1991), 46, 62–64, 167–74; Horn, *Army of Tennessee*, 406–407, 417; Hattaway and Jones, *How the North Won*, 649–50.

drawing. Nothing came of this scheme, and, in fact, after the first week, there was little change in the army's line, although both Stewart and Lee retired their lines on December 10 to gain better access to firewood.[46]

Deployed on the army's left, Stewart's Corps was stretched to the utmost, the effective total strength of the corps, with artillery, at 5,216. Its final line extended across the Granny White Pike to a hill near the Hillsboro Pike. Loring's Division occupied a solid entrenched line facing the Federal lines. To protect the corps' (and the army's) left flank, five redoubts were constructed along the Hillsboro Pike, the rearmost about a mile and a half from the end of the main entrenched line. Similar redoubts were built in the sectors of the other two corps, and Stewart, Lee, and Cheatham were directed by Hood to supervise the construction personally as much as possible. These works were to be armed with artillery, each with infantry support of a hundred men. Hood believed these semi-independent redoubts would keep a flanking column from gaining the rear of the army. A skeletal line stretched from the Hillsboro Pike toward the Cumberland to the west of the city, consisting of a line of cavalry and Ector's Brigade of French's Division. Its command structure already weakened by the slaughter at Franklin, Stewart's Corps lost one of its division commanders, French, who was placed on leave suffering from a severe eye infection. His division, now the corps' smallest, with fewer than 800 effectives, was placed under Walthall. The remnant of Cockrell's Brigade was detached and marched to the west to build a fort to interdict the Tennessee River. With Ector's Brigade on picket service, this meant that the only addition to Walthall's force was Sears's effective strength of 210 men.[47]

As the ice melted on December 14, Thomas planned a holding attack the next day on the Confederate right with Steedman's force, while Wood's veterans occupied the Confederate center. The main Federal effort would be made against Stewart and the Confederate left. A. J. Smith's Sixteenth Corps of the Army of the Tennessee and Wilson's reinforced and rejuvenated Federal cavalry would make this attack pivoting on Wood. Schofield

46. Connelly, *Autumn of Glory*, 508; *OR* 45(1):672, 45(2):669.

47. Field Returns, December 10, 1864, Jones Collection, Tulane; *OR* 45(1):679–80, 709, 711, 722, 45(2):669, 672, 676, 691; Application for Leave, December 6, 1864, French Papers, RG 109, NA; Special Order No. 10, Stewart's Corps, December 15, 1864, E. C. Walthall Papers, RG 109, NA; Sword, *Embrace an Angry Wind*, 314–15.

would be held in reserve, near the Federal left center, to be used as events dictated.[48]

December 15 became a relatively warm, sunny Middle Tennessee winter morning, although the day started with a dense fog. Early that morning, Stewart gamely wrote S. D. Lee that he felt his new line was tenable, and made it clear he was ready to fight on either the old or the new line. Stewart soon got his wish. About 9 A.M., Gale received a report that the Federals were advancing in heavy force on Loring's front and on the Hillsboro Pike. When Gale informed him of the Yankee advance, Old Straight rode out to the line along the Hillsboro Pike to order Walthall to put his command, including Sears's Brigade, under arms and man the redoubts extending along the left. Stewart found that an attack was under way and that the Confederate cavalry on the left, supported by Ector's Brigade, was being forced back. Stewart ordered Colonel David Coleman, commanding Ector's men, to report to Walthall, who placed the unit on the left of his line. Walthall's line extended south at right angles from that of Loring, Sears in the interval between the two divisions, with the brigades of Quarles, Shelly, and Reynolds extending to the left, positioned behind a stone wall along the Hillsboro Pike. Walthall manned the two leftmost redoubts, Nos. 4 and 5, with a hundred men each from Quarles's and Shelly's brigades. The only artillery on that portion of the line were the six pieces in these two redoubts, as the rest of the division's artillery was spaced at other points along the main line.[49]

Reports began to reach Stewart of the Federal buildup all along the line, but especially on the left. The Federals strangely were not pressing forward, however, at least at first. Loring reported that the Federals had moved out in front of his left brigade, Adams', and then lain down on the ground. The great Federal wheel against Stewart's line had not completed its move on the outer arc. Stewart knew he was in trouble, and must have been reminded of his experience just over a year before at Missionary Ridge. A Federal column moved beyond the corps' flank on the Hillsboro Pike. Stewart, in consultation with Walthall, ordered Colonel Coleman to march Ector's Brigade to interdict that move. Stewart then informed

48. Stone, "Repelling Hood's Invasion," 457.
49. Ibid.; APS to S. D. Lee, December 15, 1864, S. D. Lee Papers, SHC; W. D. Gale to wife, January 19, 1865, in Ridley, *Battles and Sketches*, 413; *OR* 45(1):709, 722.

Hood of the Federal advance, and Hood ordered two brigades of Johnson's Division, Manigault's and Brigadier General Zachariah C. Deas's, to the left to Stewart's aid. Portions of Smith's infantry and a brigade of Wilson's cavalry overran the most southerly redoubt, No. 5. Redoubt No. 4 was occupied by Captain Charles L. Lumsden's Alabama battery of four 12-pound Napoleons. Lumsden's infantry support scattered, but the battery was ordered by Stewart to hold as long as possible. Lumsden resisted for three hours before finally having to abandon his guns. He later complained to Stewart about the sacrifice, and was told that it could not have been avoided. With his line stretched "to its utmost tension," Stewart directed Manigault's and Deas's brigades to the left to help shore up the now-endangered flank, as Coleman was cut off from the corps by the Federal penetration.[50]

Manigault's and Deas's brigades were both veteran units, and they were closely followed by their division commander, Major General Edward "Allegheny" Johnson. Stewart ordered Manigault's men into line parallel to the Hillsboro Pike opposite to Redoubt No. 4. Johnson was directed to place Deas's men between Manigault's and Walthall, forming a continuous line to check the oncoming bluecoats. To Stewart's chagrin, however, "the two brigades named, making but feeble resistance, fled, and the enemy crossed the pike, passing Walthall's left." Stewart ordered a battery withdrawn from Loring's line, which he posted on a commanding hill to provide a rallying point for Johnson's scattering men. The two brigades reformed around the battery briefly, but then fled once more, leaving the battery to be overrun by the enemy. In the meantime, Walthall refused Reynolds' Brigade to cover his left flank, in hopes that Johnson's reinforcements would restore the situation. When Johnson's men scattered, all Stewart could do was warn Walthall, about 3:30 P.M., that Johnson's men had fallen back. Walthall was ordered to watch his flanks and hold on as long as possible, in hopes that reinforcements would arrive from Cheatham. Even the arrival of Johnson's other two brigades could not halt the flanking Unionists.[51]

50. *OR* 45(2):691–92; 45(1):709, 722–23; Sword, *Embrace an Angry Wind*, 334–38; James R. Maxwell, "Lumsden's Battery at the Battle of Nashville," *CV* 12 (October 1904): 484–85.

51. *OR* 45(1):709, 723, 45(2):693.

With his extreme left no longer in existence, Stewart held the remainder of his line "to the last possible moment," in hope of reinforcement from other parts of the line. The presence of the Federals in their rear soon made Walthall's and Loring's position "perilous in the extreme." Finally, it reached the point that Stewart was compelled to order a general withdrawal. He found that Walthall had anticipated that order, as Reynolds' holding force could not hold back the mass of Yankees in the corps' rear. Walthall later reported that he extricated his men "with difficulty." Naturally, Walthall's retreat necessitated Loring abandoning his line, which he had successfully held for most of the day. The presence of Federals in the corps' rear soon threatened Stewart's headquarters, manned by Gale. When the enemy advanced to within three hundred yards, Gale and his clerks escaped through the back yard to join Stewart. Not far from their meeting place, General Sears was seriously wounded and captured.[52]

The corps made good its withdrawal to a point between the Granny White and Franklin Pikes, nightfall having brought an end to the day's fighting. Gale felt that the men demonstrated a never-before-seen lethargy and lack of enthusiasm. He hoped that Hood would retreat south to the Duck River that night, and then stop and fight. Hood formed a new line, however, in the Brentwood Hills along the general line of the present Harding Place—Cheatham now on the left holding an eminence (soon to be known as Shy's Hill) with Bate's Division, supported by Ector's Brigade in reserve. On the right, Lee's Corps occupied a hill hard by the Franklin Pike, known as either Overton's Hill or the more local usage, Peach Orchard Hill. Stewart's Corps, down to Loring and Walthall with Sears's frazzled brigade of one hundred fifty men, occupied the army's center, from the side of Shy's Hill east along a stone wall.[53]

The grimness of the army's situation was reflected in Hood's orders to Stewart the morning of December 16, which, like the day before, dawned unusually mild. Prefaced by the phrase "Should any disaster happen to us to-day," Hood ordered Stewart to withdraw his corps by the Frankin Pike, covered by Lee, and once past Brentwood, form "in the best position you

---

52. *OR* 45(1):709–10, 723; W. D. Gale to wife, January 19, 1865, in Ridley, *Battles and Sketches*, 413; Reynolds Diary, December 15, 1864, Reynolds Papers, UAR.

53. W. D. Gale to wife, January 19, 1865, in Ridley, *Battles and Sketches*, 413; *OR* 45(1):712; Horn, *Decisive Battle of Nashville*, 108–12.

can find, and let the whole army pass through you." Stewart instructed his subordinate commanders accordingly. In the same event, Cheatham was to withdraw by the Granny White Pike. By contrast, Thomas' orders to his troops was simply to attack if Hood was still in their front, otherwise to pursue.[54]

As the chief Union efforts were against the Confederate flanks, Stewart's lines were confronted with only occasional attacks, which Walthall characterized as "feeble." The corps, however, was subjected to a heavy artillery fire, although not as heavy or effectual as that suffered by Bate's men on Shy's Hill, just to Walthall's left. Late in the morning, the only reserve on the left, Ector's Brigade, was directed to the rear to head off a penetration behind the army's left by Wilson's dismounted cavalrymen. The morning became afternoon, and the bombardment and desultory Federal attacks continued. A cold rain began. The ineffectiveness of the Federal attacks into the afternoon was demonstrated by the simple fact that, notwithstanding the two terrible beatings it had taken in the space of seventeen days, the Army of Tennessee was holding on. The Federal threat in the left rear continued, to the point that the Granny White Pike, one of the army's two escape routes, was interdicted. At 3:15 P.M., Stewart called on Walthall for Reynolds' Arkansas brigade, which was dispatched to the left rear to assist Ector's (Coleman's) Brigade in regaining control of the Granny White Pike escape route. Walthall took care that Reynolds' line was covered by the remnants of Sears's Brigade and Shelly's Brigade and that officers spread the word to the troops to prevent confusion. These two brigades were able to temporarily halt Wilson's advance, but could not regain the pass where the Granny White Pike crossed the ridge in the army's rear.[55]

As was the case the day before, the danger to the army was on the left, which was now held by Cheatham. While Wilson was moving to cut the pike in Cheatham's rear, pressure on Lee's Corps on the army's right caused Hood to send all but one brigade of Cleburne's old division to that quarter. With no reserve, Cheatham did not have the strength to hold

54. *OR* 45(1):710, 45(2):696; Sword, *Embrace an Angry Wind*, 350; Horn, *Decisive Battle of Nashville*, 113.

55. *OR* 45(1):710–11, 723, 45(2):696–97; Horn, *Decisive Battle of Nashville*, 117–18, 122–26.

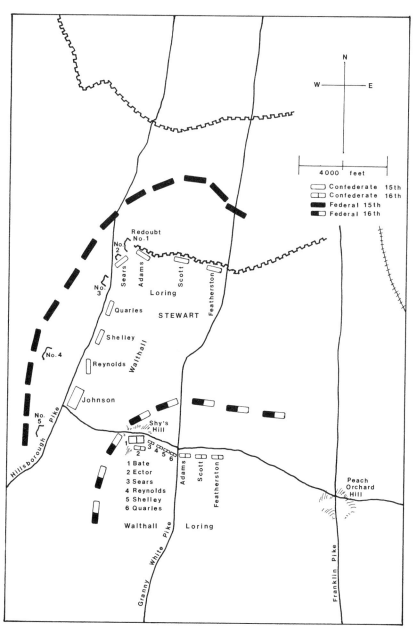

Nashville

Map by Blake Magner

against a determined Federal attack, which was finally launched about 4 P.M. At that point, Stewart was in conference with Hood at army headquarters. Doubtless, Stewart was confident to that point of his corps' ability to hold, as it had repulsed every attack made on its lines during the day. While Stewart and Hood were in conversation, a member of Hood's staff announced that the line had given way.[56]

It was obvious through the day that Bate's position on Shy's Hill was the focal point of the Federal attack. At 2 P.M., Old Straight directed that if Bate fell back, Walthall, on his left, should keep his left connected with Bate, falling back from the left toward the right and forming a new line in the hills in the rear of his position. A later dispatch directed Walthall to "hold everything in readiness to retire to-nite [*sic*]," indicating that at least Stewart knew that the army had been pushed past its limit. Nonetheless, Walthall and Loring continued to repulse attacks on their line until 4 P.M., when matters began to unravel. First, Walthall noticed a line of bluecoats "distinctly visible on the hills in our rear, covering much of our corps, which was the center in the army line." Once again, the Federals in his front launched an attack on Walthall's front, but it was "repulsed without difficulty." To Walthall's left, Shy's Hill was just then carried by a determined Federal attack. His rear already threatened, Walthall immediately ordered a withdrawal. With Federals at their front, flank, and rear, the men of the corps streamed toward the Franklin Pike, in "disorder [that] was great and general." Despite the chaos, Stewart's men were not in a panic. Stewart's staff engineer, Major Wilbur Foster, later recalled moving along the foot of the Brentwood Hills, with a group of the men, none of whom cried in terror but in fact made gibes and sarcastic remarks. With the knowledge of veterans, they fled, "not because they were panic-stricken, but because it was the proper thing to do."[57]

Stewart's headquarters was located where the Granny White Pike crossed the heights in the rear of the army. From that point, the corps' whole line could be observed, and every move by either side. Gale marveled at the panoramic view of Thomas' masses set against the backdrop of the church spires and the Tennessee capitol in Nashville. There was, more-

---

56. Horn, *Decisive Battle of Nashville*, 123–28; *OR* 45(1):711.

57. *OR* 45(1):723–24, 45(2):696–97; Wilbur J. Foster, Letter, *CV* 12 (June 1904): 274.

over, considerable concern at the fact that Wilson's men had crossed the pike in the rear of the headquarters. As the collapse began, and with Stewart absent from his headquarters, Gale prevailed upon General Reynolds to deploy his brigade as a rallying point for the men streaming south in flight. The Arkansas men fought a heroic series of rearguard actions on the Confederate left. A veteran of Brown's Division recalled that some of Stewart's men stemmed the Federal tide in the Confederate rear, enabling his division to escape. In the end, the effort to rally became futile, and Gale barely escaped. Moving in the gathering darkness through the woods to the Franklin Pike, Gale found Stewart, who had heard that Gale had been either killed or captured. Stewart moved on to Brentwood, whither he had dispatched his staff engineer, Major Foster, in accordance with Hood's "disaster" order, to lay out a line of defense.[58]

At Brentwood, Lee's largely intact corps formed the rear guard. Stewart was not allowed to rest and collect his men, but was ordered on to Franklin, where elements of the corps arrived around 3 A.M. on December 17. Once the men were across the Harpeth, they were permitted to rest for a few hours before they started for Columbia and the Duck River crossing there. Stewart arrived at Columbia the morning of December 18 and formed on the north bank of the Duck, Loring on the right and Walthall on the left, covering the passage of the army. During the night of December 19–20, the corps made a harrowing crossing besides which, according to Gale, Washington's crossing of the Delaware eighty-eight years before seemed insignificant. The men encamped a short distance from Columbia on the road to Pulaski.[59]

Hood hoped to remain on the Duck River line for the winter, but the condition of the army was such that when he reached Columbia, he became convinced that safety lay only on the other side of the Tennessee. On the morning of December 20, Walthall organized a special command to assist Forrest and his cavalry in covering the retreat of the army. In addition to four of Cheatham's brigades, Walthall took two of his brigades, Reyn-

58. W. D. Gale to wife, January 19, 1865, in Ridley, *Battles and Sketches*, 414–15; *OR* 45(1):711; Reynolds Diary, December 16, 1864, Reynolds Papers, UAR; Frank S. Roberts, "Spring Hill—Franklin—Nashville, 1864," *CV* 27 (February 1919): 60.

59. *OR* 45(1):655, 711, 724; W. D. Gale to wife, January 19, 1865, in Ridley, *Battles and Sketches*, 415.

olds' and Quarles's, one of French's, Ector's Texans, and one of Loring's, Featherston's Mississippians. With Cockrell gone, it was fully half of Stewart's Corps. Under Forrest's command, Walthall and his men fought an inspiring rearguard action as the army limped toward the crossing of the Tennessee at Bainbridge, Alabama. The remnant of the corps marched southward, through ice, rain, and snow. The road south from Pulaski was strewn with dead horses and mules, broken wagons, and, ominously, fifteen broken pontoons.[60]

Why was Stewart not personally placed in command when half his corps was detached to the rear guard? An artilleryman of Cheatham's Corps observed Hood, Stewart, Cheatham, and Carter Stevenson late on December 16. While Stewart and the others "were doing what they could to bring order out of chaos," Hood did little to rally his disintegrating army. Throughout the retreat, it appeared to the same observer that Stewart was "our real leader throughout the retreat and directed the passage of the river." No doubt Hood overcame his mortification over the smashing of his army and played a large part in supervising its retreat. Nonetheless, Stewart unquestionably had a significant role in directing the retreat, as dictated by his being the army's second-ranking officer and having better mobility than the disabled Hood.[61]

Christmas Day found the army at the Tennessee River. Stewart was detached at Shoal Creek, about two miles north of Bainbridge, Alabama, to form a line of battle with the remaining part of his corps to cover the crossing. Between the remnants of the army's pontoon train and some enemy pontoons captured by Brigadier General Philip D. Roddey's cavalry, Hood was able to construct a bridge. Thomas, however, dispatched gunboats down the Tennessee to destroy the bridge. Stewart ordered three guns—all that remained of Captain James A. Hoskins' Mississippi battery and Cowan's (Lieutenant George H. Tompkins') Vicksburg battery—down the river to Florence, Alabama, to contest the passage. One gunboat tried to make the run, but the three field pieces drove it away. On December 27, Walthall and the corps' four detached brigades were back under Stewart's

60. *OR* 45(1):655, 711, 724; General Order No. 1, December 20, 1864, Walthall Papers, RG 109, NA; W. D. Gale to wife, January 19, 1865, in Ridley, *Battles and Sketches*, 415.

61. Stephenson, *Civil War Memoir*, 334, 344. Sam Watkins saw Hood in a similar state during the retreat. Watkins, *Co. Aytch*, 241.

command, and the reunited corps crossed the river at daylight on December 28, taking up the pontoon bridge behind it.[62]

The corps marched on to Burnsville, Mississippi, on the Memphis and Charleston Railroad, arriving on January 2. From that point, the corps proceeded further south to Tupelo, and went into camp much reduced, Walthall observing that his whole division numbered less than one of its brigades had when he'd assumed command eight months before. The corps headquarters was established at the house of the Widow Sample, who suggested a belated Christmas dinner. Stewart's staff contributed the delicacies that they had been able to salvage out of the debacle in Tennessee, and the widow made available some of her own foodstuffs, thus enabling Stewart and his staff to host Beauregard, Hood, Walthall, and Loring at a feast like none had seen for many months. Ridley and another young officer on the staff, possibly Stewart's son Caruthers, imbibed too much from a supply of gin a friend had given Stewart in Tennessee. They drew the attention of the assembled generals: the "big hearted, impetuous" Hood, the "polite little Frenchman" Beauregard, the "good hearted, impulsive" Loring, Walthall, fresh off of his successful covering of the army's retreat, and Stewart, an "unobtrusive, stern West Pointer" who "look[ed] daggers" at the two young men. After a night of nausea, Ridley and the other young officer received a mild yet devastating rebuke from Old Straight the next day: "Young men, I was mortified at your action yesterday."[63]

This moment of levity was probably Hood's last with the Army of Tennessee. On January 13, Hood requested to be relieved from command, and departed for Richmond on January 23. Beauregard placed Lieutenant General Richard Taylor, commander of the Department of East Louisiana, Mississippi, and Alabama, in command. It was a hollow honor. Beauregard began dispatching elements of the Army of Tennessee to the Carolinas to help resist Sherman. By the time Hood relinquished command, Stevenson, commanding Lee's Corps since Lee was wounded on the retreat from Nashville, had departed for Augusta, Georgia, with orders having been issued to Cheatham to follow.[64]

---

62. *OR* 45(1):711, 724; W. D. Gale to wife, January 19, 1865, in Ridley, *Battles and Sketches*, 415; Dabney, "Gen. A. P. Stewart on Strong Topics," 31.

63. *OR* 45(1):674, 724; Ridley, *Battles and Sketches*, 444–46.

64. Hood, *Advance and Retreat*, 307–308; Horn, *Army of Tennessee*, 422–23.

Thus ended what Stewart later termed "the disastrous campaign into Tennessee." Stewart did not disagree with the strategy of the campaign. "I deem it proper to say that after the fall of Atlanta the condition of the army and other considerations rendered it necessary, in my judgment, that an offensive campaign should be made in the enemy's rear and on his line of communications. It is not my purpose, nor does it pertain to me, to explain the reasons which prompted the campaign, but simply to express my concurrence in the views which determined the operations of the army." There is no such direct statement of Stewart's views on the conduct of the campaign, but he obviously did not concur with the rash assault at Franklin, although he was willing to absolve Hood of the ill motive of taking the Spring Hill debacle out on the Army of Tennessee on November 30, 1864. The only indication that Old Straight disagreed with Hood at Nashville is Gale's letter indicating that at least members of Stewart's staff hoped that the army would withdraw behind the Duck after the first day of fighting on December 15.[65]

Stewart's personal performance in the campaign is obscured by the general disaster that befell the army, but enough evidence remains to make several conclusions. First, the only shadow on Stewart's performance at Spring Hill is that cast by the purported recollections of Governor Harris recorded by Major Brown, to the effect that Stewart was reluctant to put a brigade across the Franklin Pike late on the night of November 29. If that is discounted—and there is ample reason to do so—Stewart followed Hood's orders to the letter. Stewart correctly believed that the failure at Spring Hill was ultimately Hood's. Such was also the case at Franklin, where Hood's orders and the tactical situation left little for either Stewart or Cheatham to do except order their men into the firestorm generated by the entrenched Federal troops. Finally, at Nashville, the corps was stretched to the limit on the Confederate left on December 15, in much the same way as Stewart's division had been on Missionary Ridge. The real break on the left occurred when the isolated redoubts fell and the brigades of Johnson's Division were unable (and unwilling) to restore the situation. The corps held the center on December 16 until the collapse of the position on Shy's Hill and Wilson's flanking cavalrymen caused the collapse of

65. Lindsley, ed., *Military Annals*, 106; *OR* 45(1):712; W. D. Gale to wife, January 19, 1865, in Ridley, *Battles and Sketches*, 415.

the army's position. Hood and the army as a whole appear to have retained confidence in Stewart to the end. In fact, Stewart appears to have had a significant role in leading the army to safety. Stewart's Corps covered the army's retreat across the Tennessee in December, much the same as Stewart and his division had covered the withdrawal across the Oostanaula in May.

In early 1865, only the most unperceptive of men could fail to see that the end of the Confederacy was near. Nonetheless, Stewart, and the other thin and tattered Tennesseans who stayed with the colors, "remained . . . true to the cause they had espoused, and a *third time* left their State in the hands of the enemy to follow the fortunes of the 'Southern Cross.'" On January 30, 1865, Old Straight and the remnants of his corps began their long, torturous trip east, for one more fight under Old Joe against Sherman.[66]

66. Lindsley, ed., *Military Annals*, 106–107; Horn, *Army of Tennessee*, 430.

— 13 —

The Noble Army of
Tennessee Disbanded

The Carolina Campaign and the End of the War

While Hood took his forlorn hope into Tennessee, William Tecumseh
Sherman and 60,000 of his hardiest veterans marched almost unopposed
to Savannah. The seaport fell to the Federals on December 20, 1864, even
as the Army of Tennessee endured its terrible retreat to the Tennessee
River. Among the civilians Sherman encountered in Savannah was Harriet
Stewart, who applied to the Federal conqueror for protection and news of
her husband. Sherman assured Harriet that Stewart had not been killed or
captured. Learning she was from Ohio, he advised her to go to her relatives in Cincinnati to await the end of the war.[1]

Sherman planned to rest, resupply, and reorganize his men, and then to
move into the Carolinas, marching to join Grant in the Richmond area,
but in the meantime wrecking anything of military value to the shrinking
Confederacy in his path. Faced with the prospect of an irresistible combination of the Union's two best generals commanding the Union's two
greatest field armies, Jefferson Davis ordered Beauregard to transfer the
remnants of the Army of Tennessee to South Carolina, to join the other
ragged remnants of Confederate divisions, brigades, and regiments gathering to resist Sherman.[2]

1. William T. Sherman, *Memoirs of General William T. Sherman* (New York: Charles L.
Webster, 1890), 2:235–36.
2. Hattaway and Jones, *How the North Won*, 654–56.

Originally, Stewart's Corps, no doubt because it was the old Army of Mississippi, was slated to stay with Taylor. The remnant of the Confederate heartland was open to an onslaught from the victorious bluecoats in Middle Tennessee that spring. The practicalities of the situation soon changed that thinking, as Beauregard notified Davis on February 2, 1865: "General Taylor reports that a victory over Sherman is essential, and that he can resist a raid without Stewart's corps [but] cannot fight a battle with it against an army; that French's division is sufficient to fully garrison Mobile and Choctaw Bluff, and proposes to send balance of corps [to Augusta, Georgia]. I have accordingly ordered it [to Augusta], with a battalion of artillery." By the time this message was sent, the corps, without French's Division, had entrained at Tupelo and begun a trip to Augusta via Mobile, Montgomery, and Macon.[3]

After riding the almost bankrupt Confederate railroad system for over two weeks, the greater part of the corps was in Augusta by February 15. As reduced as it was by the detachment of French's Division and the winter campaign into Tennessee, Stewart's Corps was still further diminished by a furlough program approved by Hood and Beauregard, which one report indicated lowered the corps' strength by 2,500 men. One of Beauregard's staff reported that the entire corps would number only 1,000 effectives, and was "in bad condition."[4]

With the Confederacy *in extremis*, Jefferson Davis appointed Robert E. Lee as general-in-chief of its shrinking armies. Always diplomatic in his relations with Davis, Lee broached the possibility of Davis' ultimate *persona non grata*, Joe Johnston, returning to command the Confederacy's second army in a letter to new Secretary of War John C. Breckinridge on February 19. Noting that Beauregard was not able to articulate any proposals, and further that the Creole general was of indifferent health, Lee expressed the view that Johnston was the only officer who had the confidence of the army and the people. Securing authorization, on February 22 Lee ordered Johnston to assume command of the Army of Tennessee, and all troops in

    3. Ibid.; *OR* 47(2):1078; Ridley, *Battles and Sketches*, 455; Reynolds Diary, January 30–February 15, 1865, Reynolds Papers, UAR. Beauregard later had to explain to Joe Johnston why French and two of Lee's brigades were not with the rest of the army. See *OR* 47(3):694, 699, 700–701.

    4. Hood, *Advance and Retreat*, 308–309; *OR* 47(2):1174, 1194.

the Departments of Georgia, South Carolina, and Florida. Johnston was given one overriding task: "Concentrate all available forces and drive back Sherman."[5]

When Johnston assumed command on February 22, Stewart and his men were at Newberry, a railroad junction thirty-five miles up the Saluda River from Columbia, by then a smoldering ruin. From Newberry, the corps, in line of march with Cheatham and his men, moved on to Chester, between Newberry and Charlotte, North Carolina. On March 5, Stewart's reduced corps began a slow movement along the Carolina railroads through Charlotte, Salisbury, and Raleigh to Smithfield, North Carolina, a railroad junction between Raleigh and Goldsboro.[6]

By March 13, Stewart was at Smithfield. Johnston directed him to remain there and stop all the troops arriving from the West. Johnston arrived at Smithfield on March 15, and was met by a band from the Army of Tennessee that played "Dixie" in his honor. At Smithfield, Johnston formed what he termed the Army of the South, a combination of Hardee's troops from the Charleston and Savannah garrisons, Bragg's Department of North Carolina forces, Hampton's cavalry, and the three decimated corps of the Army of Tennessee. The next day, Johnston appointed Beauregard his second-in-command and placed Stewart in command of the infantry and artillery of the Army of Tennessee. Stewart assumed command of only 5,306 total present as half of Cheatham's Corps, most of the furloughed troops, and the artillery having not yet arrived. Stewart's own corps, now commanded by Loring, numbered but 1,349 total present.[7]

On that March 16, Hardee's two divisions under Virginia veterans Brigadier General William B. Taliaferro and Major General Lafayette McLaws clashed at Averasboro with Major General Henry W. Slocum's Army of Georgia. Slocum's force included the Fourteenth and Twentieth

5. Dowdy, *Wartime Papers of R. E. Lee*, 904–906; *OR* 47(2):1247.

6. Ridley, *Battles and Sketches*, 455; *OR* 47(1):1049–50, 1053; Henry W. Slocum, "Sherman's March from Savannah to Bentonville," *B&L* 4:687.

7. Ridley, *Battles and Sketches*, 452; *OR* 47(2):1385, 1388, 1394, 1399, 1402, 1408; Mark L. Bradley, *Last Stand in the Carolinas: The Battle of Bentonville* (Campbell, Calif.: Savas Woodbury, 1996), 137–38. More of the army was on the way, however, as Stephen D. Lee reported from Augusta on March 13 that he was preparing to march with about 3,000 men and that about 4,000 more, probably stragglers and troops returning from furlough, were expected soon with the army's wagon train. *OR* 47(2):1384.

Corps, about 15,000 men each. After a day-long fight, Hardee withdrew his outnumbered men under darkness, having given the Federals their stiffest fight since leaving Atlanta. Hardee stalled Sherman for a day while Johnston gathered his scattered forces to make a stand. Hardee also felt that he had given his men, primarily garrison troops from Savannah and Charleston, a valuable taste of combat.[8]

Sherman veered toward Goldsboro, where he expected to rendezvous with Schofield's Twenty-third Corps, which was shipped to the North Carolina coast from Tennessee. Slocum's wing marched on the Federal left, Major General Oliver O. Howard's wing several miles away on the Federal right. Late on the night of March 17, Johnston inquired of his cavalry commander, Wade Hampton, as to the position of Sherman's corps and as to any ideas that he may have had concerning an attack. Hampton was at that point two miles south of Bentonville, which was itself about sixteen miles from Smithfield. Hampton replied immediately, to the effect that the Fourteenth Corps was in his immediate front and the Twentieth Corps was five or six miles to the rear, and that Howard's force was some miles to the south on a parallel road. Hampton urged a concentration at that point, which Johnston undertook.[9]

Johnston may well have discussed his possibilities with Stewart, as Old Joe visited the new headquarters of the Army of Tennessee on March 17. Bromfield Ridley found Johnston "surpassingly social," and he told Johnston, no doubt truthfully, of the joy that swept the army when its men learned that Johnston was assuming command. Johnston said he was equally gratified, but sadly observed that it was "too late to make it the same army." Still solicitous of the comfort and morale of the men, Johnston directed Stewart to communicate to them that furloughs were suspended because of the presence of the enemy, but that they would be recommenced on a liberal basis when consistent with the good of the service. The next morning, March 18, Johnston ordered Stewart to move his command to Bentonville.[10]

8. Bradley, *Last Stand*, 121–33.

9. Slocum, "Sherman's March," 692; Wade Hampton, "The Battle of Bentonville," *B&L* 4:701.

10. Ridley, *Battles and Sketches*, 452; *OR* 47(2):1402, 1413, 1428.

On March 18, the various components of his command marched to effect Johnston's concentration at Bentonville. Bragg's troops and the Army of Tennessee camped at a point south of Bentonville that night. Due to a faulty map, Hardee's march took considerably longer than anticipated, but his corps was expected early the next day. At Bentonville that night, Stewart was ordered to have his command quietly under arms early in the morning, and was advised that Hardee would march the final six miles to Bentonville at 3:00 A.M. Stewart was also given intelligence as to the location of the Federal army, which Hampton reported to be three miles out the Goldsboro Road from the point the road from Bentonville intersected it. Ridley noticed that the army "was in high spirits and ready to brave the coming storm."[11]

Early the morning of March 19, the Army of Tennessee moved into position on the Confederate right, positioned to attack the flank of any Federal force advancing against Bragg's men, who blocked the Goldsboro Road. Unfortunately, only one road was available to Stewart through the pine thickets, occasioning Johnston to remark that his movement "consumed a weary time."[12]

As the Army of Tennessee filed into position, the reliable Daniel H. Reynolds, commanding what was now only a nominal brigade in Walthall's Division, was struck by a Yankee shell, losing his left leg. Stewart directed Walthall to take the left flank, covering the artillery posted there. Walthall was touched beyond measure when he rode down his line and the familiar cheers of his decimated division burst forth. As D. H. Hill brought Lee's Corps on to the field, Stewart told him to not bother entrenching, as the Rebels were awaiting orders to advance. A former classmate (and superior) of Stewart's, Hill openly disagreed with the order. To keep the troops employed before the advance, Hill ordered them to throw up breastworks. Stewart obviously acquiesced with this insubordination, and in the event, Hill was right. The work was about half done at about 1 P.M. when two Federal brigades struck Hill in the Army of Tennessee's center on the front of Stovall's Brigade, and Bate on the army's right, on the

11. *OR* 47(1):1056, 47(2):1428; Ridley, *Battles and Sketches*, 452.
12. *OR* 47(1):1056, 1089; Hughes, *Bentonville: The Final Battle of Sherman and Johnston*, 52–53; Bradley, *Last Stand*, 162, 302.

front of Daniel Govan's brigade. After a "sharp engagement," the Federals were repulsed.[13]

Unfortunately for the Confederates, another of those incidents that had plagued the Army of Tennessee throughout its history now intervened. Johnston planned to throw Stewart and Hardee on the flank of the Federals massing to force the road in Bragg's front. As soon as Hardee's column reached the field, however, the Federals launched a heavy attack on Major General Robert F. Hoke's Division on Bragg's front. Bragg called on Johnston for reinforcements. Over Hampton's protest, Johnston sent Bragg one of Hardee's two divisions, that of Lafayette McLaws, the strongest in Johnston's army. As it turned out, Hoke easily repulsed the attack against his front. McLaws was thus not available for Johnston's counterstroke, conceived to crush the Fourteenth Corps.[14]

Now on the field, Hardee was placed in command of the Confederate right wing, and Bragg the left. This did not leave Stewart without a command. Hardee assumed direct supervision of the division of his current corps under Taliaferro, and that portion of his old corps, which was then Cheatham's Corps, present under Bate. Stewart then took direct command of the rest of the Army of Tennessee contingent, that is, Lee's Corps under D. H. Hill and his own corps under Loring. Hardee thus commanded the extreme right, Stewart the center, and Bragg the left. The attack was set for 2:45 P.M., and young Ridley was dispatched to advise the corps commanders under Stewart of the plan.[15]

At about 3:00 P.M., Hardee ordered the Confederate right and center to advance against the exposed position of Brigadier General William P. Carlin's division of the Fourteenth Corps. The last great attack of the Army of Tennessee swept forward, and pushed Carlin several hundred yards back to a point where Federal troops of the Twentieth Corps arriving on the field solidified the Federal front. On Stewart's front, Hill and Loring advanced through Carlin's line and struck Morgan's division from the flank and rear.

13. *OR* 47(1):1101, 1103, 1089–90, 1106; Reynolds Diary, March 19, 1865, Reynolds Papers, UAR; Alfred W. Garner, "Public Services of E. C. Walthall," *Publications of the Mississippi Historical Society* 9 (1906): 239, 241; Bradley, *Last Stand*, 167; Hughes, *Bentonville*, 54, 57–59.

14. Hampton, "Bentonville," 702–703, 705; Hughes, *Bentonville*, 60–61.

15. Bradley, *Last Stand*, 193; Hughes, *Bentonville*, 120, 123; *OR* 47(1):1056; Ridley, *Battles and Sketches*, 452–53.

A counterattack cut off elements of Hill's Corps, forcing them to make a fighting retreat out of the pocket. The Confederates restored the line, however, before too much damage was done.[16]

Unfortunately, Bentonville was the one major battle where Stewart was present but, apparently, never wrote a report. There are small bits of information recorded as to his presence at various spots on the battlefield on March 19, but nothing on which to base any evaluation of his performance, especially during the attack that afternoon. Johnston's report of the battle mentions Hardee's charge and notes that Old Reliable was "gallantly seconded by Stewart, Hill, Loring and the officers under them." While Johnston's statement indicates that Stewart performed as expected, detailed analysis of Old Straight's role as the commander of the Army of Tennessee in its last attack is not possible.[17]

While the Confederates fought hard and suffered high casualties, Johnston failed in his effort to destroy one of Sherman's exposed wings. Given the state of affairs at that stage of the war, even the destruction of Slocum's entire wing would not have substantially changed the outcome. In any event, Slocum survived, and Sherman marched to his relief with Howard's wing, the Army of the Tennessee. The issue for Johnston was what to do next, in the face of the vastly superior Federal force. Consolidation seemed to be the first order of business, so Johnston returned to his jumping-off point and established a defensive position.[18]

By noon on March 20, most, and perhaps even all, of Sherman's united army was on Johnston's front. That afternoon, the Federals made several attacks on Hoke's Division from the east. Johnston obstinately maintained the field, although the position of the army was, in Hampton's words, "extremely perilous." The Confederates confronted a force twice their size.

---

16. Bradley, *Last Stand*, 202–70; Hughes, *Bentonville*, 123–32.

17. See discussions in Bradley, *Last Stand*, 504, n. 14; Hughes, *Bentonville*, 225. For Johnston's laudatory reference, see *OR* 47(1):1056. Stewart appears to have monitored Hill's advance (see *OR* 47[1]:1090), and no doubt Loring and Walthall's (ibid., 1101–1103). Stewart's message reporting Carlin's attack and repulse appear in *OR* 47(2):1437. A reference in Bradley, *Last Stand*, 256, shows Stewart on the Goldsboro Road during the retreat of Hill's men from the attack on Morgan's division. Other references are in Bradley, *Last Stand*, 204, 223, 262–63.

18. See Bradley, *Last Stand*, 309, 320–22; Slocum, "Sherman's March," 695; *OR* 47(1):1056; Ridley, *Battles and Sketches*, 453.

Johnston's paper-thin lines rested on no natural defenses, and the army had its back to a deep and rapid stream, Mill Creek, over which there was but a single bridge. Johnston basically had two reasons to stay, the humanitarian reason of removing his wounded, and the strategic reason of hoping Sherman might make a ruinous frontal assault similar to that at Kennesaw Mountain, which would give the Confederates a defensive victory.[19]

Within Stewart's command, Loring became ill and had to go to the rear. The stout warrior Walthall assumed command of Stewart's Corps. Ridley noted that the Federals were "remarkably quiet" on the Army of Tennessee's front, but that there were heavy demonstrations against Hoke. This comported with a report that Loring sent before he left, to the effect that the Federals on his front were either fortifying or cutting a road to the left. Stewart sent forward skirmishers and determined that the Federals were still on his front. D. H. Hill expressed displeasure over a salient in the Army of Tennessee's line, but Stewart insisted the troops remain. On this occasion, Stewart was right, as Hill later used the salient as a good artillery position. The gathering Yankee host and the Confederate army's exposed condition concerned Stewart. Late in the day, he informed Johnston's headquarters that if the army was to withdraw that night, it would be well to give the artillery on his line early notice so that they could be prepared to move. Stewart himself received a report from the Army of Tennessee's medical director, Dr. J. T. Darby, that the 624 wounded under his care could not all be removed unless all the army's wagons were placed at his disposal.[20]

The next morning, March 21, the sky began to threaten rain. Stewart got a report of Federals trying to turn Taliaferro's Division on the right flank of the Army of Tennessee, and reported it to Johnston. Fortunately, it turned out to be Federal skirmishers who were making a reconnaissance of the Confederate right, and they mistakenly reported that the Confederate right was strongly defended. Stewart and Taliaferro later threw out heavy skirmish lines and drove back probing Federals. This inconclusive skirmishing effectively ended the Battle of Bentonville on Stewart's front.[21]

The story was different on the Confederate left. A heavy Federal attack

19. Hampton, "Bentonville," 704; Bradley, *Last Stand*, 343.
20. Ridley, *Battles and Sketches*, 453; Hughes, *Bentonville*, 172; *OR* 47(2):1442.
21. Bradley, *Last Stand*, 353–57.

against the extreme Confederate left forced Johnston out of his headquarters and threatened to cut off the army's line of retreat across Mill Creek. Hardee led an attack that restored the situation. Old Reliable performed well that afternoon, but his moment of triumph was blasted when his only son, sixteen-year-old Willie, was mortally wounded.[22]

With Taliaferro dispatched along with three of his brigades to restore the situation on the left, the afternoon of March 21 must have been an anxious time for Stewart. While the Federals were quiet on the Army of Tennessee's front, Bate reported that his men on the extreme right were from three to five feet apart in single rank, and that he was not supported by cavalry on his flank. Bluntly, Stewart's old brigadier observed: "The enemy can come in there with impunity." Faced with the sparsity of his line, Stewart and his staff could hear the roar of battle far to the left, on their line of retreat. Eventually, even Walthall was pulled out of the line to reinforce the far left. Fortunately, the Federals did not test Stewart's line. After dark on March 21, the Confederates retreated. By dawn the next day, the Army of the South was across Mill Creek and on the road for Smithfield. Sherman moved on to Goldsboro, to effect his long-anticipated junction with Schofield.[23]

Since the Army of the South was no longer in touch with the enemy, on March 23 the men were allowed to wash up and put on clean clothes. Johnston reported to Lee from Smithfield, making a complimentary reference to the men of his old army: "Troops of Tennessee army have fully disproved slanders that have been published against them. Evening and night of 21st enemy moved toward Goldsborough, where Schofield joined him, and yesterday we came here. Sherman's course cannot be hindered by the small force I have. I can do no more than annoy him. I respectfully suggest that it is no longer a question whether you leave present position; you have only to decide where to meet Sherman. I will be near him."[24]

The period between the retreat from Bentonville to Smithfield and April 10 was a time of respite for Stewart and his men. Likewise, Sherman's junction with Schofield at Goldsboro was accompanied by a period

22. Ibid., 374–96.

23. Ibid., 400; *OR* 47(2):1447; Hughes, *Bentonville*, 193–97; Ridley, *Battles and Sketches*, 453.

24. *OR* 47(2):1454; for washing and clean clothes, see Ridley, *Battles and Sketches*, 453.

of rest and replenishment for the Federal army. Sherman made use of the interval to make plans to join with Grant.[25]

For Stewart, this interval was an unhappy one, in which his greatest solace must have been his religious faith. During this period, he learned of the death on March 13 of his young son, Gustavus Woodson Smith Stewart. The boy died at the age of four at the home of Stewart's brother Dr. O. W. Stewart in Auburn, Alabama. Rejecting Sherman's advice, Harriet and the two younger boys went to Auburn from Savannah. Bromfield Ridley observed that the general took his son's death very hard, writing in his diary: "Notwithstanding his stern military character he is a tender hearted man."[26]

Stewart must have derived great comfort from the presence of his two oldest sons, Caruthers and Alphonso, the latter of whom now joined him. Alphonso's adventures were many and varied. Leaving his school in Middle Tennessee in the late summer of 1864, he joined the 4th Tennessee Cavalry at Bristol, Tennessee, that September. He fought in several skirmishes with his new comrades until his father got word of his situation. Orders were issued for Alphonso to join Stewart, then marching north from Atlanta. Stewart sent him to Harriet in Savannah, but he left the town the day before it was occupied by Sherman. Alphonso was then sent to a military school at Tuscaloosa, Alabama, discharged from the army on account of his minority. The adventurous young man wrote Stewart seeking his consent to go on active service, threatening to do so even if not given parental permission. Stewart relented, and the boy traversed the tottering Confederacy to join his father's staff as an unofficial staff member. Previously, Stewart had made an effort to secure the boy a cadetship in the Confederate army. The application was erroneously denied by the War Department because such appointments required prior service in the army. The government appeared to be unaware of his time in the cavalry, or perhaps the service was insufficient because of his discharge as underage.[27]

---

25. Henry W. Slocum, "Final Operations of Sherman's Army," *B&L* 4:754–55.

26. Wingfield, *Stewart*, 213; Ridley, *Battles and Sketches*, 456. Hood's report as to Spring Hill came in during these days as well, implying, as noted above, that Stewart might have been delinquent at Spring Hill, which Hood later denied. See Ridley, *Battles and Sketches*, 455; *OR* 45(1):712–13.

27. Clement A. Evans, ed., *Confederate Military History* (1899; reprint, Wilmington, N.C.: Broadfoot Publishing, 1988), 12:419; APS to Jefferson Davis, December 11, 1864,

Stewart seems to have felt the impending demise of the Confederacy deeply. A few days after the retreat from Bentonville, Ridley observed that the general was depressed. Stewart had cast his lot with the Confederacy, believed in what it stood for, and had watched its young men bleed from Belmont to Bentonville. Defeat was at hand. If things went according to plan, the skeletal remains of the Army of Tennessee would combine with what was left of Robert E. Lee's Army of Northern Virginia in one last battle, where more would die even if Lee pulled off one of his miracles.[28]

Even after more arrivals from the West, the Army of Tennessee was still a shadow. A return dated March 23 showed 7,052 total present, but only 5,174 effectives. A report dated March 26 indicated that the command structure of the army was as thin as the numbers of soldiers who remained with the colors. Of the twenty-one shadow-like brigades with the army on that date, only two were under the direction of the commander for whom they were named. With French detached to Mobile, Loring absent with his illness, and Walthall in actual command of the corps, Stewart's own corps on that date was without any of its normal division commanders. Only five of the corps' six remaining brigades were present, Shelly's Brigade not having returned from furlough. Within a few days, however, some of the familiar names began to arrive along with a few thousand of the troops strung out on the long route from Tupelo.[29]

Johnston sought to reinstill some *esprit de corps* in the motley collection of troops under his command, and reviewed Hardee's Corps the morning of April 3. The next day, Ridley observed the last review of the old Army of Tennessee:

> April 4th: I witnessed to-day the saddest spectacle of my life, the review of the skeleton Army of Tennessee, that but one year ago was replete with men, and now filed by with tattered garments, worn out shoes, bare-footed and ranks so depleted that each color was supported by only thirty or forty men. Desertion, sickness, deaths, hard-

_____
with endorsement of February 2, 1865, Confederate Citizens' or Business Firms File, RG 109, NA; see Ridley, *Battles and Sketches*, 464.

28. Ridley, *Battles and Sketches*, 453.

29. *OR* 47(3):697–98; Ridley, *Battles and Sketches*, 455; R. Hugh Simmons, "Analysis of Historical Data Pertaining to Stewart's Corps, the Confederate Army of Tennessee, in North Carolina in 1865" (1993; copy in possession of author).

ships, perils and vicissitudes demonstrated themselves too plainly upon that old army not to recur to its history. Oh, what a contrast between the Dalton review and this one! The march of the remnant was so slow—colors tattered and torn with bullets—that it looked like a funeral procession. The countenance of every spectator who saw both reviews was depressed and dejected, and the solemn, stern look of the soldiery was so impressive—Oh! it is beginning to look dark in the east, gloomy in the west, and like almost a lost hope when we reflect upon the review of to-day![30]

In the context of the news of Lee's retreat from Richmond and with prisoners reporting that Sherman would move his immense force on April 10, Johnston for the last time on April 9 reorganized his forces, incorporating all of his troops into the Army of Tennessee. In the reorganization, Hardee was assigned a polyglot of his old corps, which had been Cheatham's after Atlanta, and Hoke's Division, formerly part of Bragg's command. Bragg was no longer with Johnston's army. Stewart was assigned command of a second corps, which included divisions under Loring, Patton Anderson, who was assigned command of Taliaferro's men, and Walthall, who assumed command of the division lately led by McLaws. Stephen D. Lee commanded a third corps, made up of divisions under D. H. Hill and Carter Stevenson. Each of the new corps contained elements of the old Army of Tennessee, but the shadow-like nature of the Confederate organization remained. Several of the regiments in Stewart's new brigades were "consolidated" regiments made up of the fragments of three, four, or even five of the old regiments. Stewart's old brigade of Tennesseans was now in the new 3rd Tennessee, along with the fragments of three other brigades.[31]

Fortunately, this brave remnant of a once-proud army would fight no more. Even as Sherman moved out of Goldsboro, Johnston's army fell back toward Raleigh, and word began to trickle in from Appomattox Court House concerning the surrender of the Army of Northern Virginia. Although hopeful reports to the contrary were also received, Jefferson Davis himself notified Johnston that even without official confirmation,

30. Ridley, *Battles and Sketches*, 455–56; John Johnson Diary, April 4, 1865, DU.
31. Ridley, *Battles and Sketches*, 456–57; *OR* 47(3):1061–66.

"there is little room for doubt as to result." On April 11, Stewart's Corps marched through Raleigh on the retreat west, where the impending gloom of defeat did not keep some of the younger members of Stewart's staff from stopping to flirt with the students of a girls' school.[32]

As the "new" Army of Tennessee marched on toward Goldsboro on April 11, Johnston departed from the army to meet with Davis, Beauregard, and the Confederate cabinet at Goldsboro. Anticipating the cessation of hostilities, Johnston ordered Stewart to suspend the execution of four condemned men in the corps. The army moved in two columns west from Raleigh, Hardee leading his corps, Stewart commanding his and that of Lee. Johnston's meeting with Davis led Old Joe to determine that the bankrupt Confederacy was no longer worth the blood of his army.[33]

On April 17, Johnston and Sherman met at the Bennett House near Durham to negotiate terms for the surrender of the Army of Tennessee. After the initial terms were rejected in Washington as too generous, Sherman had to go back and offer the same terms Grant offered Lee, which Johnston had no choice but to accept.[34]

The final days before the surrender were passed by its general officers struggling to keep the army together. News of Lee's collapse and the impending surrender was accompanied by desertion and open thievery by marauding soldiers at Stewart's very headquarters. Stewart and Loring spoke to a large assembly of the rank and file on April 20, explaining the initial surrender terms concluded by Johnston with Sherman.[35]

On April 25, Stewart went to Old Joe's headquarters and found that Johnston was waiting to conclude the final surrender terms. By this time, only the army's regard for Johnston seems to have held it together, as Ridley observed that "the eagerness of the men to get to their homes now is beyond picture." Stewart made speeches to three different segments of his command, "explaining to them the reason General Johnston refuses the acceptance of the terms, the same being that all over a certain rank will be held for treason." Obviously, Stewart was not above an uncharacteristic

---

32. Lindsley, ed., *Military Annals*, 110; *OR* 45(3):777, 789, 793; Ridley, *Battles and Sketches*, 457–58.

33. Ridley, *Battles and Sketches*, 457; Connelly, *Autumn of Glory*, 533–34.

34. Slocum, "Final Operations," 755–57; Connelly, *Autumn of Glory*, 534.

35. Ridley, *Battles and Sketches*, 458–59; *OR* 47(3):835.

white lie to hold the army together long enough for Johnston to conclude a proper surrender, although there must have been some uncertainty about the very possibility of prosecution.[36]

The final surrender was concluded April 26, 1865. Stewart spent the following days attending to the final affairs of his corps, including reporting on the arms, ammunition, and equipment held by his command, trying to straighten out transportation for his men, and waiting to see his men paroled. On a more personal level, the general spent time exchanging farewells with various officers in the army. On May 2, the army marched in its organized corps to Salisbury, where on May 5, it separated into three columns, one marching via Morganton, North Carolina, another via Spartanburg and Abbeville, South Carolina, and the remainder via Chester and Newberry, South Carolina. Thus, "the noble Army of Tennessee was disbanded."[37]

Stewart and his party chose to move through Spartanburg and Abbeville and on across the Savannah River into Georgia, a roundabout route into Tennessee to avoid bushwhackers in the mountains. Accompanied part of the way by his escort company, Captain Greenleaf's Light Horse from New Orleans, and Colonel Sevier of his staff, Stewart finally met with the party in which his sons and Ridley were traveling on May 17. The cavalry company and Sevier departed in Hancock County, Georgia, and, by May 25, other members of the party separated. Around May 25, Harriet Stewart and young Alex joined the general at Cornucopia, Georgia. There, they rested ten days before making the final trip into Tennessee.[38]

The trip to Lebanon took approximately six weeks. The party moved on the outskirts of Atlanta to avoid the Federal occupation troops, who supposedly cut the buttons, bars, stars, and lace off all Confederate uniforms. Stewart likely avoided the route between Dalton and Atlanta taken by the armies twice the year before, as it was a barren wasteland. Navigating by his headquarters maps, Stewart and his family finally made it back to Lebanon over Short Mountain in Cannon County, Tennessee, arriving by the end of June or the first of July.[39] The Stewart family's war was over.

36. Ridley, *Battles and Sketches*, 464.
37. *OR* 47(3):856–57; APS to E. J. Harris et al., May 2, 1865, Louisiana Historical Association Collection, Tulane; Johnston, *Narrative*, 418; Lindsley, ed., *Military Annals*, 111.
38. Ridley, *Battles and Sketches*, 472–79, 482.
39. Ibid., 482–84.

— 14 —

A Quiet, Peaceable, Law-Abiding Citizen

Educator and Businessman, 1865–1889

When he arrived home in the summer of 1865, Alexander Peter Stewart was a general without an army, a professor without a university, a revolutionary without a revolution. Stewart and his family returned to a Tennessee in a semi-anarchic condition, the rural regions infested by guerrillas and the cities occupied by Federal troops who either did little to fight a crime wave that troubled urban citizens or who actually committed crimes themselves. Freedmen clashed with the poor whites of Memphis and Nashville, and Wilson County itself was still in an uproar over the ax murder of a prominent doctor and his wife during the winter, allegedly by marauding blacks.

Returning Confederates met hostility from Union men all over the state. In rural areas, ex-Confederates were beaten and terrorized, although things seem to have settled down in the course of the year in the middle and western parts of the state. Ex-Confederates in East Tennessee experienced the greatest hostility, fueled primarily by the abuse the Unionist majority there suffered during Confederate occupation. Eventually, most of these former Rebels moved out of state or to Middle or West Tennessee.

Because it had been a primary battleground of the late war, much of the state was desolate, with railroads in disrepair, bridges ruined, roads out, and farmland lying untended. Many inhabitants, especially those who had measured their wealth in money and securities issued by the vanished Richmond government, were reduced to slow starvation. Habitations

whose structures had been spared by the contending armies had nevertheless in many cases been looted, and many households made do with broken
implements that the owners could no longer afford to replace. Furthermore, in the farming areas of Middle and West Tennessee, the vast amount
of capital invested in slaves was now gone.[1]

Conditions in Lebanon were similar to those elsewhere in the state.
Wilson County was not the venue of any major battles, but during the interlude after the Battle of Murfreesboro in 1863, Lebanon served as a
haven for spies of both sides and a place from which medical supplies
smuggled out of occupied Nashville were directed to the Rebel army. In
late 1864, the main building of Cumberland University, already stripped
bare by occupying Federals, was burned by a party of Confederate soldiers
led by a man who had once been a student there. As men returned from
both armies, they came to a town with fences gone, trees cut down, and
some houses burned. As if the desolation of war were not bad enough, the
day after a group of ex-Confederates arrived from the surrender in North
Carolina on May 26, 1865, the town was flooded, with six feet of water on
the town square.[2]

While Stewart must have been as impoverished as most ex-Confederates, he and his family were fortunate in that their relatively large home in
Lebanon survived the war. Once the university started functioning again in
1866, Harriet took in students as boarders. The resumption of classes,
however, did not mean that Professor Stewart was back in the classroom.
In the immediate period after his return to Lebanon in the summer of
1865, Stewart found work surveying in the Lebanon and Nashville areas.
Concerned for the welfare of his family in a now-desolate South, Old
Straight began a phase of entrepreneurship.

By January, 1866, Stewart was on the road, traveling as far as New Orleans and Texas to establish a cotton brokerage business in the Crescent
City with his brother Charles S. Stewart, who had lived in Louisiana for
some years. The general could thus provide his eldest son, Caruthers, with

1. Thomas B. Alexander, "Neither Peace nor War: Conditions in Tennessee in 1865,"
East Tennessee Historical Society's Publications 21 (1950): 33–51.

2. Burns, *Wilson County*, 43–45; Bone, *History of Cumberland University*, 87. Bone states
that the university's building was burned in 1863, "the blame for which rests on the soldiers
of both armies."

a career, and replace or at least supplement his salary at the university. As early as May 15, 1866, a newspaper reported Stewart was a cotton broker in New Orleans, a vocation also being pursued there by his former compatriots John B. Hood, Simon B. Buckner, and W. W. Loring.

In addition to extensive travel to secure "business and business connections" for his new firm, Stewart was not above using his acquaintances among the former officers of the Army of Tennessee to drum up business. Responding to a letter from S. G. French concerning some of his battle reports, Stewart slipped in a request for French and all his friends and neighbors to send their "cotton and other business" to Stewart and Brother in New Orleans. A similar request was made later in the year to Cheatham.[3]

Notwithstanding his travels, Stewart spent a substantial amount of time in Lebanon with his family in 1866. His presence there was monitored by one of the Nashville newspapers, which characterized Stewart as one of those ex-Confederates who cheerfully submitted to the fortunes of war. Indeed, within days of his return to Lebanon from the army, Stewart signed a loyalty oath and wrote President Andrew Johnson, requesting a pardon. Old Straight expressed his willingness to resume life as "a quiet, peaceable, law-abiding citizen, and a firm supporter of the Constitution & Union of the States." Privately, though, Stewart remained somewhat defiant. In a letter to Cheatham dated October 18, 1866, he asked his fellow general whether Cheatham was " 'reconstructed' yet or, like myself, still out in the cold?" Proudly noting that he was writing to Cheatham on Confederate paper enclosed in a Confederate envelope, Stewart made the following observations about the political situation: "The prospects ahead of us, politically, are, the Constitutional Amendment—the right of suffrage, homesteads & political & social equality for the negro—& possibly the perpetual disfranchisement of all rebels 'so called.' Can these or any of them be averted?"[4]

3. Wingfield, *Stewart*, 108, 202; William W. White, *The Confederate Veteran* (Tuscaloosa: Confederate Publishing, 1962), 56; APS to S. G. French, June 2, 1866, French Papers, MDAH; APS to B. F. Cheatham, October 18, 1866, Benjamin Franklin Cheatham Papers, TSLA.

4. Wingfield, *Stewart*, 108; APS Loyalty Oath, July 8, 1865, APS to Andrew Johnson, July 10, 1865, Stewart Pardon Application File, RG 74, NA; APS to Cheatham, October 18, 1866, Cheatham Papers, TSLA. The constitutional amendment appears to have been the Fourteenth, which attached certain disqualifications upon persons involved in insurrections

The letter to Cheatham and one to Bromfield Ridley dated April 13, 1866, provide valuable insight into Stewart's state of mind a year after the surrender. The letter to Ridley noted the younger man's positive contributions "in the great struggle for constitutional liberty" and Stewart's hope that he would distinguish himself in the stirring times to come. Yet, still the schoolmaster, Stewart wrote: "It behooves every young man in the South to do the best that is possible with his time, talents and physical powers. The South needs workers, and she needs men of high moral and religious character, as well as cultivated intellectually, so while improving your mind, do not neglect the body, and remember that the moral education is the most important of all."[5]

The general's natural inclination as an educator competed with his efforts to break into a more lucrative line of work. Cumberland still beckoned. In October, 1866, Stewart was offered the presidency of the university, which became vacant in August when longtime president T. C. Anderson resigned in order to allow a younger man to lead the debt-burdened institution into the postwar era. Tantalized by this offer at the very time an investor, Dr. H. H. Bennett of Alabama, was to join the brokerage business and infuse new capital into it, Stewart wrote his mentor, Judge Caruthers, that if he could get the business situated through the end of the year, he would accept the post. No doubt haunted by his earlier years with the university, Stewart expressed concern to Judge Caruthers as to whether the Cumberland Presbyterian Church would support the university financially. Financial support from the church would give the school a chance to succeed, and Stewart a chance to be paid. Eventually, for these very reasons, Stewart declined the post, and moved to Memphis to aid his new business and "*get rid* of *teaching*." Explaining his decision to Judge Caruthers in February, 1867, Stewart surmised that if he stayed with teaching, it would take him several years to get out of debt, and in the meantime, he would lose his home at Lebanon in clearing himself. Racial tensions in Tennessee made him take a dim view of the future, lending his normal desire to be out of debt greater force: "I am *extremely anxious* to get out of

---

against the United States. See Thomas B. Alexander, *Political Reconstruction in Tennessee* (1950; reprint, New York: Russell & Russell, 1968), 98–112, 118–21. Stewart received his pardon on February 19, 1868. Stewart Pardon Application File, RG 74, NA.

　　5. Ridley, *Battles and Sketches*, 484–85.

debt; because, for one reason, within a very few years, this country, in fact the whole world, will again be convulsed. I wish to be free of all encumbrances of that kind, if possible—& so, am ready to take hold wherever there is a prospect of making a little money, legitimately."[6]

Stewart's concerns about indebtedness and continued conflict were reflected in a letter he wrote earlier that same month to former Whig governor and then "Conservative" congressman William B. Campbell regarding a debt to the government secured by a mortgage on his house. While a Unionist during the war, Campbell supported leniency for ex-Confederates and opposed the Radical regime in Tennessee. Stewart expressed his appreciation for Campbell's assistance and his hope that while he tried to pay off his debt, the government would not seize his property. Stewart went on to note that he had never been a politician and had participated in the war as a soldier only from a sense of duty. Stewart desired that harmony would soon be restored between the sections and, doubtlessly thinking of French interference in Mexico, predicted that the North would soon need ex-Rebels, as a great war with Europe would not be too far in the future.[7]

Although the general sought to "get rid of teaching" in 1867, his old mentor Caruthers once more was able to induce him to return to Cumberland, late in the 1866–67 school year, again with a promise of a sufficient salary. The cotton brokerage business seems to have been just adequate, but nothing more, and apparently Stewart's involvement in it did not last out 1867. Judge Caruthers induced Stewart to return with a promise of a salary equal to the university president's—twenty-five hundred dollars a year. As events would transpire, Cumberland would again fail to pay all that was promised.[8]

Tennessee continued to be a hotbed of controversy, as Governor Wil-

6. APS to B. F. Cheatham, October 18, 1866, Cheatham Papers, TSLA; Bone, *History of Cumberland University*, 89, 103, 107; Pollard, *Lee and His Lieutenants*, 716; APS to R. L. Caruthers, October 23, 1866, February 22, March 17, 1867, Robert L. Caruthers Papers, SHC.

7. APS to W. B. Campbell, February 9, 1867, photocopy in Campbell Collection, Stockton Archives, Cumberland University; Alexander, *Political Reconstruction in Tennessee*, 86. Valuable insight on Campbell and on Stewart's life and home in Lebanon was provided by Cumberland's university historian, G. Frank Burns.

8. APS to R. L. Caruthers, March 17, 1867, September 28, 1870, Caruthers Papers, SHC; Bone, *History of Cumberland University*, 89, 103, 106.

liam G. Brownlow and his Radicals kept an iron grip on the state. In 1868, Brownlow pushed for legislation to suppress the Ku Klux Klan, which had initially been a social organization of ex-Confederates but which had quickly grown into a monstrosity. Fearing more civil strife and further repression of ex-Confederates, Tennessee's former Confederate generals Forrest, Cheatham, Bate, Brown, Bushrod Johnson, Pillow, Quarles, S. R. Anderson, George G. Dibrell, and Maney addressed a memorial to the legislature as a protest of Brownlow's proposed legislation, with the sensible observation that much dissatisfaction among white men would be assuaged if their disenfranchisement were removed. Stewart is conspicuous in his absence from this list, but he appears to have been active enough in the rebuilding Tennessee Democratic Party to be selected a member of a committee at the 1868 state convention that addressed a protest to the national convention that year against the "carpetbag and scalawag" governments in the South.[9]

In 1869, Stewart's long service at Cumberland came to an end. According to the minutes of the board of trustees of Cumberland University of September 2, 1869, it had been communicated to the board that Stewart "would probably be unable from affliction {diseased throat} to perform the duties assigned to his department unless speedily relieved, and on that account desires to retire from the labors and confinement incident to the situation." Another account indicates that Stewart felt the need to leave his professorship for financial reasons. Both appear to have been true, as Stewart wrote Judge Caruthers a year later complaining once more about unpaid salary due from Cumberland and mentioning that he was still experiencing difficulty with his throat. Stewart moved with Harriet and his sons Caruthers and Alex to St. Louis, where he became assistant secretary and assistant actuary of the St. Louis Mutual Life Insurance Company, at a salary of six thousand dollars a year. Alphonso, admitted a member of the Tennessee bar in 1868, remained for an interval practicing law in Winches-

9. John Trotwood Moore and Austin P. Foster, *Tennessee: The Volunteer State* (Chicago: S. J. Clarke, 1923), 1:538–40; Wingfield, *Stewart*, 109. There is a remote possibility that Stewart was among the generals who made the protest, as another Tennessee historian mentions that thirteen generals were involved, although he doesn't name them. See Philip M. Hamer, ed., *Tennessee: A History, 1673–1932* (New York: American Historical Society, 1933), 2:638.

ter among his father's family. It was probably during or near the time of Alphonso's stay in Winchester that A. P. Stewart's father, William Stewart, died.[10]

Originally incorporated in 1857, the St. Louis Mutual Life Insurance Company insured the lives of people and livestock as well as the health of people. When a new charter was issued on March 27, 1861, the company was limited to the human life insurance business alone. As an officer, Stewart would likely have had the duty imposed by the company charter to prepare a year-end financial statement showing premiums and other income received, expenses and other liabilities, losses, and the assets of the company, such as cash on hand, secured loans, and the like.

Given these mundane duties, it is not surprising that Stewart was dissatisfied with his career in the insurance business. Nevertheless, the Stewart family settled into their new life and home for a time. The general's two older sons, Caruthers and Alphonso, moved to St. Louis, Caruthers with his parents, Alphonso in 1873. Interestingly, both remained in close proximity to their father, Caruthers working as a clerk at St. Louis Mutual Life and Alphonso opening his law office in the company's office building. Stewart was promoted to secretary, and his name was used in company advertisements. Both of the older boys married girls from St. Louis and began to raise families there. Yet despite these growing family roots, Stewart did not have the classroom out of his blood. When, in 1874, word came that the University of Mississippi was seeking a new chancellor, Old Straight submitted his name for consideration. Stewart was the only applicant for the job, and his election by the university's board of trustees was unanimous. Stewart was notified of his election by telegraph, and he promptly replied, entering into his new position on October 19, 1874, shortly after his fifty-third birthday. His formal inauguration was held on

---

10. Board of Trustees Minute Book 1842–1871, Stoughton Archives, Cumberland University (braces appear in the original); APS to R. L. Caruthers, September 28, 1870, Caruthers Papers, SHC; Evans, ed., *Confederate Military History*, 12:420; Wingfield, *Stewart*, 109–10; *Edwards' Annual Director [sic] to the Inhabitants, Institutions, Incorporated Companies, Manufacturing Establishments . . . in the City of St. Louis for 1871* (St. Louis: Southern Publishing–Edwards & Company Publishers, 1871), 782. A report in the *Nashville Republican Banner* of July 8, 1868, indicated that William Stewart died a few days previous to that date. Jill L. Garrett, ed., *Obituaries from Tennessee Newspapers* (Easley, S.C.: Southern Historical Press, 1980), 364.

November 10 at the Cumberland Presbyterian Church in Oxford. Congressman L. Q. C. Lamar delivered the address, to which Stewart made a suitable reply.[11]

Founded in 1848, the University of Mississippi occupied a mostly wooded section of land in Lafayette County, lying partly in the town of Oxford. The university managed to survive the war in the keeping of one of its faculty members. When it reopened in 1865, most of its students were former soldiers, a trend that was ending by the time Stewart took office. The university consisted of nine professor's residences, three dormitories, a chapel, an observatory, a preparatory department, a gymnasium, six boardinghouses, and the famed Lyceum.[12]

Stewart was not a stranger in Oxford; he had commanded a corps with a large contingent of Mississippi troops, and was thus known throughout the state. Furthermore, old comrades were involved with the university in 1874. Stewart's former brigadier Claudius Sears was a professor of mathematics, and his division commander at Shiloh, Charles Clark, was a member of the board of trustees. In addition to his administrative duties as chancellor, Stewart taught moral science and Christian education. Apparently, the years out of the classroom had cleared up his throat ailment. His teaching duties shifted to a professorship of history during his second year, and then of history and political economy for his remaining years at the university.[13]

11. *Laws of the State of Missouri* (Jefferson City: C. J. Corwin Public Printer, 1857), 14:466; *Laws of the State of Missouri* (Jefferson City: W. G. Cheeney, 1861), 17:158; *Edwards' Annual Director* [*sic*], 782; *Gould and Aldrich's Annual Directory for the City of St. Louis, for 1872* (St. Louis: Review Steam Press, 1872), 724; *Gould's St. Louis City Directory for 1873* (St. Louis; David B. Gould, 1873), 818; *Gould's St. Louis Directory for 1874* (St. Louis: David B. Gould, 1874), 855; Evans, ed., *Confederate Military History*, 12:420; Wingfield, *Stewart*, 110; Wingfield, "Old Straight," 113; James A. Cabiness, *A History of the University of Mississippi* (University, Miss.: University of Mississippi Press, 1949), 90.

12. Dunbar Rowland, *Encyclopedia of Mississippi History* (Madison, Wis.: Selwyn A. Brant, 1907), 2:844; Cabiness, *University of Mississippi*, 92. Though no other source indicates so, Stewart may not have been a stranger to the university, as a catalog summarizing the various faculty members published in 1887 indicates he was professor of physics, astronomy, and civil engineering in 1865, along with the former artillery chief and chief of staff of the Army of Tennessee, F. A. Shoup. Stewart may have found the position at the university at that time compatible with his cotton brokerage business in New Orleans. See *Bulletin of the University of Mississippi* vol. 35 (Oxford, Miss.: University of Mississippi, 1887).

13. *Bulletin of the University of Mississippi*, 22:3–4, 23:4, 24:4, 25:4; APS to W. H. McCardle, April 30, 1878, McCardle Papers, MDAH.

Although he had been the only candidate, Stewart's appointment had some political significance in Mississippi, in that it was yet another signal that the Radical Republican rule in the state was coming to an end. Certainly, Stewart's status as a lieutenant general of the defunct but lamented Confederacy would have convinced the whites of the state (the only segment of society eligible to send their sons to Ole Miss) that there would be no Radical influence at the university. Stewart realized the value of such influence and, on numerous occasions, went on voluntary speaking tours about the state promoting the university and its work, a practice that was both encouraged and complimented by the board of trustees.[14]

Life in Oxford agreed with Stewart, Harriet, and young Alex. Soon after he accepted the chancellorship, Stewart wrote his older sister Catherine Jones with news of his family, and indicated that his years after the war had been spent with some "wandering, partly for conscience sake." Alex entered the university, and Stewart and Harriet must have felt great pride at their son's academic achievements, as each year of his education there he won a prize or received an honor for his oratorical abilities. Stewart's nephew Charles Spyker Stewart also matriculated at the university, two years behind his cousin. Harriet took a leadership role in the community after Francis Willard, president of the Women's Christian Temperance Union, gave an address there in 1882. Sixteen ladies thereafter formed the first WCTU chapter in the state, and Harriet became its president. While his salary at Mississippi remained low throughout his tenure, Stewart acquired some amenities, including a personal library, which he encouraged his family to use, and two dogs, a large Newfoundland called Pup, and a small, black, ill-tempered terrier, El Mahdi.[15]

Stewart's role in the war was not forgotten. He was visited on at least one occasion by Jefferson Davis, who during these years was involved in a

14. James B. Lloyd, *The University of Mississippi: The Formative Years, 1848–1906* (Oxford: University of Mississippi Department of Archives and Special Collections, 1979), 43; Board of Trustees Minutes 1860–1882, June 18, 1875, pp. 297–98, January 27, 1877, pp. 335, 337, June 26, 1879, p. 395, June 26, 1882, p. 472; Board of Trustees Minutes 1883–1897, June 25, 1883, p. 14, June 23, 1886, p. 74, UM.

15. APS to Catherine Jones, January 7, 1877, in Wingfield, *Stewart*, 117; *Bulletin of the University of Mississippi*, 25:10, 26:20, 27:15, 18, 28:15, 20, 29:16; W. H. Patton, "History of the Prohibition Movement in Mississippi," *Publications of the Mississippi Historical Society* 10 (1909): 181–82; Wingfield, *Stewart*, 118; see Board of Trustees Minutes, 1860–1882, pp. 296–97; 1883–1897, pp. 35, 72, UM.

literary battle with Joe Johnston over the events of the war, including Davis' removal of Johnston from command of the Army of Tennessee in July, 1864. Stewart had corresponded with Davis in 1873 about the plan to invade Tennessee after the fall of Atlanta. An 1868 letter from Stewart to Johnston concerning the latter's removal was published in Johnston's vehemently anti-Davis *Narrative of Military Operations Directed During the Late War Between the States*. These contacts did not alter Stewart's conviction that removing Johnston was a mistake, as is evidenced by the publication in 1886 of Old Straight's historical sketch of the Army of Tennessee, which appeared as part of *The Military Annals of Tennessee: Confederate*, a memorial volume sold by subscription "to the fame and memory of the Confederate soldiery of Tennessee." Johnston's *Narrative* is cited several times in Stewart's sketch, and Stewart maintained that Johnston's removal was a great error. To ensure a proper awareness of the war among his students, in 1880 Stewart placed an order for a copy of the *Official Records* for the university library.[16]

The primary issues at the University of Mississippi during Stewart's tenure were money, the admittance of women, and the decline of discipline. Stewart's low salary was just one indication of the economic difficulty of the university, which was voted money by the state legislature that never materialized. To a large degree, the university's financial problems could be traced to the fact that the trustees during most of Stewart's tenure abolished tuition for Mississippi residents. The university's historian cites this and other actions, such as the one-day abolition of fraternities, as part of a conscious effort to portray the university as a "poor man's college." Some economy efforts bordered on the ridiculous, such as the board's combining of the jobs of janitor and librarian. Fortunately, state funds began to flow to the university during the later years of Stewart's tenure.[17]

Although there is no evidence that Stewart pushed for the acceptance of women at the university, certainly any opposition of his would have been recorded, and none was. Although there had been a movement in favor of state-supported education for women as early as 1856, agitation had in-

16. Wingfield, *Stewart*, 118; APS to Jefferson Davis, September 6, 1873, Davis Papers, Tulane; Johnston, *Narrative*, 367–69; Lindsley, ed., *Military Annals*, 6, 52–111; APS to Marcus J. Wright, October 12, 1880, Wright Papers, SHC.

17. Cabiness, *University of Mississippi*, 94–101.

creased in 1879 and into the early 1880s. Under the leadership of Hampton M. Sullivan, an Oxford attorney, the trustees voted to admit women in 1882. The new coeds were to have the same status as the male students, except they were allowed to live on-campus only in the homes of faculty members. The success of this progressive move was demonstrated in the fact that the highest-ranked honor student in the first class that graduated women was a woman, Sally Vick Hill. Another blow was struck for equal rights when, in 1885, the university acquired its first female faculty member, Sarah McGee Isom, teacher of elocution.[18]

Discipline became an increasing problem as the students who had endured the privations of the war gave way to those who had little, if any, memory of the conflict. In an 1877 letter to his sister Catherine, Stewart wrote that life at a university was not necessarily conducive to piety, an observation that might be characterized as having touched upon a timeless truth. At the trustee's meeting in June, 1878, Stewart asked for clarification of the university's code of conduct to subject the law students to the same standards as the other students. During that meeting, it was noted that there was great potential for disorder from such practices as "bumping the seniors," kangaroo courts, and hazing.[19]

Two years later, one of the trustees notified Stewart that word was spreading throughout the state concerning immorality and intemperance at the university. Efforts were made to increase supervision by the faculty, and it was resolved by the board of trustees in 1881 that a member of the faculty would visit each student's room once a day at irregular times. On alternate Saturdays, the rooms were to be cleaned and an inspection would be made "as is customary at West Point and other military schools." For his part, Stewart supplemented these more stringent measures by private conferences, chapel talks, and exhortations to individual students to pray for their unconverted classmates, belying any impression of Old Straight as a stern old soldier. Though his disapproving looks and mild rebukes had controlled the boisterousness of the young members of his staff during the war, they apparently were not adequate for a generation that had not known the war. Problems continued, including a "lewd woman" being dis-

18. Ibid., 102–103.
19. Ibid., 107; APS to Catherine Jones, January 7, 1877, in Wingfield, *Stewart*, 117; Board of Trustees Minutes 1860–1882, June 27, 1878, pp. 363–64, UM.

covered in the room of a student, underage voting, and rock-throwing at passing trains.[20]

Stewart's losing struggle with disciplinary matters, as well as his advancing age, appears to have been a catalyst for his resignation as chancellor on July 29, 1886. Already in 1884, one of the trustees called for the resignation of Stewart and the rest of the faculty, an initiative which was defeated. On June 23, 1886, at the annual meeting of the trustees, a similar measure declaring that the offices of the chancellor and the faculty were vacant was carried. Notwithstanding his immediate reelection, Stewart determined that his tenure at the University of Mississippi was at an end. He therefore submitted a dignified resignation, and was accorded the benefit of his home in Oxford until October 1 and his salary until the end of the year.[21]

Stewart's career in formal education was over. He continued his efforts with his grandchildren and their friends on an informal basis when he returned to St. Louis, accompanying them on expeditions to manufacturing plants and other concerns, where he explained the workings and processes of such operations. In fact, Stewart was admired for his full attention to the questions of young people, to each of whom he gave a "full and painstaking reply." While his administration at Ole Miss was a success overall, no doubt his best efforts were in the classroom, where he had the day-to-day contact with students that he enjoyed. Recognizing his efforts, his fellow faculty members in 1885 petitioned the board of trustees to confer on the general the degree of doctor of laws. Unfortunately, the board received the faculty's request only an hour or so after voting not to award the degree on an honorary basis any longer. Stewart had received this honor from Cumberland in 1875, and was later made a fellow of the Royal Historical Society.[22]

After their departure from Oxford, the general and Harriet traveled in the West, frequently stopping to live with their son, Caruthers, who by this

20. Cabiness, *University of Mississippi*, 107–109; Board of Trustees Minutes 1860–1882, June 27, 1881, p. 451, UM; APS to A. A. Walter, November 27, 1876, Walter W. Harvey Papers, SHC.

21. Cabiness, *University of Mississippi*, 110; Wingfield, *Stewart*, 123; Board of Trustees Minutes, 1883–1897, June 23, 1886, p. 79, July 29, 1886, pp. 85, 88, UM.

22. Wingfield, "Old Straight," 115; "Glorying in Their Name," *Chattanooga Times*, September 15, 1908; Cabiness, *University of Mississippi*, 107; Cumberland University Commencement Program, June, 1875, Stoughton Archives, Cumberland University.

time lived in New Mexico with his family. The years 1888–1890 were spent in the home of Alphonso, in St. Louis. Although Stewart could have lived out the remainder of his life among his family in St. Louis in religious contemplation and the study and discussion of history, an opportunity arose in 1890 to preserve in a unique way the history of which he was a part.[23]

23. Wingfield, "Old Straight," 115.

— 15 —

A Dream of the Past

Confederate Veteran and Park Commissioner,
1890–1908

The Civil War remained the central event of the lives of those who had memory of that great struggle, and especially those, Union and Confederate, who had fought and survived. In the summer of 1888, two veterans of the Army of the Cumberland, Ferdinand Van Derveer and Henry V. Boynton, visited the once-blasted woods and fields of Chickamauga. They came away with the conviction that the field should be preserved and marked. Boynton wrote a series of newspaper articles proposing that veterans of both sides come together to establish the field as a park. Such were the beginnings of the Chickamauga-Chattanooga National Military Park, the nation's oldest and largest.[1]

In 1889, veterans of the battle incorporated a joint memorial association of fifty men from each side, each state to be represented in proportion to the number of troops it had engaged in the battle. The list of incorporators was a "who's who" of surviving veterans: William S. Rosecrans, Absalom Baird, John M. Palmer, John M. Brannan, and Thomas J. Wood on the Union side, and James Longstreet, Joseph Wheeler, John C. Brown, William B. Bate, J. T. Holtzclaw, Edward C. Walthall, Randall L. Gibson, and Alexander P. Stewart on the Confederate side.[2]

1. H. V. Boynton, "Chickamauga-Chattanooga National Military Park," *Chattanooga Times*, July 1, 1903; James W. Livingood, "Chickamauga and Chattanooga National Military Park," *Tennessee Historical Quarterly* 23 (March 1964): 3, 7.

2. Boynton, "Chickamauga-Chattanooga"; Livingood, "Chickamauga and Chatta-

Eventually, the aid of Congress was solicited, resulting in the remarkably swift passage of a bill through both houses. The bill was signed into law by President Benjamin Harrison on August 19, 1890. The bill provided for an appropriation of $125,000 to purchase the Chickamauga battlefield and approach roads, which included the crest road along Missionary Ridge, the La Fayette Road, and others. Section 5 of the act provided that "the affairs of the . . . Park shall, subject to the supervision and direction of the Secretary of War, be in the charge of three commissioners, each of whom shall have actively participated in the battle of Chickamauga or one of the battles about Chattanooga, two to be appointed from civil life by the Secretary of War, and a third, who shall be detailed by the Secretary of War from among those officers of the army best acquainted with the details of the battles."[3]

While the act did not specifically provide for the division of the two civilian posts between a Union and a Confederate veteran, such was what transpired. The Union veteran appointed was General Joseph S. Fullerton, chief of staff to Major General Gordon Granger during the campaign. The second civilian position was to be an ex-Confederate. That appointment came at the instance of southern congressmen, who, at the time, included William B. Bate, Edward C. Walthall, Randall L. Gibson, and Francis M. Cockrell, all of whom had served under Stewart during the war. As Stewart some months later wrote to an acquaintance, "My southern friends in Congress thought I was the proper person to represent the Confederate side in this enterprise." Accordingly, on September 8, 1890, it was announced that Fullerton and Stewart were appointed commissioners by the secretary of war, along with Colonel S. C. Kellogg, George Thomas' nephew and a former member of his staff. Boynton was appointed the historian of the commission.[4]

The general and Harriet moved to north Georgia near the new park, where Stewart took up duties as the resident commissioner. The commission's first duty was to acquire the land for the park, and so its members

---

nooga," 8–9; H. V. Boynton, *The National Military Park: Chickamauga-Chattanooga, An Historical Guide* (Cincinnati: Robert Clarke, 1895), 248–49.

  3. Boynton, *National Military Park*, 263–64; Livingood, "Chickamauga and Chattanooga," 15.

  4. Wingfield, *Stewart*, 124–26; Boynton, *National Military Park*, 267–68; Livingood, "Chickamauga and Chattanooga," 16.

and agents began negotiations with and, when necessary, condemnation proceedings against, the various owners of the property that constituted the Chickamauga battlefield.[5]

The park's enabling act contemplated the active participation of veterans from the various states in assisting the commission in marking the troop positions and battle lines. The states accordingly created commissions themselves to undertake this work, or at least promised to. The work of the park commission then involved hearing evidence on the proper placement of each position, which records reveal was a tedious process.[6]

As resident commissioner, Stewart spent a great deal of time in the park, supervising engineer Atwell Thompson in road construction, the erection of towers and bridges, and the general engineering work of the park, and engineer E. E. Betts in topographical engineering, mapping, and the erection of monuments. Early efforts included the clearing of the fields to restore them to their condition at the time of the battle, surveying the park, the extension and improvement of roads, and the erection of the unique pyramids of shells that commemorated the brigade commanders who were killed or mortally wounded during the battle. There was also the continuous work of consultation with the commissions of the various states and answering questions about the development of the park. Stewart, now past seventy, learned to ride a bicycle, and by that means or on horseback traveled all about the park. He suffered some injuries from a fall from his bicycle, yet gamely replied to the awkward inquiry of one of his fellow commissioners that he was laid up because his wisdom teeth were coming in. A more dangerous fall occurred on March 30, 1893, when a freight train crossing a trestle on which Stewart was standing suddenly backed up, knocking him off the structure twenty feet to the ground. Not only was Stewart badly bruised, but he broke his right arm at the wrist and above the elbow. By that summer, the arm was on the mend, but the general was still having some pain and difficulty in using the arm to write.[7]

5. Wingfield, *Stewart*, 124; Boynton, "Chickamauga-Chattanooga"; "The Park Lands," *Chattanooga News*, February 14, 1892.

6. Boynton, *National Military Park*, 275; transcript of Proceedings of Chickamauga Park Commission, November 8, 1892, CCNMP.

7. Boynton, *National Military Park*, 273; Boynton, "Chickamauga-Chattanooga"; Proceedings of Park Commission, October 3, 1893, CCNMP; APS to R. A. Brock, May 25, June 2, 1891, Brock Collection, Huntington Library; APS to Owen McGarr, November 19, 1892, Chattanooga Historical Society Papers, C-HCBL; Wingfield, *Stewart*, 125–26.

The work of the park naturally brought Stewart into contact with veterans of both sides, and old controversies were still the subject of discussion. While on the battlefield with members of the Tennessee commission, Stewart, Bate, and others of those present discussed Hood's decision to attack at Franklin. Stewart's last meeting with his old classmate Rosecrans was at Chickamauga in September, 1892. Rosecrans and Stewart discussed the relative strength of the two armies at Chickamauga, Rosecrans admitting that "we always overestimated your numbers." A month later, Stewart wrote another old classmate, James Longstreet, inviting him to visit the park and promising not to "make a fuss" over "Old Peter."[8]

By 1895, the park had progressed to the point where Congress resolved to have a great dedication ceremony on the thirty-second anniversary of the battle, September 19 and 20, 1895, and to invite the surviving participants, the president, the Congress, Supreme Court, the cabinet, the senior officers of the army and navy, and the governors of the several states. Twenty thousand dollars was appropriated for the ceremony, which spotlighted Chattanooga in a way that had not occurred since the momentous events of the war. Several state monuments were dedicated, and Vice President Adlai E. Stevenson, four cabinet members, fifteen governors, and twenty congressmen were among the attendees.[9]

Although the dedicatory ceremony must have been a personal triumph for Stewart and a vindication of five years of work, he was not well enough to attend the ceremonies. In the summer of 1895, Stewart came down with a malarial fever which was misdiagnosed by the local physicians as "fatty degeneration of the heart." Stewart's condition was such that on August 8, Boynton thought it appropriate to write General Fullerton to suggest possible replacements for Stewart on the commission. Boynton ad-

8. John P. Hickman, Letter, *CV*, 15; APS to Charles D. McGuffey, November 17, 1905, Chattanooga Historical Society Papers, C-HCBL; APS to James Longstreet, October 31, 1892, James Longstreet Collection, GA. Stewart always maintained that Confederate numbers at Chickamauga were between 40,000 and 50,000, based upon a conversation he had with Bragg a day or two after the battle, when Stewart encountered his commander on the march to Chattanooga. Bragg indicated at that time that his army at the time of the battle was closer to 40,000 men in strength. APS to Charles Todd Quintard, October 18, 1895, Charles T. Quintard Papers, DU. In light of the casualties sustained by the Army of Tennessee at Chickamauga, a day-of-battle strength of 40,000 men seems to be too low.

9. Boynton, *National Military Park*, 269–70; Livingood, "Chickamauga and Chattanooga," 16–18.

mitted that it seemed "pretty harsh business" to be discussing such matters "while Gen. Stewart is thought to be dying—but, with all our high regard and affection for him, it is of such importance as to relieve our work of harshness." Summoned to the general's bedside that same August week, his son Alphonso was asked by the doctors to prepare Harriet for her husband's imminent death. Fortunately, Alex, who was by this time a physician of some experience, arrived to correctly diagnose his father's condition and save his life. Even under his son's careful attention, Stewart remained seriously ill for some weeks. On September 19, the day of the ceremonies, a Middle Tennessee newspaper reported that Stewart was seriously ill at Chattanooga and not expected to recover. By the middle of October, 1895, however, Stewart was able to write Bishop Charles Todd Quintard at Sewanee that he was "thankful that I have escaped so well from a severe attack of illness and a much severer attack of doctors."[10]

Stewart's work at the park, was, of course, only one aspect of his life during the last decade of the nineteenth century. Stewart's correspondence of a historical nature with former Confederates has already been noted, but as a prominent ex-Confederate, Stewart received communications from friends and, indeed, from out of the blue seeking his viewpoints, photographs, or souvenirs of the war. Irritated by an article in the *Southern Historical Society Papers* that misrepresented his order of rank among the Confederate lieutenant generals and misnamed him "Ambrose P. Stewart," Stewart wrote the publication's editor with a correction. Writing to E. C. Brown of New York during his last months in Oxford, Stewart indicated he had no "old war letter" to send Brown, noting that his supply of such was either with the War Records office or had been doled out to other friends. Stewart offered to sum up for Brown his conclusions relative to the war, and that was that Providence had a great deal to do with the affairs of men, and that human efforts, even those of men who were considered great, had very little to do with great achievements. On another occasion, writing from Chickamauga, Stewart wrote to Marcus J. Wright, seeking

---

10. Jack D. Welsh, *Medical Histories of Confederate Generals* (Kent, Ohio: Kent State University Press, 1995), 207–208; H. V. Boynton to J. S. Fullerton, August 8, 1895, Correspondence of Park Commission, CCNMP; A. C. Stewart to L. H. Stewart, August 9, 1895, in Wingfield, *Stewart*, 211; Garrett, ed., *Obituaries from Tennessee Newspapers*, 363; APS to Charles Todd Quintard, October 18, 1895, Quintard Papers, DU.

information for a friend in California who was writing an article on the war.[11]

The United Confederate Veterans was organized in 1889, and the general and his wife had occasion to attend at least two of its functions. At the meeting held in New Orleans in April, 1892, Stewart had a busy schedule of attending church, receiving the visits of his old comrades, assisting in the decoration services, feasting at the annual banquet of the Army of Tennessee, and being honored at a reception. Stewart also made an excursion to view the New Orleans riverfront. In June, 1897, Stewart and Harriet attended the reunion at Nashville, where it was particularly noted that the wives and daughters of Confederate heroes, including Harriet, would be there, along with every living Confederate general who could be present.[12]

The general and his wife must have derived great satisfaction in their old age from the success of their sons. Caruthers, in New Mexico with his wife, son, and daughter since 1883, became grand master of the Grand Lodge of the Free Masons of the state. Alphonso remained in St. Louis with his family and became a notable lawyer. After graduating from medical school in 1888, Alex moved to Dallas in 1890, where he married a schoolteacher from Wisconsin. The couple had no children before her death in 1900.[13]

The elder Stewarts enjoyed the occasional company of and correspondence with their sons and grandchildren during these years, as well as contact with other members of the family. The old general often corresponded with Alphonso's daughter, Harriet, whom the family called "Hattie." Letters from 1896 reflect that she accompanied her grandparents on a trip to

11. APS to Marcus J. Wright, October 30, 1880, Wright Papers, SHC; APS to E. C. Brown, February 16, 1886, APS to Marcus J. Wright, August 18, 1891, Civil War Times Illustrated Collection, United States Army Military History Institute, Carlisle, Pa. (the original of the letter to Brown is in the University of Mississippi Archives); APS to R. A. Brock, June 2, 1891, Brock Collection, Huntington Library; APS to James W. Eldridge, July 1, 1895, Eldridge Collection, Huntington Library; APS to L. T. Dickinson, June 29, 1895, Chattanooga Historical Society Papers, C-HCBL.

12. Wingfield, *Stewart*, 131; Ridley, *Battles and Sketches*, 540–41. Stewart may have visited the Murfreesboro battlefield in the company of Bromfield Ridley on the occasion of the visit to Nashville, pointing out the scenes of battle. John Trotwood Moore, "Historic Highways of the South: The Battle of Stone [*sic*] River," *Taylor-Trotwood Magazine* 6 (February 1908): 505, 507.

13. Wingfield, *Stewart*, 208–12.

New Orleans, and then the two Harriets, grandmother and granddaughter, visited family friends in Oxford while Stewart returned to Chickamauga. Stewart was photographed in New Orleans, and enjoyed the company of veterans of his staff and corps, including Douglas West and Aristide Hopkins. Writing Hattie from Chickamauga, Stewart noted he had received the pictures as published in the newspaper in the Crescent City and joked that he considered having her father, Alphonso, sue the paper for publishing a caricature.[14]

In addition to the former members of his staff, Stewart was also consulted by higher-ranking veterans, such as Samuel G. French, who asked his former corps commander to review a manuscript on which he was working. In reply, Stewart related that he derived his philosophy concerning events of the war from Robert E. Lee, keeping a "dignified silence" and "all causes of complaint among ourselves, *to* ourselves." Accordingly, he advised French to avoid "any severe reflections on Hood."[15]

Notwithstanding Stewart's mishaps in the park and his near death from the fever, Harriet was the first to pass away. In 1892, she wrote Hattie complaining of weak eyes and noting her white hair and wrinkles. By the time of their trip to the Confederate reunion in Nashville in 1897, she and the general were living in Chattanooga at the home of Mrs. Euclid Waterhouse at 451 Oak Street. There, on the morning of January 4, 1898, Harriet died of a cerebral hemorrhage. Stewart took her body to St. Louis and laid her to rest in the company of all of the couple's children and grandchildren. Writing a week later to thank the Chattanooga chapter of the United Daughters of the Confederacy for their sympathy, the general said of his wife: "None could know her as I did after more than fifty-two years of happy married life. She was the very highest type of a true, lovely, Christian woman, and was in every way worthy of the love and admiration that followed her everywhere she went." In addition to the Daughters of the Confederacy, the Chattanooga chapter of the United Confederate Veterans, the Nathan Bedford Forrest Camp, passed a resolution expressing in poetic terms the sympathy of its members at Stewart's bereavement, which was published in the *Chattanooga News*. Stewart expressed his "warmest thanks" to the camp for its sympathy and the "beautiful resolutions."[16]

14. APS to Harriet Chase Stewart, April 11, 17, 1896, in Wingfield, *Stewart*, 135–38.

15. APS to S. G. French, March 25, April 29, May 11, 1897, French Papers, MDAH.

16. Wingfield, *Stewart*, 131–32; APS to Mrs. Carrie R. Rowles, January 11, 1898, Papers of A. P. Stewart Chapter, UDC, C-HCBL; Minutes, January 4, 1898, Papers of the Na-

While Stewart spent time in St. Louis and Dallas in the months after Harriet's death visiting with his sons, he looked forward to the dedication, in May, 1898, of the Tennessee monuments in the park. As the Confederate representative on the commission, he must have felt regret that the southern states had been slow to erect monuments. Starting in 1892, Stewart considered trips to Atlanta and to the capitals of the other southern states to try to drum up support for monuments commemorating the sacrifice of the Confederate troops. As late as 1900, Stewart was in Richmond lobbying the Virginia legislature to memorialize its troops at the park, an effort that did not succeed. As it turned out, his home state of Tennessee was the first of the former Confederate states to dedicate monuments at the park.[17]

The Tennessee dedication took place on the extension of Snodgrass Hill now known as Horseshoe Ridge on May 12, 1898. At the time of the ceremony, the reunited United States was at war with Spain, and references were made to the progress of that new struggle. Stewart spoke on behalf of the federal government in accepting the Tennessee monuments. He took the occasion to speak upon the great history of the state of Tennessee and his own Tennessee roots. Perhaps reflecting upon the work of his later years and his own decline, Stewart noted with sadness the passing of his great friend and subordinate Walthall, observing: "Comrades, we are passing away, passing away. It will not be long until the Confederate soldier will be a dream of the past, but his name will live. It will live in history, in story, in song and in tradition while the world stands." Stewart, never repentant about the justification for or role of the Confederacy in American

---

than Bedford Forrest Camp, UCV, C-HCBL; APS to L. T. Dickinson, January 23, 1898, Forrest Camp Papers, C-HCBL.

17. Wingfield, *Stewart*, 134, 140–43; APS to Mary Coles Carrington, March 5, 1900, I. H. Carrington Papers, DU; Livingood, "Chickamauga and Chattanooga," 22. Several members of the Tennessee Chickamauga Park Commission, each of whom fought in the battle, were well known to Stewart. In addition to Senator Bate, members who were friends of the general included ex-governor James D. Porter, formerly a member of Cheatham's staff; R. B. Snowden, who commanded a regiment in Bushrod Johnson's brigade; and Moses H. Clift, who had been on the staff of a cavalry command, and in whose home Stewart resided for a portion of his remaining time in Chattanooga. Ironically, Clift's father had been one of the staunchest Unionists in the Chattanooga area. Alternates included Marcus J. Wright; J. Minnick Williams, a member of Polk's staff; J. Polk Smartt, a Chattanooga merchant who had served in the 16th Tennessee as a private; and Bromfield Ridley, then a Murfreesboro lawyer. Ridley, *Battles and Sketches*, 602–603.

history, also asked the rhetorical question: "Why did the South fail?" The answer was not in who had the bigger armies or who was in the right or wrong, but in God's own design: "The one sole reason why the South failed—you may see it in the events transpiring around us today—was that Almighty God had need of this Union. He presided at its birth; all these years He has held it in the hollow of his hand; He still needs it for the accomplishment of His great designs." In the view of the correspondent of the *Confederate Veteran* on the scene, "those present . . . were almost lifted out of their seats by [Stewart's] eloquence."[18]

During 1899, Stewart continued his day-to-day work as a commissioner, accepting bids for houses in the park and directing engineer Betts to investigate reports of water rushing off of Missionary Ridge and onto a resident's place. The park was used as a camp by soldiers assembling for the Spanish-American War, and the park commission complained to the secretary of war about the deplorable condition in which the men left the park, necessitating $11,630 in repairs. Stewart was so protective of the park grounds that he was accused by some of thinking more of the trees than of the troops. By this time, the park had 228 monuments, 237 guns, 554 historical markers, 448 distance and locality markers, and 341 other markers. Stewart continued his work at the park, even though he was now seventy-eight, and was driven about in a buggy by the celebrated Mark Thrash, an ex-slave who is supposed to have been the general's near equal in age but who lived until 1944, dying at the reported age of 124.[19]

The turn of the century saw Stewart continuing his work as commissioner, supervising the restoration of the woods that existed at the time of the battle but which had been cleared since that time, and ensuring that the livestock of surrounding farmers stayed out of the park. The commission invited a general inspection of its work in October, 1900, to ensure that any errors in the text on or location of the tablets and markers at the park

18. Ridley, *Battles and Sketches*, 618–25; Note, *CV*, 6 (October 1898): 456. During Stewart's "extemporaneous" speech, Joe Wheeler, a guest at the ceremony, received a telegram ordering him to immediate duty in the Spanish-American War. Moore, "Historic Highways of the South," *Taylor-Trotwood Magazine* 5 (September, 1907): 716, 719–20.

19. APS to Betts, February 13, APS to E. E. Betts, February 23, Betts to APS, March 10, APS to F. G. Smith, March 11, APS to Betts, April 10, 1899, Correspondence of the Park Commission, CCNMP; "In Honor of Gen. Stewart," *Chattanooga Times*, April 22, 1919; "The Chickamauga National Park," *Chattanooga Times*, December 25, 1899.

were detected. The old general participated in a fund drive for a monument to Confederate hero Sam Davis by sending in a five-dollar contribution. He also wrote to the *Confederate Veteran* to endorse the "Game of Confederate Heroes" as "well calculated to aid the young in gaining some knowledge of the events of the Confederate war and of those who took part in it on the Confederate side." Writing a letter to be read at the 1900 meeting of the United Confederate Veterans, Stewart repeated his views as to the right of secession and God's will in the result of the war, and sought to encourage relief for infirm veterans and the training of their children as good citizens. Old Straight was surely gratified by the statement in the *Confederate Veteran* in March of that year that he was "beloved all over the South." In July, Stewart was honored as the senior living Confederate commander of the Battle of Peachtree Creek.[20]

The *Confederate Veteran* provides valuable insight into Stewart's veteran activities in the first years of the new century. The United Confederate Veterans passed a resolution to collect funds for a monument to southern women. With the recently departed Harriet no doubt on his mind, Stewart had made a tribute to the women of the South in his speech at the Tennessee monument dedication in 1898. He was named treasurer of this new effort, and he published letters encouraging veteran camps to receive contributions for the monument. Stewart later resigned this position on account of his age. Stewart also endorsed General Samuel G. French's book, *Two Wars*, as a "thoroughly correct" narrative, and expressed an interest in the educational work done by Peabody College.[21]

On August 1, 1903, while vacationing with Senator Bate at Epsom Springs in Sumner County, Tennessee, not far from Nashville, the general suffered a stroke, which paralyzed the right side of his face and the left side of his body. Fortunately, Alex had been living with Stewart since the previ-

20. H. V. Boynton to APS, October 17, 22, 1900, with APS note of October 24, 1900, Correspondence of the Park Commission, CCNMP; Note, *CV* 8 (January 1900): 34; "Invited to Chickamauga Park in October," *CV* 8 (March 1900): 115; Alexander P. Stewart, Letter, *CV* 8 (June 1900): 248; "Atlanta Battlefield Reunion," *CV* 8 (June 1900): 257.

21. "Memphis Reunion—Notes from Proceedings," *CV* 9 (June 1901): 246; Alexander P. Stewart, "The Southern Women's Memorial Fund," CV 9 (August 1901): 343; Alexander P. Stewart, Letter, *CV* 9 (September 1901), 396; "Southern Women's Monument," *CV* 10 (July 1902): 304; Alexander P. Stewart, "Monument to the Women," *CV* 11 (July 1903): 310; Tennie P. Dozier, "Confederate Educational Home," *CV* 11 (August 1903): 358.

ous year and was nearby. Alex wrote Aristide Hopkins on August 5 that Stewart's mind had been spared and was "clear and bright as ever." Another correspondent on the scene wrote Hopkins the same day that Stewart was calm and cheerful without fear of death. Many expressions of sympathy were made, perhaps the most notable being from the Frank Cheatham Bivouac of the United Confederate Veterans, which expressed its high esteem and appreciation that Stewart's high position with the Federal government did not induce him to apologize for the actions of the South during the war. By the time this communication was received, Stewart, who was on the way to a full recovery, was able to defiantly reply that "the action of the Southern people was legally, constitutionally, and morally right." While there is some indication that Stewart retired to St. Louis and conducted park business by correspondence from this point onward, correspondence in the park files suggests that he continued to spend a large amount of time in Chattanooga as late as 1905.[22]

While Stewart's health limited his time in Chattanooga, there is no question that he was held in high regard by many there. For example, in February, 1904, the Chattanooga chapter of the United Daughters of the Confederacy voted unanimously to rename their chapter after "our most distinguished Gen. A. P. Stewart." Extremely proud of this honor, Stewart called upon the ladies of the chapter to thank them for the courtesy, and later provided the chapter with a photograph. In keeping with his usual expressions of humility, Stewart thanked the women for their compliments, feeling they were undeserved. "There is one thing however to which I can lay claim. Firmly believing in the righteousness of the Southern Cause, I did my best to defend it."[23]

22. Wingfield, *Stewart*, 112, 212–13; Alexander P. Stewart, Jr., to Aristide Hopkins, August 5, Frances P. Clift to Aristide Hopkins, August 5, 1903, Louisiana Historical Association Collection, Tulane; APS quoted in "Right of South to Secede," *CV* 11 (October 1903): 447; APS to Boynton, February 27, 1905, APS to F. G. Smith, May 18, 1905, Correspondence of the Park Commission, CCNMP; see also Stewart's introduction to Ridley's *Battles and Sketches*, xii, dated August 15, 1905, from Chattanooga. The 1905 and 1906 editions of *Gould's St. Louis Directory* do not list Stewart as a resident. *Gould's St. Louis Directory for 1905* (St. Louis: Gould Directory, 1905); *Gould's St. Louis Directory for 1906* (St. Louis: Gould Directory, 1906).

23. Minutes of A. P. Stewart Chapter, UDC, 1904–1908, APS to Mrs. James A. Cash, October 17, 1905, Stewart Chapter Papers, C-CHBL; "Birthday of Rebel Gen. A. P. Stewart

During a celebrated visit to Borden-Wheeler Springs in May, 1905, at which time he shared the spotlight at the resort with Mrs. Stonewall Jackson and two of her grandchildren, Stewart wrote fellow commissioner F. G. Smith to give him dates as to when he might possibly return to Chattanooga, stating that he was far from well and hoped to stay at the springs as long as possible. Stewart asked Smith to hold his pay for the month, obviously because he felt he had not earned anything while at the springs. He closed his letter: "Let the following now be strictly confidential with you and General Boynton, for the present. About or soon after July 1, I expect to go to St. Louis to spend the rest of my days. Either I will retain membership in the Commission, but without compensation; or if it be preferred will resign." As events transpired, the general retained his seat on the commission to his dying day, when on his desk were found park papers ready to be mailed. Stewart refused, however, to collect any further compensation.[24]

Stewart's last stay in St. Louis ended in late 1906. Alex determined that the climate in Biloxi, Mississippi, was the most beneficial to the general's health, so Stewart, Alex, and Alex's new wife found a house on Beach Boulevard there, next door to Stewart's former staff officer, Aristide Hopkins. There, Stewart's last years involved his recollections of the war and contemplation of new religious teaching.[25]

In his later years, Stewart became a follower of Charles Taze Russell, the founder of the modern-day Jehovah's Witnesses. It is beyond the scope of this book and the ability of the author to fully explain the doctrinal differences between Stewart's former Cumberland Presbyterianism and Russell's teachings, but Russell's doctrine involved significant deviations from orthodox Christianity. Marshall Wingfield, Stewart's biographer and himself a man of the cloth, undertook to explain these differences and why, after so many years of mainstream Christianity, Stewart would embrace Russell's peculiar teachings. Supported by Stewart's last letter, an epistle to his son Alphonso, Wingfield concluded that Stewart's writings indicated

---

Celebrated by 'Miss Mamie' Tucker," *Chattanooga News–Free Press*, October 2, 1971; "In Honor of Gen. Stewart," *Chattanooga Times,* April 22, 1919.

24. Wingfield, *Stewart,* 112–13, 149; APS to F. G. Smith, May 18, 1905, Correspondence of the Park Commission, CCNMP.

25. Wingfield, *Stewart,* 146.

he had trouble with the orthodox concept of eternal punishment, something the general felt was inconsistent with the great love of God. To Stewart, Russell's alternative, that of eternal death for sinners rather than eternal punishment, was more worthy of God. As a possible confirmation of Wingfield's analysis, in the months after Stewart's death the *Confederate Veteran* promised an account of Stewart in its December, 1908, issue that would "refer specially to the General's religious belief in which there is much interest by those who knew him." Unfortunately, for some unknown reason this article never appeared.[26]

In 1904, and perhaps as a result of the lingering effects of his stroke, Stewart wrote in response to a request that he comment on the Battle of Nashville that his recollections of that struggle were "hazy," and asked his former engineer, Major W. F. Foster, to reply on his behalf. However, in 1907 and 1908, the last two years of his life, Stewart on occasion commented on the events of the war in a fashion that indicated he still had good recollection of the events of over forty years before. In March, 1907, "in full enjoyment of his mental faculties, though enfeebled in body," he wrote J. A. Chalaron concerning the position of the 5th Company, Washington Artillery, on Missionary Ridge. In 1908, he became aware of certain statements made by E. P. Alexander, formerly Longstreet's chief of artillery, in his book *Military Memoirs of a Confederate*, to the effect that Stewart and Cheatham had been absent from their corps on the night of November 29, 1864, at Spring Hill. In a reply in *Confederate Veteran* published just after his death, Stewart felt it necessary to publish his own report of Spring Hill, and Hood's letter of absolution to him in April, 1865. The old soldier thundered that Alexander had uncritically accepted rumor as to Spring Hill and Hood's version as to Franklin, and noted, once again, that the failure was Hood's. Stewart scathingly wrote: "It is worse than a waste of time to read such a book."[27]

Even as late as a few days before his death, Stewart was able to discuss with one of his veterans, T. G. Dabney, two significant events after he became corps commander, the removal of Joe Johnston and the Spring Hill

---

26. Ibid., 152–61; Hopkins, Le Moncier, and Chalaron, "Tributes to Gen. A. P. Stewart," 595.

27. "Corps Commanders' Reports of the Battle," *CV* 12 (June 1904): 273; Stewart, "A Critical Narrative," 462–63.

affair. Dabney's visit and the recollections it stirred must have had an effect on Stewart, because in a letter written a day or two later to Alphonso, he indicated that certain of his "Confederate friends" wanted him to relate all that he knew about Johnston's removal and the campaign into Tennessee. True to his principle that ex-Confederates should not squabble among themselves, Stewart worried about offending the friends of the men he would have to criticize, presumably Davis and Hood. As it turned out, Dabney's publication of the account of his last visit with the general seems to have provided the insight on these subjects that Stewart had to offer.[28]

Having in a sense fired his last shot of the war, Stewart died on Sunday morning, August 30, 1908, at his home in Biloxi. In his final days, Stewart wrote to a friend who was believed to be near death: "It is a simple thing but to die. As you enter the valley you have but to put your hand in that of the God who made you. Trust yourself entirely to Him. He will lead you forth into eternal life and light. The passage is but a little way and there is nothing to fear if you cling to Him." Having suffered with organic heart disease for over a year, Stewart was forced to bed with the malady for the last two weeks of his life. At 3:00 A.M. on August 30, he suddenly took a turn for the worse. Alex and his wife, along with the general's faithful collie Duke, were present in his final hours. Aristide Hopkins received his dying ex-chief's sword. Unlike some of his fellow Confederate generals, Stewart did not spend his last moments in a delirium calling out orders to Strahl, Clayton, Bate, or Walthall, but, at peace, he simply said to the dog, "Well, Duke, are you here?" Stewart was taken back to St. Louis and buried in Bellefontaine Cemetery. The funeral services were conducted in accordance with the regulations of the United Confederate Veterans, and were presided over by Charles Taze Russell.[29]

It can be fairly said that Stewart pronounced the manner of his own death some ten years before at the dedication of the Tennessee monuments on the Chickamauga battlefield, a day of great emotion and remembrance

28. Dabney, "Gen. A. P. Stewart on Strong Topics," 31–32; APS to Alphonso C. Stewart, August 26, 1908, in Wingfield, *Stewart*, 147–49.

29. Wingfield, *Stewart*, 149–50; "Glorying in Their Name," *Chattanooga Times*, September 15, 1908; "Last Roll Call," *CV*, 33, 346; "General Stewart Dead, Leader in Confederacy," *New Orleans Times-Democrat*, August 31, 1908; "Gen. Stewart Passes Away," Chattanooga News, August 31, 1908.

for a true soldier of Tennessee: "It will not be long until the summons shall come for us every one. Let us so live that when it does come we may go 'not like the galley slave at night, scourged to his dungeon?' 'but every duty performed, life work done, conscience clear, like one who wraps the drapery of his couch about him and lies down to pleasant dreams;' or else that, like the immortal Stonewall, there may remain for us only to glide peacefully over the placid bosom of the waters and rest forever, in companionship with all the gallant throng who have gone before, under the shade of the eternal trees."[30]

30. Ridley, *Battles and Sketches*, 624–25.

Conclusion

A Man Growing Before Our Eyes

A biographical sketch of Stewart and other Confederate generals published in 1867 quoted a lengthy letter from one of Stewart's friends at Cumberland, Dr. N. L. Lindsley. After listing the many virtues Stewart possessed, Lindsley concluded that his friend was "undeniably one of the most useful of men, and a living proof that pure patriotism is not a delusion, nor virtue an empty name."[1] Although a friend's admiration may often be discounted, in this case it was deserved. Similarly, Old Straight deserves in our own time recognition for a long life that can fairly be characterized as useful, patriotic, and virtuous.

From the start of his life, Stewart was fortunate. His mother, father, and extended family instilled in him early the educational and religious values that supported him for the rest of his life. His family also provided the means for an education sufficient to qualify him for West Point, and the influence necessary to secure an appointment there.

West Point played a significant role in Stewart's growth. Not only did it provide him with the knowledge and contacts he would need for his career as a soldier, but it formed the basis for his lifelong calling as an educator. West Point was Stewart's first job in education, and we find him applying its methods of discipline in his last position as an educator, at the University of Mississippi. Somewhat more serendipitously, a friend at West Point

---

1. Pollard, *Lee and His Lieutenants*, 716–17.

introduced Stewart to Harriet Byron Chase. Their solid marriage of over
fifty years had an incalculable effect on the man that Stewart became.

The few details available as to Stewart's experience at Cumberland provide an outline of the various positions he held and was offered in the years
before and after the war. Behind this impressive listing, however, stood a
man concerned not so much with gaining a wide range of experience as
with maintaining a growing family. Financial pressure caused Stewart to
leave education in exasperation more than once. Yet in every case he returned to teaching, until finally a combination of age and institutional
changes caused him to leave the classroom for good.

Stewart's deeply held convictions eventually led to his joining the Confederacy when Tennessee seceded in May, 1861. Although Stewart owned
no slaves, his sense of social order, his ideological bent regarding the prior-
ity of states' rights and regarding the Constitution as it was written, his vis-
ceral belief in the inferiority of people of African descent and distaste for
blacks' being on an equal social footing with whites, his resistance to what
he perceived to be northern political and social aggression, and his desire
to stand with his fellow southerners all played a part in his decision. Like
many other Tennesseans who never owned slaves, Stewart answered Governor Harris' call in 1861 for the defense of the legal rights he deemed protected by the Constitution.

As a major of artillery, Stewart proved to his superiors at Columbus that
he was an officer of promise. Albert Sidney Johnston perceived this and insisted on Stewart's promotion to brigadier general. This promotion was
the first of a series that culminated in Stewart's elevation to lieutenant general, becoming Tennessee's highest-ranking Confederate officer. Virtually
every officer of high rank in what would become the Army of Tennessee
would at one time or another recommend him for promotion.

As a brigadier, Stewart showed steady improvement. New Madrid was
a slow start. In a sense, it was not a fair test of Stewart's abilities as a general officer, owing to the overwhelming superiority of Pope's army and artillery and to the precarious position of the Confederates against the river.
At Shiloh, Stewart, like others, was unable to keep his brigade together on
April 6, 1862. The impromptu commands that he formed fought well, and
in fact covered the retreat on his portion of the field on April 7, 1862. At
Perryville, Stewart's brigade of Tennesseans were part of a single division
that virtually wrecked the entire left wing of the Federal army. In the sec-

ond line of Cheatham's Division, Stewart's Brigade provided important support to an already successful attack. At Murfreesboro, Stewart's Tennesseans routed the Federals out of the cedars along the Wilkinson Pike, Stewart insisting that his men attack as one unit so as to strike the Federals there with a decisive hammer blow.[2]

Stewart's competence on and off the battlefield and the respect the officers and men of his brigade had for him did not go unnoticed by the Army of Tennessee's high command. When the command of one of the army's five divisions came temporarily open, Stewart was elevated to that post. Thus, when the time came for the creation of a new division in 1863, Stewart was the only choice for that important post, and he commanded that division for over a year. He saw it change from the Little Giant Division of mostly Tennesseans to the steady body of troops from the Deep South he led to the gates of Atlanta. Stewart's performance as a division commander was extremely competent. The attack of the Little Giant Division on September 19, 1863, at Chickamauga both restored the army's center and temporarily split that of the Federals. Defensively, the repulse of the Twentieth Corps at New Hope Church on May 25, 1864, was one of the few highlights of the Atlanta campaign for the Confederacy. Stewart's unsuccessful battles as a division commander can be attributed to either the lack of men to cover his front, such as at Hoover's Gap and Missionary Ridge, or, in the case of the failed attack at Resaca, the fault of others.

Stewart's performance around Atlanta was uneven. Certainly, his attack at Peachtree Creek was the army's highlight in the first of Hood's attempts to drive Sherman away from Atlanta. Stewart's attack at Ezra Church was unsuccessful, but if he had any fault at all it was in following orders and reinforcing Stephen D. Lee's failed attack, rather than exercising more discretion, as a corps commander facing unexpected circumstances might have done.

It is difficult to evaluate Stewart's overall performance in the period between the advance into Tennessee and the final surrender of the army. There were no successes to credit to Old Straight in the strictest military sense. Sheer bad luck and Hood's failure to coordinate matters ruined the Army of Tennessee's chances at Spring Hill; Hood's obstinacy caused the disaster at Franklin; and the army's inability to offset Federal mobility and

2. Lindsley, ed., *Military Annals*, 111.

numerical superiority effectively doomed it at Nashville. Stewart did a
commendable job keeping the left flank from completely dissolving on December 15, 1864, at Nashville, and kept his corps in hand until Cheatham's
flank dissolved the next day. Stewart assumed a large portion of the burden
of the terrible withdrawal from Nashville, keeping the army intact during
the retreat across the Tennessee. Once again, Old Straight guarded the rear
of the army as it recrossed the river. His activity at Bentonville remains
shrouded in mystery. Yet even if the army's last battles were such that no
amount of leadership could have altered its fate, Stewart had a positive influence on his men and the army in the closing months of the war, if nothing else by example—as when he helped the men of Tarrant's Battery free
their piece from the mud.

Stewart's career with the Army of Tennessee had one other significant
facet. Alone among its senior officers, he seemed to rise above the constant
conflict in its high command. Polk, Hardee, Breckinridge, Cheatham, Cleburne, D. H. Hill, Buckner, and Hindman, among others, came into conflict with Bragg. Hood fought with Johnston. Hardee and Cheatham
fought with Hood. Stewart, the modest Christian soldier, managed good
relations with each of the army's four commanders, as well as its corps and
division commanders. Albert Sidney Johnston, Joseph E. Johnston, Leonidas Polk, William J. Hardee, and others all considered Stewart's character
and service in recommending him for promotion. When Polk died in June,
1864, Johnston notified Richmond that Stewart was the most qualified officer among the army's major generals to fill the departed bishop's place.
John Bell Hood, too, thought Stewart worthy of this promotion. The history of Stewart's relationship with Hood reflects Hood's reliance on Stewart to handle the most difficult assignments. Hood considered Stewart a
friend, although Stewart was active in trying to suspend Davis' order removing Johnston and elevating Hood into his place. As the war ended,
Hood made sure that Stewart knew he placed no blame on Old Straight
for the debacle at Spring Hill.

A commander is first and foremost a leader of men. The rank and file of
the Army of Tennessee joined its generals in their approbation of Stewart
as a general, and their appreciation of him as a man. The men, too, saw
Stewart grow as a soldier:

> Lt. Gen. Alex P. Stewart had been with the Army of Tennessee
> from its first organization, and may be said to have grown with it,

and developed both as to experience and efficiency. His promotion was steady and every time deserved. Indeed, Stewart, I was used to, from the start at Columbus, as with Cheatham. Although never regarded by the men as having the qualities of greatness, we yet felt that he was a man growing before our eyes. He never seemed to make a mistake! Painstaking, obedient to orders, cool and courageous, that was Stewart. As a man he was dignified but considerate of his men, and we liked him, gave him both our esteem and confidence. His high Christian character commanded our respect. His greatest peculiarity as a soldier was, perhaps, his imperturbable temper. Nothing could startle Stewart. In battle, and defeat especially, this trait became heroism. By no sign did he ever give evidence of excitement, uneasiness, confusion, anxiety. To look at his calm tranquil face in a time of peril or doubt was to get inspiration, regain confidence and courage.[3]

In a large sense, Alexander Peter Stewart was the embodiment of the Army of Tennessee. Only Frank Cheatham could rival his service with the army from its earliest beginnings at Columbus and Belmont, yet Cheatham was first and last identified with a faction in the army. Old Straight was associated with the Army of Tennessee as a whole—not just his fellows of Tennessee, but men of Georgia, Alabama, Mississippi, Arkansas, Louisiana, Texas, and North Carolina.

It is fitting that in the Army of Tennessee's last battle, Old Straight was at its head. Stewart was not only its senior officer on the field, but the embodiment of the virtues that kept its men fighting from first to last: constancy, belief in the Confederate cause, and the ability to endure the endless infighting and the string of defeats and return to the line of battle again and again. As a veteran of that unfortunate host, Stewart would have agreed with the sentiments of a speaker at the dedication of a Confederate monument in Murfreesboro in 1901 who eloquently described the career of the Army of Tennessee:

> The Army of Tennessee, never the best equipped of Confederate forces, met more defeats without destruction, endured more hardships without complaint, made longer marches with less straggling,

3. Stephenson, *Civil War Memoir*, 212.

followed more unfortunate leaders with fewer desertions, showed more cheerfulness in distress and exhibited greater fortitude in disaster than any military organization known in history. It was always hopeful in misfortune, brave in action, patient in privation, valiant in conflict, constant in trials, unmurmuring in difficulties and unconquerable in spirit.[4]

It is not surprising that Stewart's place in history, as in much of his life, is forever linked with the Army of Tennessee. Unfortunately, as has been noted by Richard M. McMurry and Thomas Connelly, the Army of Tennessee, along with its officers and men, has been relatively neglected until recently. In contrast, as McMurry has observed, even brigadiers, colonels, and majors of the Army of Northern Virginia are the subject of new works.[5]

In addition to the limitations associated with service with the Army of Tennessee, Stewart's tendency to avoid the limelight has also affected his place in history. Writing his sketch of the Army of Tennessee for the *Military Annals* in 1886 was the perfect opportunity to present his story as a soldier. While this piece gives insight into Stewart's attitude toward Bragg, the Johnstons, and other issues, it fails to provide any idea of what Stewart himself did on the army's many bloody battlefields. As late as 1904, a fellow Tennessee veteran published a sketch of Stewart for the *Confederate Veteran* and encouraged Stewart to come forth with his view of the momentous events to which he was a witness:

> Gen. Stewart, with his lifelong persistency in avoiding notoriety, has kept himself out of sight. The time has come when it is due Tennessee and the men he commanded that he allow those of us who knew him long and well to speak the truth in part at least. He must permit the State to bear the honors he won for her. He must grant the request of his old students and soldiers to crown his closing years with at least a modest statement of the truth evidenced by our best generals that there was no conflict between Christian faith and Con-

---

4. Colonel Bennett Young at Murfreesboro, November 7, 1901, in Ridley, *Battles and Sketches*, 591.

5. McMurry, *Two Great Rebel Armies*, 1–9; Connelly, *Army of the Heartland*, viii–ix.

federate service. Of this fact there has been through the years no brighter example than Gen. Alex P. Stewart.[6]

History being as it is, the four years of Stewart's participation in the Civil War will likely stir more interest than his forty years after it. Yet the end of the war did not signal the end of his growth. After the demise of the revolution he had fought to sustain, and in the disruption and devastation of the South, he picked himself up and began a new phase of his life, looking to new careers and new possibilities. In so doing, he left a more enduring legacy, as an educator, devout Christian, and mentor to several generations of young people. Bromfield Ridley's admiration for Stewart must have been shared by thousands of young people through the years. Further, as if to vindicate Stewart's belief that "through the overruling providence of God great virtues may be born of war," Stewart's other great peacetime legacy is the Chickamauga-Chattanooga National Military Park.[7] A wonderful example of historic preservation, created in a joint effort with former enemies such as Fullerton, Smith, and Boynton, the park is an enduring memorial to the men who fought there. Through the park, perhaps more than any single one of his other works, Stewart helped preserve the memory of the Army of Tennessee.

6. D. C. Kelley, "Lieut. Gen. Alex. P. Stewart," *CV* 12 (August 1904): 392–95.
7. Lindsley, ed., *Military Annals*, 55.

BIBLIOGRAPHY

PRIMARY SOURCES

Manuscripts

Alabama Department of Archives and History, Montgomery, Ala.
      Alpheus Baker Diary
Chattanooga–Hamilton County Bicentennial Library, Chattanooga, Tenn.
      Papers of the Chattanooga Historical Society
      Papers of the Nathan Bedford Forrest Camp, United Confederate
        Veterans
      Papers of A. P. Stewart Chapter, United Daughters of the Confed-
        eracy
Chickamauga-Chattanooga National Military Park, Ga.
      Milton P. Jarnigan Reminiscences
      Correspondence of Park Commission
      Proceedings of Park Commission
      Edwin H. Rennolds Diary
      20th Tennessee File
      33rd Tennessee File
Cumberland University, Stoughton Archives, Lebanon, Tenn.
      Board of Trustees Minute Book, 1842–1871
      William Campbell Collection
      1875 Commencement Program
Duke University, William R. Perkins Library, Special Collections, Durham, N. C.
      I. H. Carrington Papers
      Confederate States Archives, Miscellaneous Letters
      Confederate Veteran Papers
      William B. Dupree Papers
      John Johnson Diary
      John Euclid Magee Papers
      Charles T. Quintard Papers
      Alexander P. Stewart Papers
      Oliver W. Stickland Papers
      Joseph Milner Wrightman Papers

Georgia Department of Archives and History, Atlanta, Ga.
    James Longstreet Collection
    Catherine Barnes Whitehead Rowland Diary
    Charles Alden Rowland Diary and Letters
    O. F. Strahl and W. A. Taylor Civil War Letters
Georgia Historical Society, Savannah, Ga.
    Confederate States Army Papers
Huntington Library, San Marino, Calif.
    Alonzo Brock Collection
    Simon Bolivar Buckner Collection
    Eldridge Collection
    Joseph E. Johnston Collection
Kennesaw Mountain National Battlefield Park, Ga.
    William A. Brown Diary
    Columbus Sykes Letters
Library of Congress, Washington, D.C.
    Braxton Bragg Papers
    William J. Hardee Papers
    Isham G. Harris Papers
    Leonidas Polk Papers
Mississippi Department of Archives and History, Jackson, Miss.
    S. G. French Papers
    William H. McCardle Papers
    Daniel Ruggles Papers
National Archives, Washington, D.C.
  Record Group 74
    A. P. Stewart Pardon Application File
  Record Group 109
    Army of Tennessee, General Orders, 1862
    Army of Tennessee, General Orders and Circulars, 1863–1865
    Army of Tennessee, Special Orders, 1864–1865
    Army of Tennessee, Telegrams Sent, 1864
    Chief Engineer, Western Department, Letters Sent, 1861–1862
    Compiled Service Records—General and Staff Officers' Papers
    Confederate Citizens or Business Firms File
    Departmental Records, Army and Department of Tennessee
    Samuel G. French Papers
    Officers File
    Leonidas Polk Papers

Polk's Corps Army of the Mississippi/Army of Tennessee, Special Or-
    ders, 1862

32nd Tennessee Regiment, Issuances Received

E. C. Walthall Papers

Western Department and Department of Mississippi, Letters Sent,
    1861–1863

North Carolina State Archives, Raleigh, N.C.

James Patton Anderson Papers

Shiloh National Military Park, Shiloh, Tenn.

W. A. Howard Letters

Tennessee State Library and Archives, Nashville, Tenn.

Campbell Brown–Richard Stoddart Ewell Papers

Terry Cahal Letter

Benjamin Franklin Cheatham Papers

W. D. Gale Letters

Tulane University, Howard-Tilton Memorial Library, New Orleans, La.

Joseph Jones Collection

Louisiana Historical Association Collection, Jefferson Davis Papers

United States Army Military History Institute, Carlisle, Pa.

Civil War Times Illustrated Collection

United States Military Academy, West Point, N.Y.

Alexander P. Stewart Cadet Records

University of Alabama, W. S. Hoole Special Collections Library, Tuscaloosa, Ala.

Henry Delamar Clayton Papers

University of Arkansas, Fayetteville, Ark.

Daniel H. Reynolds Papers

University of Georgia, Hargett Library, Athens, Ga.

Alexander P. Stewart Letter

University of Mississippi Archives and Special Collections, University, Miss.

Board of Trustees Minutes, 1860–1882

Board of Trustees Minutes, 1883–1897

W. S. Featherston Papers

Alexander P. Stewart Correspondence

University of North Carolina, Wilson Library, Chapel Hill, N.C.

Southern Historical Collection

Robert L. Caruthers Papers

Gale-Polk Papers

Walter W. Harvey Papers

Daniel Harvey Hill Papers

Aristide Hopkins Diary
Stephen D. Lee Papers
W. W. Mackall Papers
Leonidas Polk Papers
Marcus Wright Papers
University of the South, Dupont Library, Sewanee, Tenn.
Leonidas Polk Papers
Western Reserve Historical Society, Cleveland
William P. Palmer Collection of Bragg Papers
Alexander P. Stewart Letter

Newspapers

Atlanta Daily Intelligencer
Augusta Daily Chronicle and Sentinel
Chattanooga Daily Rebel
Chattanooga News
Chattanooga Times
Macon Daily Telegraph
Memphis (Atlanta) Daily Appeal
New Orleans Times-Democrat
Savannah Republican
Southern Confederacy (Atlanta)

Microfilm

U.S. Military Academy Cadet Application Papers, 1805–1866, National Archives
Microfilm Publication 688.

Government Publications

Journal of the Congress of the Confederate States of America, 1861–1865. 7 vols. Washington, D.C.: U.S. Government Printing Office, 1904.
Laws of the State of Missouri, vol. 14. Jefferson City: C. J. Corwin Public Printer, 1857.
Laws of the State of Missouri, vol. 17. Jefferson City: W. G. Cheeney, 1861.

United States Military Academy. *Official Register of the Officers and Cadets of the U.S. Military Academy, June, 1839.* West Point, N.Y.: N.p., 1839.

———. *Official Register of the Officers and Cadets of the U.S. Military Academy, June, 1840.* West Point, N.Y.: N.p., 1840.

———. *Official Register of the Officers and Cadets of the U.S. Military Academy, June, 1841.* West Point, N.Y.: N.p., 1841.

———. *Official Register of the Officers and Cadets of the U.S. Military Academy, June, 1842.* West Point, N.Y.: N.p., 1842.

———. *Official Register of the Officers and Cadets of the U.S. Military Academy, June, 1844.* West Point, N.Y.: N.p., 1844.

———. *Regulations Established for the Organization and Government of the Military Academy.* New York: Wiley & Putnam, 1839.

War of the Rebellion: A Compilation of the Official Records of the Union and Confederate Armies. 128 vols. Washington, D.C.: U.S. Government Printing Office, 1880–1901.

Books and Pamphlets

Buck, Irving A. *Cleburne and His Command.* 1908. Reprint, Wilmington, N.C.: Broadfoot Publishing, 1987.

Bulletin of the University of Mississippi. Vols. 22–29, 35. Oxford, Miss.: University of Mississippi, 1874–1881, 1887.

Cannon, J. P. *Bloody Banners and Barefoot Boys: A History of the 27th Regiment Alabama Infantry, C.S.A.* Ed. Neil Crowson and John V. Brogden. Shippensburg, Pa.: Burd Street Press, 1997.

Cater, Douglas John. *As It Was: Reminiscences of a Soldier of the Third Texas Cavalry and the Nineteenth Louisiana Infantry.* 1981. Reprint, Austin, Texas: State House Press, 1990.

Chambers, William Pitt. *Blood and Sacrifice: The Civil War Journal of a Confederate Soldier.* Ed. Richard A. Baumgardner. Huntington, W.Va.: Blue Acorn Press, 1994.

"Correspondence Relating to Chickamauga and Chattanooga." In *Papers of the Military Historical Society of Massachusetts.* Vol. 8, *The Mississippi Valley, Tennessee, Georgia, Alabama, 1861–1864.* Boston: Military Historical Society of Massachusetts, 1910.

Dowdy, Clifford, ed. *The Wartime Papers of R. E. Lee.* New York: Bramhall House, 1961.

Freeman, D. S., and Grady McWhiney, eds. *Lee's Dispatches to Jefferson Davis.* New York: Putnam, 1957.

Fremantle, James A. L. *The Fremantle Diary*. Ed. Walter Lord. Boston: Little, Brown, 1954.

French, S. G. *Two Wars: An Autobiography of Gen. Samuel G. French*. Nashville: Confederate Veteran, 1901.

Hood, John B. *Advance and Retreat*. New Orleans: G. T. Beauregard, 1880.

Hoole, William Stanley, and Martha DuBose Hoole, eds. *Historical Sketches of Barton's (Later Stovall's) Georgia Brigade, Army of Tennessee, C.S.A.* University, Ala.: Confederate Publishing, 1984.

Johnson, Robert Underwood, and Clarence Clough Buel, eds. *Battles and Leaders of the Civil War*. 4 vols. 1884–1887. Reprint, New York: Thomas Yoseloff, 1956.

Johnston, Joseph E. *Narrative of Military Operations Directed During the Late War Between the States*. New York: D. Appleton, 1874.

Johnston, William Preston. *The Life of Albert Sidney Johnston*. New York: D. Appleton, 1878.

Jones, Edgar W. *History of the 18th Alabama Regiment*. Ed. Zane Grier. Mountain Brook, Ala.: Privately published, 1994.

Liddell, St. John R. *Liddell's Record*. Ed. Nathaniel Cheairs Hughes, Jr. 1985. Reprint, Baton Rouge: Louisiana State University Press, 1997.

Lindsley, John Berrian, ed. *The Military Annals of Tennessee: Confederate*. Nashville: J. M. Lindsley, 1886.

Longstreet, James. *From Manassas to Appomattox*. 1896. Reprint, Secaucus, N.J.: Blue & Gray Press, 1984.

McMurray, W. J. *History of the Twentieth Tennessee Regiment Volunteer Infantry, C.S.A.* Nashville: Publications Committee, 1904.

Manigault, A. M. *A Carolinian Goes to War*. Ed. R. Lockwood Tower. Columbia: University of South Carolina Press, 1983.

Moser, Harold D., David R. Hoth, and George Hoemann, eds. *The Papers of Andrew Jackson*. Vol. 5, *1821–1824*. Knoxville: University of Tennessee Press, 1996.

Patrick, Robert. *Reluctant Rebel: The Secret Diary of Robert Patrick, 1861–1865*. Ed. F. Jay Taylor. 1959. Reprint, Baton Rouge: Louisiana State University Press, 1996.

Ridley, Bromfield. *Battles and Sketches of the Army of Tennessee*. 1906. Reprint, Dayton: Morningside Bookshop, 1995.

Roman, Alfred. *The Military Operations of General Beauregard*. New York: Harper, 1884.

Rowland, Dunbar, ed. *Jefferson Davis–Constitutionalist: His Letters, Papers and Speeches*. Jackson: Mississippi Department of Archives and History, 1923.

Sheridan, Philip H. *Personal Memoirs*. New York: Charles L. Webster, 1888.

Sherman, William T. *Memoirs of General William T. Sherman*. New York: Charles L. Webster, 1890.

Sorrel, G. Moxley. *Recollections of a Confederate Staff Officer*. 1905. Reprint, New York: Bantam Books, 1992.

Stephenson, Philip Daingerfield. *The Civil War Memoir of Philip Daingerfield Stephenson, D.D.* Ed. Nathaniel Cheairs Hughes, Jr. Conway, Ark.: University of Central Arkansas Press, 1995.

Stevenson, Alexander F. *The Battle of Stone's River*. Boston: James R. Osgood, 1884.

Warner, J. H. *Personal Glimpses of the Civil War*. Chattanooga: Privately published, 1914.

Watkins, Sam R. *Co. Aytch*. 1900. Reprint, New York: Collier, 1962.

Willett, Elbert D. *History of Company B (Originally Pickens Planters), 40th Alabama Regiment, Confederate States Army, 1862 to 1865*. Northport, Ala.: Colonial Press, 1963.

Williams, Hiram Smith. *This War So Horrible: The Civil War Diary of Hiram Smith Williams*. Ed. Lewis N. Wynne and Robert A. Taylor. Tuscaloosa: University of Alabama Press, 1993.

Worsham, W. J. *The Old Nineteenth Tennessee Regiment, C.S.A.: June, 1861–April, 1865*. Knoxville: Paragon Printing, 1902.

Articles and Essays

Alderson, William T., ed. "The Civil War Diary of Captain James Litton Cooper, September 30, 1861, to January, 1865." *Tennessee Historical Quarterly*, vol. 15 (June 1956).

"Atlanta Battlefield Reunion." *Confederate Veteran*, vol. 8 (June 1900).

Boyce, Joseph. "Missourians in the Battle of Franklin." *Confederate Veteran*, vol. 24 (March 1916).

Cheatham, Benjamin F. "The Battle of Perryville." *Southern Bivouac* (April 1886).

———. "The Lost Opportunity at Spring Hill, Tenn.—General Cheatham's Reply to General Hood." *Southern Historical Society Papers*, vol. 9 (October, November, and December, 1881).

Copely, John M. "Battle of Franklin, with Reminiscences of Camp Douglas." *Journal of Confederate History*, vol. 2, no. 1 (1989).

Corn, T. I. "Brown's Brigade at Chickamauga." *Confederate Veteran*, vol. 21 (March 1913).

"Corps Commanders' Reports of the Battle." *Confederate Veteran,* vol. 12 (June 1904).

Curry, J. H. "A History of Company B, 40th Alabama Infantry, C.S.A., from the Diary of J. H. Curry." *Alabama Historical Quarterly,* vol. 17 (1955).

Dodd, W. O. "Reminiscences of Hood's Tennessee Campaign." *Southern Historical Society Papers,* vol. 9 (October, November, and December 1881).

Dozier, Tennie P. "Confederate Educational Home." *Confederate Veteran,* vol. 11 (August 1903).

Earp, Charles A., ed. "A Confederate Aide-de-Camp's Letters from the Chattanooga Area, 1863." *Journal of East Tennessee History,* vol. 67 (1995).

Gentry, W. M. "Surgeons of the Confederacy," *Confederate Veteran,* vol. 40 (September–October 1932).

Hickman, John P. Letter. *Confederate Veteran,* vol. 22 (January 1914).

Hopkins, Aristide, Y. R. Le Moncier, and J. Adolph Chalaron. "Tributes to Gen. A. P. Stewart." *Confederate Veteran,* vol. 16 (November 1908).

Howard, N. C. "An Incident of Missionary Ridge." *Confederate Veteran,* vol. 21 (June 1913).

Howe, Robert. "Dead at New Hope Church." *Confederate Veteran,* vol. 5 (October 1897).

"Invited to Chickamauga Park in October." *Confederate Veteran,* vol. 8 (March 1900).

Law, J. G. "Diary of the Rev. J. G. Law." *Southern Historical Society Papers,* vol. 10 (December 1882).

Lea, H. J. "In the Battle of New Hope Church." *Confederate Veteran,* vol. 31 (February 1923).

Lee, James W. Letter. *Confederate Veteran,* vol. 12 (October 1909).

McMurray, W. J. "The Gap of Death at Chickamauga." *Confederate Veteran,* vol. 2 (November 1894).

McNeilly, James H. "A Great Game of Strategy." *Confederate Veteran,* vol. 27 (October 1919).

———. "Franklin—Incidents of the Battle." *Confederate Veteran,* vol. 25 (March 1918).

Maxwell, James R. "Lumsden's Battery at the Battle of Nashville." *Confederate Veteran,* vol. 12 (October 1904).

Meadows, A. J. "The Fourth Tennessee Infantry." *Confederate Veteran,* vol. 14 (July 1906).

"Memphis Reunion—Notes from Proceedings." *Confederate Veteran,* vol. 9 (June 1901).

Mott, Charles R., Jr., ed. "War Journal of a Confederate Officer." *Tennessee Historical Quarterly,* vol. 5 (September 1946).

Murphree, Joel. "Autobiography and Civil War Letters of Joel Murphree of Troy, Alabama, 1864–1865." *Alabama Historical Quarterly*, vol. 19 (1957).

Note. *Confederate Veteran*, vol. 4 (October 1896).

Note. *Confederate Veteran*, vol. 6 (October 1898).

Note. *Confederate Veteran*, vol. 8 (January 1900).

Pickett, William D. "The Bursting of the Lady Polk." *Confederate Veteran*, vol. 12 (June 1904).

Porter, James D. "Criticisms by Friends of General Johnston." *Confederate Veteran*, vol. 4 (August 1896).

Read, C. W. "Reminiscences of the Confederate States Navy." *Southern Historical Society Papers*, vol. 1 (May 1876).

Ridley, Bromfield L. "Daring Deeds of Staff and Escort." *Confederate Veteran*, vol. 4 (September 1896).

"Right of the South to Secede." *Confederate Veteran*, vol. 11 (October 1903).

Roberts, Frank S. "Spring Hill—Franklin—Nashville, 1864." *Confederate Veteran*, vol. 27 (February 1919).

Smith, Frank H. " 'The Duck River Rifles,' the Twenty-Fourth Tennessee Infantry." In *The Civil War in Maury County, Tennessee*, ed. Jill K. Garrett and Marise P. Lightfoot. Columbia, Tenn.: Privately published, 1966.

"Southern Women's Monument." *Confederate Veteran*, vol. 10 (July 1902).

Stewart, Alexander P. Letter. *Confederate Veteran*, vol. 8 (June 1900).

———. "The Southern Women's Memorial Fund." *Confederate Veteran*, vol. 9 (August 1901).

———. Letter. *Confederate Veteran*, vol. 9 (September 1901).

———. "Monument to the Women." *Confederate Veteran*, vol. 11 (July 1903).

———. "A Critical Narrative." *Confederate Veteran*, vol. 16 (September 1908).

Tarrant, E. W. Letter. *Confederate Veteran*, vol. 17 (April 1909).

Willoughby, C. L. "Eclipse of the Moon at Missionary Ridge." *Confederate Veteran*, vol. 21 (December 1913).

Wright, J. W. A. "Bragg's Campaign Around Chattanooga." *Southern Bivouac*, vol. 2 (1886/87).

SECONDARY SOURCES

Books

Alexander, Thomas B. *Political Reconstruction in Tennessee*. 1950. Reprint, New York: Russell & Russell, 1968.

Allardice, Bruce S. *More Generals in Gray*. Baton Rouge: Louisiana State University Press, 1995.

Barnard, Harry V. *Tattered Volunteers: The Twenty-seventh Alabama Infantry Regiment, C.S.A.* Northport, Ala.: Hermitage Press, 1965.

Bergeron, Arthur W., Jr. *Guide to Louisiana Confederate Military Units, 1861–1865*. Baton Rouge: Louisiana State University Press, 1989.

Bone, Winstead P. *A History of Cumberland University, 1842–1935*. Lebanon, Tenn.: Winstead P. Bone, 1935.

Boynton, H. V. *The National Military Park: Chickamauga-Chattanooga, An Historical Guide*. Cincinnati: Robert Clarke, 1895.

Bradley, Mark L. *Last Stand in the Carolinas: The Battle of Bentonville*. Campbell, Calif.: Savas Woodbury, 1996.

Bridges, Hal. *Lee's Maverick General: Daniel Harvey Hill*. New York: McGraw-Hill, 1961.

Brown, Russell K. *To the Manner Born: The Life of General William H. T. Walker*. Athens: University of Georgia Press, 1994.

Burns, G. Frank. *Wilson County*. Memphis: Memphis State University Press, 1983.

Cabiness, James A. *A History of the University of Mississippi*. University, Miss.: University of Mississippi Press, 1949.

Caldwell, Joshua W. *Sketches of the Bench and Bar of Tennessee*. Knoxville: Ogden Brothers, 1898.

Castel, Albert. *Decision in the West: The Atlanta Campaign of 1864*. Lawrence: University Press of Kansas, 1992.

Connelly, Thomas L. *Army of the Heartland*. Baton Rouge: Louisiana State University Press, 1967.

———. *Autumn of Glory*. Baton Rouge: Louisiana State University Press, 1971.

Cozzens, Peter. *No Better Place to Die*. Urbana: University of Illinois Press, 1990.

———. *This Terrible Sound: The Battle of Chickamauga*. Urbana: University of Illinois Press, 1992.

———. *The Shipwreck of Their Hopes: The Battles for Chattanooga*. Urbana: University of Illinois Press 1994.

Crawford, Charles W., ed. *Governors of Tennessee. Vol. 1, 1790–1835*. Memphis: Memphis State University Press, 1979.

Crute, Joseph E., Jr. *Confederate Staff Officers, 1861–1865*. Powhatan, Va.: Derwent Books, 1982.

Cullum, George W. *Biographical Register of the Officers and Graduates of the U.S. Military Academy at West Point, N.Y.* Boston: Houghton, Mifflin, 1891.

Cummings, Charles M. *Yankee Quaker, Confederate General: The Curious Career of Bushrod Rust Johnson*. Teaneck, N.J.: Fairleigh Dickinson University Press, 1971.

Daniel, Larry J. *Cannoneers in Gray: The Field Artillery of the Army of Tennessee, 1861–1865.* Tuscaloosa: University of Alabama Press, 1984.

———. *Soldiering in the Army of Tennessee.* Chapel Hill: University of North Carolina Press, 1991.

———. *Shiloh: The Battle That Changed the Civil War.* New York: Simon & Schuster, 1997.

Daniel, Larry J., and Lynn M. Bock. *Island No. 10: Struggle for the Mississippi Valley.* Tuscaloosa: University of Alabama Press, 1996.

Davis, William C. *Breckinridge: Statesman, Soldier, Symbol.* Baton Rouge: Louisiana State University Press, 1974.

Dyer, John P. *The Gallant Hood.* Indianapolis: Bobbs-Merrill, 1950.

Edwards' Annual Director [sic] *to the Inhabitants, Institutions, Incorporated Companies, Manufacturing Establishments . . . in the City of St. Louis for 1871.* St. Louis: Southern Publishing–Edwards & Company Publishers, 1871.

Evans, Clement A., ed. *Confederate Military History.* 1899. Reprint, Wilmington, N.C.: Broadfoot Publishing, 1988.

Faust, Patricia L., ed. *Historical Times Illustrated Encyclopedia of the Civil War.* New York: Harper, 1986.

Fleming, Thomas J. *West Point: The Men and Times of the United States Military Academy.* New York: Morrow, 1969.

Foote, Shelby. *The Civil War.* 3 vols. New York: Random House, 1958.

Freeman, D. S. *Lee's Lieutenants.* 3 vols. New York: Charles Scribner's Sons, 1942–1944.

Garrett, Jill L., ed. *Obituaries from Tennessee Newspapers.* Easley, S.C.: Southern Historical Press, 1980.

Glatthaar, Joseph T. *The March to the Sea and Beyond.* New York: New York University Press, 1985.

Goodspeed, Weston A. *Goodspeed's History of Tennessee.* 1887. Reprint, Nashville: Elder Booksellers, 1972.

———. *The Goodspeed Histories of Giles, Lincoln, Franklin and Moore Counties of Tennessee.* 1886. Reprint, Columbia, Tenn.: Woodward & Stinson Printing, 1972.

Gould and Aldrich's Annual Directory for the City of St. Louis, for 1872, St. Louis: Review Steam Press, 1872.

Gould's St. Louis City Directory for 1873. St. Louis: David B. Gould, 1873.

Gould's St. Louis Directory for 1874. St. Louis: David B. Gould, 1874.

Gould's St. Louis Directory for 1905. St. Louis: Gould Directory, 1905.

Gould's St. Louis Directory for 1906. St. Louis: Gould Directory, 1906.

Groom, Winston. *Shrouds of Glory.* New York: Atlantic Monthly Press, 1995.

Hafendorfer, Kenneth A. *Perryville: Battle for Kentucky.* Louisville: KH Press, 1991.

Hale, Will T., and Dixon L. Merritt. *A History of Tennessee and Tennesseans.* Chicago: Lewis Publishing, 1913.

Hallock, Judith Lee. *Braxton Bragg and Confederate Defeat.* Vol. 2. Tuscaloosa: University of Alabama Press, 1991.

Hamer, Philip M., ed. *Tennessee: A History, 1673–1932.* New York: American Historical Society, 1933.

Hattaway, Herman. *General Stephen D. Lee.* Jackson: University Press of Mississippi, 1976.

Hattaway, Herman, and Archer Jones. *How the North Won: A Military History of the Civil War.* Urbana: University of Illinois, 1983, 1991.

Hay, Thomas R. *Hood's Tennessee Campaign.* Dayton: Morningside Bookshop, 1975.

Hoffman, John, ed. *The Confederate Collapse at the Battle of Missionary Ridge.* Dayton: Morningside, 1985.

Hoole, William Stanley. *A Historical Sketch of the Thirty-sixth Alabama Regiment, 1862–1865.* University, Ala.: Confederate Publishing, 1986.

Hopkins, Anne H., and William Lyons. *Tennessee Votes, 1799–1976.* Knoxville: University of Tennessee Bureau of Public Administration, 1978.

Horn, Stanley F. *The Army of Tennessee.* 1941. Reprint, Wilmington, N.C.: Broadfoot Publishing, 1987.

———. *The Decisive Battle of Nashville.* 1956. Reprint, Baton Rouge: Louisiana State University Press, 1991.

Hughes, Nathaniel Cheairs, Jr. *Bentonville: The Final Battle of Sherman and Johnston.* Chapel Hill: University of North Carolina Press, 1996.

———. *The Battle of Belmont.* Chapel Hill: University of North Carolina Press, 1991.

———. *General William J. Hardee: Old Reliable.* Baton Rouge: Louisiana State University Press, 1965.

———. *The Pride of the Confederate Artillery: The Washington Artillery in the Army of Tennessee.* Baton Rouge: Louisiana State University Press, 1997.

Hughes, Nathaniel Cheairs, Jr., and Roy P. Stonsifer, Jr. *The Life and Wars of Gideon J. Pillow.* Chapel Hill: University of North Carolina Press, 1993.

Lloyd, James B. *The University of Mississippi: The Formative Years, 1848–1906.* Oxford: University of Mississippi Department of Archives and Special Collections, 1979.

Logsdon, David R., ed. *Eyewitnesses at the Battle of Shiloh.* Nashville: Kettle Mills Press, 1994.

———. *Eyewitnesses at the Battle of Stones River.* Nashville: Kettle Mills Press, 1989.

———. *Eyewitnesses at the Battle of Franklin.* Nashville: Kettle Mills Press, 1991.

Losson, Christopher. *Tennessee's Forgotten Warriors*. Knoxville: University of Tennessee Press, 1989.

McDonough, James Lee. *Shiloh: In Hell Before Night*. Knoxville: University of Tennessee Press, 1977.

———. *Stones River: Bloody Winter in Tennessee*. Knoxville: University of Tennessee Press, 1980.

———. *Chattanooga: A Death Grip on the Confederacy*. Knoxville: University of Tennessee Press, 1984.

———. *War in Kentucky: From Shiloh to Perryville*. Knoxville: University of Tennessee Press, 1994.

McDonough, James L., and Thomas Connelly. *Five Tragic Hours: The Battle of Franklin*. Knoxville: University of Tennessee Press, 1983.

McMurry, Richard M. *Two Great Rebel Armies*. Chapel Hill: University of North Carolina Press, 1989.

———. *John Bell Hood and the War for Southern Independence*. Lexington: University Press of Kentucky, 1982.

McWhiney, Grady. *Braxton Bragg and Confederate Defeat*, Vol. 1. Tuscaloosa: University of Alabama Press, 1969, 1991.

Miles, Jim. *Paths to Victory*. Nashville: Rutledge Hill Press, 1991.

Moore, John Trotwood, and Austin P. Foster. *Tennessee: The Volunteer State*. Chicago: S. J. Clarke, 1923.

Neal, Diane, and Thomas W. Kremm. *The Lion of the South: General Thomas C. Hindman*. Macon, Ga.: Mercer University Press, 1993.

Parks, Joseph H. *General Leonidas Polk, C.S.A.: The Fighting Bishop*. Baton Rouge: Louisiana State University Press, 1962.

Polk, William M. *Leonidas Polk, Bishop and General*. New York: Longmans, Green, 1893, 1915.

Pollard, Edward A. *Lee and His Lieutenants*. New York: E. B. Treat, 1867.

Raab, James W. *W. W. Loring: Florida's Forgotten General*. Manhattan, Kans.: Sunflower University Press, 1996.

Randall, J. G., and David Donald. *The Civil War and Reconstruction*. Lexington, Mass.: D. C. Heath, 1969.

Reed, David W. *The Battle of Shiloh and the Organizations Engaged*. Rev. ed. Washington, D.C.: Government Printing Office, 1913.

Reid, Richard J. *Stones River Ran Red*. Owensboro, Ky.: Commercial Printing, 1986.

Robertson, James I., Jr. *Stonewall Jackson: The Man, the Soldier, the Legend*. New York: Macmillan, 1997.

Rowland, Dunbar. *Encyclopedia of Mississippi History*. Madison, Wis.: Selwyn A. Brant, 1907.

————. *Official and Statistical Register of the State of Mississippi.* Nashville: Brandon Printing, 1908.

Savas, Theodore P., and David A. Woodbury, eds. *The Campaign for Atlanta and Sherman's March to the Sea.* Vol. 1. Campbell, Calif.: Savas Woodbury, 1992.

Sayres, Alethea D. *The Sound of Brown's Guns.* Spring Hill: Rosewood Press, 1995.

Sifakis, Stewart. *Compendium of the Confederate Armies: Alabama.* New York: Facts on File, 1992.

————. *Compendium of the Confederate Armies: Florida and Arkansas.* New York: Facts on File, 1992.

————. *Compendium of the Confederate Armies: Tennessee.* New York: Facts on File, 1992.

————. *Compendium of the Confederate Armies: South Carolina and Georgia.* New York: Facts on File, 1995.

Spruill, Matt, ed. *Guide to the Battle of Chickamauga.* Lawrence: University Press of Kansas, 1993.

Stickles, Arndt M. *Simon Bolivar Buckner: Borderland Knight.* 1940. Reprint, Wilmington, N.C.: Broadfoot Publishing, 1987.

Sunderland, Glenn W. *Lightning at Hoover's Gap: The Story of Wilder's Brigade.* New York: Yoseloff, 1969.

Sword, Wiley. *Shiloh: Bloody April.* 1974. Reprint, Dayton: Morningside, 1988.

————. *Embrace an Angry Wind: The Confederacy's Last Hurrah: Spring Hill, Franklin and Nashville.* 1992. Reprint, Lawrence: University Press of Kansas, 1992.

————. *Mountains Touched with Fire.* New York: St. Martin's Press, 1995.

Symonds, Craig L. *Joseph E. Johnston: A Civil War Biography.* New York: W. W. Norton, 1992.

————. *Stonewall of the West: Patrick Cleburne and the Civil War.* Lawrence: University Press of Kansas, 1997.

Tennessee Civil War Centennial Commission. *Tennesseans in the Civil War.* Nashville: N.p., 1964.

Tucker, Glenn. *Chickamauga: Bloody Battle in the West.* 1961. Reprint, Dayton: Morningside, 1981.

United Daughters of the Confederacy, South Carolina Division. *Recollections and Reminiscences.* 5 vols. Columbia, S.C., 1990.

United States War Department. *List of Staff Officers of the Confederate States Army.* Ed. John M. Carroll. Mattituck, N.Y.: J. M. Carroll, 1983.

Warner, Ezra. *Generals in Gray.* Baton Rouge: Louisiana State University Press, 1959.

Welsh, Jack D. *Medical Histories of Confederate Generals.* Kent, Ohio: Kent State University Press, 1995.

White, William W. *The Confederate Veteran.* Tuscaloosa: Confederate Publishing, 1962.

Wiley, Bell Irvin. *The Life of Johnny Reb: The Common Soldier of the Confederacy.* 1943. Reprint, Baton Rouge: Louisiana State University Press, 1997.

Wills, Brian Steel. *A Battle from the Start: The Life of Nathan Bedford Forrest.* New York: HarperCollins, 1992.

Wingfield, Marshall. *General A. P. Stewart: His Life and Letters.* Memphis: West Tennessee Historical Society, 1954.

Woodworth, Steven E. *Jefferson Davis and His Generals.* Lawrence: University Press of Kansas, 1990.

Wright, Marcus J. *Arkansas in the War, 1861–1865.* Batesville, Ark.: Independence County Historical Society, 1963.

Articles and Essays

Alexander, Thomas B. "Neither Peace nor War: Conditions in Tennessee in 1865." *East Tennessee Historical Society's Publications,* vol. 21 (1950).

Allardice, Bruce S. "West Points of the Confederacy: Southern Military Schools and the Confederate Army." *Civil War History,* vol. 43 (December 1997).

Allen, Stacy D. "Shiloh: The Campaign and First Day's Battle." *Blue & Gray Magazine,* vol. 14 (winter 1997).

———. "Shiloh: Grant Strikes Back." *Blue & Gray Magazine,* vol. 14 (spring 1997).

Boyle, Robert V. "Defeat Through Default: Confederate Naval Strategy of the Upper Mississippi River and Its Tributaries, 1861–1862." *Tennessee Historical Quarterly,* vol. 27 (spring 1968).

Collins, J. S. "W. W. Gist's Article Commended." *Confederate Veteran,* vol. 24 (February 1916).

Crawford, W. T. "The Mystery of Spring Hill." *Civil War History,* vol. 1 (June 1955).

Cummings, Charles M. "Otho French Strahl: Choicest Spirit to Embrace the South." *Tennessee Historical Quarterly,* vol. 24 (winter 1965).

Dabney, T. G. "Gen. A. P. Stewart on Strong Topics." *Confederate Veteran,* vol. 17 (January 1909).

Daniel, Larry. "The Quinby and Robinson Cannon Foundry at Memphis." *West Tennessee Historical Society Papers,* vol. 27 (1973).

Davis, Stephen. "Hood Fights Desperately: The Battles for Atlanta—Events from July 10 to September 2, 1864." *Blue & Gray Magazine,* vol. 6 (August 1989).

Duval, Mary Virginia. "The Chevalier Bayard of Mississippi: Edward Cary Walthall." *Publications of the Mississippi Historical Society,* vol. 4 (1901).

Ewing, Robert. "General Robert E. Lee's Inspiration to the Industrial Rehabilitation of the South, Exemplified in the Development of Southern Iron Interests." *Tennessee Historical Magazine,* vol. 9 (January 1926).

Feis, William B. "The Deception of Braxton Bragg." *Blue & Gray Magazine,* vol. 10 (October 1992).

Garner, Alfred W. "Public Services of E. C. Walthall." *Publications of the Mississippi Historical Society,* vol. 9 (1906).

Hay, Thomas Robeson. "The Battle of Spring Hill." *Tennessee Historical Magazine,* vol. 7 (July 1921).

Hill, Mrs. Bob C. "A Brief History of Decherd, Tennessee." *Franklin County Historical Review,* vol. 3 (June 1972).

Horn, Stanley F. "Isham G. Harris in the Pre-War Years." *Tennessee Historical Quarterly,* vol. 19 (September 1960).

Jacobs, Dillard. "Outfitting the Provisional Army of Tennessee: A Report on New Source Materials." *Tennessee Historical Quarterly,* vol. 40 (fall 1981).

Jones, Wharton S. "Glory Enough for All." *Confederate Veteran,* vol. 38 (June 1930).

Kelley, D. C. "Lieut. Gen. Alex. P. Stewart." *Confederate Veteran,* vol. 12 (August 1904).

Lane, Bryan. "The Familiar Road: The Life of Confederate Brigadier General John Adams." *Civil War Times Illustrated,* vol. 35 (October 1996).

"Last Roll Call." *Confederate Veteran,* vol. 10 (March 1902).

"Last Roll Call." *Confederate Veteran,* vol. 33 (September 1925).

Little, Robert D. "General Hardee and the Atlanta Campaign." *Georgia Historical Quarterly,* vol. 29 (March 1945).

Livingood, James W. "Chickamauga and Chattanooga National Military Park." *Tennessee Historical Quarterly,* vol. 23 (March 1964).

McMurry, Richard M. "Confederate Morale in the Atlanta Campaign of 1864." *Georgia Historical Quarterly,* vol. 54 (summer 1970).

———. " 'The *Enemy* at Richmond': Joseph E. Johnston and the Confederate Government." *Civil War History,* vol. 27 (March 1981).

Moore, John Trotwood. "Historic Highways of the South: The Barren Victory at Chickamauga." *Taylor-Trotwood Magazine,* vol. 5 (September 1907).

———. "Historic Highways of the South: The Battle of Stone [*sic*] River." *Taylor-Trotwood Magazine,* vol. 6 (February 1908).

Morris, Roy, Jr. "The Steadiest Body of Men I Ever Saw: John T. Wilder and the Lightning Brigade." *Blue & Gray Magazine,* vol. 10 (October 1992).

Note. *Confederate Veteran,* vol. 12 (February 1904).

Patton, W. H. "History of the Prohibition Movement in Mississippi." *Publications of the Mississippi Historical Society,* vol. 10 (1909).

Prim, G. Clinton, Jr. "Born Again in the Trenches: Revivals in the Army of Tennessee." *Tennessee Historical Quarterly,* vol. 43 (fall 1984).

Rauchle, B. C. "A Brief Account of the Early History of Franklin County." *Franklin County Historical Review,* vol. 2 (December 1970).

Secrist, Philip L. "Resaca: For Sherman a Moment of Truth." *Atlanta Historical Bulletin,* vol. 22 (1978).

Shepherd, H. R. "Gen. D. H. Hill: A Character Study." *Confederate Veteran,* vol. 25 (August 1917).

Spearman, Charles M. "The Battle of Stones River: Tragic New Year's Eve in Tennessee." *Blue & Gray Magazine,* vol. 6 (February 1989).

Tucker, Phillip Thomas. "The First Missouri Brigade at the Battle of Franklin." *Tennessee Historical Quarterly,* vol. 46 (spring 1987).

Walker, Peter Franklin. "Building a Tennessee Army: Autumn, 1861." *Tennessee Historical Quarterly,* vol. 16 (June 1957).

Wingfield, Marshall. "Old Straight: A Sketch of the Life and Campaigns of Lieutenant General Alexander Peter Stewart, C.S.A." *Tennessee Historical Quarterly,* vol. 3 (June 1944).

Woodworth, Steven E. "Braxton Bragg and the Tullahoma Campaign." In *The Art of Command,* ed. Woodward (forthcoming).

Young, J.P. "Hood's Failure at Spring Hill." *Confederate Veteran,* vol. 17 (January 1908).

Unpublished Studies

Barnett, Luke J., III. "Alexander P. Stewart and the Tactical Employment of His Division at Chickamauga." Master's thesis, United States Army Command and General Staff College, 1989.

Clauss, Errol M. "The Atlanta Campaign, 18 July–2 September, 1864." Ph.D. diss., Emory University, 1965.

McMurry, Richard M. "The Atlanta Campaign: December 23, 1863, to July 18, 1864." Ph.D. diss., Emory University, 1967.

Simmons, R. Hugh. "Analysis of Historical Data Pertaining to Stewart's Corps, the Confederate Army of Tennessee, in North Carolina in 1865." 1993 (copy in possession of author).

INDEX

Belmont, 22–23, 302; at Bentonville, 263–67, 304; birth of, 4; and Bragg, 77, 84, 140–42; business ventures of, 274–75, 276–77; and Cheatham, 50, 84; at Chickamauga, 121–35, 303; children of, 12, 63; command style of, 52, 70–71, 80, 129, 135; as Confederate veteran, 290–92, 295; at Cumberland University, 12–15; at Dalton, Ga., 167–76; and Jefferson Davis, 62–63, 218, 281–82; death of, 299; demeanor of, 27, 70–71, 80, 174–75, 178, 215, 268, 284, 304–305; early education of, 5, 6; employment opportunities of, 12–14, 274–75, 276; esteemed by troops, 81, 85, 196, 304–305; at Ezra Church, 212–14, 303; financial concerns of, 13–14, 276–77; at Franklin, 238–45, 303; health of, 11, 278, 288, 289–90, 295–96; honorary degrees of, 284; and Hood, 208–10, 304; and Hoover's Gap, Tenn., 88–95, 303; and A. S. Johnston, 21–22, 33–34; and J. E. Johnston, 84, 165, 191, 200–201, 298; and Kentucky Campaign, 52–60, 302; and McLemore's Cove, 116–19; marriage of, 12; and Mill Creek Gap, 175–76; at Missionary Ridge, 146–64, 303; at Murfreesboro, 65–75; at Nashville, 248–54, 303; at New Hope Church, 184–89, 303; at New Madrid, 26–32, 302; nickname of, 80; pardon of, 275, 276n; as park commissioner, 287–89, 293–94, 297; at Peachtree Creek, 202–209; physical description of, 27; political support for, 77–78, 84; political views of, 15, 18–19, 275–77; and Polk, 23, 81, 84, 191; promotions of, 23, 85, 191–94, 194–95n; in Provisional Army of Tennessee, 19–20; religious beliefs of, 7, 15, 196, 297–98; at Resaca, 177–83, 303; at Shiloh, 38–46; siblings of, 7; on slavery and African Americans, 7, 18, 168–69, 169n, 275–76, 302; and Spring Hill, Tenn., 227–35,

298; staff of, 79, 215n; at surrender of Army of Tennessee, 271–72; and Tullahoma Campaign, 87–98; at University of Mississippi, 279–84; at University of Nashville, 13, 14; as U.S. Army officer, 10–12; at U.S. Military Academy, 7–10, 11; wounds of, 132, 212, 214; writings of, 17n, 282
Stewart, Alexander P., Jr., 12, 272, 278, 281, 290–91, 295–96, 297, 299
Stewart, Alphonso Chase, 12, 174, 268, 278–79, 290–92, 297, 299
Stewart, Charles S., 274
Stewart, Charles Spyker, 281
Stewart, Elizabeth Decherd, 4, 7–8, 14–15
Stewart, Gustavus Woodson Smith, 12, 267
Stewart, Harriet, 291–92
Stewart, Harriet Byron Chase, 11–12, 63, 91, 93, 174, 259, 268, 272, 278, 281, 284, 287, 290, 292–93, 295, 302
Stewart, James, 15
Stewart, James, Jr., 4
Stewart, James, III, 4, 9
Stewart, John, 79, 152
Stewart, O. W., 268
Stewart, R. A., 28
Stewart, Robert Caruthers, 12, 79, 188, 190, 256, 268, 274, 278–79, 284, 291
Stewart, Samuel, 14
Stewart, William, 4, 7–9, 279
Stovall, Marcellus A., 138, 141, 150, 155, 159, 183; brigade of, 130, 141, 146, 149–50, 152, 154, 161, 175, 179, 183–84, 186, 188, 263
Strahl, Otho French, 40, 78, 81–82, 141, 159, 244; brigade of, 141, 149–50, 152, 158–61, 170
Sullivan, Hampton M., 283
Sumner County, Tenn., 295
Sykes, Columbus, 195–96
Sykes, George, 9

Taliaferro, William B., division of, 261, 264, 266–67, 270